HUNGRY FOR THE
FLESH OF THE LIVING

written by JOHN RUSSO & MIKE WOLFER
covers JACEN BURROWS
cover color JUANMAR

chapters 1-4
artwork SEBASTIAN FIUMARA
color ANDREW DALHOUSE

chapter 5
artwork EDISON GEORGE
color GURU FX

chapter 6
artwork RYAN WATERHOUSE
color GREG WALLER

chapter 7
art EDISON GEORGE, LUIS CZERNIAWSKI
color ANDREW DALHOUSE

chapter 8
art FABIO JANSEN
color DIGIKORE

chapter breaks & cover gallery
art JACEN BURROWS, SEBASTIAN FIUMARA,
EDISON GEORGE, MIKE WOLFER, TIM VIGIL,
DHEERAJ VERMA
color ANDREW DALHOUSE, GURU FX

avatar press
editor in chief WILLIAM CHRISTENSEN
creative director MARK SEIFERT
director of sales KEITH DAVIDSEN
marketing director DAVID MARKS
production assistant ARIANA OSBORNE

atarpress.com
ter.com/avatarpress
ebook.com/avatarpress

NIGHT OF THE LIVING DEAD VOLUME 1. May 2010. Published by Avatar Press, Inc., 515 N. Century Blvd.
Rantoul, IL 61866. ©2010 Avatar Press, Inc. Night of the Living Dead and all related properties TM &
©2010 Image Ten. All characters as depicted in this story are over the age of 18. The stories,
characters, and institutions mentioned in this magazine are entirely fictional. Printed in Canada.

D1288495

AVATAR
™

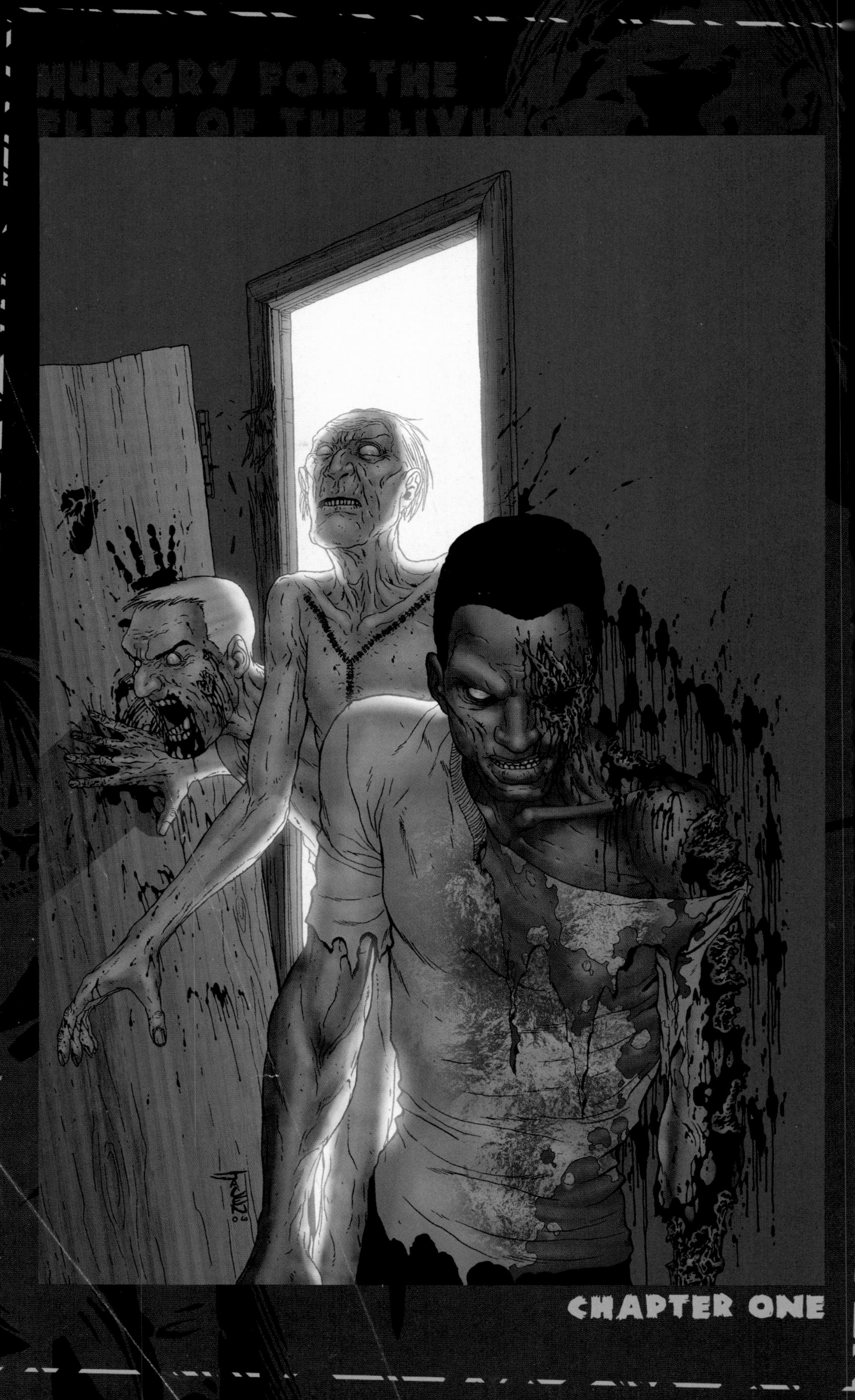
HUNGRY FOR THE
FLESH OF THE

CHAPTER ONE

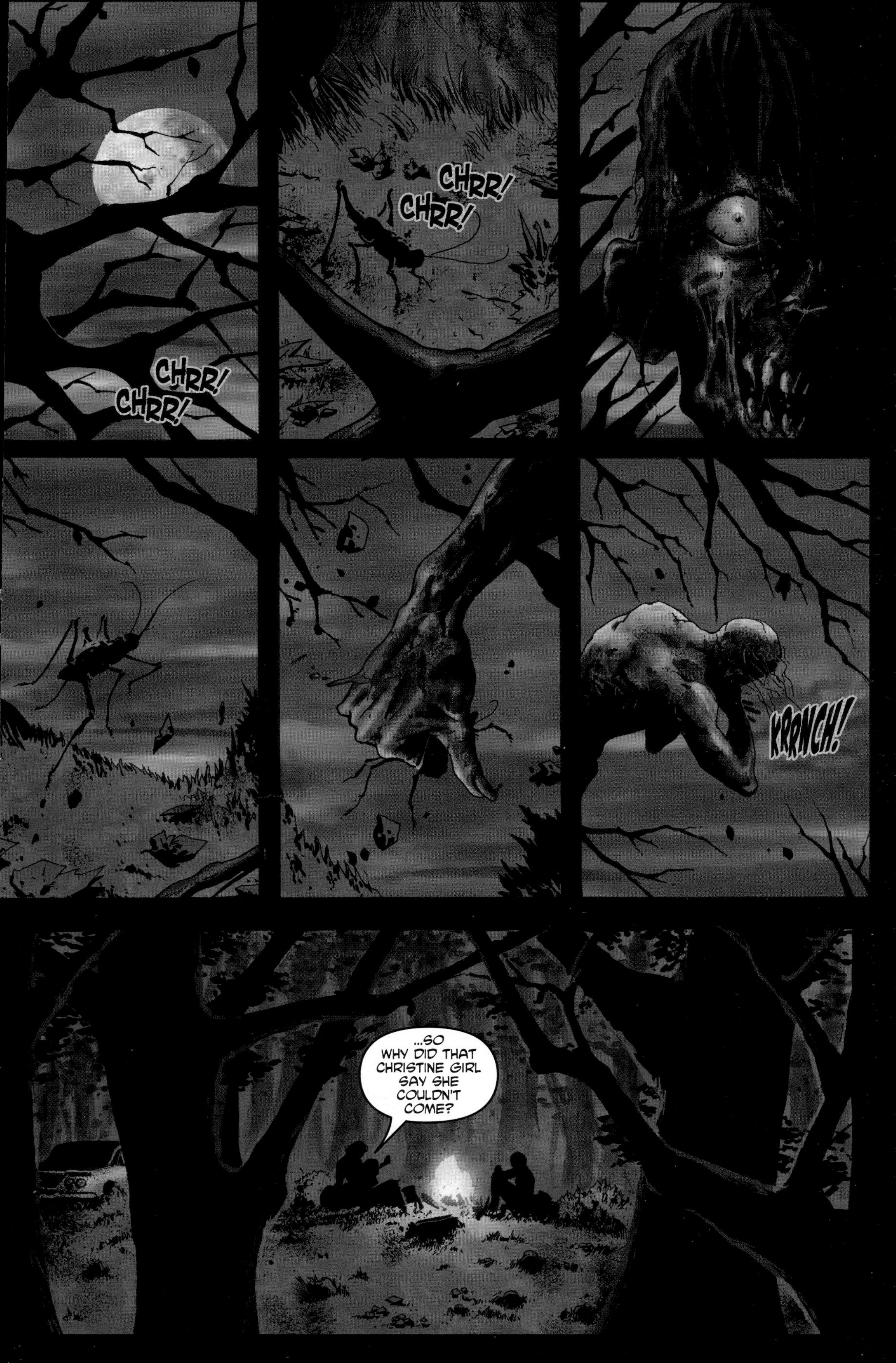
CHRR!
CHRR!
CHRR!
CHRR!
KRRNCH!
...SO WHY DID THAT CHRISTINE GIRL SAY SHE COULDN'T COME?

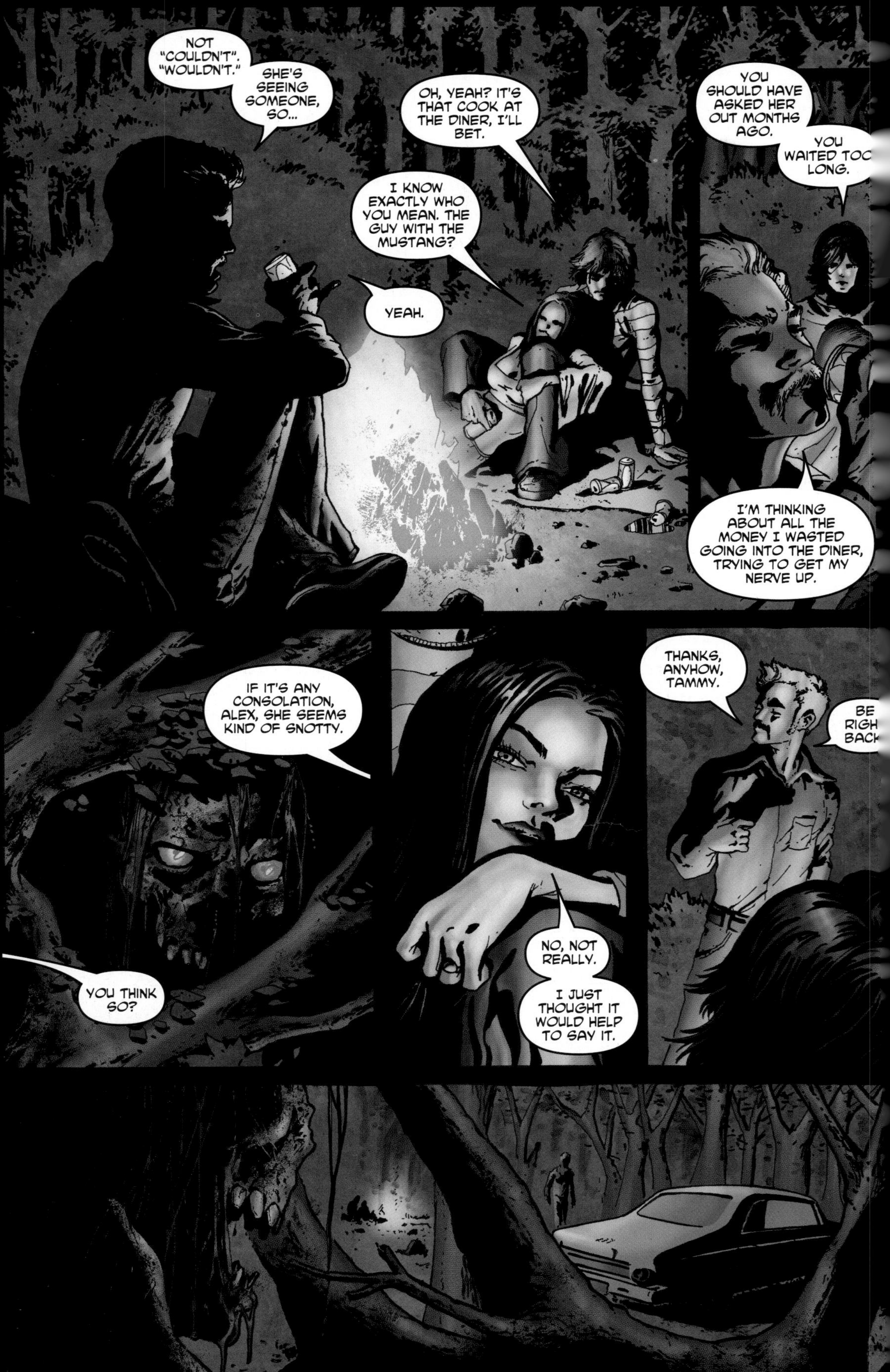
NOT "COULDN'T". "WOULDN'T."
SHE'S SEEING SOMEONE, SO...
OH, YEAH? IT'S THAT COOK AT THE DINER, I'LL BET.
I KNOW EXACTLY WHO YOU MEAN. THE GUY WITH THE MUSTANG?
YEAH.
YOU SHOULD HAVE ASKED HER OUT MONTHS AGO.
YOU WAITED TOO LONG.
I'M THINKING ABOUT ALL THE MONEY I WASTED GOING INTO THE DINER, TRYING TO GET MY NERVE UP.
IF IT'S ANY CONSOLATION, ALEX, SHE SEEMS KIND OF SNOTTY.
YOU THINK SO?
NO, NOT REALLY.
I JUST THOUGHT IT WOULD HELP TO SAY IT.
THANKS, ANYHOW, TAMMY.

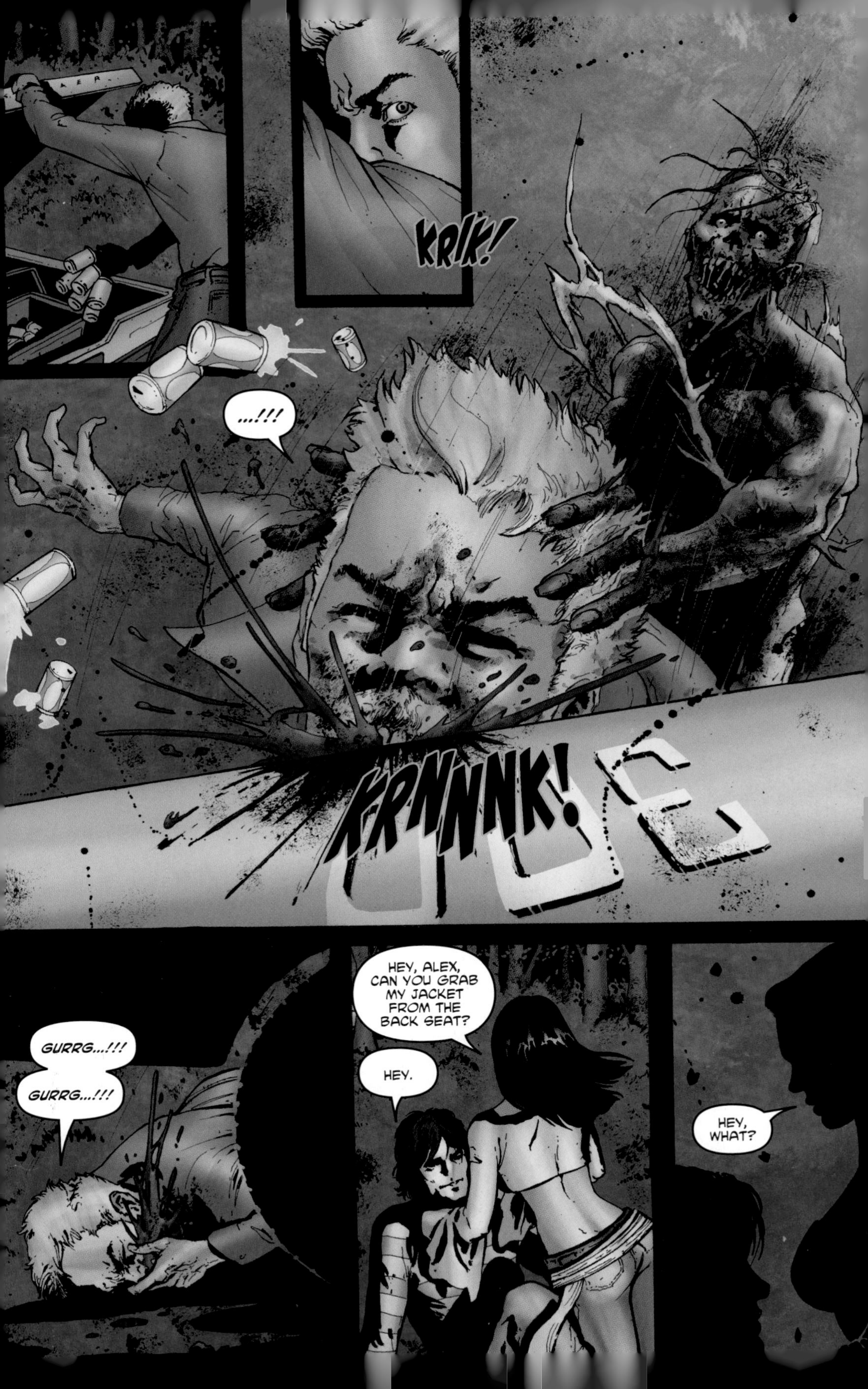
KRIK!
...!!!
KRNNNK!
GURRG...!!!
GURRG...!!!
HEY, ALEX, CAN YOU GRAB MY JACKET FROM THE BACK SEAT?
HEY.
HEY, WHAT?

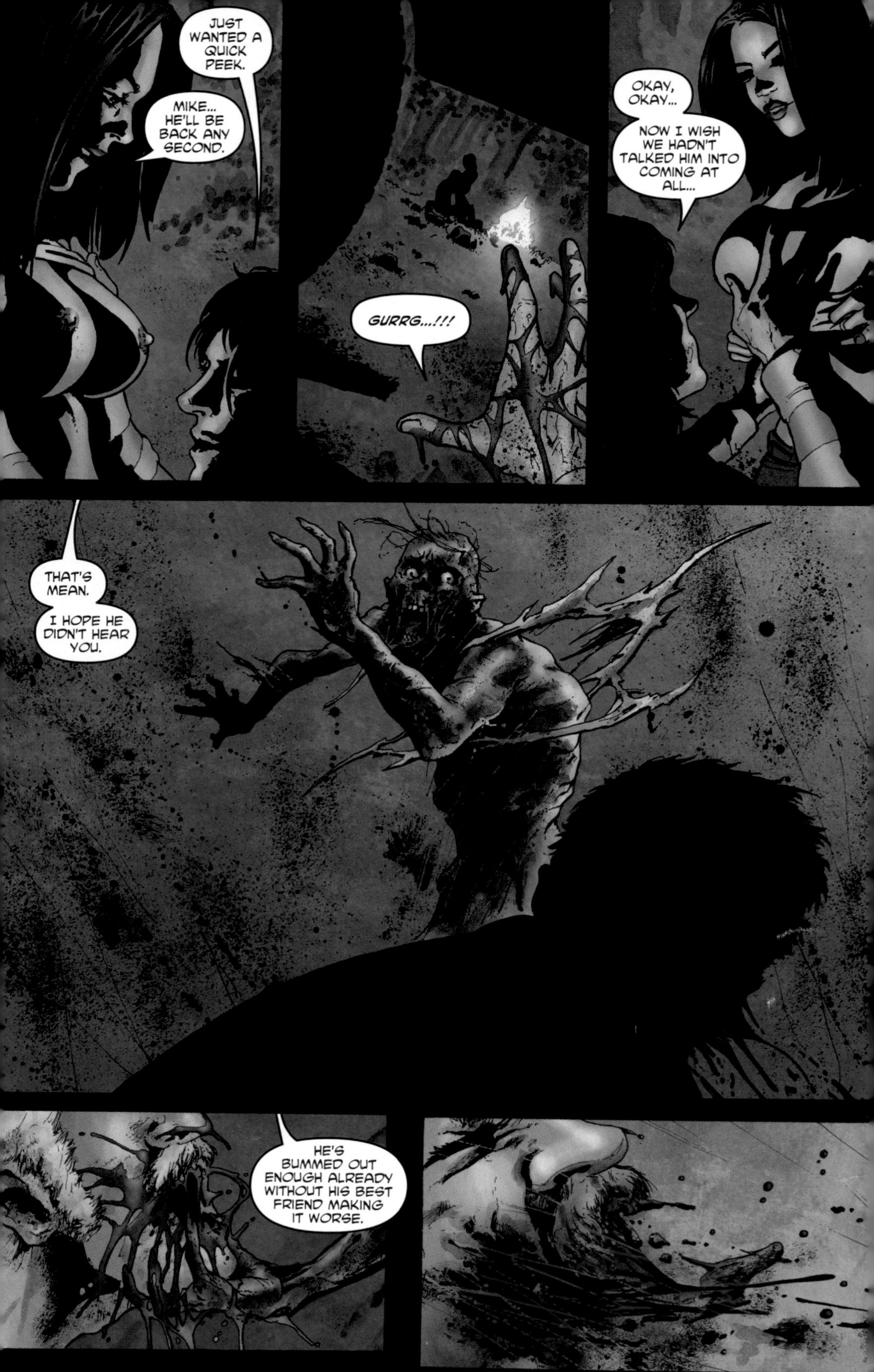
JUST WANTED A QUICK PEEK.
MIKE... HE'LL BE BACK ANY SECOND.
GURRG...!!!
OKAY, OKAY...
NOW I WISH WE HADN'T TALKED HIM INTO COMING AT ALL...
THAT'S MEAN.
I HOPE HE DIDN'T HEAR YOU.
HE'S BUMMED OUT ENOUGH ALREADY WITHOUT HIS BEST FRIEND MAKING IT WORSE.

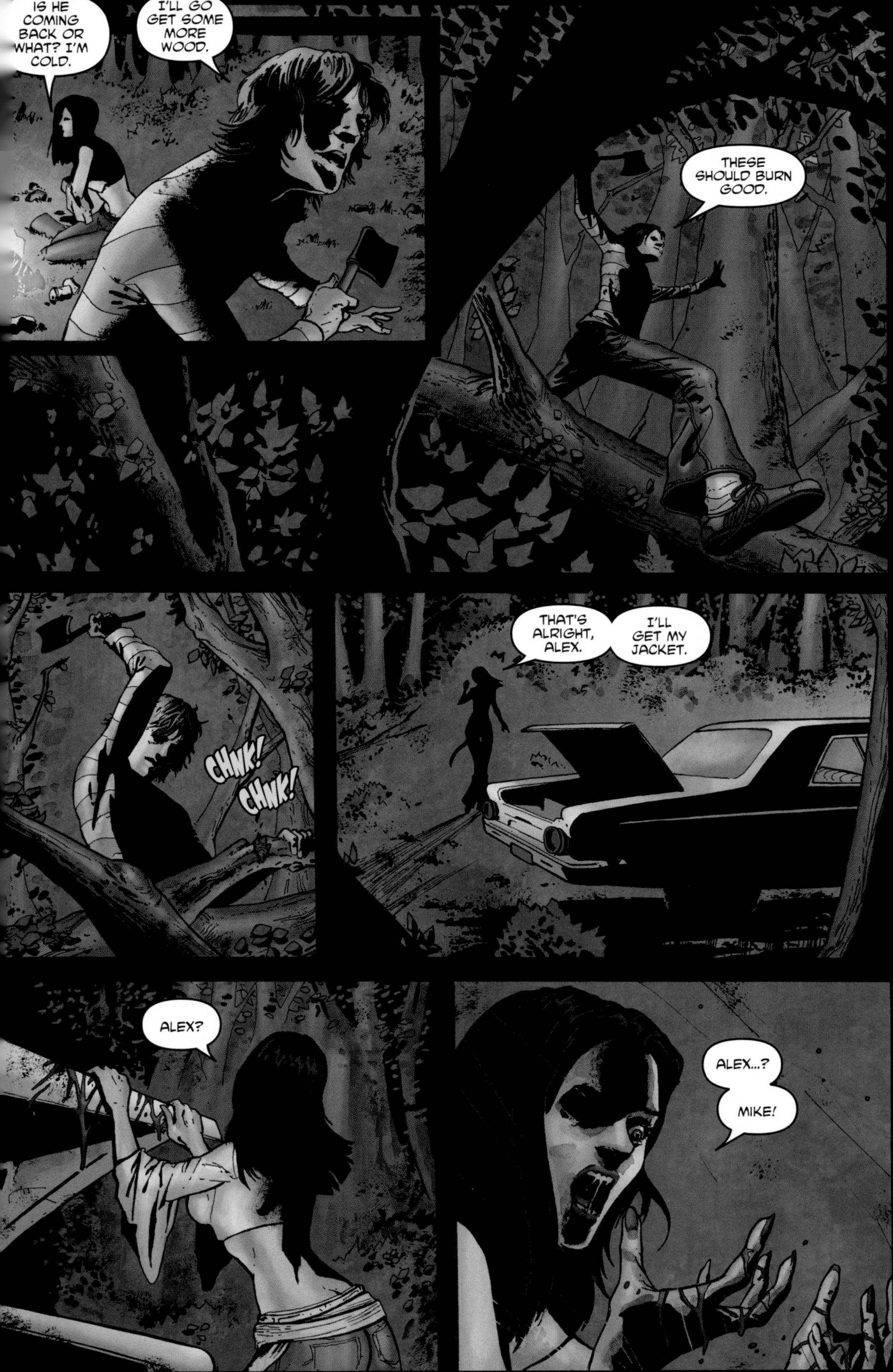
IS HE COMING BACK OR WHAT? I'M COLD.
I'LL GO GET SOME MORE WOOD.
THESE SHOULD BURN GOOD.
CHNK! CHNK!
THAT'S ALRIGHT, ALEX.
I'LL GET MY JACKET.
ALEX?
ALEX...?
MIKE!

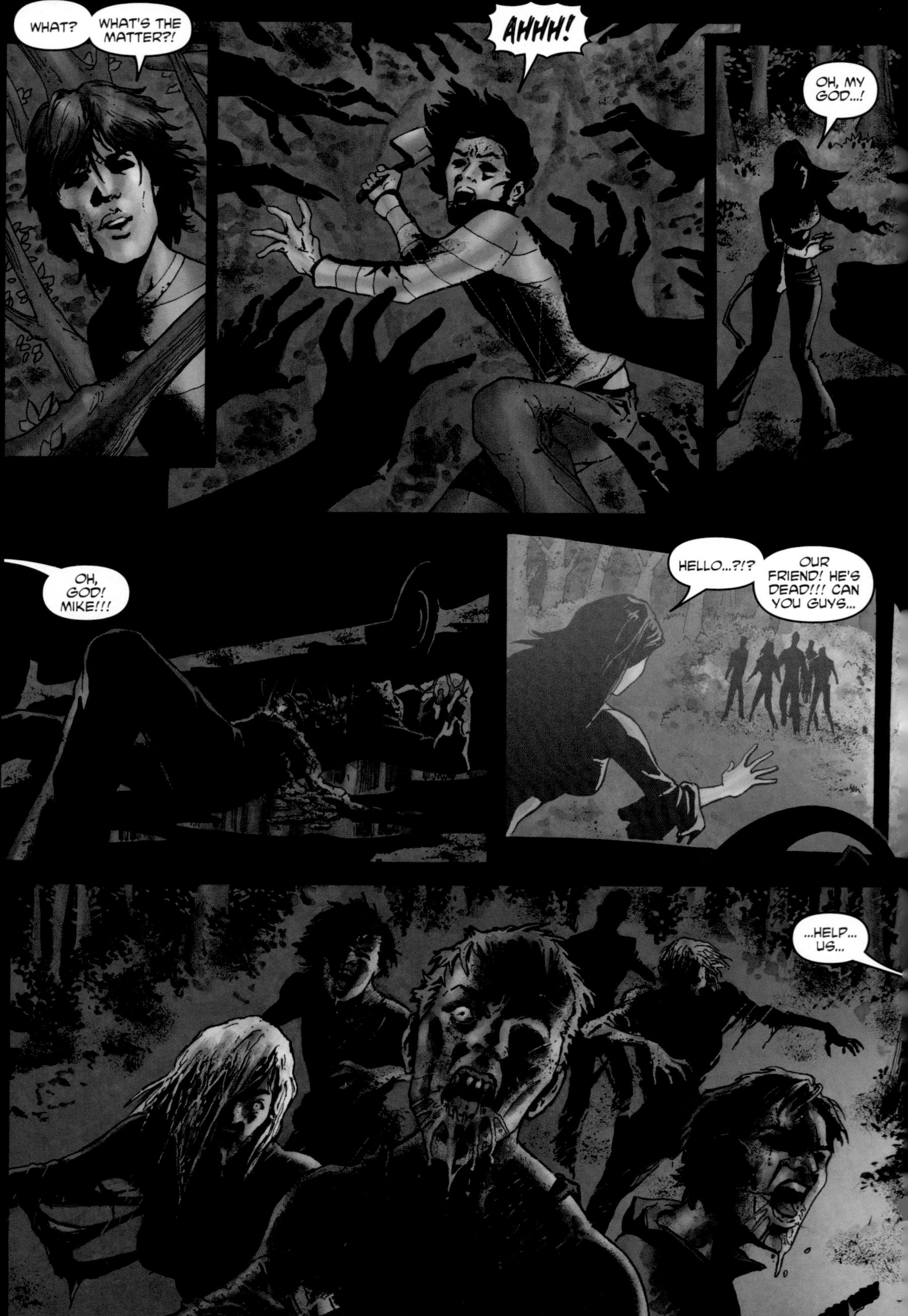
WHAT?
WHAT'S THE MATTER?!
AHHH!
OH, MY GOD...!
OH, GOD! MIKE!!!
HELLO...?!?
OUR FRIEND! HE'S DEAD!!! CAN YOU GUYS...
...HELP... US...

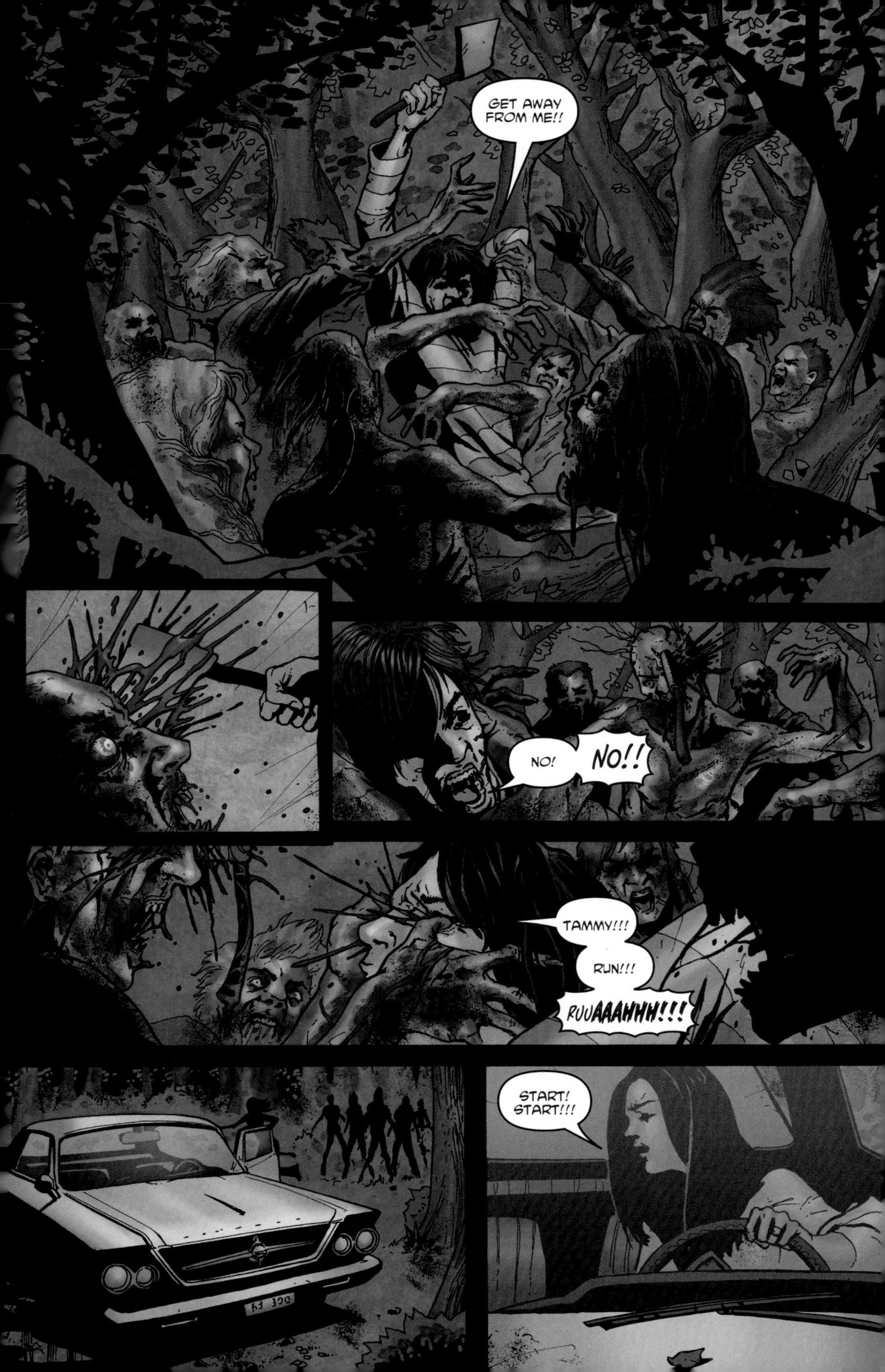
GET AWAY FROM ME!!
NO!
NO!!
TAMMY!!!
RUN!!!
RUUAAAHHH!!!
START! START!!!

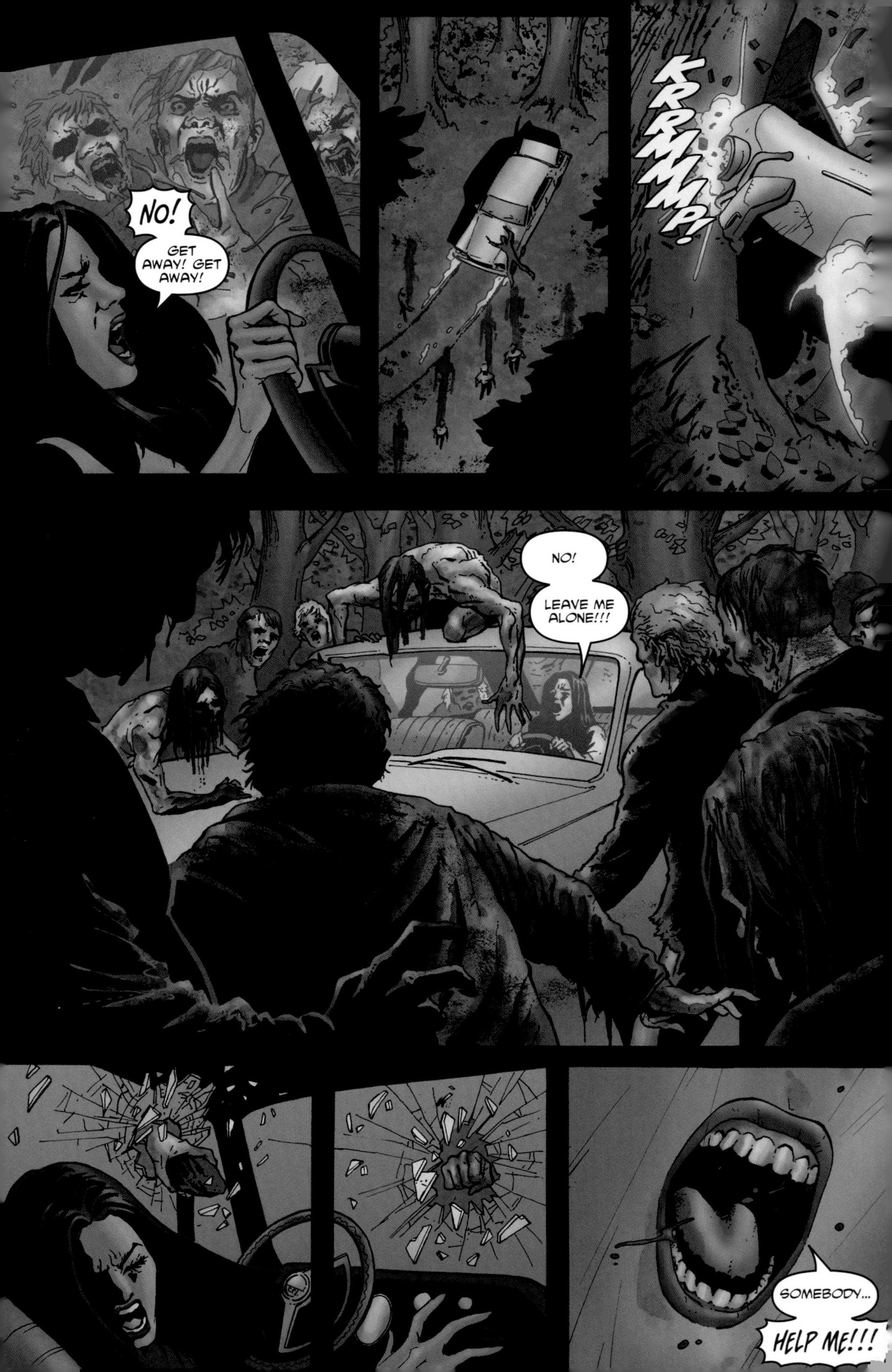
NO!
GET AWAY! GET AWAY!
KRRMMP!
NO!
LEAVE ME ALONE!!!
SOMEBODY...
HELP ME!!!

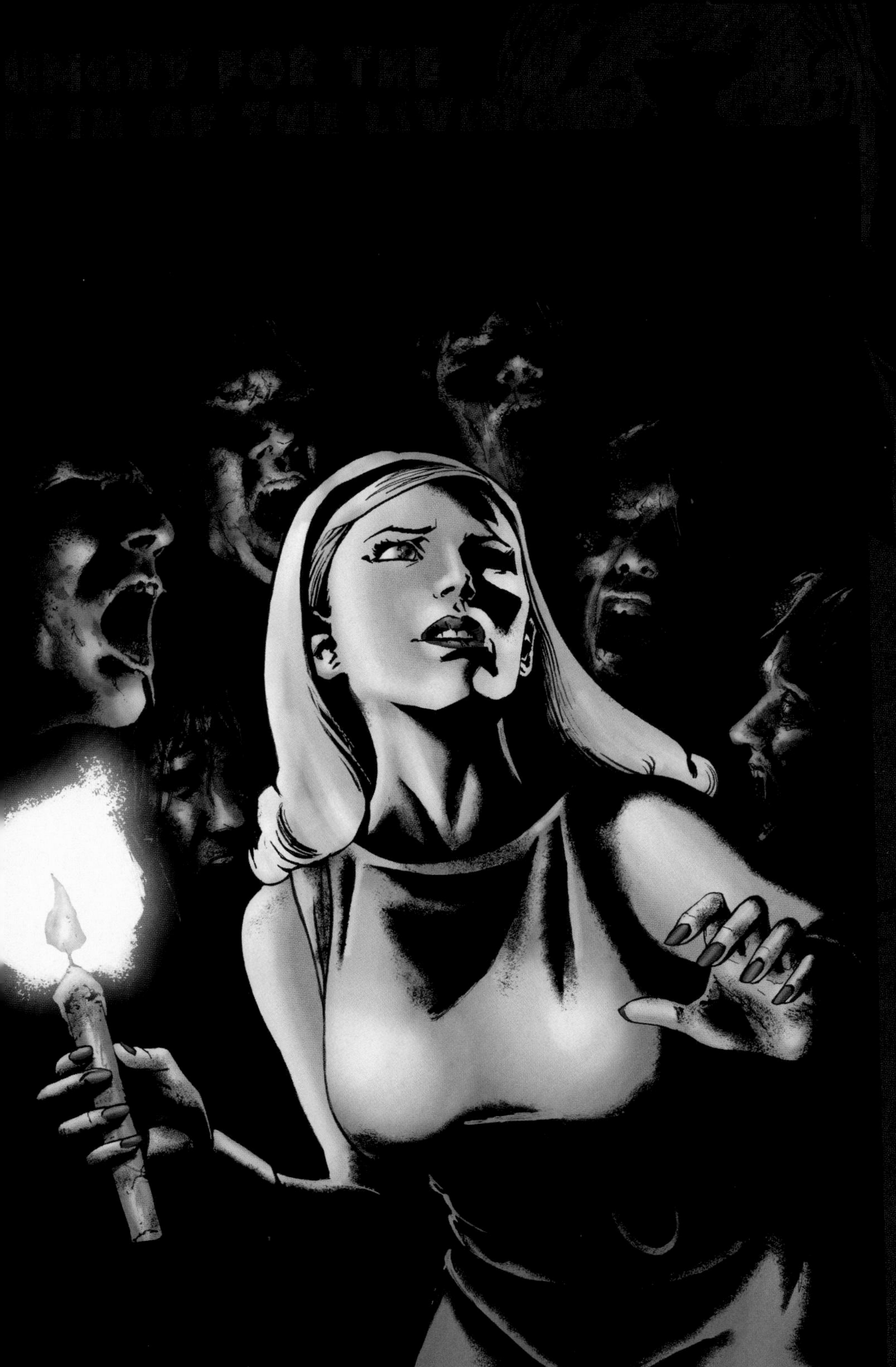

CHAPTER TWO

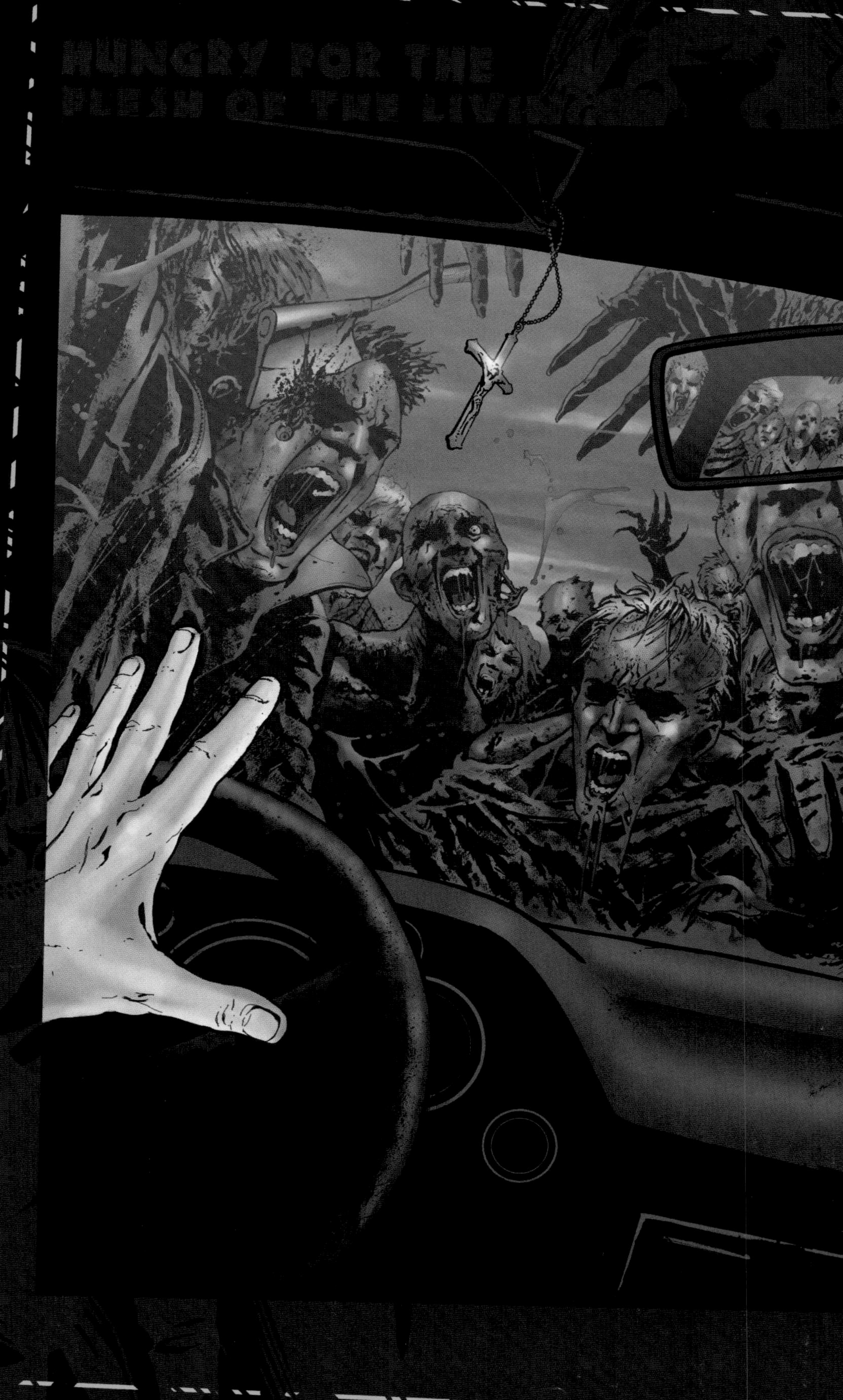
HUNGRY FOR THE
FLESH OF THE LIVIN

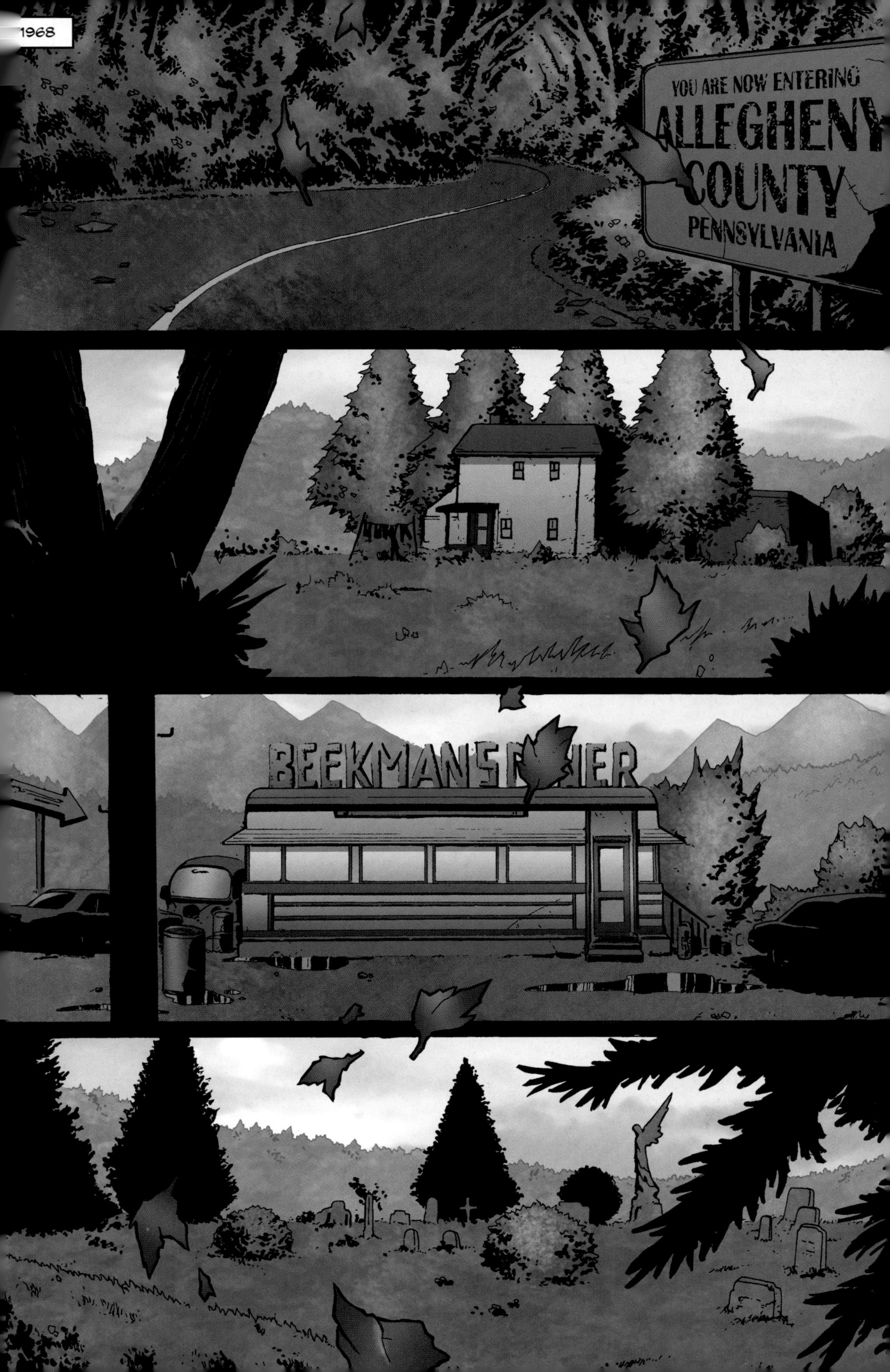
1968
YOU ARE NOW ENTERING
ALLEGHENY
COUNTY
PENNSYLVANIA
BEEKMANS

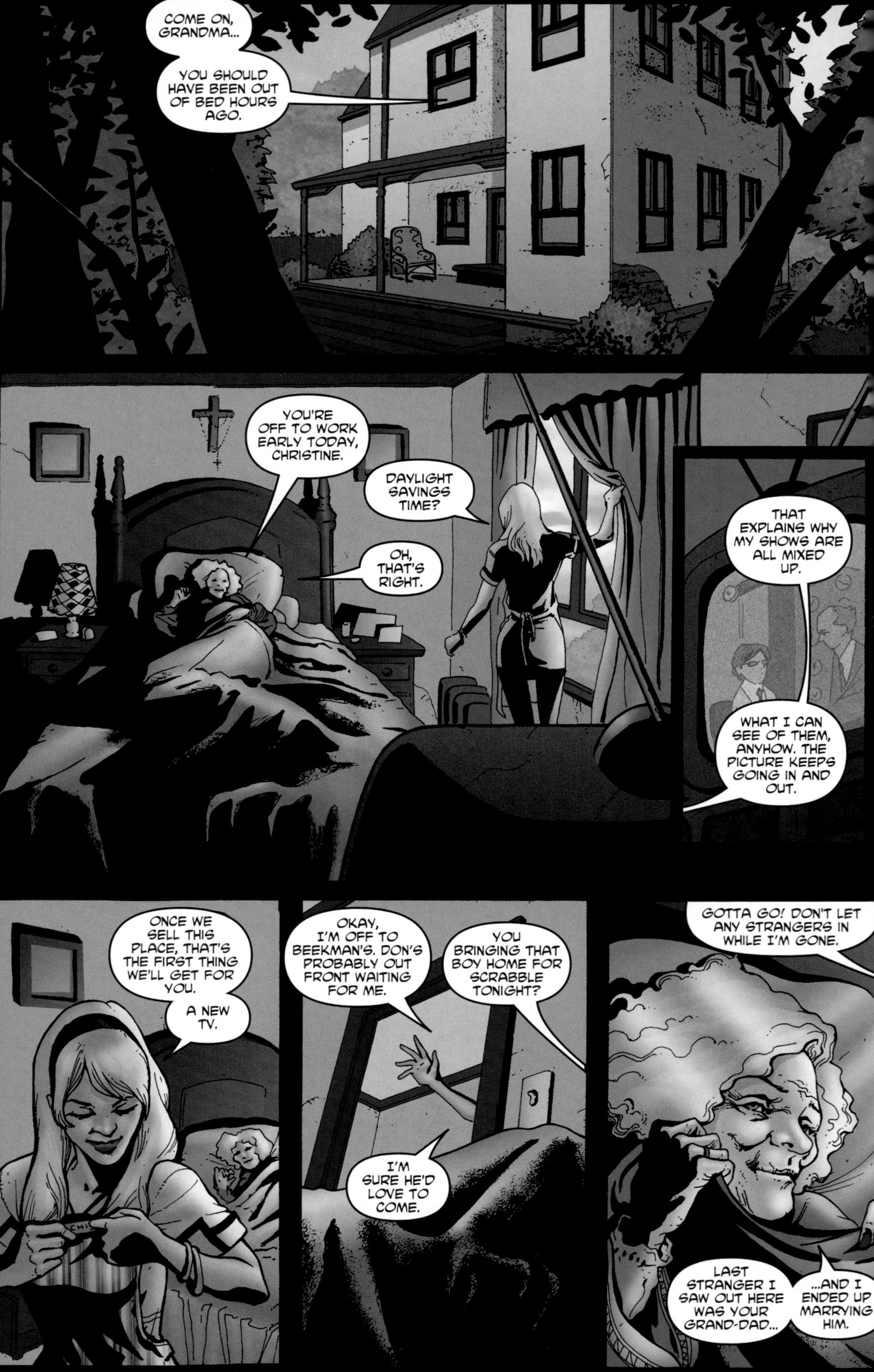
COME ON, GRANDMA...
YOU SHOULD HAVE BEEN OUT OF BED HOURS AGO.
YOU'RE OFF TO WORK EARLY TODAY, CHRISTINE.
DAYLIGHT SAVINGS TIME?
OH, THAT'S RIGHT.
THAT EXPLAINS WHY MY SHOWS ARE ALL MIXED UP.
WHAT I CAN SEE OF THEM, ANYHOW. THE PICTURE KEEPS GOING IN AND OUT.
ONCE WE SELL THIS PLACE, THAT'S THE FIRST THING WE'LL GET FOR YOU.
A NEW TV.
OKAY, I'M OFF TO BEEKMAN'S. DON'S PROBABLY OUT FRONT WAITING FOR ME.
YOU BRINGING THAT BOY HOME FOR SCRABBLE TONIGHT?
I'M SURE HE'D LOVE TO COME.
GOTTA GO! DON'T LET ANY STRANGERS IN WHILE I'M GONE.
LAST STRANGER I SAW OUT HERE WAS YOUR GRAND-DAD...
...AND I ENDED UP MARRYING HIM.

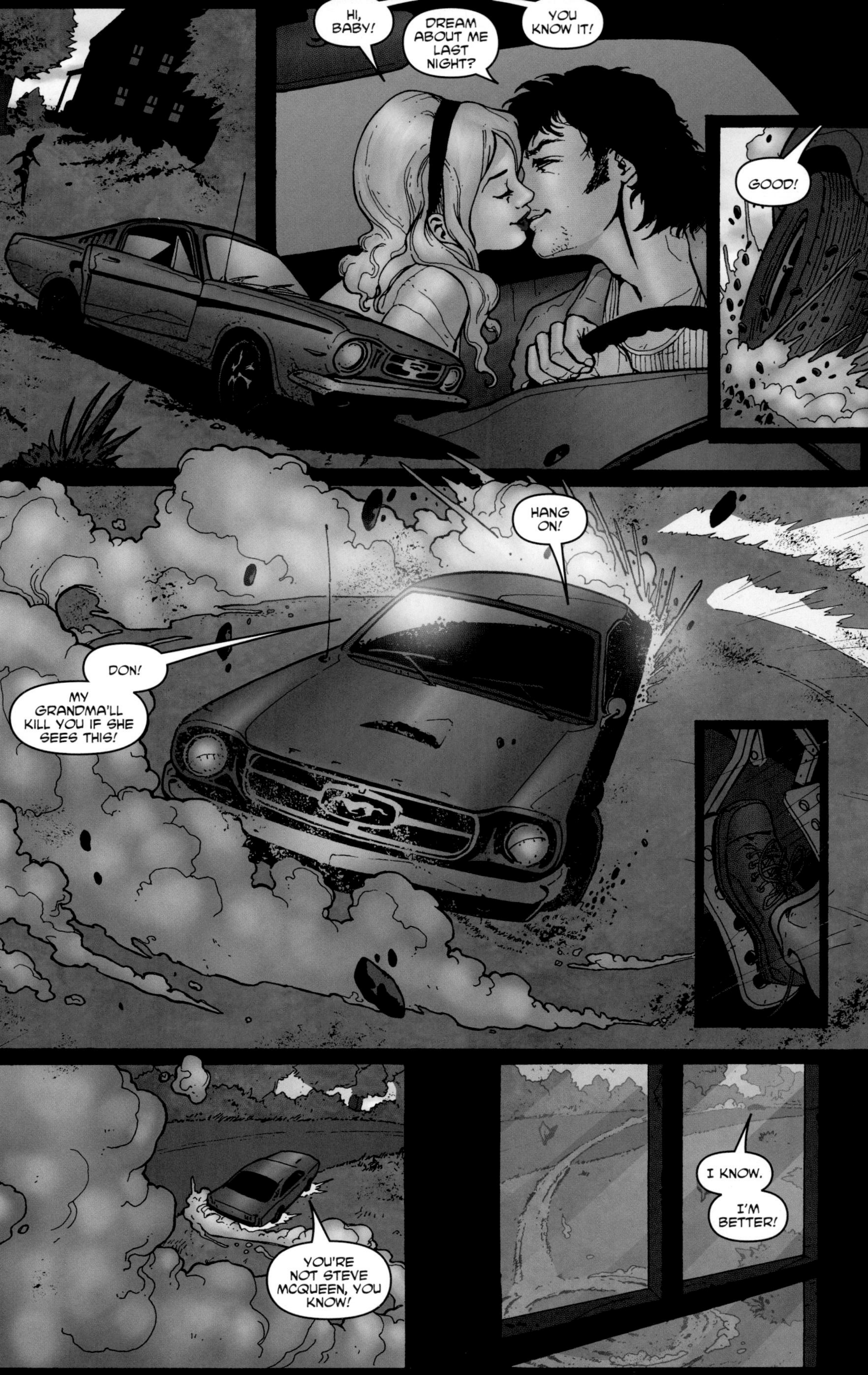
HI, BABY!
DREAM ABOUT ME LAST NIGHT?
YOU KNOW IT!
GOOD!
HANG ON!
DON!
MY GRANDMA'LL KILL YOU IF SHE SEES THIS!
YOU'RE NOT STEVE MCQUEEN, YOU KNOW!
I KNOW.
I'M BETTER!

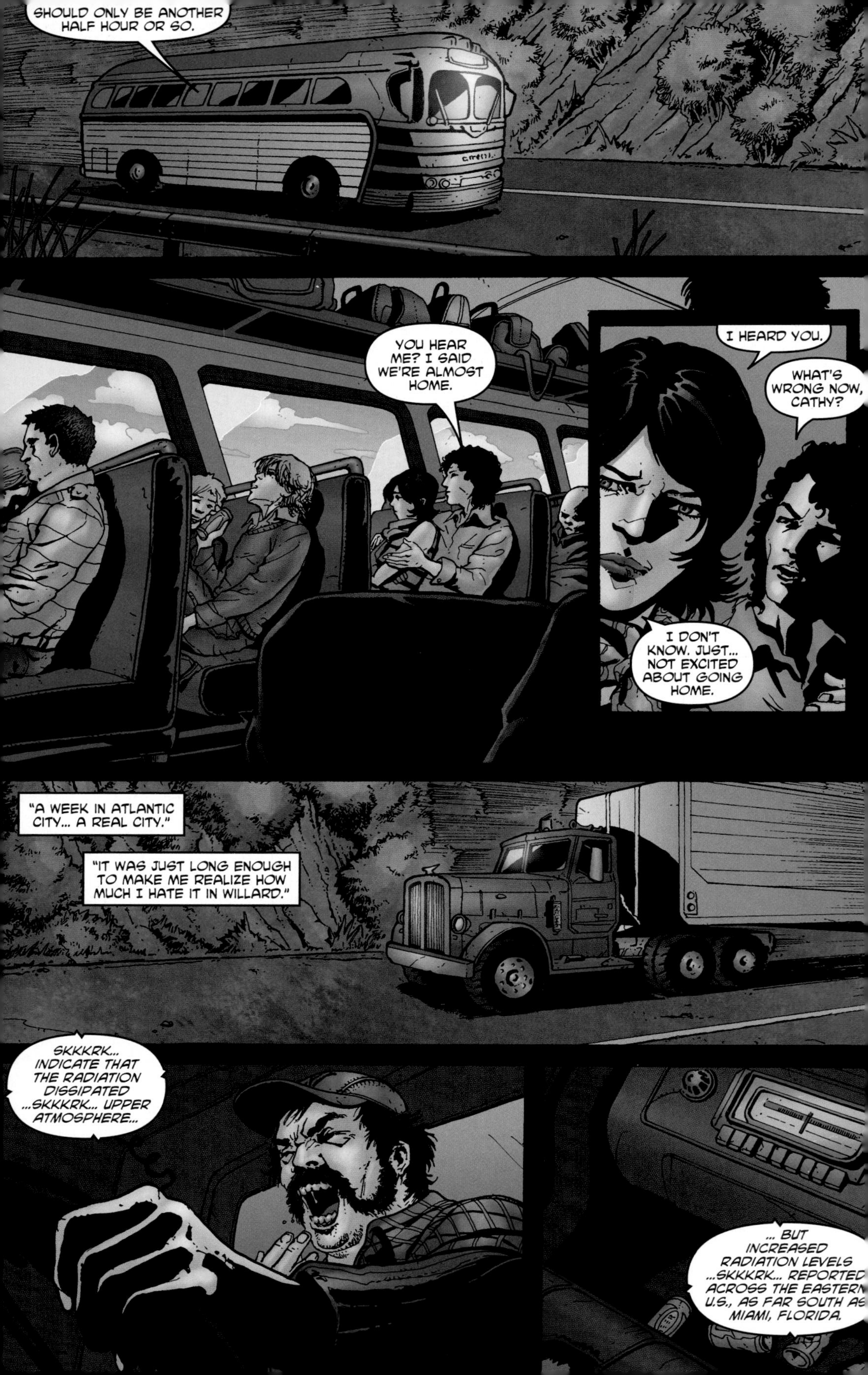
SHOULD ONLY BE ANOTHER HALF HOUR OR SO.
YOU HEAR ME? I SAID WE'RE ALMOST HOME.
I HEARD YOU.
WHAT'S WRONG NOW, CATHY?
I DON'T KNOW. JUST... NOT EXCITED ABOUT GOING HOME.
"A WEEK IN ATLANTIC CITY... A REAL CITY."
"IT WAS JUST LONG ENOUGH TO MAKE ME REALIZE HOW MUCH I HATE IT IN WILLARD."
SKKKRK... INDICATE THAT THE RADIATION DISSIPATED ...SKKKRK... UPPER ATMOSPHERE...
... BUT INCREASED RADIATION LEVELS ...SKKKRK... REPORTED ACROSS THE EASTERN U.S., AS FAR SOUTH AS MIAMI, FLORIDA.

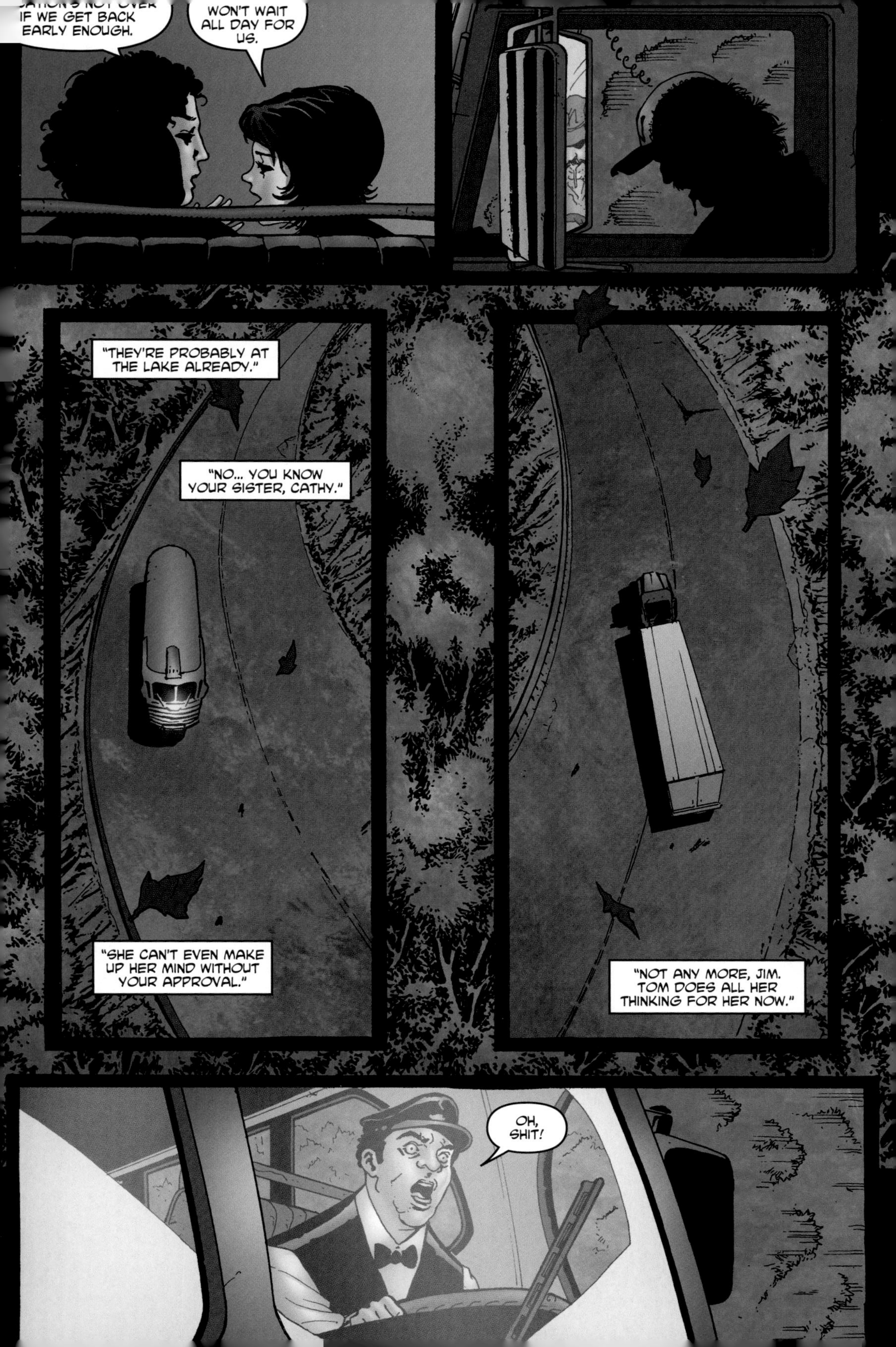
IF WE GET BACK
EARLY ENOUGH.
WON'T WAIT
ALL DAY FOR
US.
"THEY'RE PROBABLY AT
THE LAKE ALREADY."
"NO... YOU KNOW
YOUR SISTER, CATHY."
"SHE CAN'T EVEN MAKE
UP HER MIND WITHOUT
YOUR APPROVAL."
"NOT ANY MORE, JIM.
TOM DOES ALL HER
THINKING FOR HER NOW."
OH,
SHIT!

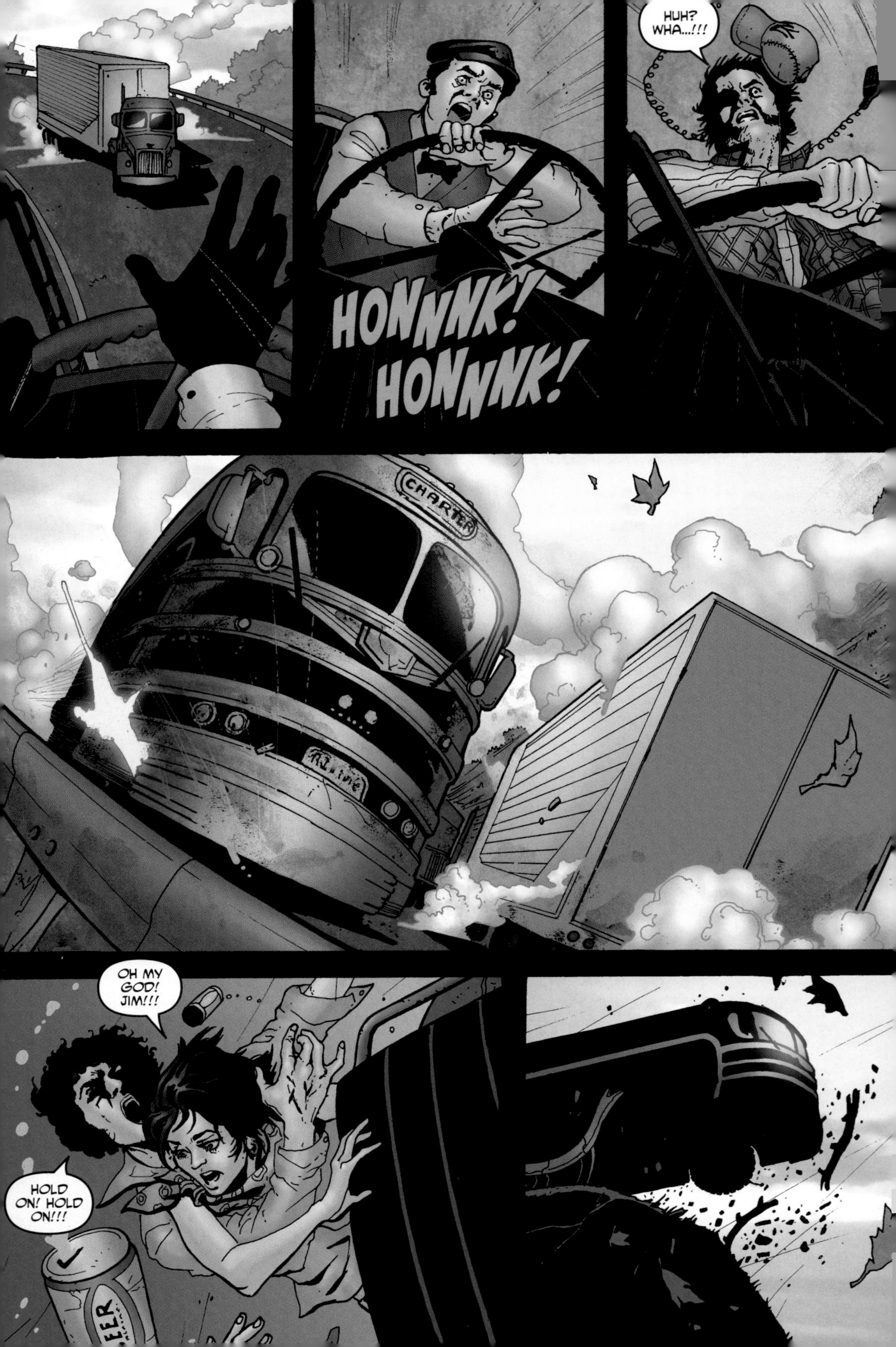
HONNNK! HONNNK!
HUH? WHA...!!!
CHARTER
OH MY GOD! JIM!!!
HOLD ON! HOLD ON!!!
EER

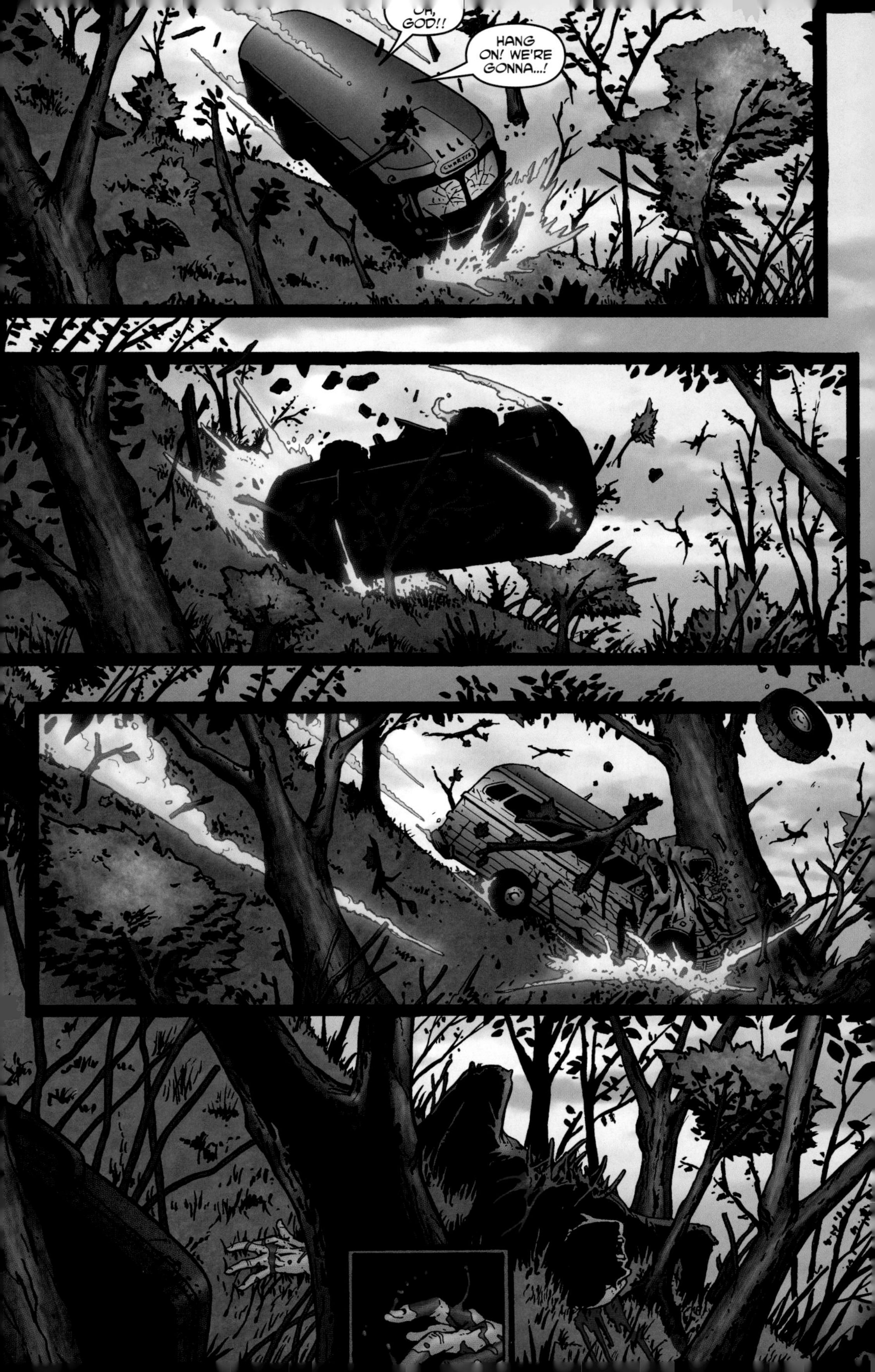
GOD!!
HANG ON! WE'RE GONNA...!

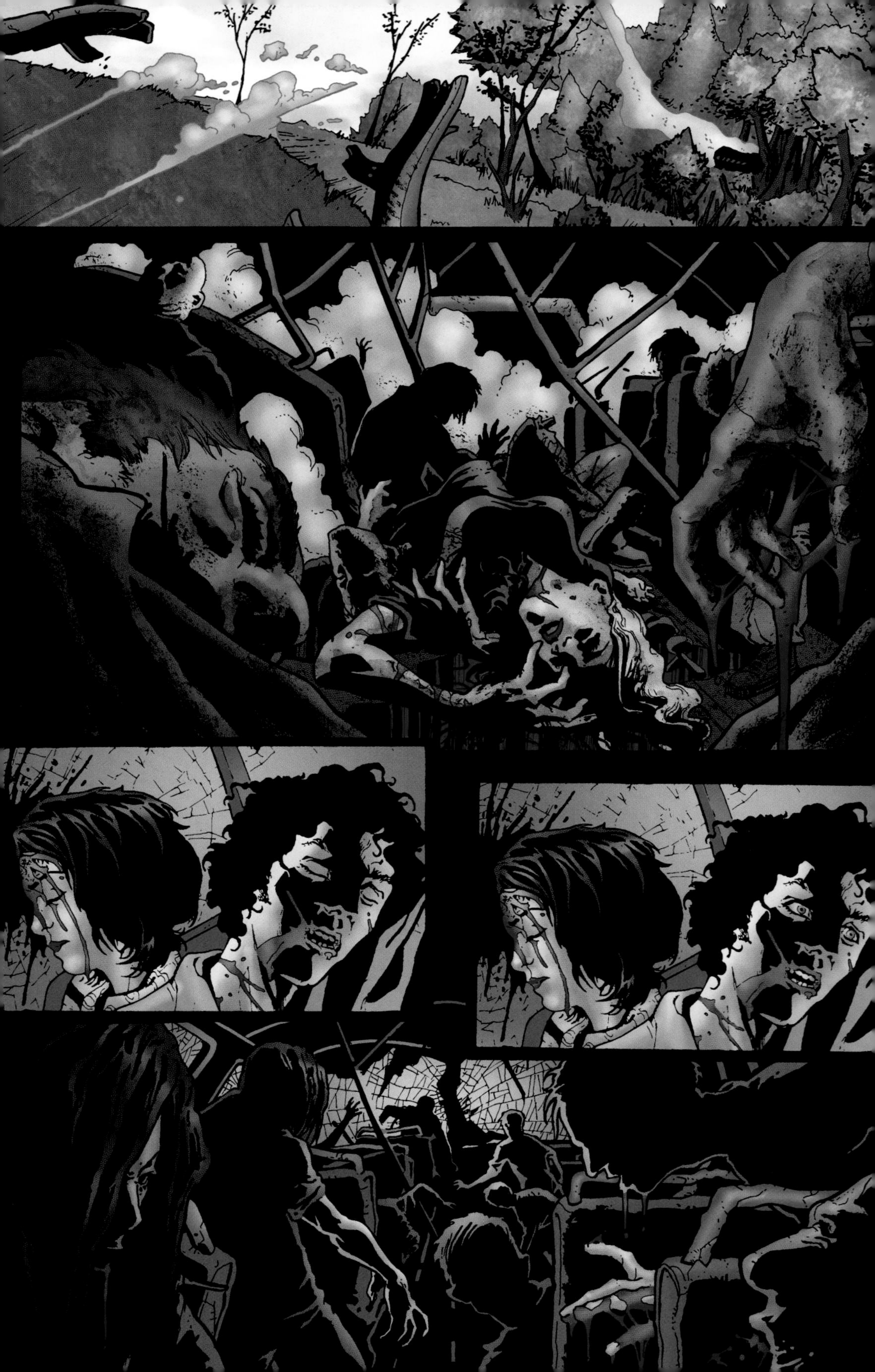

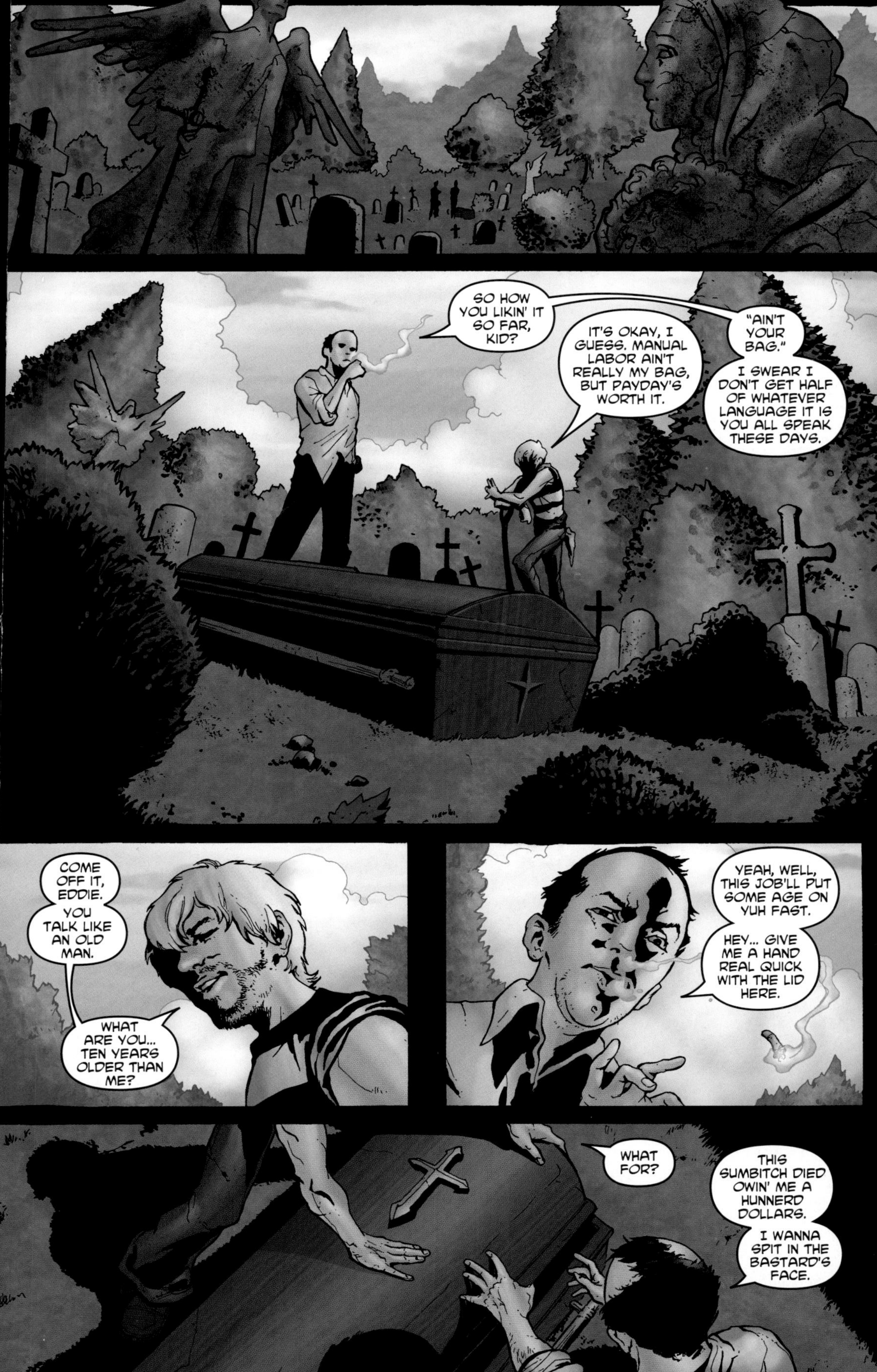
SO HOW YOU LIKIN' IT SO FAR, KID?
IT'S OKAY, I GUESS. MANUAL LABOR AIN'T REALLY MY BAG, BUT PAYDAY'S WORTH IT.
"AIN'T YOUR BAG."
I SWEAR I DON'T GET HALF OF WHATEVER LANGUAGE IT IS YOU ALL SPEAK THESE DAYS.
COME OFF IT, EDDIE.
YOU TALK LIKE AN OLD MAN.
WHAT ARE YOU... TEN YEARS OLDER THAN ME?
YEAH, WELL, THIS JOB'LL PUT SOME AGE ON YUH FAST.
HEY... GIVE ME A HAND REAL QUICK WITH THE LID HERE.
WHAT FOR?
THIS SUMBITCH DIED OWIN' ME A HUNNERD DOLLARS.
I WANNA SPIT IN THE BASTARD'S FACE.

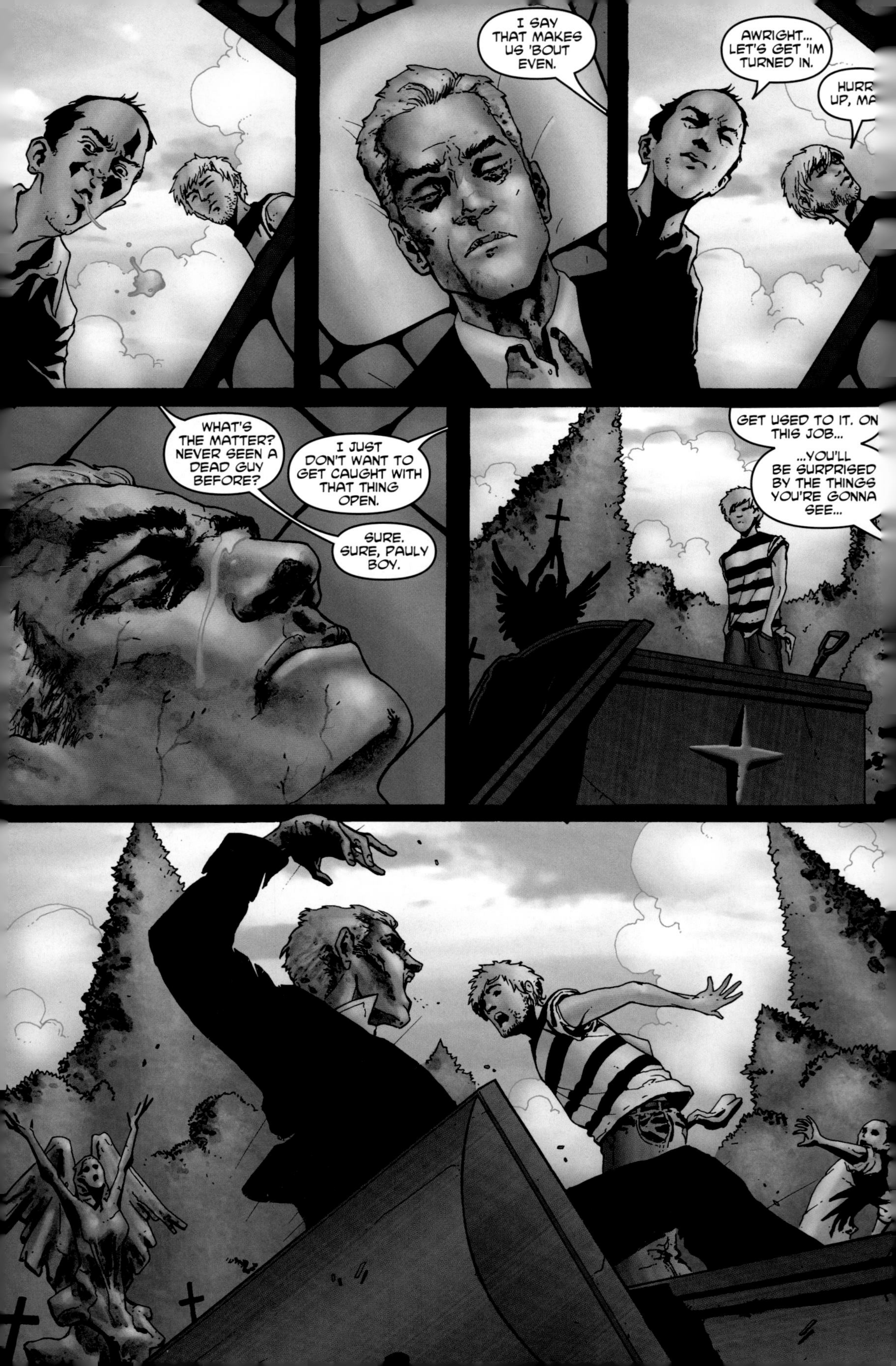
I SAY THAT MAKES US 'BOUT EVEN.
AWRIGHT... LET'S GET 'IM TURNED IN.
WHAT'S THE MATTER? NEVER SEEN A DEAD GUY BEFORE?
I JUST DON'T WANT TO GET CAUGHT WITH THAT THING OPEN.
SURE. SURE, PAULY BOY.
GET USED TO IT. ON THIS JOB...
...YOU'LL BE SURPRISED BY THE THINGS YOU'RE GONNA SEE...

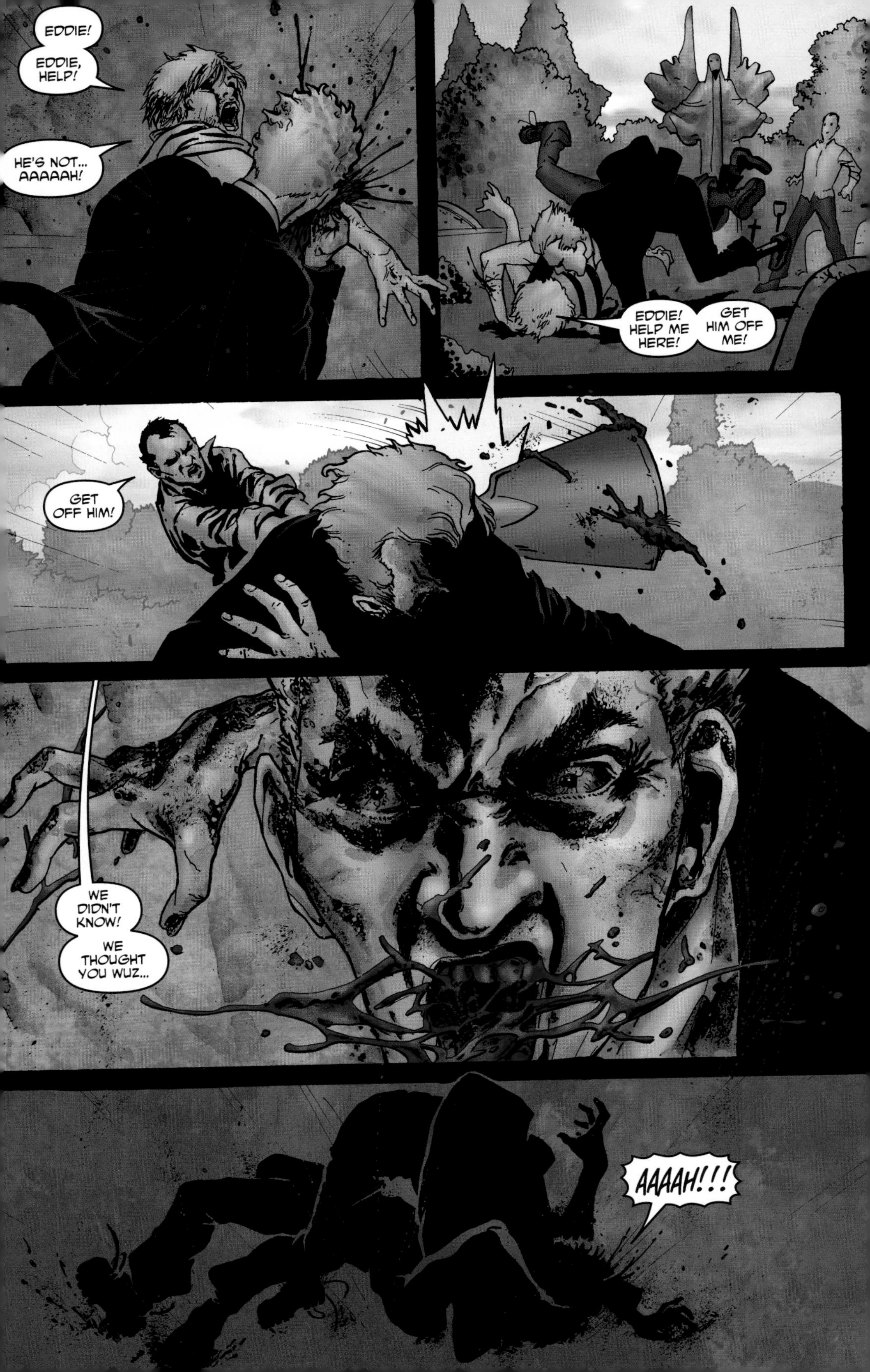
EDDIE!
EDDIE, HELP!
HE'S NOT... AAAAAH!
EDDIE! HELP ME HERE!
GET HIM OFF ME!
GET OFF HIM!
WE DIDN'T KNOW!
WE THOUGHT YOU WUZ...
AAAAH!!!

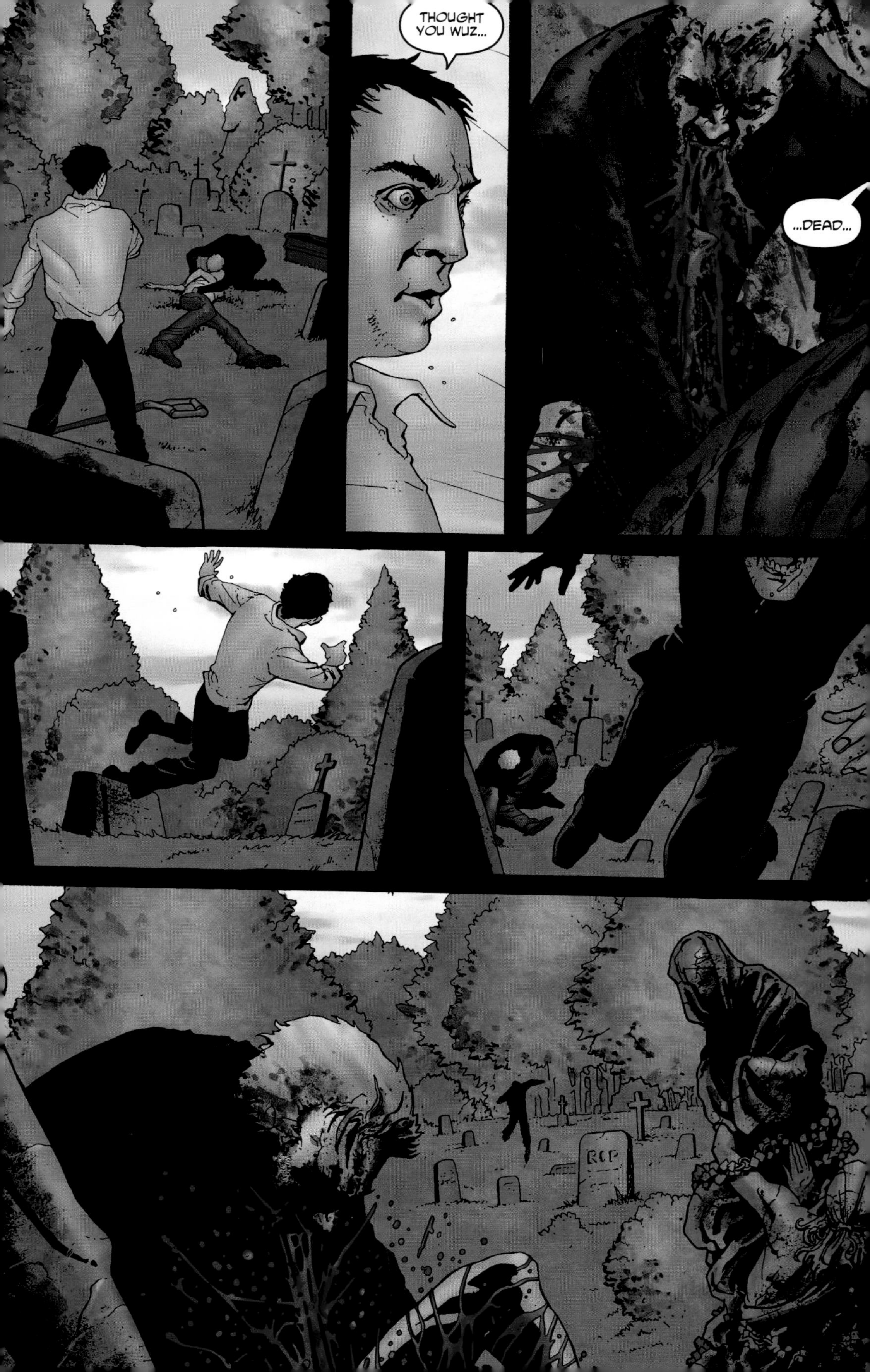
THOUGHT YOU WUZ...
...DEAD...
RIP

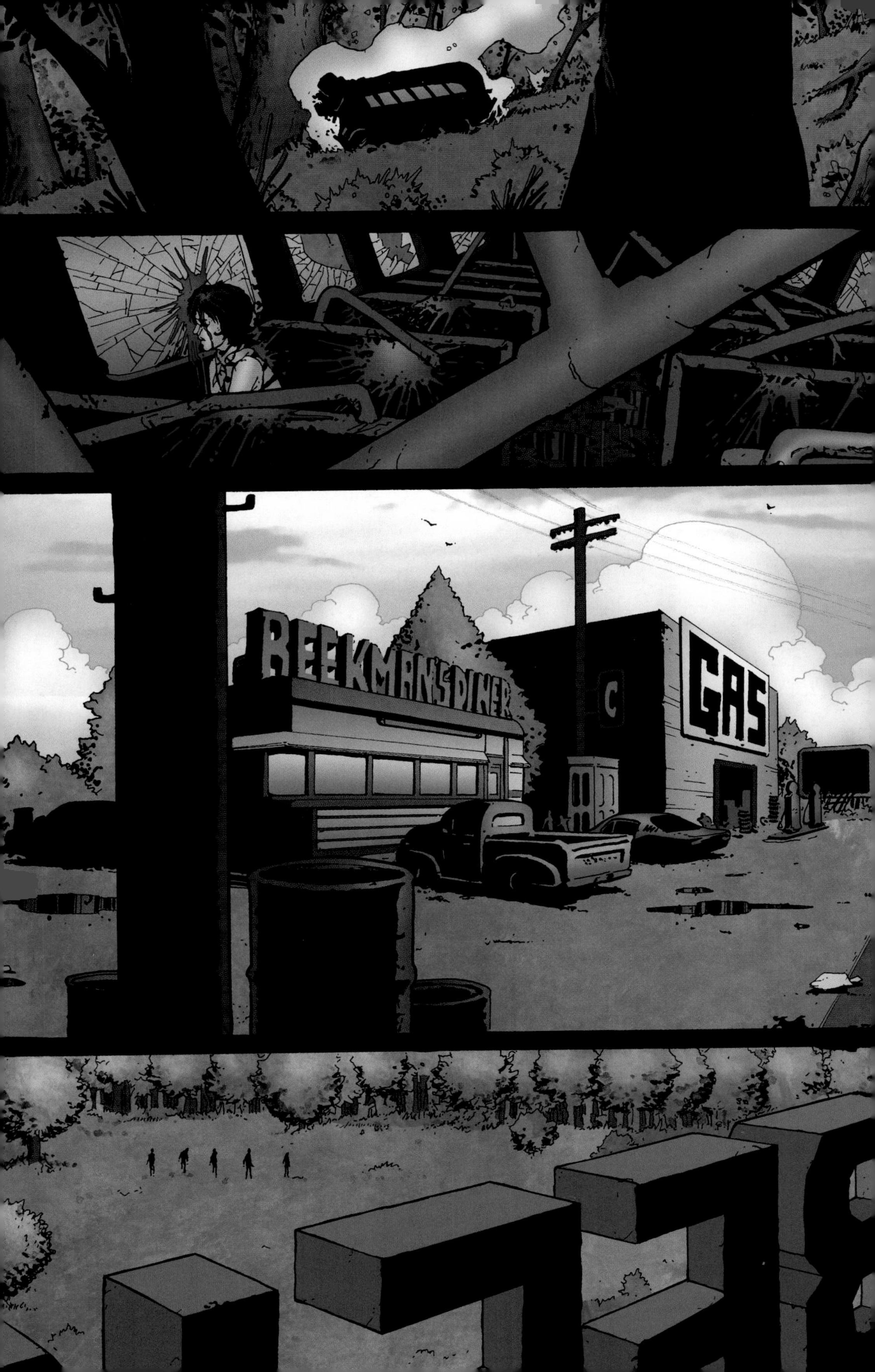
BEEKMAN'S DINER
C
GAS

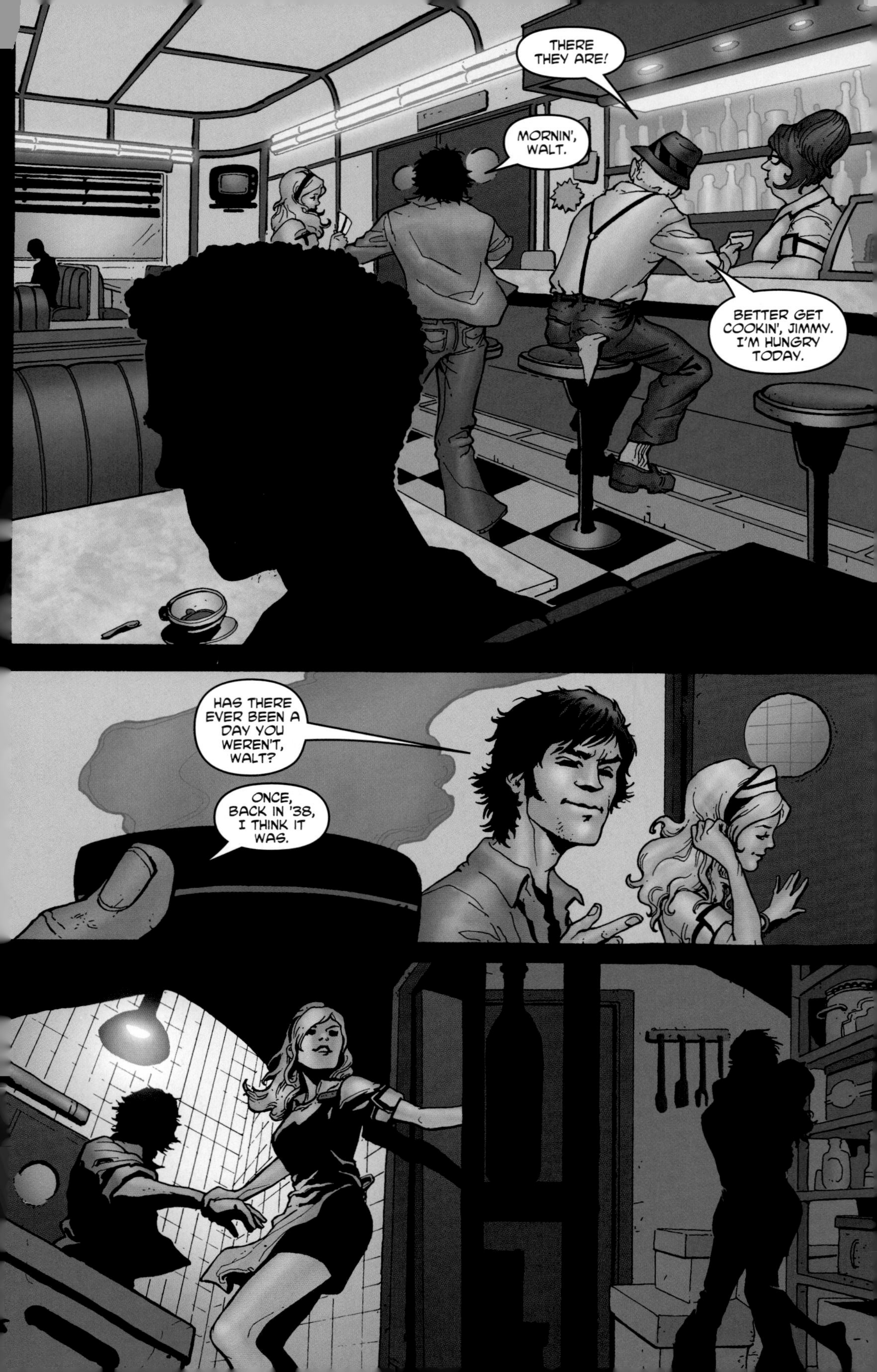
THERE THEY ARE!
MORNIN', WALT.
BETTER GET COOKIN', JIMMY. I'M HUNGRY TODAY.
HAS THERE EVER BEEN A DAY YOU WEREN'T, WALT?
ONCE, BACK IN '38, I THINK IT WAS.

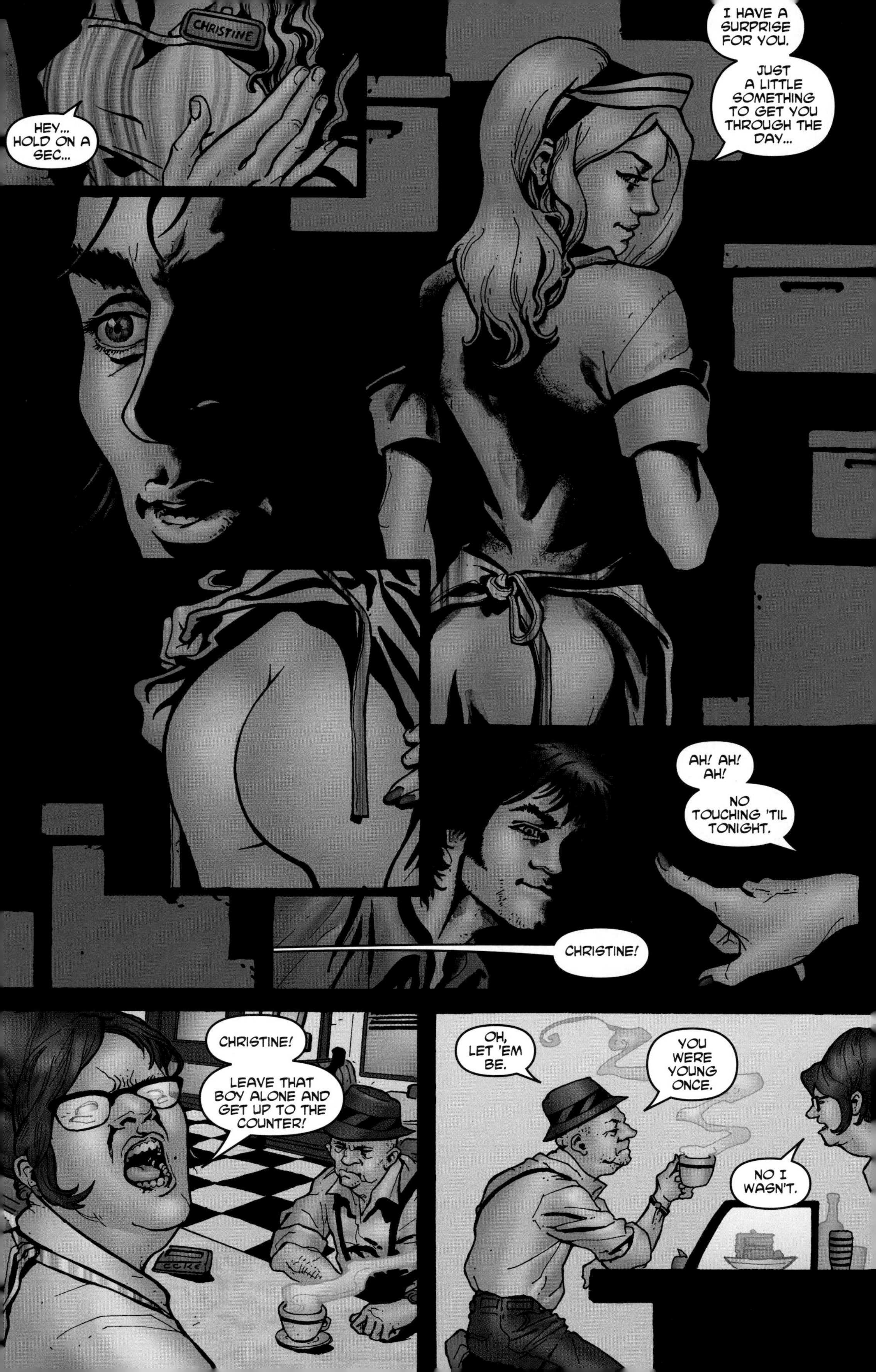
CHRISTINE
HEY... HOLD ON A SEC...
I HAVE A SURPRISE FOR YOU.
JUST A LITTLE SOMETHING TO GET YOU THROUGH THE DAY...
AH! AH! AH!
NO TOUCHING 'TIL TONIGHT.
CHRISTINE!
CHRISTINE!
LEAVE THAT BOY ALONE AND GET UP TO THE COUNTER!
OH, LET 'EM BE.
YOU WERE YOUNG ONCE.
NO I WASN'T.

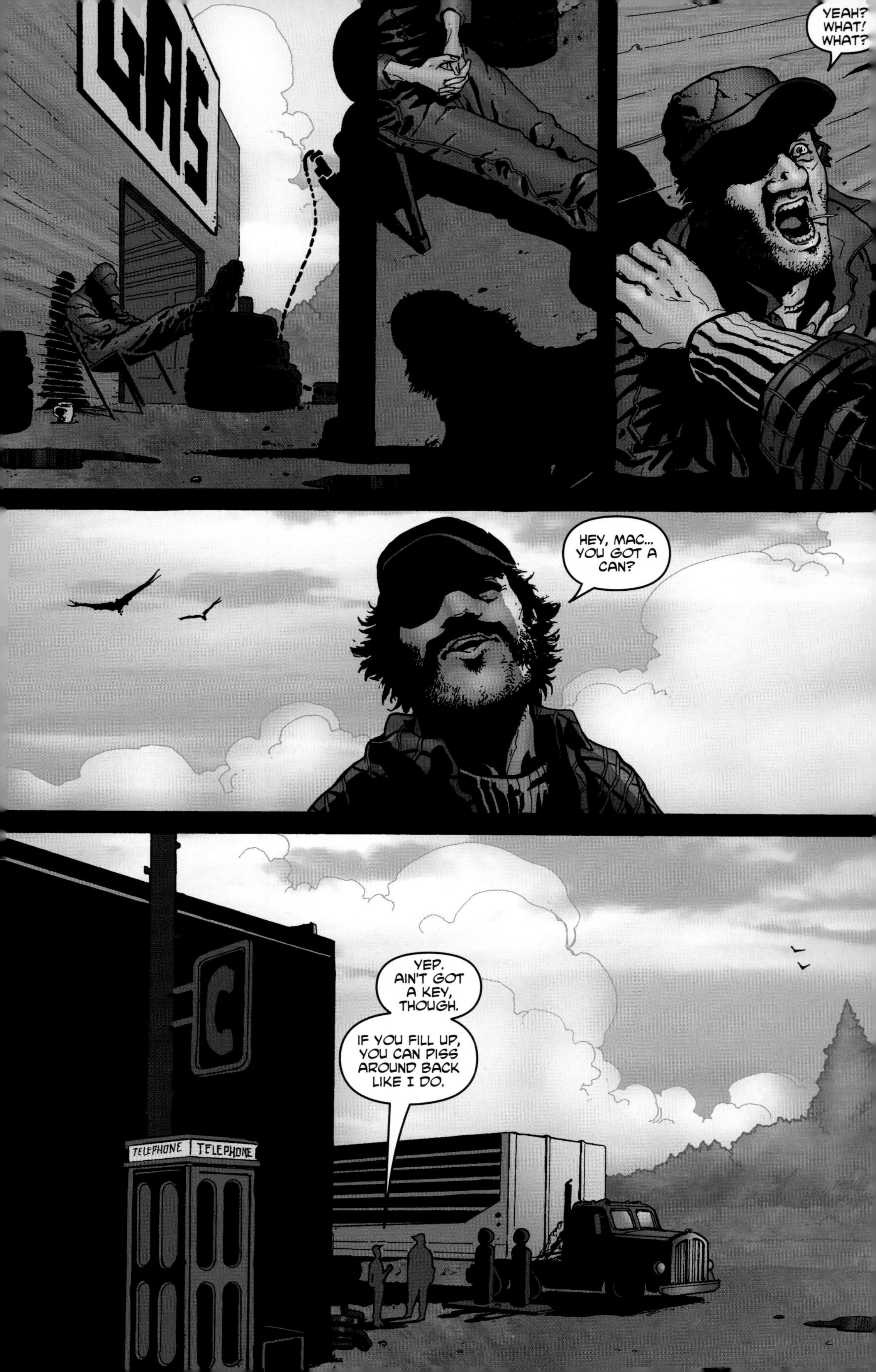
YEAH? WHAT! WHAT?
HEY, MAC... YOU GOT A CAN?
YEP. AIN'T GOT A KEY, THOUGH.
IF YOU FILL UP, YOU CAN PISS AROUND BACK LIKE I DO.
GAS
TELEPHONE
TELEPHONE

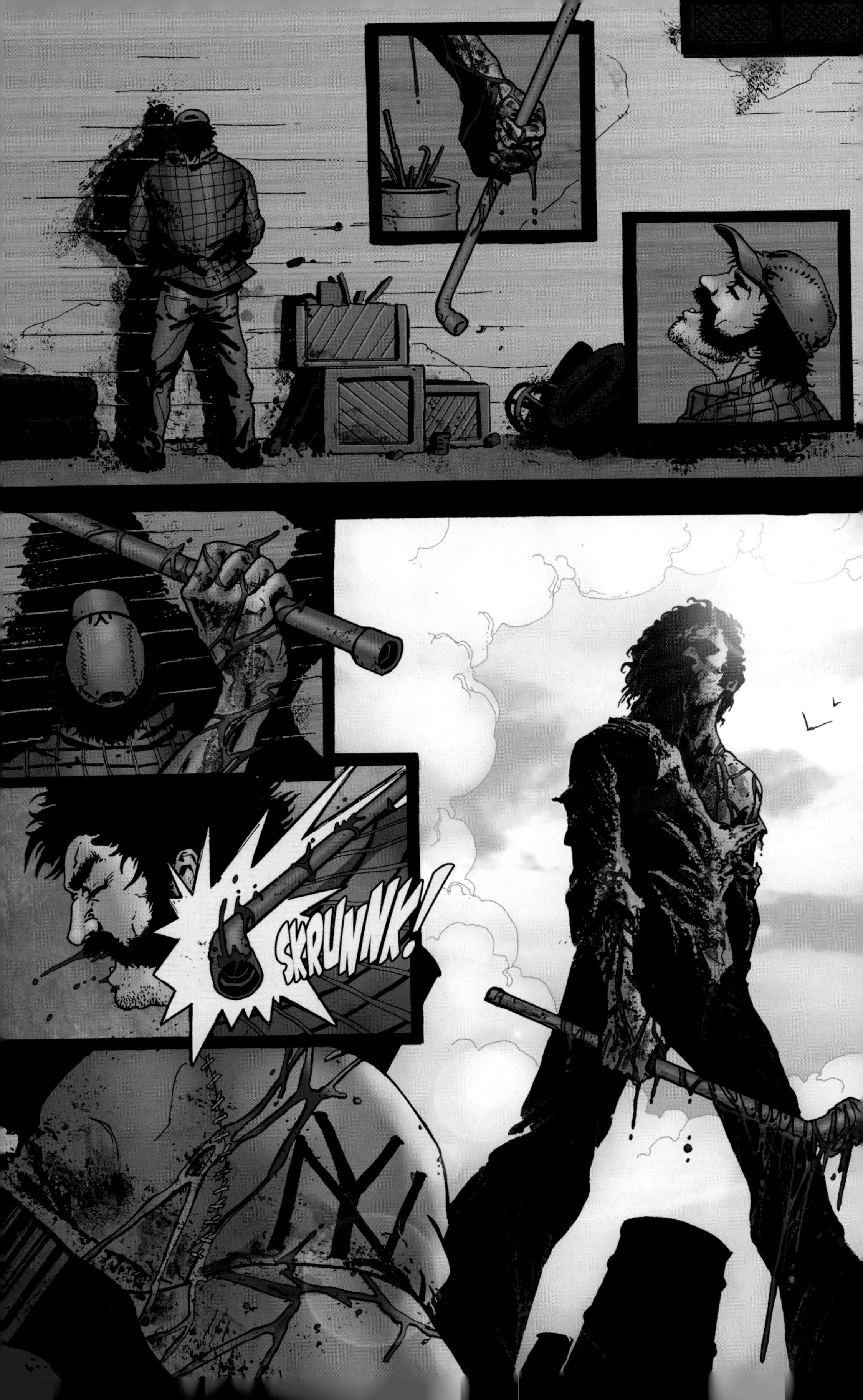
SKRUNNK!

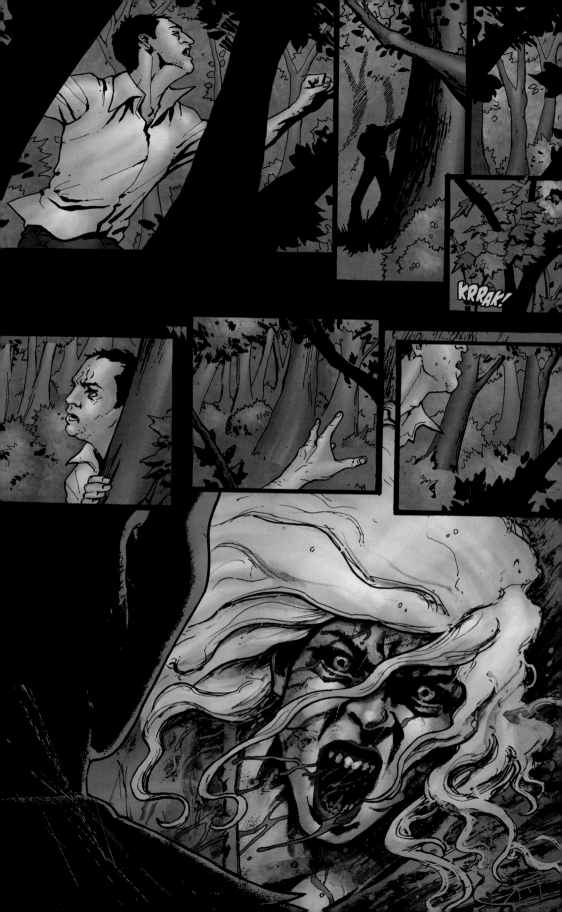

KRRAK!

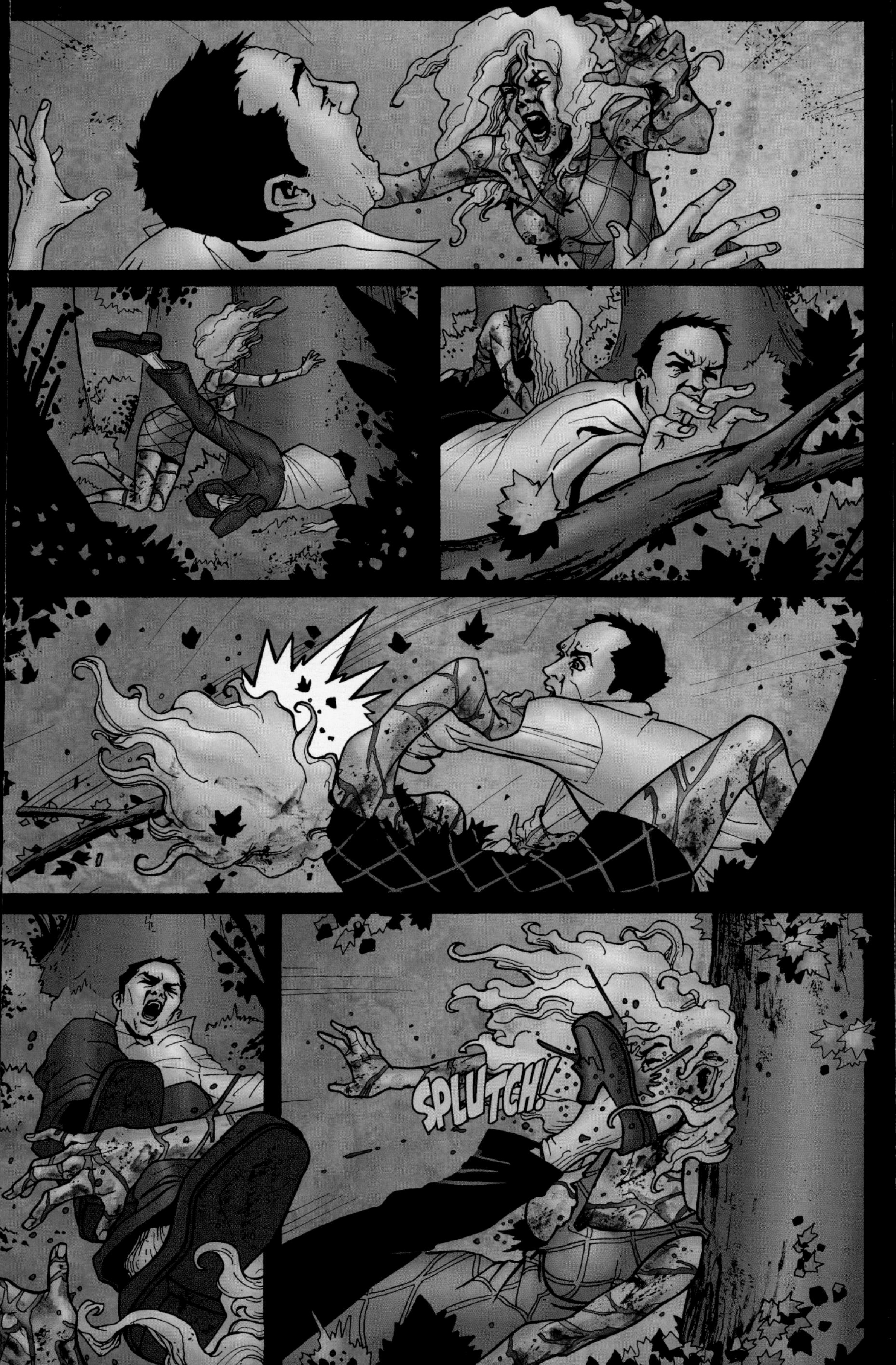
SPLUTCH!

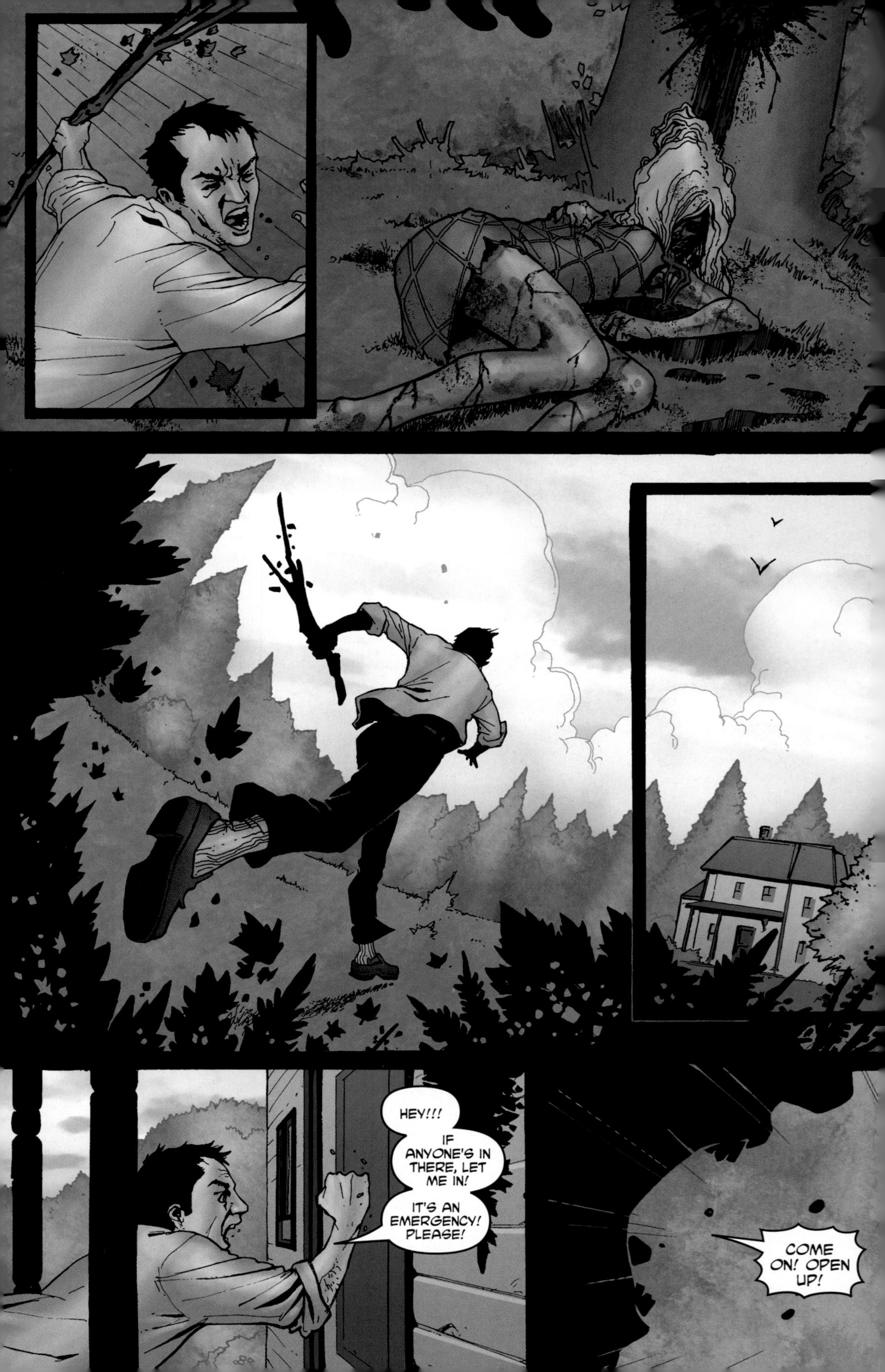
HEY!!!
IF ANYONE'S IN THERE, LET ME IN!
IT'S AN EMERGENCY! PLEASE!
COME ON! OPEN UP!

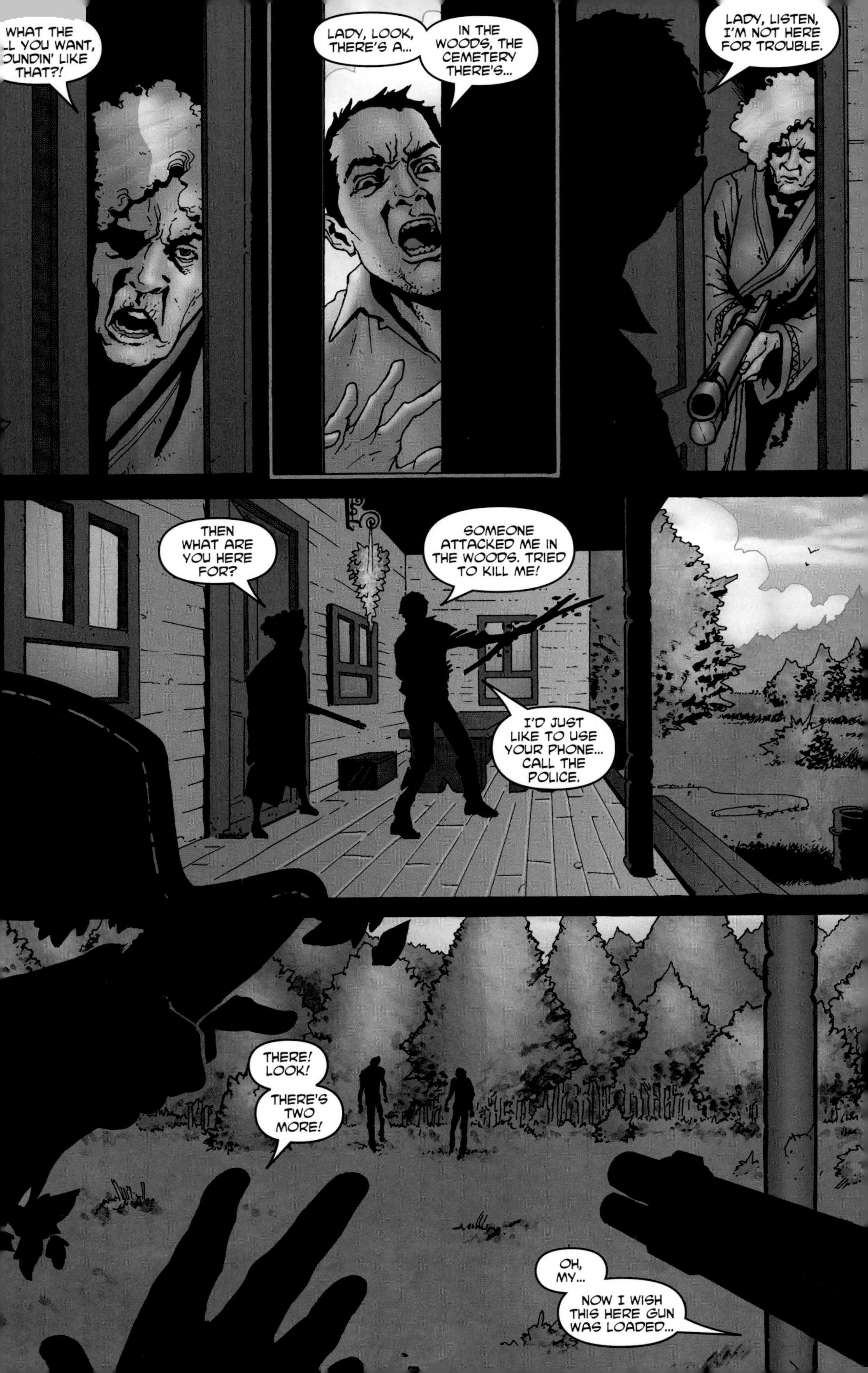
WHAT THE
LL YOU WANT,
OUNDIN' LIKE
THAT?!
LADY, LOOK, THERE'S A...
IN THE WOODS, THE CEMETERY THERE'S...
LADY, LISTEN, I'M NOT HERE FOR TROUBLE.
THEN WHAT ARE YOU HERE FOR?
SOMEONE ATTACKED ME IN THE WOODS. TRIED TO KILL ME!
I'D JUST LIKE TO USE YOUR PHONE... CALL THE POLICE.
THERE! LOOK!
THERE'S TWO MORE!
OH, MY...
NOW I WISH THIS HERE GUN WAS LOADED...

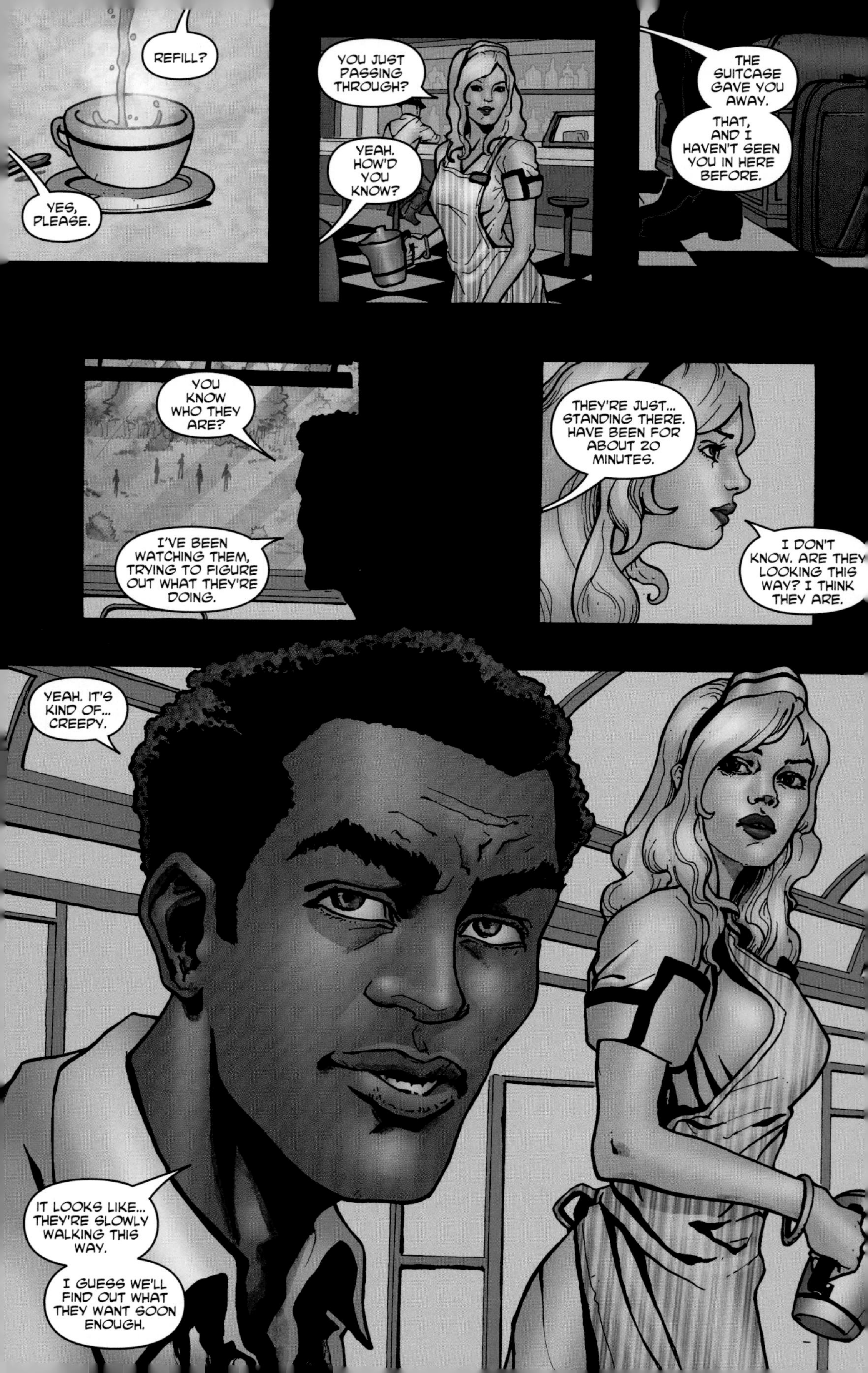
REFILL?
YES, PLEASE.
YOU JUST PASSING THROUGH?
YEAH. HOW'D YOU KNOW?
THE SUITCASE GAVE YOU AWAY.
THAT, AND I HAVEN'T SEEN YOU IN HERE BEFORE.
YOU KNOW WHO THEY ARE?
I'VE BEEN WATCHING THEM, TRYING TO FIGURE OUT WHAT THEY'RE DOING.
THEY'RE JUST... STANDING THERE. HAVE BEEN FOR ABOUT 20 MINUTES.
I DON'T KNOW. ARE THEY LOOKING THIS WAY? I THINK THEY ARE.
YEAH. IT'S KIND OF... CREEPY.
IT LOOKS LIKE... THEY'RE SLOWLY WALKING THIS WAY.
I GUESS WE'LL FIND OUT WHAT THEY WANT SOON ENOUGH.

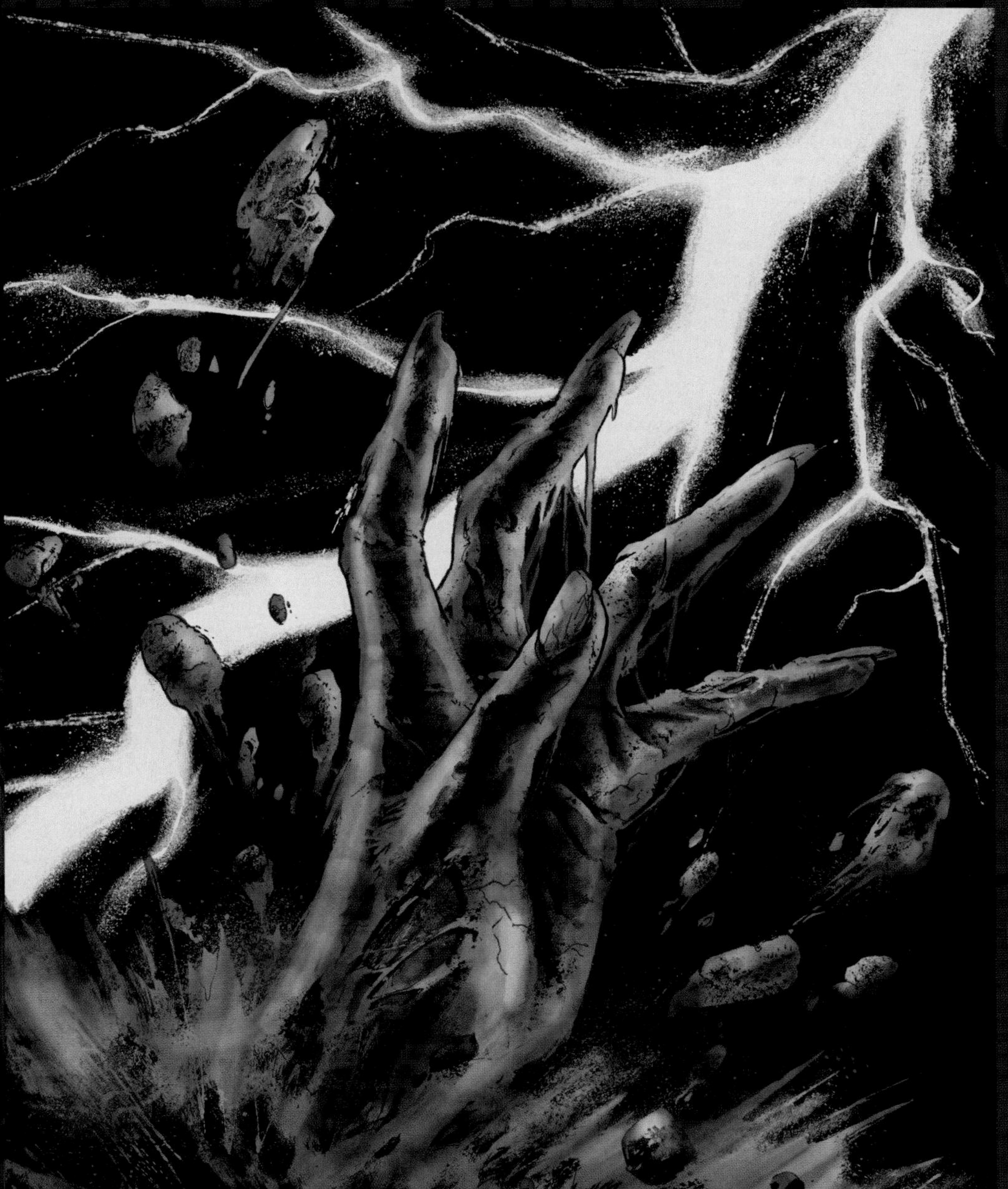

CHAPTER THREE

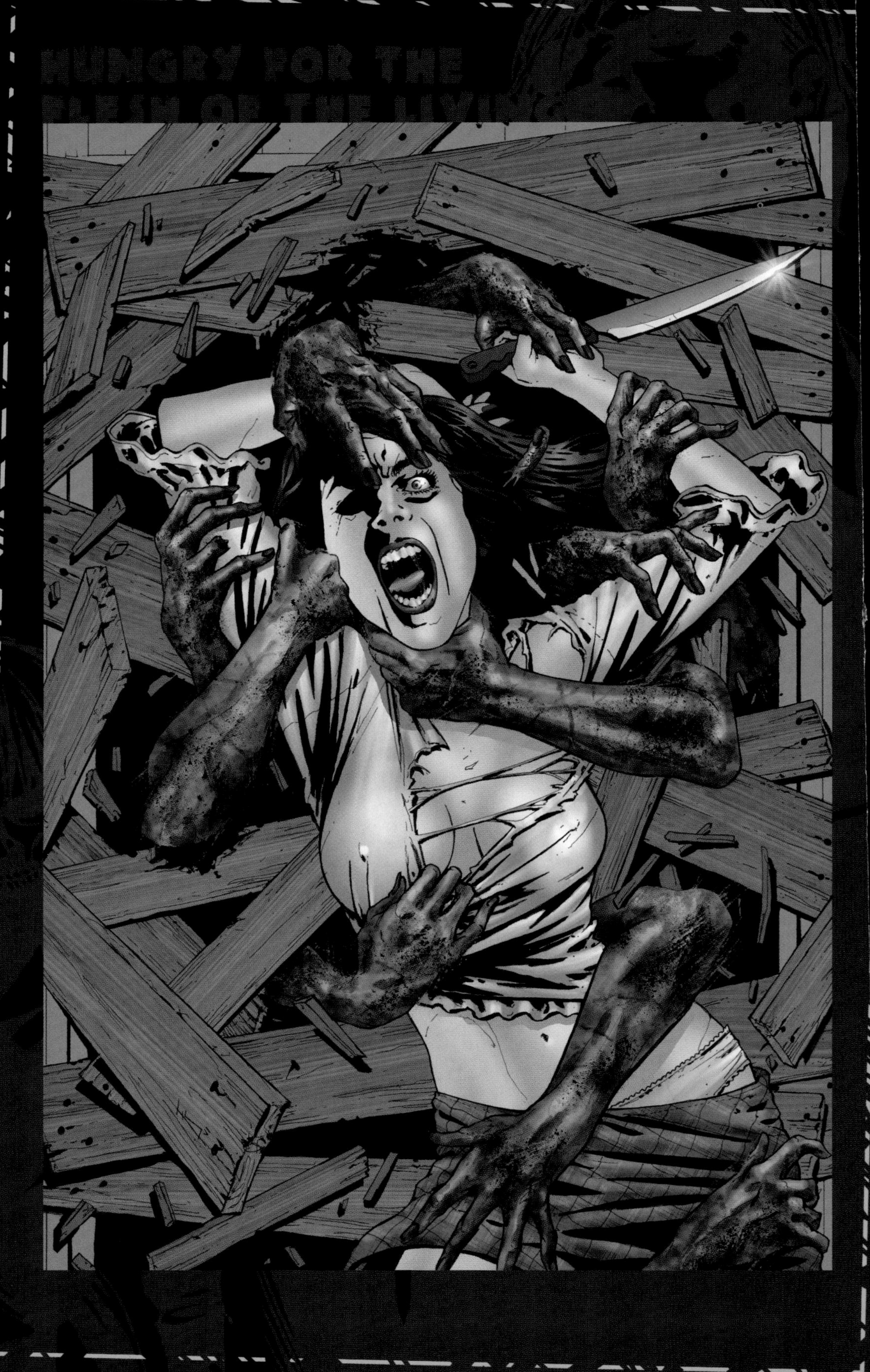
HUNGRY FOR THE
FLESH OF THE LIVIN

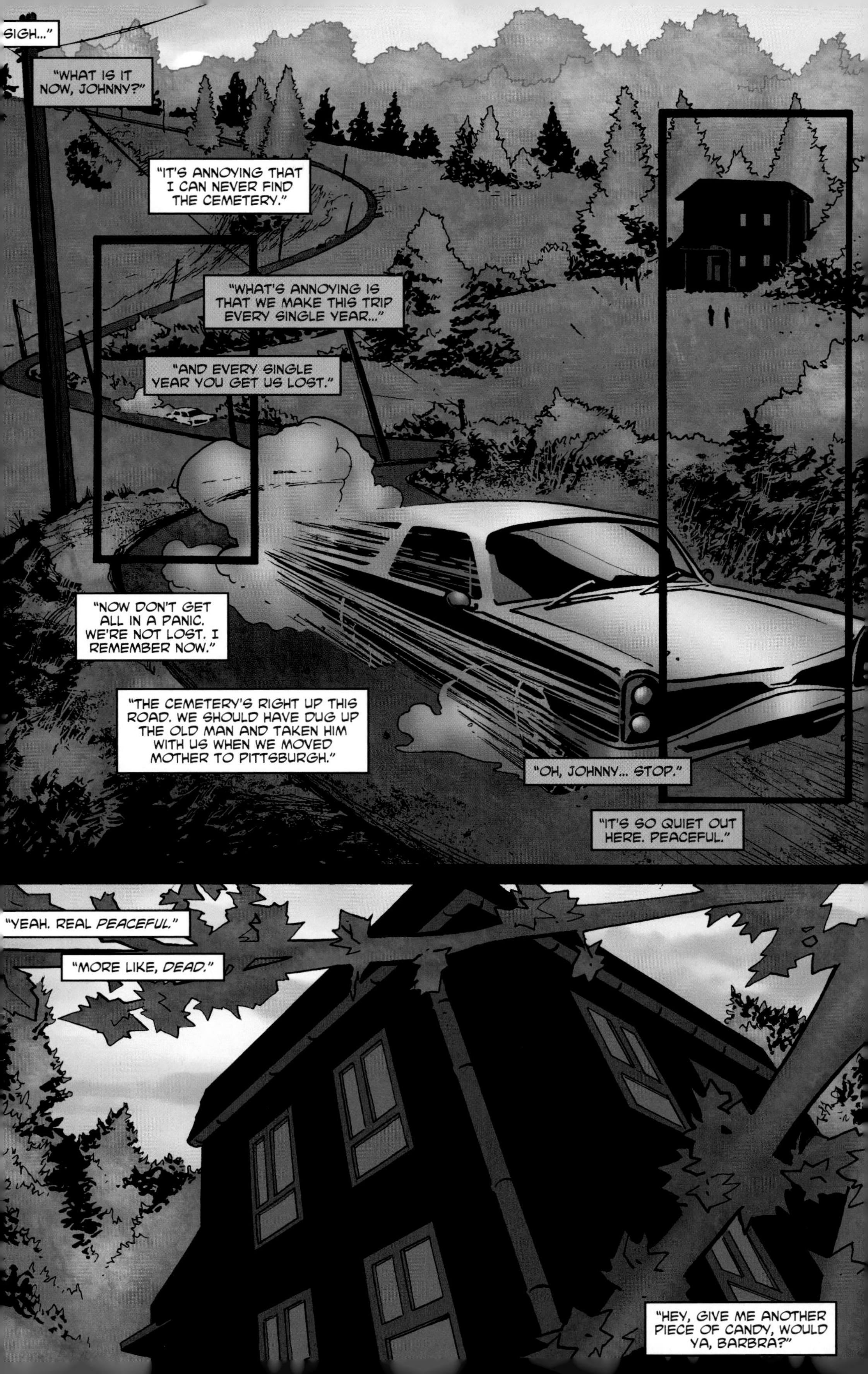
SIGH..."
"WHAT IS IT NOW, JOHNNY?"
"IT'S ANNOYING THAT I CAN NEVER FIND THE CEMETERY."
"WHAT'S ANNOYING IS THAT WE MAKE THIS TRIP EVERY SINGLE YEAR..."
"AND EVERY SINGLE YEAR YOU GET US LOST."
"NOW DON'T GET ALL IN A PANIC. WE'RE NOT LOST. I REMEMBER NOW."
"THE CEMETERY'S RIGHT UP THIS ROAD. WE SHOULD HAVE DUG UP THE OLD MAN AND TAKEN HIM WITH US WHEN WE MOVED MOTHER TO PITTSBURGH."
"OH, JOHNNY... STOP."
"IT'S SO QUIET OUT HERE. PEACEFUL."
"YEAH. REAL *PEACEFUL.*"
"MORE LIKE, *DEAD.*"
"HEY, GIVE ME ANOTHER PIECE OF CANDY, WOULD YA, BARBRA?"

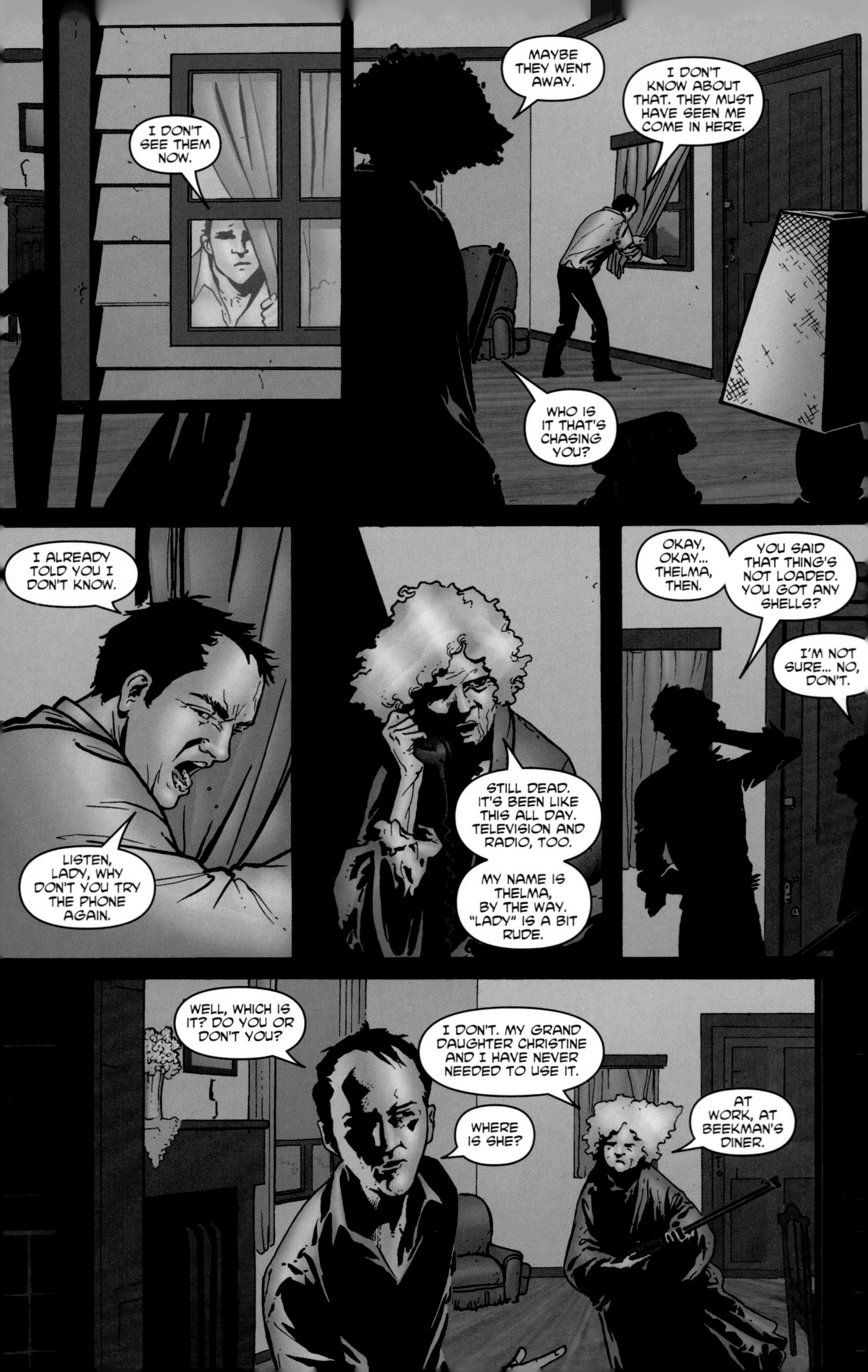
I DON'T SEE THEM NOW.
MAYBE THEY WENT AWAY.
I DON'T KNOW ABOUT THAT. THEY MUST HAVE SEEN ME COME IN HERE.
WHO IS IT THAT'S CHASING YOU?
I ALREADY TOLD YOU I DON'T KNOW.
LISTEN, LADY, WHY DON'T YOU TRY THE PHONE AGAIN.
STILL DEAD. IT'S BEEN LIKE THIS ALL DAY. TELEVISION AND RADIO, TOO.
MY NAME IS THELMA, BY THE WAY. "LADY" IS A BIT RUDE.
OKAY, OKAY... THELMA, THEN.
YOU SAID THAT THING'S NOT LOADED. YOU GOT ANY SHELLS?
I'M NOT SURE... NO, DON'T.
WELL, WHICH IS IT? DO YOU OR DON'T YOU?
I DON'T. MY GRAND DAUGHTER CHRISTINE AND I HAVE NEVER NEEDED TO USE IT.
WHERE IS SHE?
AT WORK, AT BEEKMAN'S DINER.

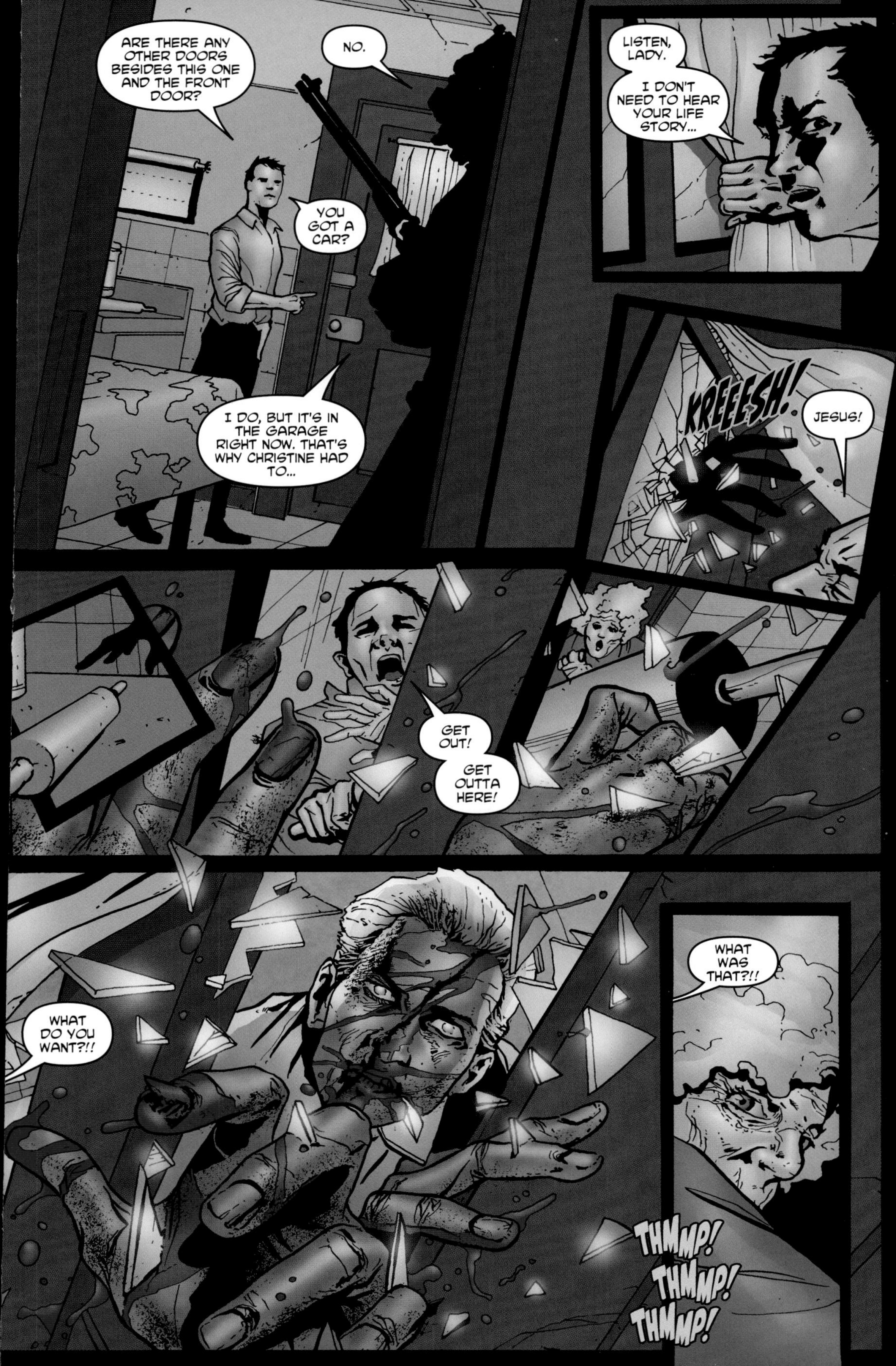
ARE THERE ANY OTHER DOORS BESIDES THIS ONE AND THE FRONT DOOR?
NO.
YOU GOT A CAR?
I DO, BUT IT'S IN THE GARAGE RIGHT NOW. THAT'S WHY CHRISTINE HAD TO...
LISTEN, LADY.
I DON'T NEED TO HEAR YOUR LIFE STORY...
KREEESH!
JESUS!
GET OUT!
GET OUTTA HERE!
WHAT DO YOU WANT?!!
WHAT WAS THAT?!!
THMMP! THMMP! THMMP!

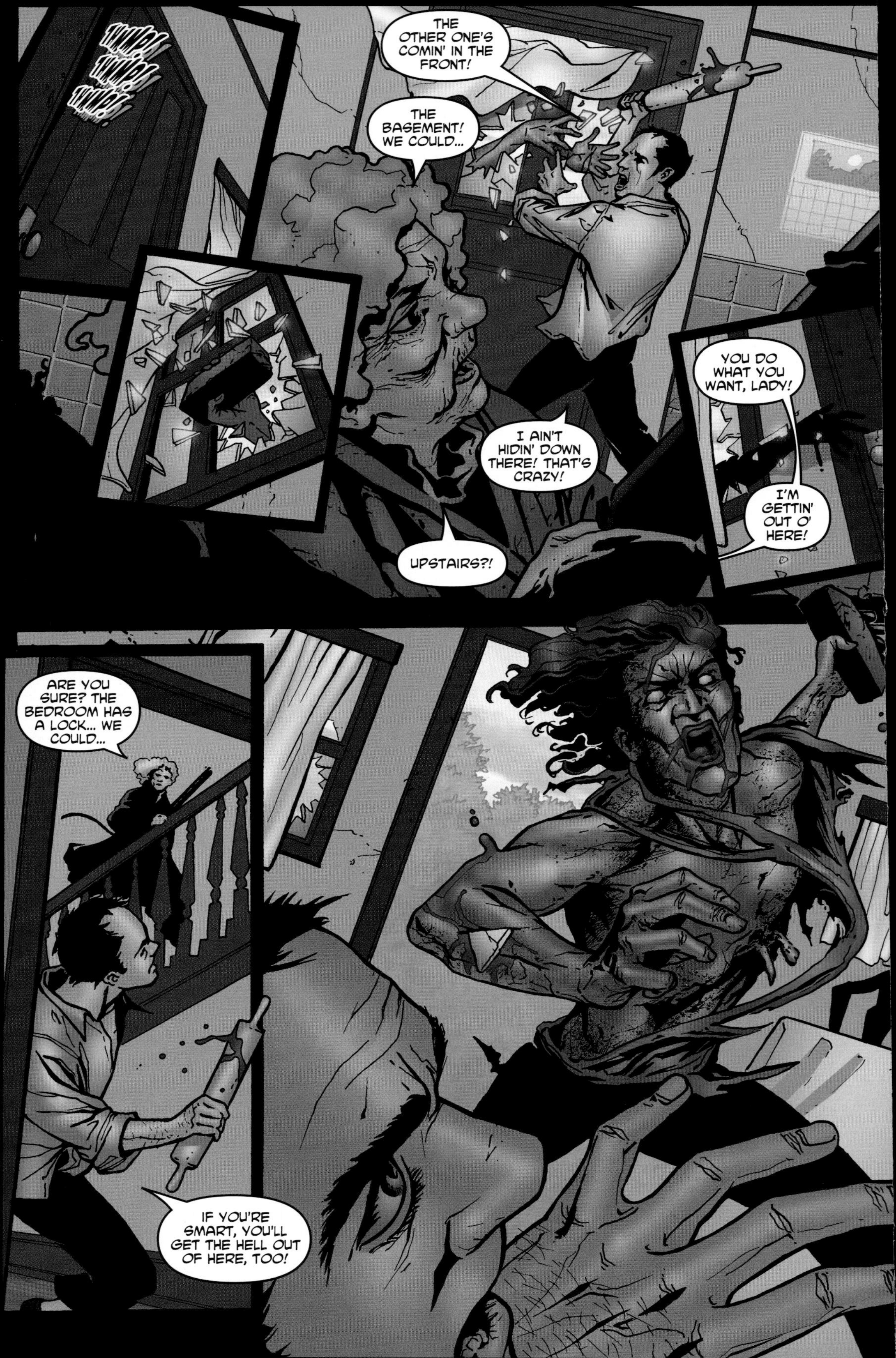
THWMP! THWMP! THWMP!
THE OTHER ONE'S COMIN' IN THE FRONT!
THE BASEMENT! WE COULD...
I AIN'T HIDIN' DOWN THERE! THAT'S CRAZY!
UPSTAIRS?!
YOU DO WHAT YOU WANT, LADY!
I'M GETTIN' OUT O' HERE!
ARE YOU SURE? THE BEDROOM HAS A LOCK... WE COULD...
IF YOU'RE SMART, YOU'LL GET THE HELL OUT OF HERE, TOO!

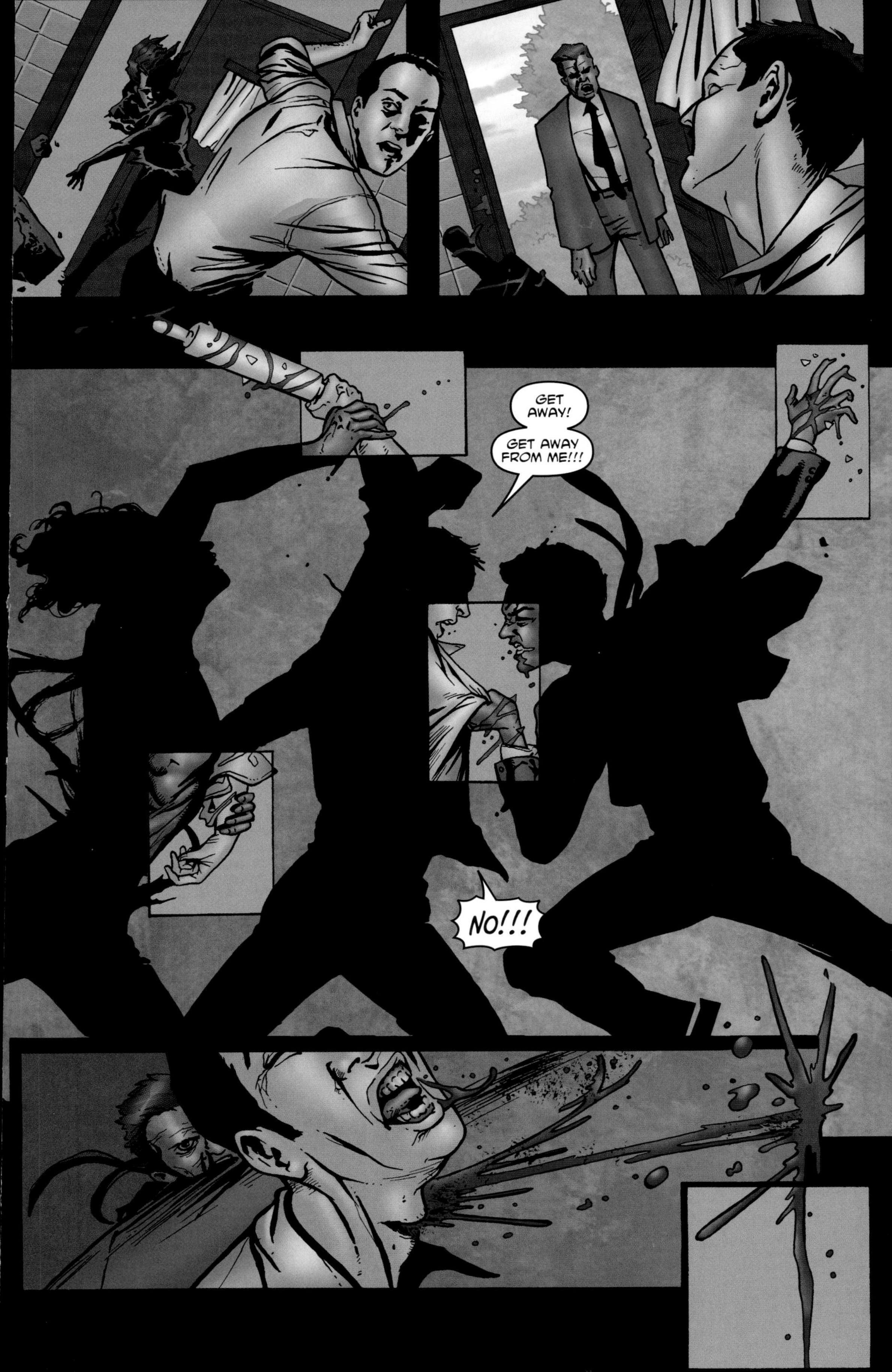
GET AWAY!
GET AWAY FROM ME!!!
NO!!!

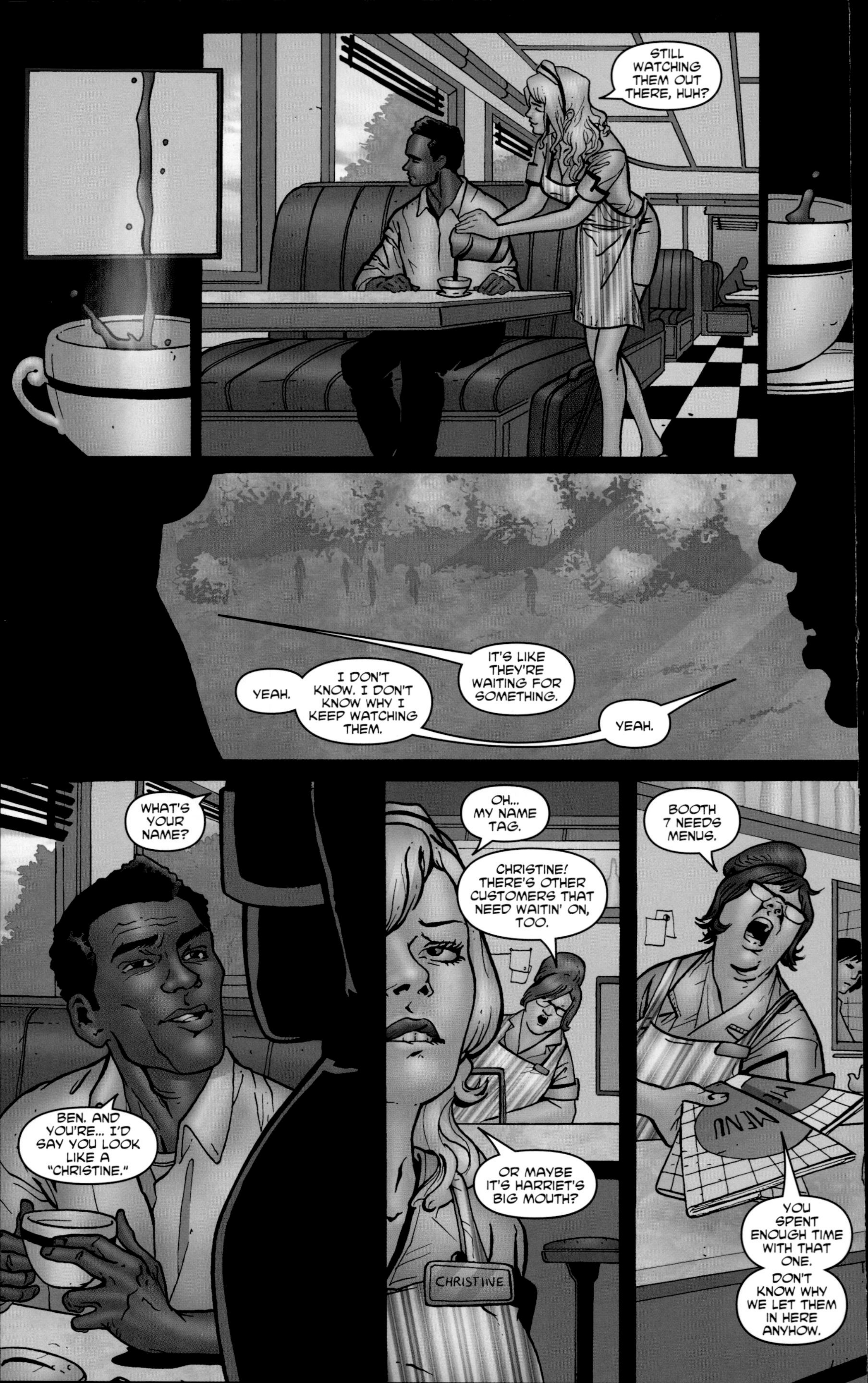
STILL WATCHING THEM OUT THERE, HUH?
YEAH.
I DON'T KNOW. I DON'T KNOW WHY I KEEP WATCHING THEM.
IT'S LIKE THEY'RE WAITING FOR SOMETHING.
YEAH.
WHAT'S YOUR NAME?
BEN. AND YOU'RE... I'D SAY YOU LOOK LIKE A "CHRISTINE."
OH... MY NAME TAG.
CHRISTINE! THERE'S OTHER CUSTOMERS THAT NEED WAITIN' ON, TOO.
OR MAYBE IT'S HARRIET'S BIG MOUTH?
CHRISTINE
BOOTH 7 NEEDS MENUS.
MENU
YOU SPENT ENOUGH TIME WITH THAT ONE.
DON'T KNOW WHY WE LET THEM IN HERE ANYHOW.

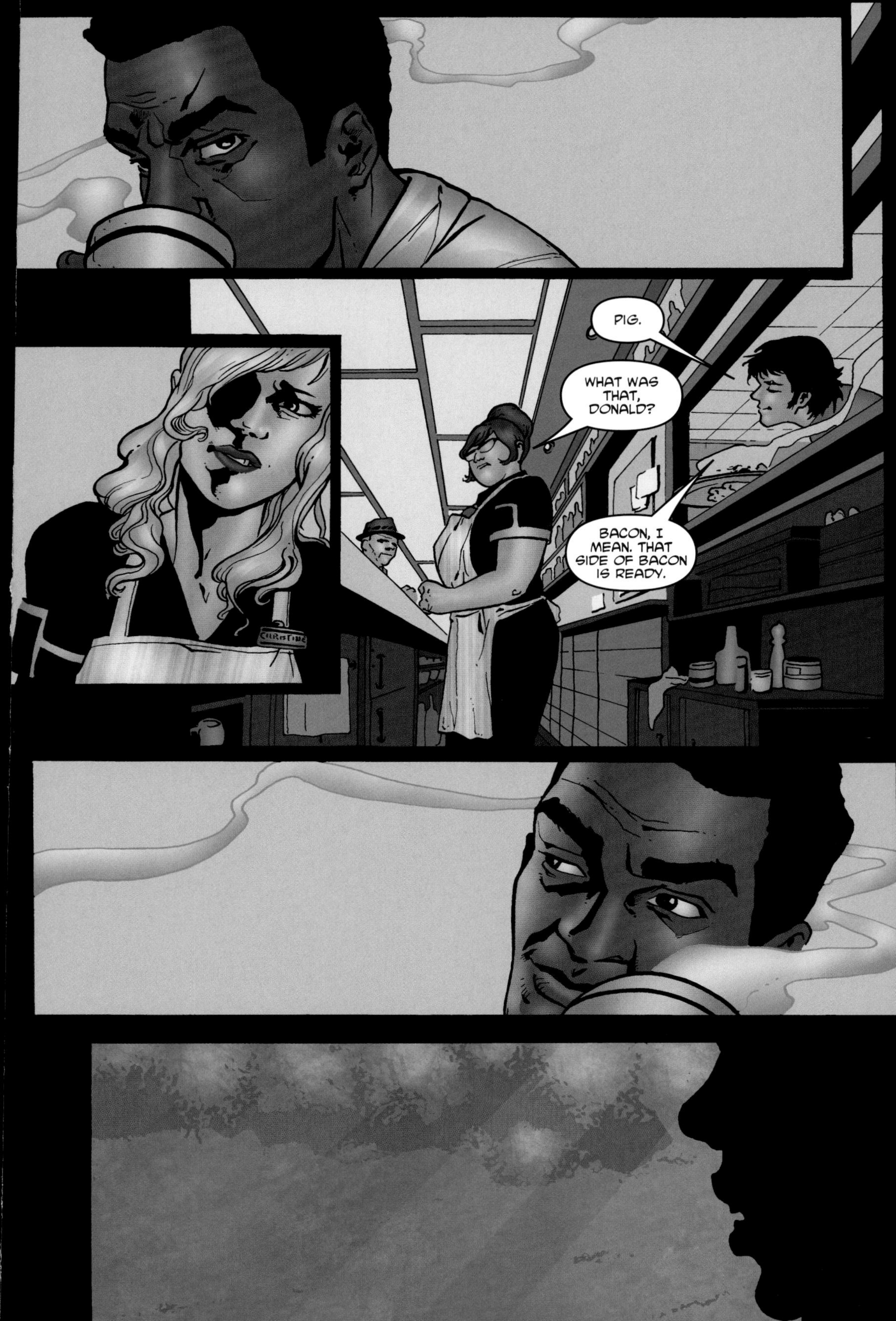
PIG.
WHAT WAS THAT, DONALD?
BACON, I MEAN. THAT SIDE OF BACON IS READY.

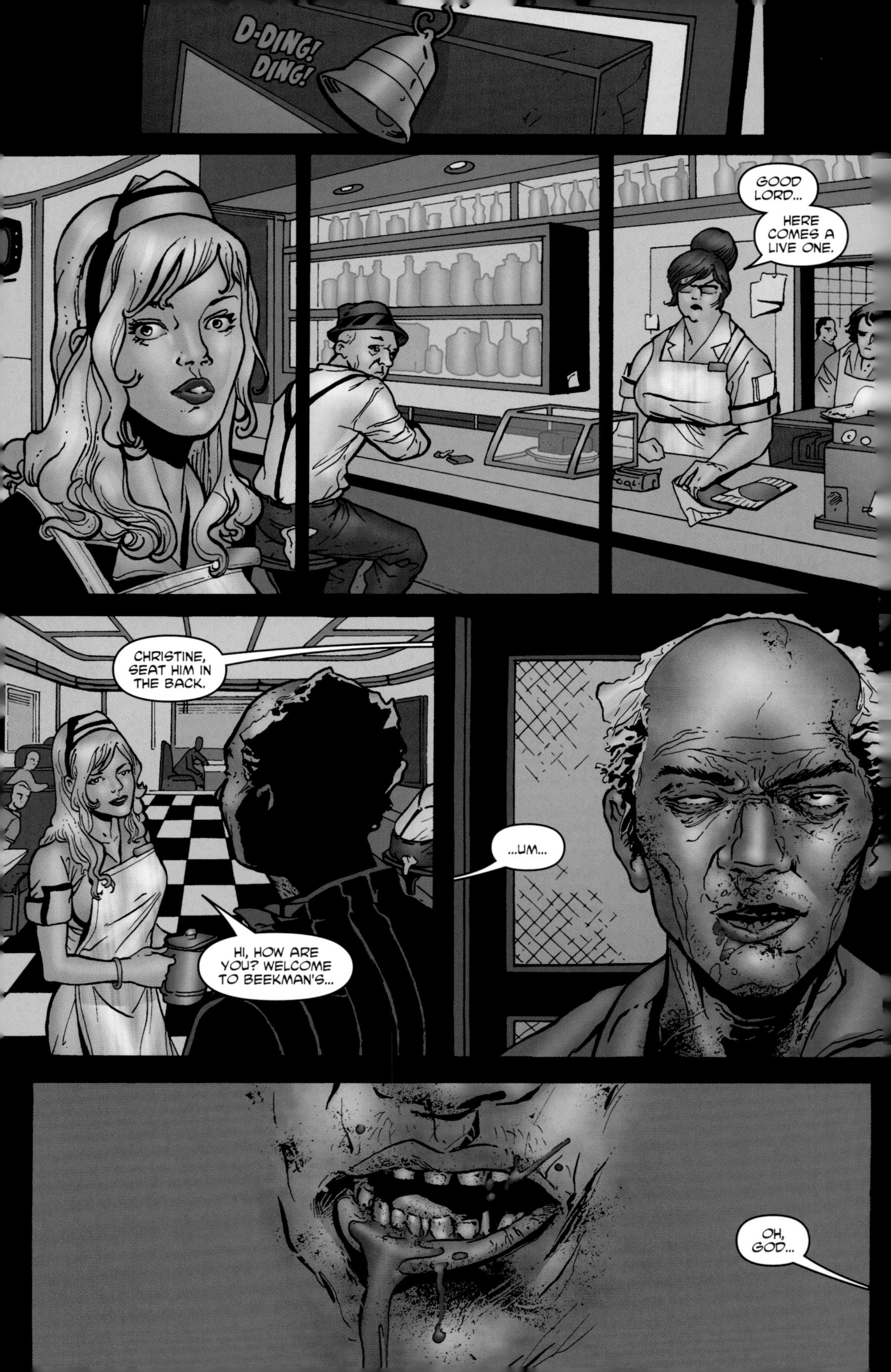
D-DING! DING!
GOOD LORD...
HERE COMES A LIVE ONE.
CHRISTINE, SEAT HIM IN THE BACK.
HI, HOW ARE YOU? WELCOME TO BEEKMAN'S...
...UM...
OH, GOD...

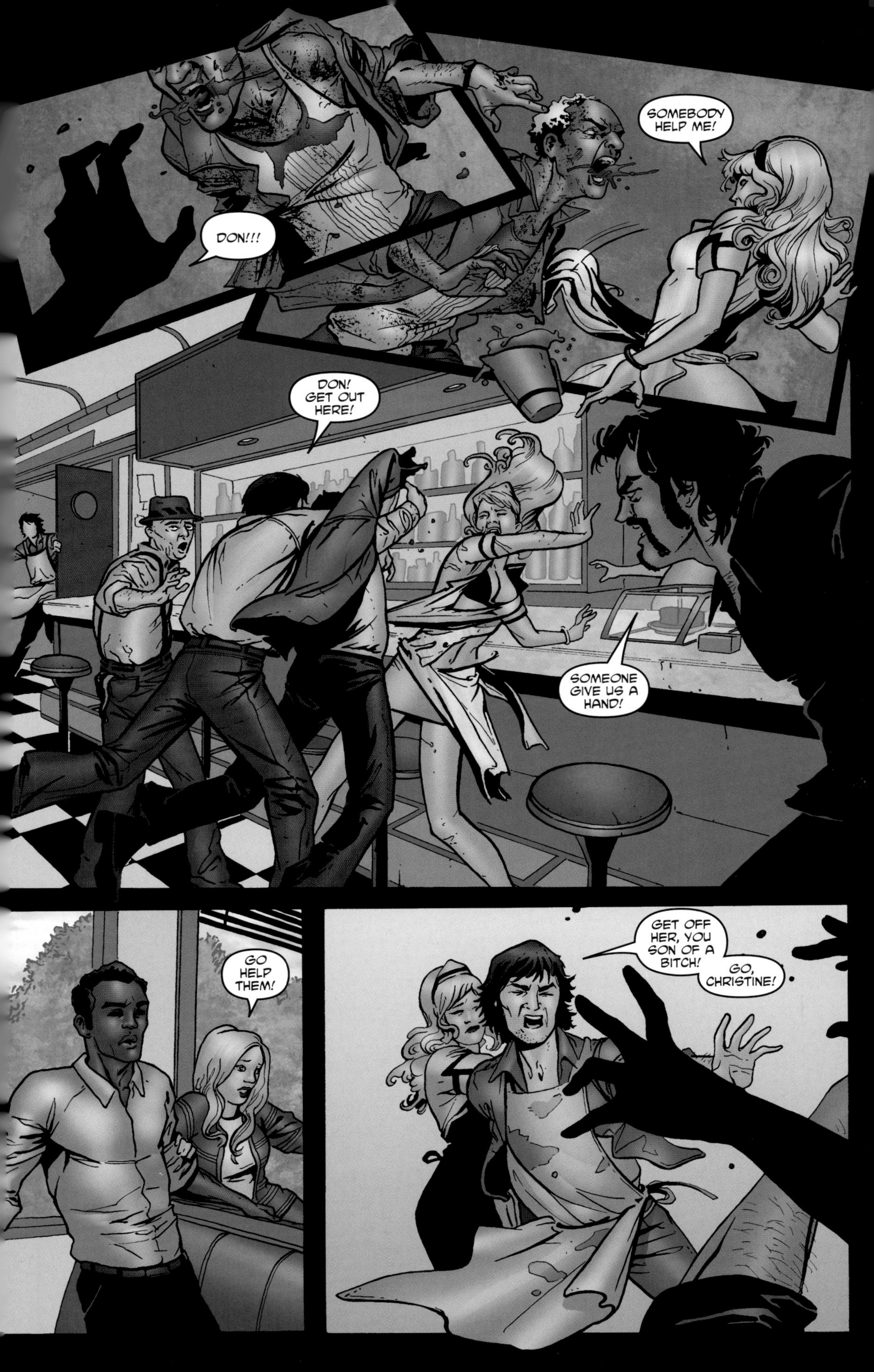
SOMEBODY HELP ME!
DON!!!
DON! GET OUT HERE!
SOMEONE GIVE US A HAND!
GO HELP THEM!
GET OFF HER, YOU SON OF A BITCH!
GO, CHRISTINE!

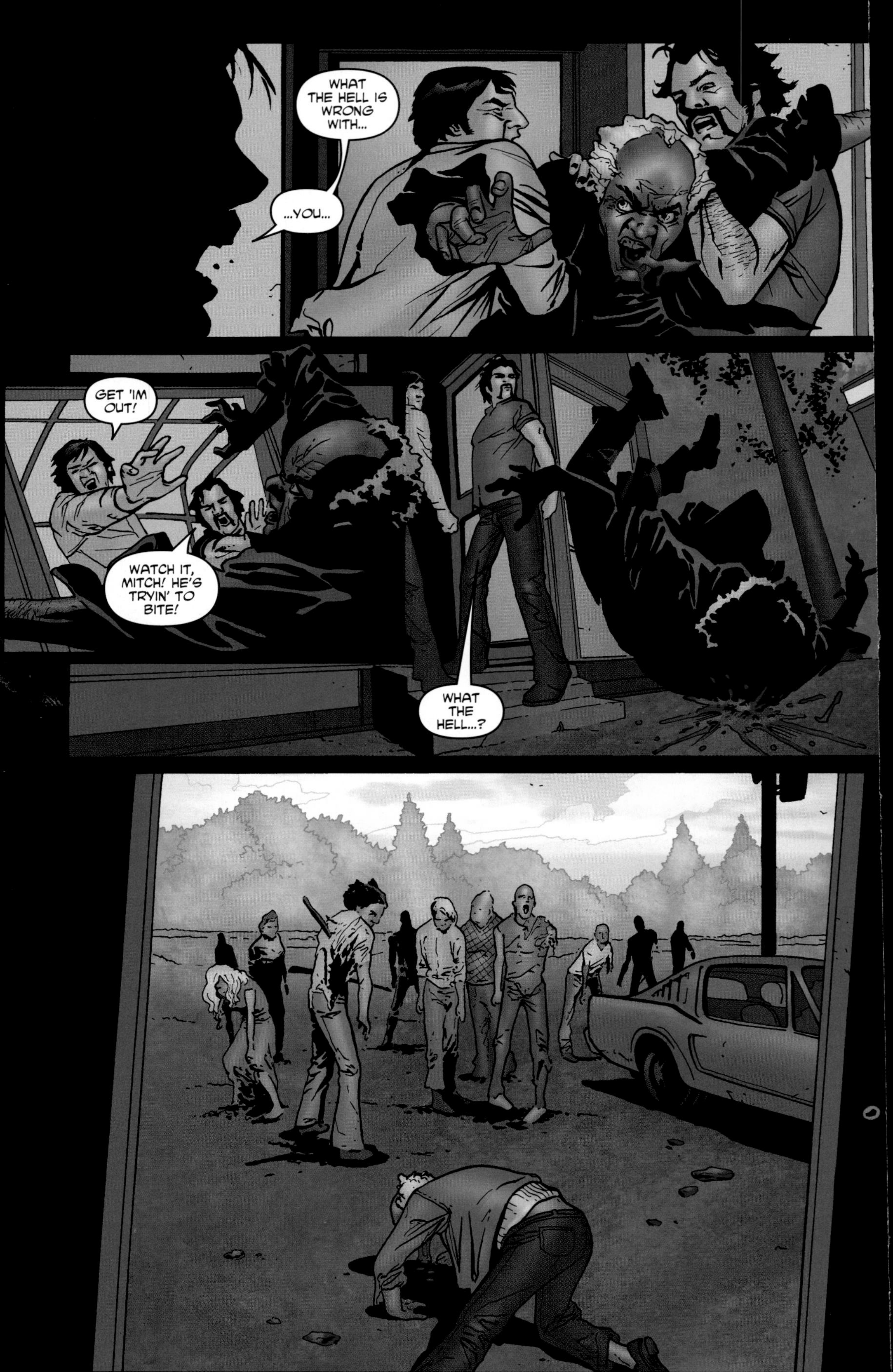
WHAT THE HELL IS WRONG WITH...
...YOU...
GET 'IM OUT!
WATCH IT, MITCH! HE'S TRYIN' TO BITE!
WHAT THE HELL...?

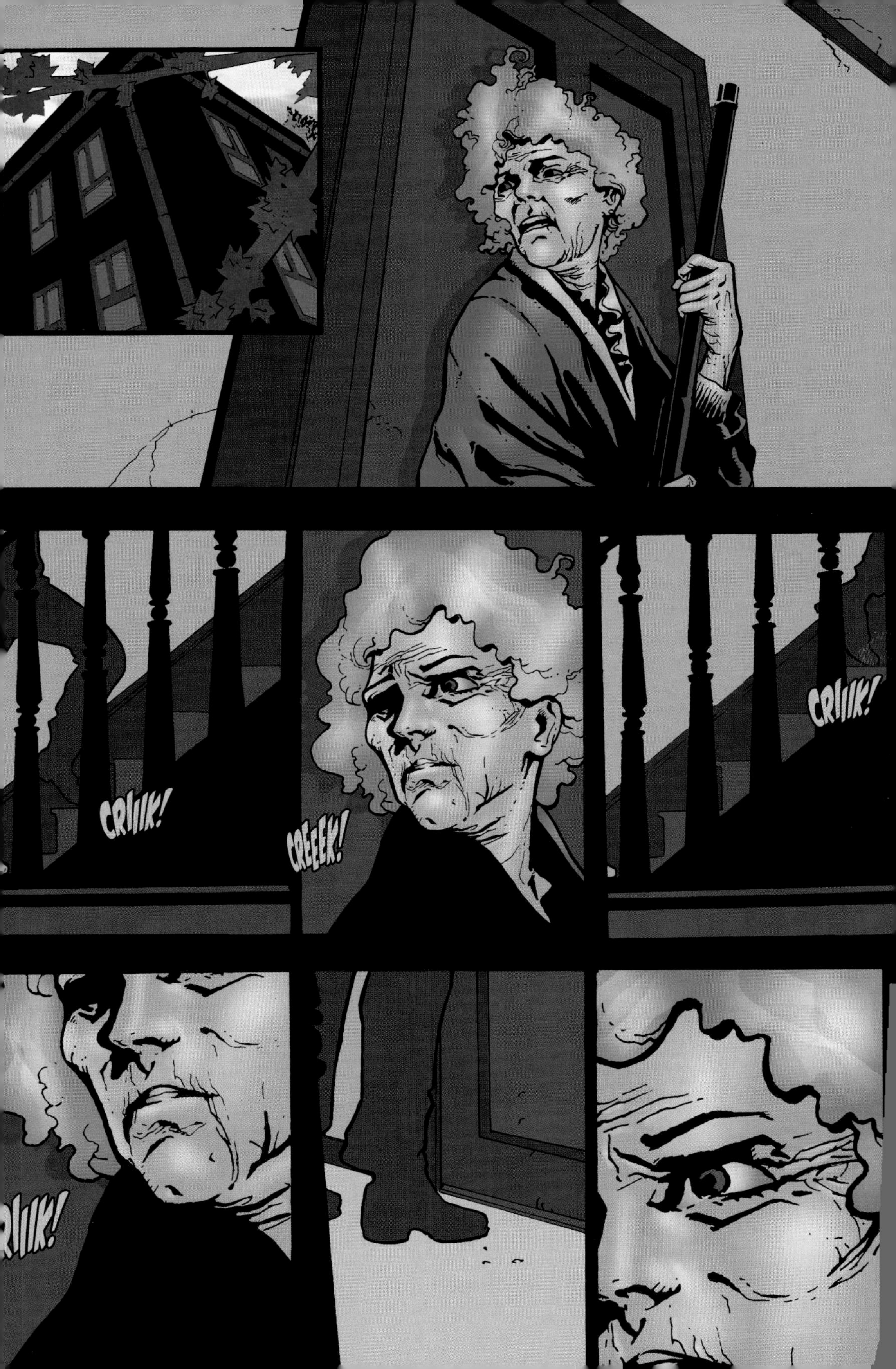
CRIIIK!
CREEEK!
CRIIIK!
RIIIK!

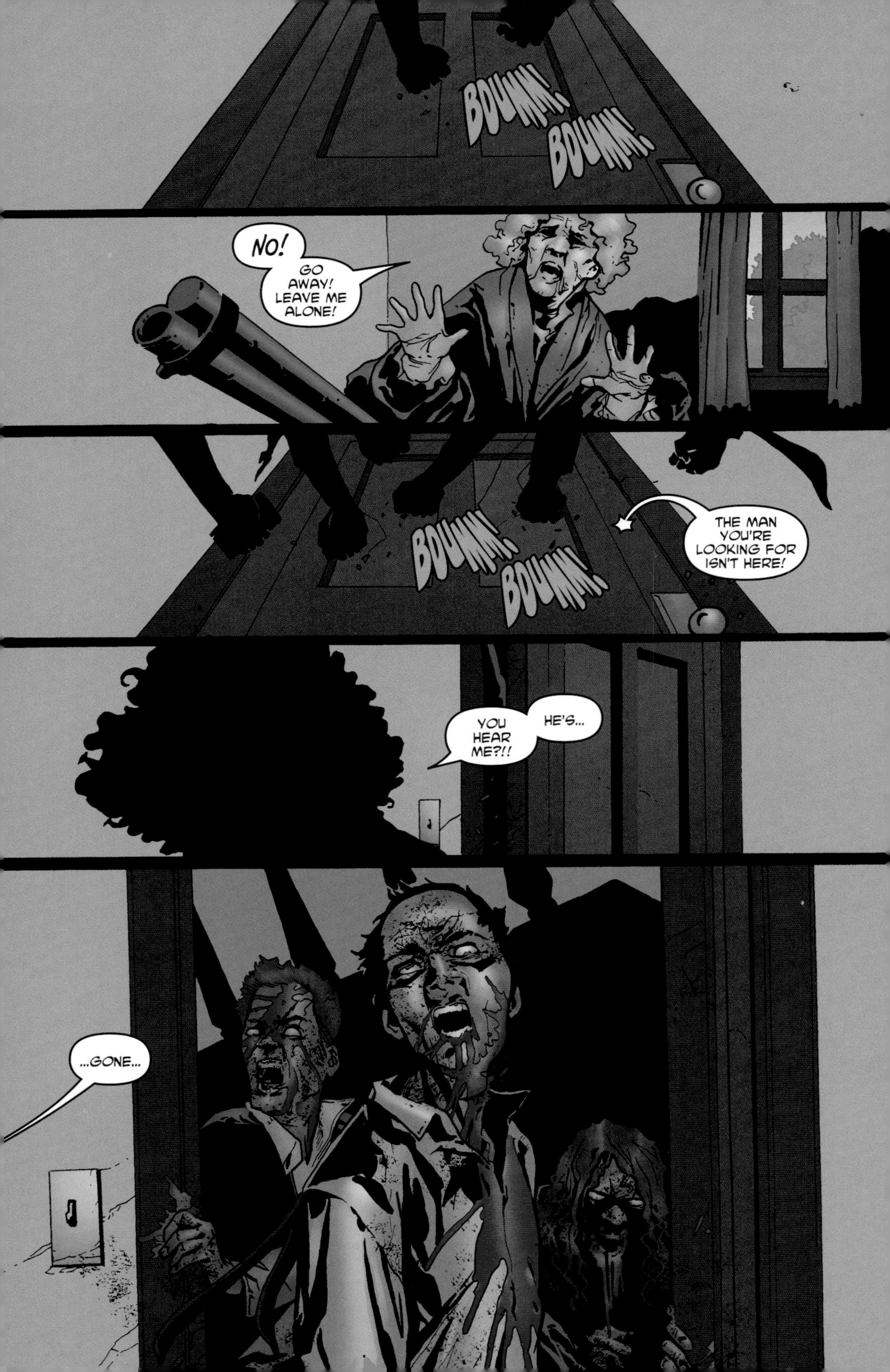
BOUMM! BOUMM!
NO! GO AWAY! LEAVE ME ALONE!
BOUMM! BOUMM!
THE MAN YOU'RE LOOKING FOR ISN'T HERE!
YOU HEAR ME?!!
HE'S...
...GONE...

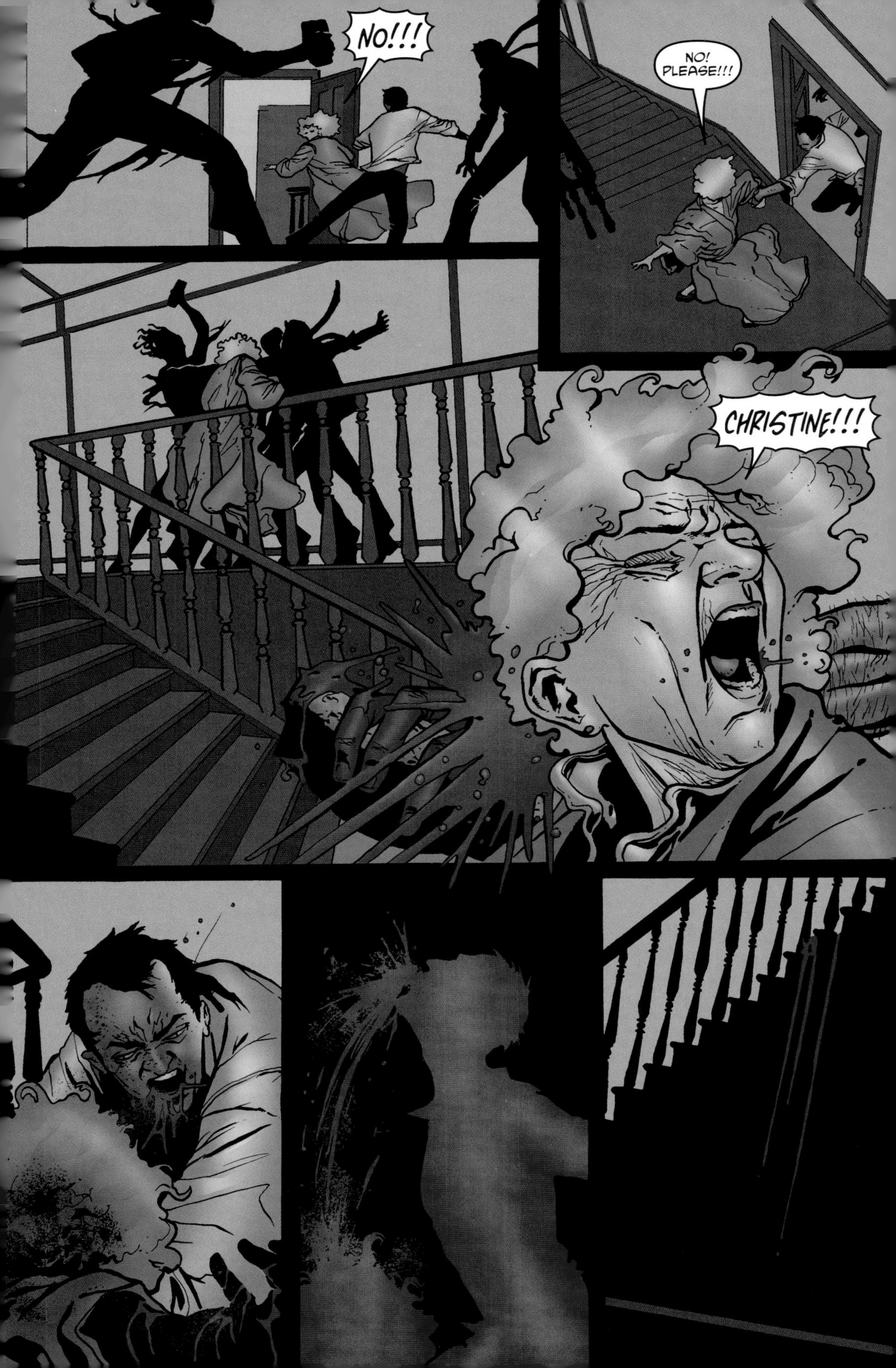
NO!!!
NO! PLEASE!!!
CHRISTINE!!!

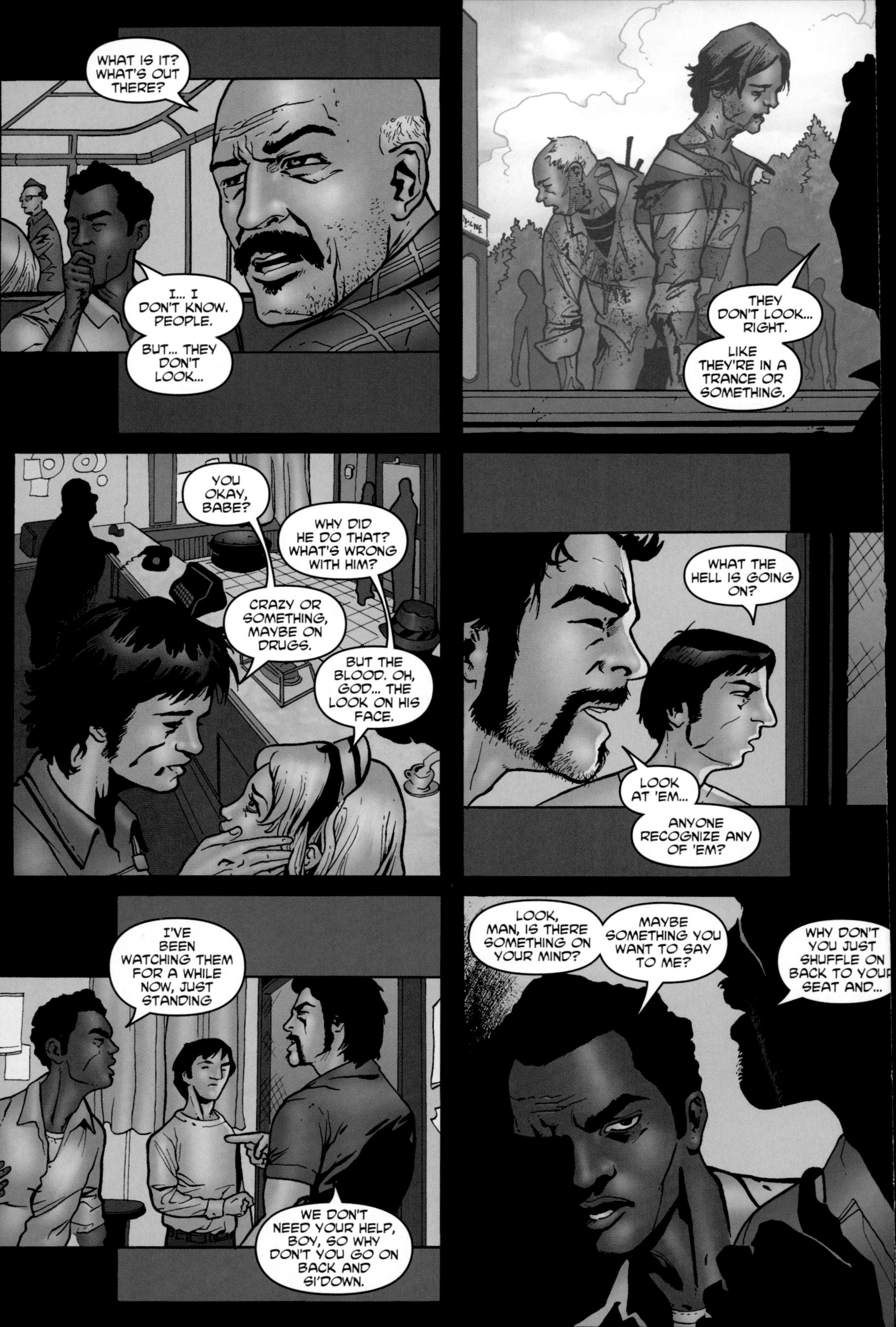
WHAT IS IT? WHAT'S OUT THERE?
I... I DON'T KNOW. PEOPLE.
BUT... THEY DON'T LOOK...
THEY DON'T LOOK... RIGHT.
LIKE THEY'RE IN A TRANCE OR SOMETHING.
YOU OKAY, BABE?
WHY DID HE DO THAT? WHAT'S WRONG WITH HIM?
CRAZY OR SOMETHING, MAYBE ON DRUGS.
BUT THE BLOOD. OH, GOD... THE LOOK ON HIS FACE.
WHAT THE HELL IS GOING ON?
LOOK AT 'EM...
ANYONE RECOGNIZE ANY OF 'EM?
I'VE BEEN WATCHING THEM FOR A WHILE NOW, JUST STANDING
WE DON'T NEED YOUR HELP, BOY, SO WHY DON'T YOU GO ON BACK AND SI'DOWN.
LOOK, MAN, IS THERE SOMETHING ON YOUR MIND?
MAYBE SOMETHING YOU WANT TO SAY TO ME?
WHY DON'T YOU JUST SHUFFLE ON BACK TO YOUR SEAT AND...

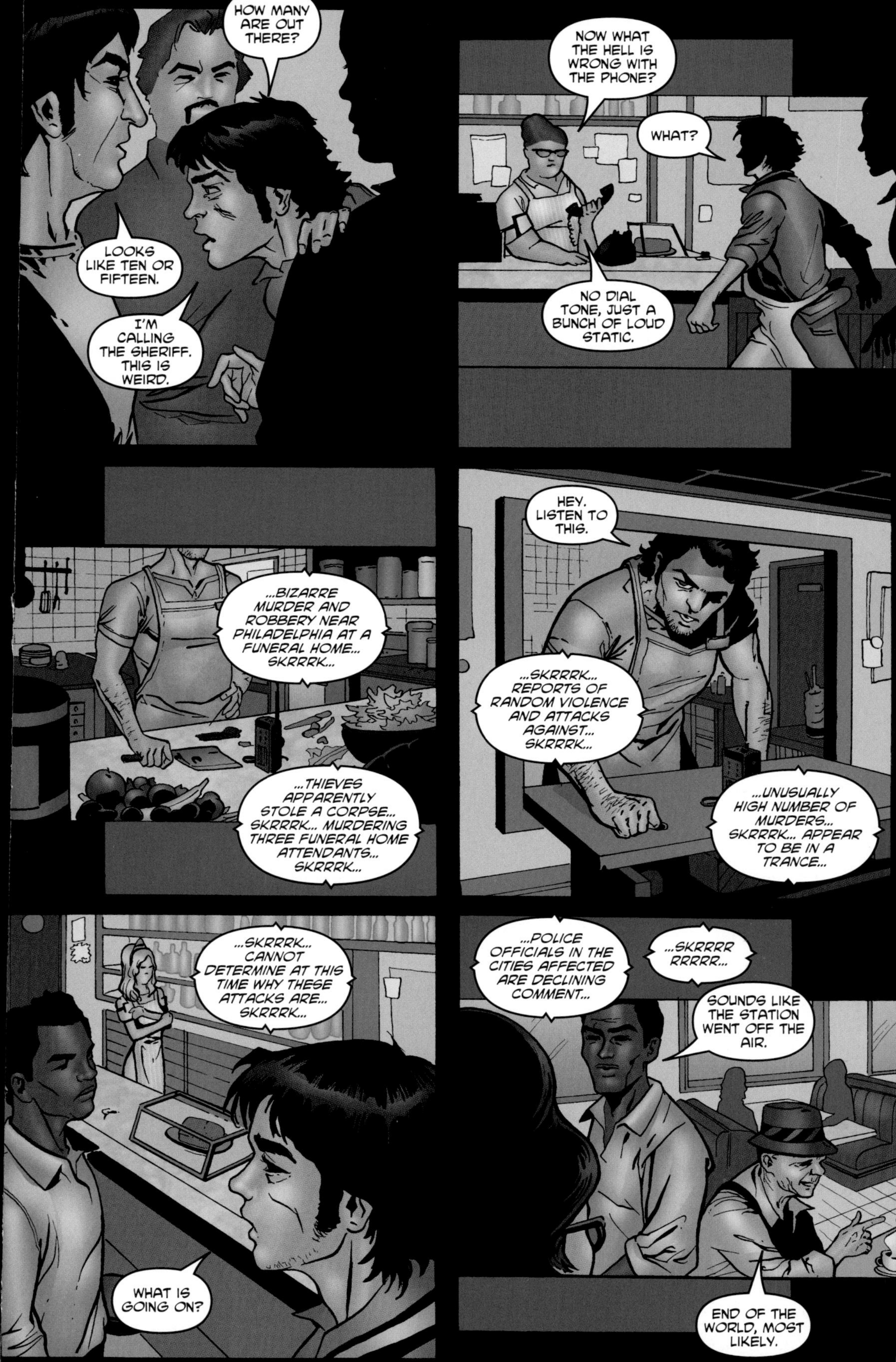
HOW MANY ARE OUT THERE?
LOOKS LIKE TEN OR FIFTEEN.
I'M CALLING THE SHERIFF. THIS IS WEIRD.
NOW WHAT THE HELL IS WRONG WITH THE PHONE?
WHAT?
NO DIAL TONE, JUST A BUNCH OF LOUD STATIC.
...BIZARRE MURDER AND ROBBERY NEAR PHILADELPHIA AT A FUNERAL HOME... SKRRRK...
...THIEVES APPARENTLY STOLE A CORPSE... SKRRRK... MURDERING THREE FUNERAL HOME ATTENDANTS... SKRRRK...
HEY. LISTEN TO THIS.
...SKRRRK... REPORTS OF RANDOM VIOLENCE AND ATTACKS AGAINST... SKRRRK...
...UNUSUALLY HIGH NUMBER OF MURDERS... SKRRRK... APPEAR TO BE IN A TRANCE...
...SKRRRK... CANNOT DETERMINE AT THIS TIME WHY THESE ATTACKS ARE... SKRRRK...
WHAT IS GOING ON?
...POLICE OFFICIALS IN THE CITIES AFFECTED ARE DECLINING COMMENT...
...SKRRRR RRRRR...
SOUNDS LIKE THE STATION WENT OFF THE AIR.
END OF THE WORLD, MOST LIKELY.

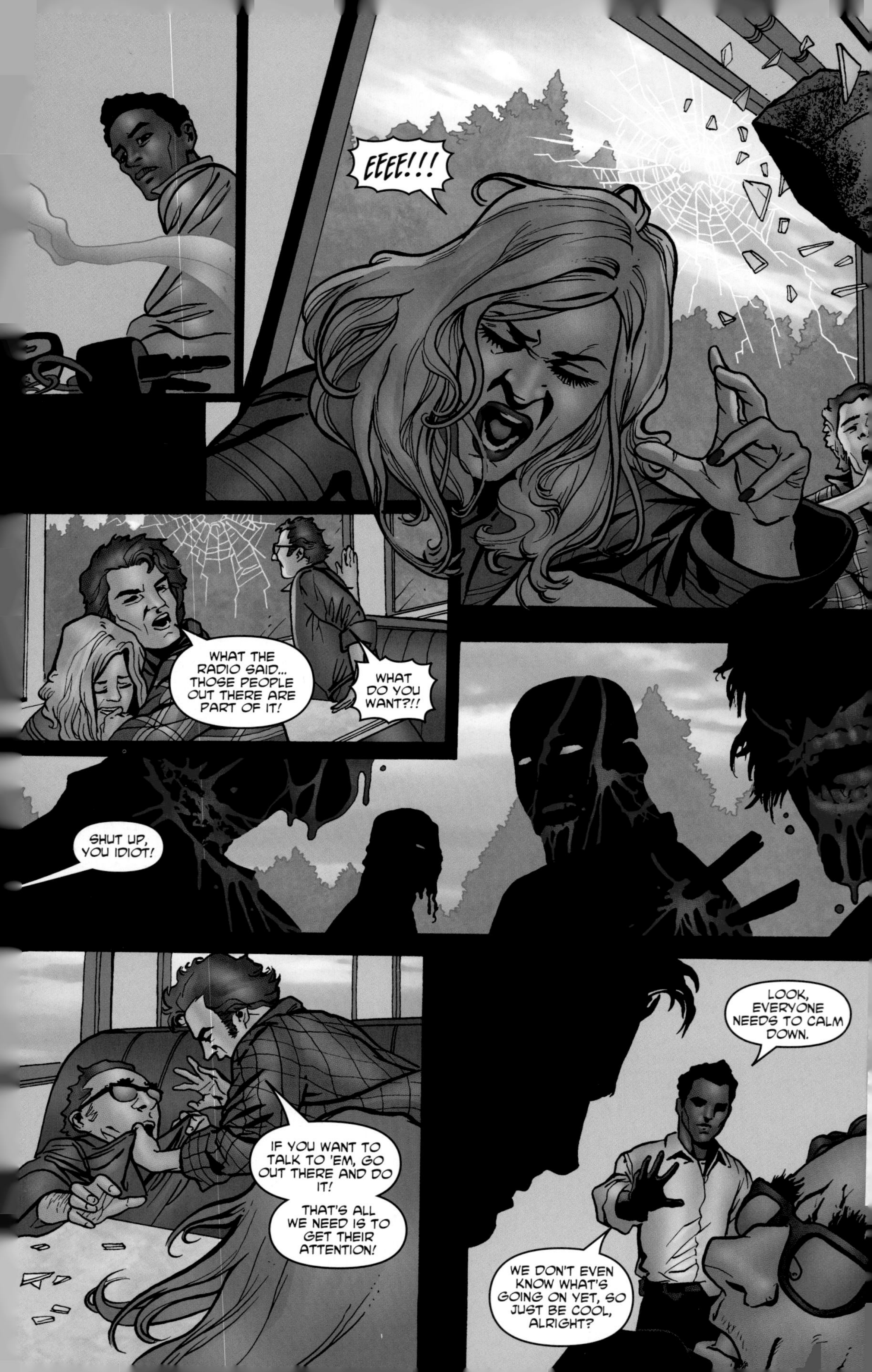
EEEE!!!
WHAT THE RADIO SAID... THOSE PEOPLE OUT THERE ARE PART OF IT!
WHAT DO YOU WANT?!!
SHUT UP, YOU IDIOT!
IF YOU WANT TO TALK TO 'EM, GO OUT THERE AND DO IT!
THAT'S ALL WE NEED IS TO GET THEIR ATTENTION!
LOOK, EVERYONE NEEDS TO CALM DOWN.
WE DON'T EVEN KNOW WHAT'S GOING ON YET, SO JUST BE COOL, ALRIGHT?

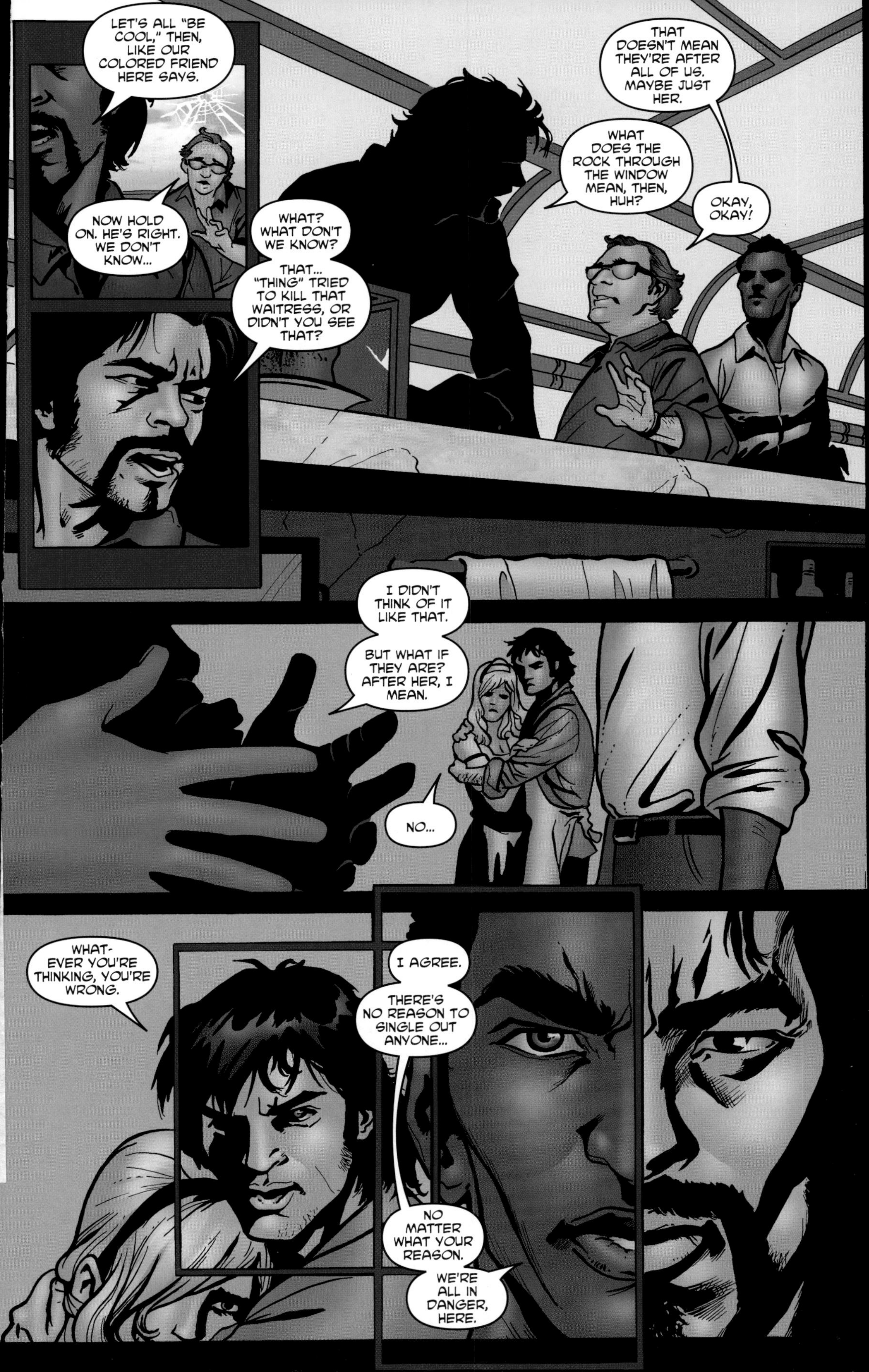
LET'S ALL "BE COOL," THEN, LIKE OUR COLORED FRIEND HERE SAYS.
NOW HOLD ON. HE'S RIGHT. WE DON'T KNOW...
WHAT? WHAT DON'T WE KNOW?
THAT... "THING" TRIED TO KILL THAT WAITRESS, OR DIDN'T YOU SEE THAT?
THAT DOESN'T MEAN THEY'RE AFTER ALL OF US. MAYBE JUST HER.
WHAT DOES THE ROCK THROUGH THE WINDOW MEAN, THEN, HUH?
OKAY, OKAY!
I DIDN'T THINK OF IT LIKE THAT.
BUT WHAT IF THEY ARE? AFTER HER, I MEAN.
NO...
WHAT-EVER YOU'RE THINKING, YOU'RE WRONG.
I AGREE.
THERE'S NO REASON TO SINGLE OUT ANYONE...
NO MATTER WHAT YOUR REASON.
WE'RE ALL IN DANGER, HERE.

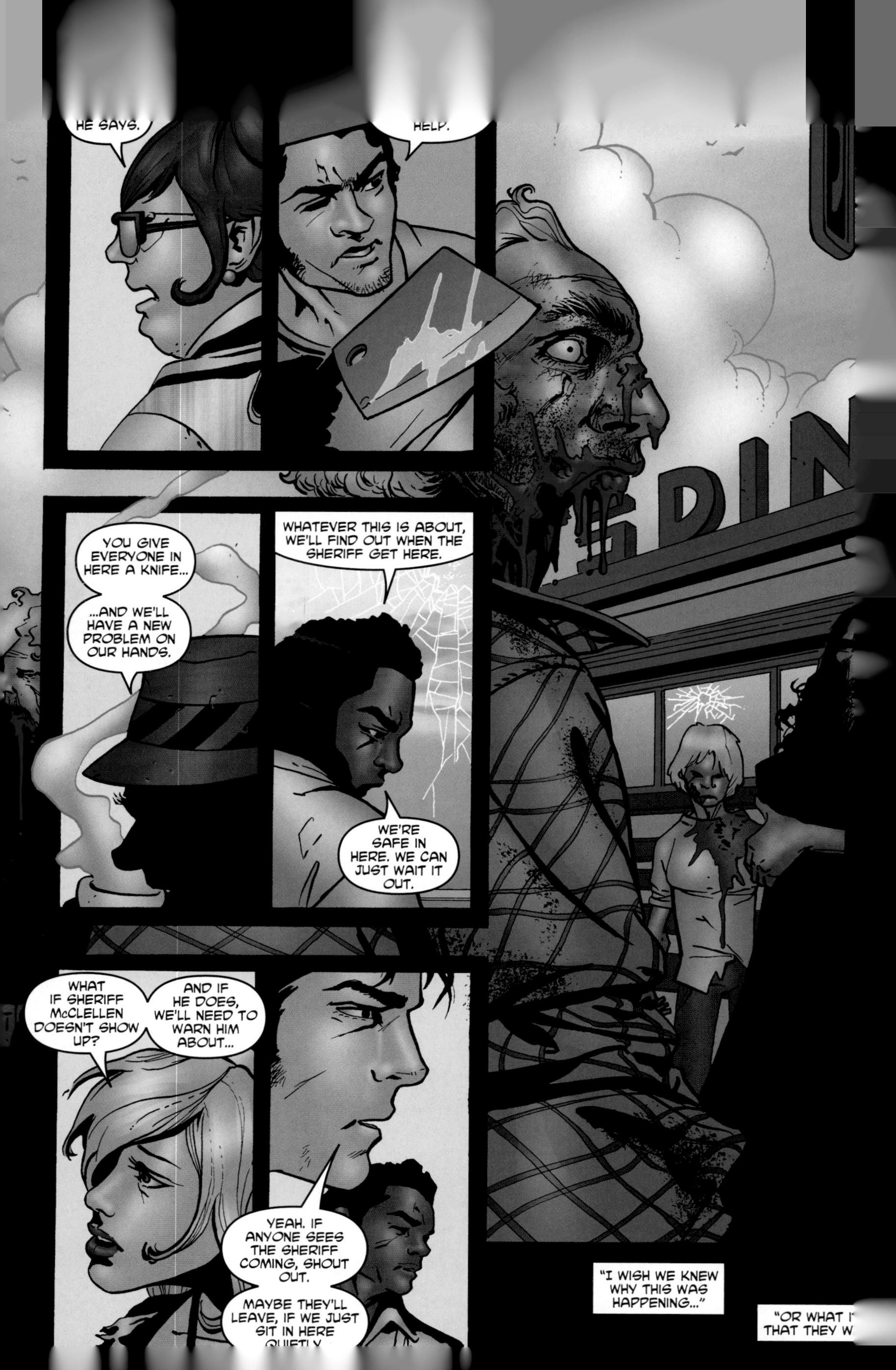
HE SAYS.
HELP.
YOU GIVE EVERYONE IN HERE A KNIFE...
...AND WE'LL HAVE A NEW PROBLEM ON OUR HANDS.
WHATEVER THIS IS ABOUT, WE'LL FIND OUT WHEN THE SHERIFF GET HERE.
WE'RE SAFE IN HERE. WE CAN JUST WAIT IT OUT.
WHAT IF SHERIFF McCLELLEN DOESN'T SHOW UP?
AND IF HE DOES, WE'LL NEED TO WARN HIM ABOUT...
YEAH. IF ANYONE SEES THE SHERIFF COMING, SHOUT OUT.
MAYBE THEY'LL LEAVE, IF WE JUST SIT IN HERE
"I WISH WE KNEW WHY THIS WAS HAPPENING..."
"OR WHAT
THAT THEY W

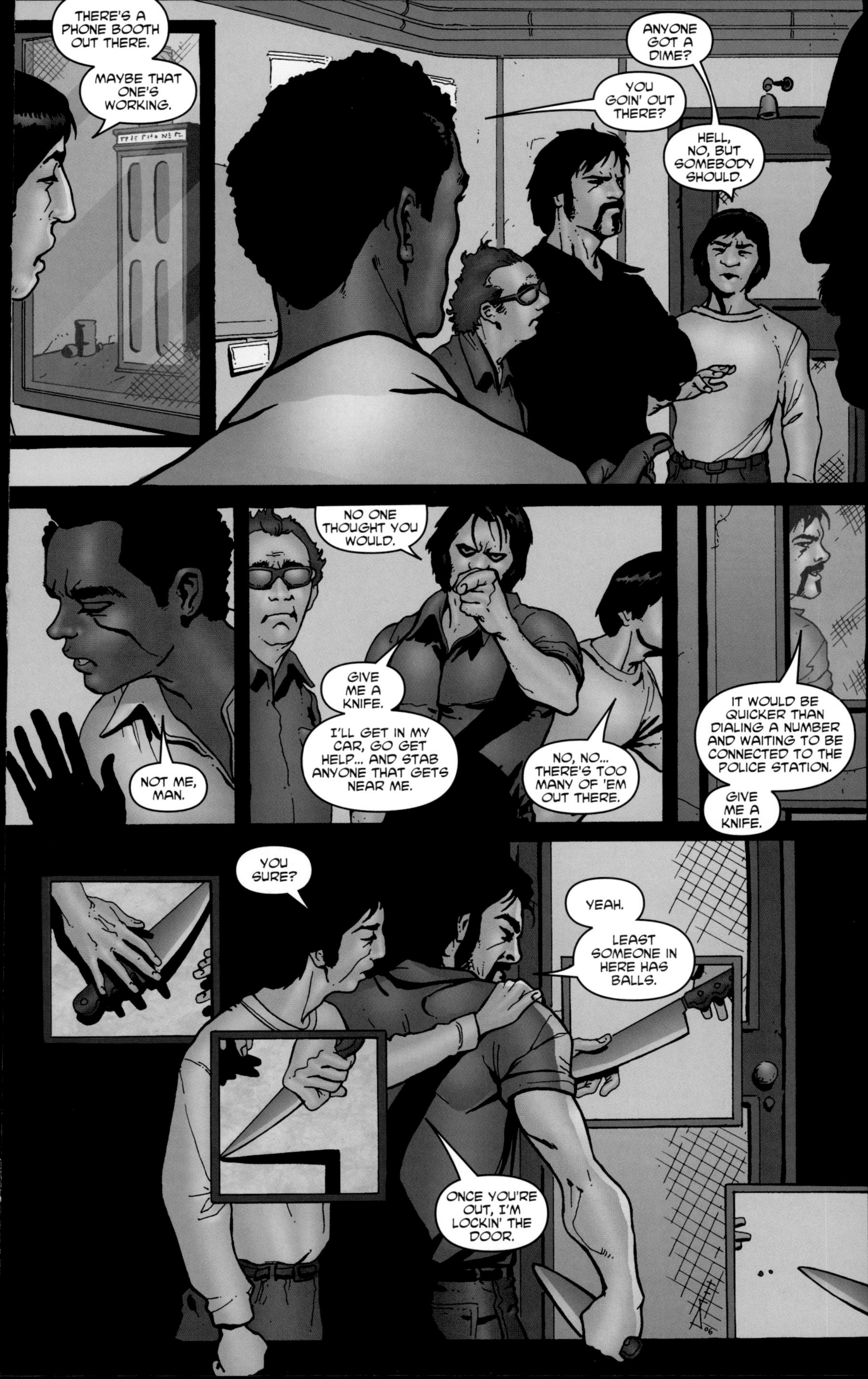
THERE'S A PHONE BOOTH OUT THERE.
MAYBE THAT ONE'S WORKING.
ANYONE GOT A DIME?
YOU GOIN' OUT THERE?
HELL, NO, BUT SOMEBODY SHOULD.
NOT ME, MAN.
NO ONE THOUGHT YOU WOULD.
GIVE ME A KNIFE.
I'LL GET IN MY CAR, GO GET HELP... AND STAB ANYONE THAT GETS NEAR ME.
NO, NO... THERE'S TOO MANY OF 'EM OUT THERE.
IT WOULD BE QUICKER THAN DIALING A NUMBER AND WAITING TO BE CONNECTED TO THE POLICE STATION.
GIVE ME A KNIFE.
YOU SURE?
YEAH.
LEAST SOMEONE IN HERE HAS BALLS.
ONCE YOU'RE OUT, I'M LOCKIN' THE DOOR.

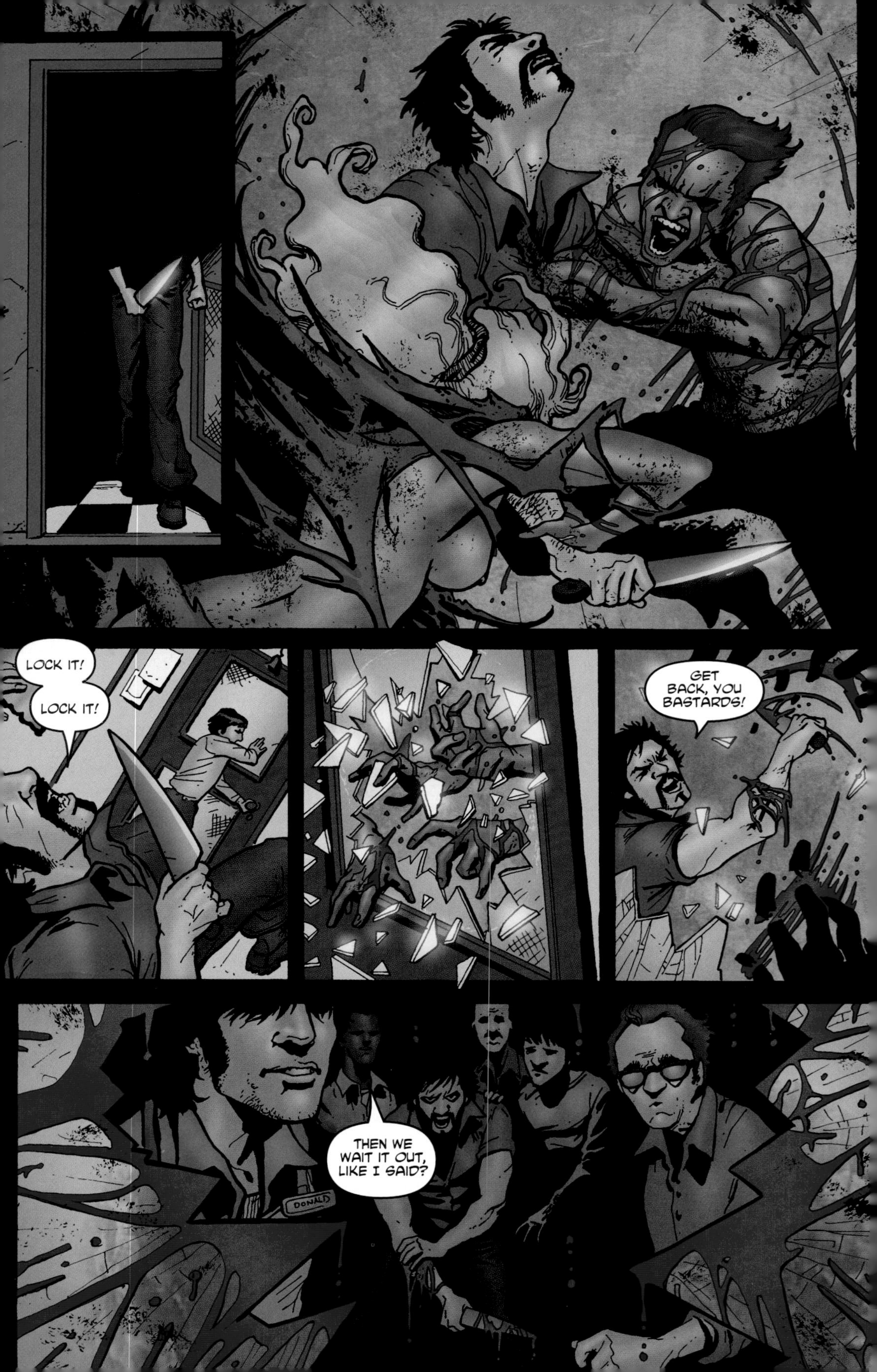
LOCK IT!
LOCK IT!
GET BACK, YOU BASTARDS!
DONALD
THEN WE WAIT IT OUT, LIKE I SAID?

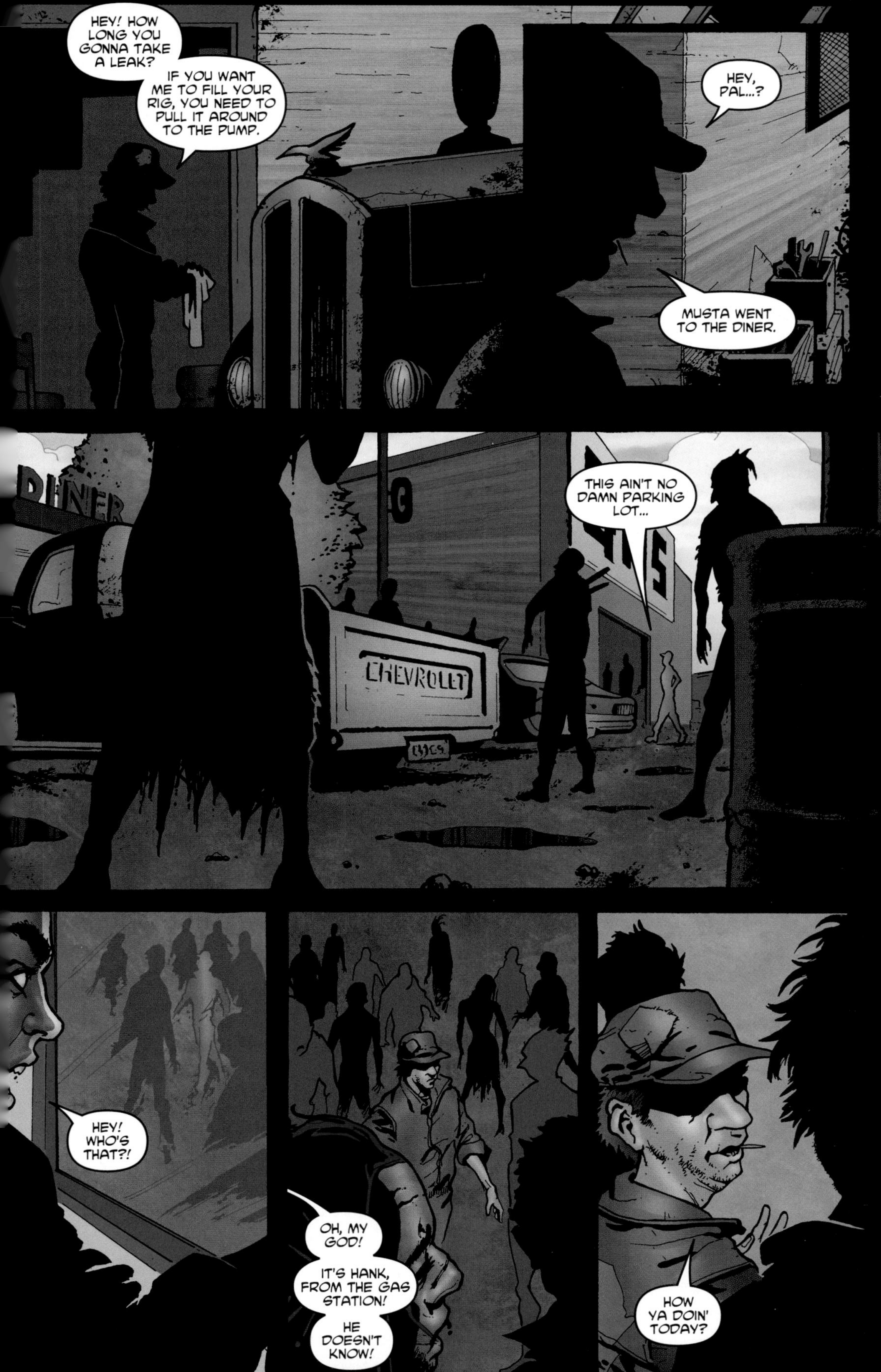
HEY! HOW LONG YOU GONNA TAKE A LEAK?
IF YOU WANT ME TO FILL YOUR RIG, YOU NEED TO PULL IT AROUND TO THE PUMP.
HEY, PAL...?
MUSTA WENT TO THE DINER.
DINER
CHEVROLET
THIS AIN'T NO DAMN PARKING LOT...
HEY! WHO'S THAT?!
OH, MY GOD!
IT'S HANK, FROM THE GAS STATION!
HE DOESN'T KNOW!
HOW YA DOIN' TODAY?

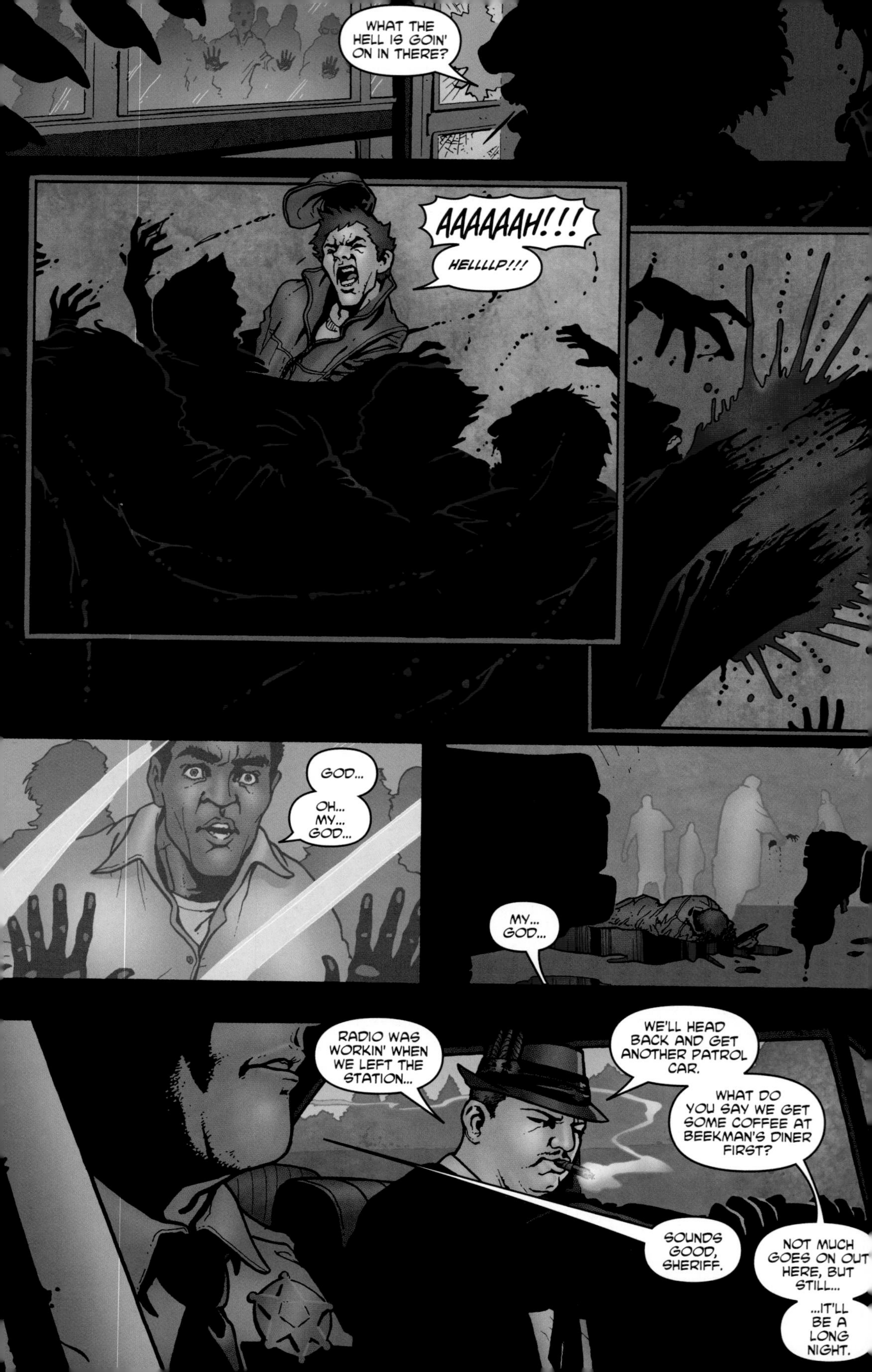
WHAT THE HELL IS GOIN' ON IN THERE?
AAAAAAH!!!
HELLLLP!!!
GOD...
OH... MY... GOD...
MY... GOD...
RADIO WAS WORKIN' WHEN WE LEFT THE STATION...
WE'LL HEAD BACK AND GET ANOTHER PATROL CAR.
WHAT DO YOU SAY WE GET SOME COFFEE AT BEEKMAN'S DINER FIRST?
SOUNDS GOOD, SHERIFF.
NOT MUCH GOES ON OUT HERE, BUT STILL...
...IT'LL BE A LONG NIGHT.

HUNGRY FOR THE FLESH OF THE LIVI

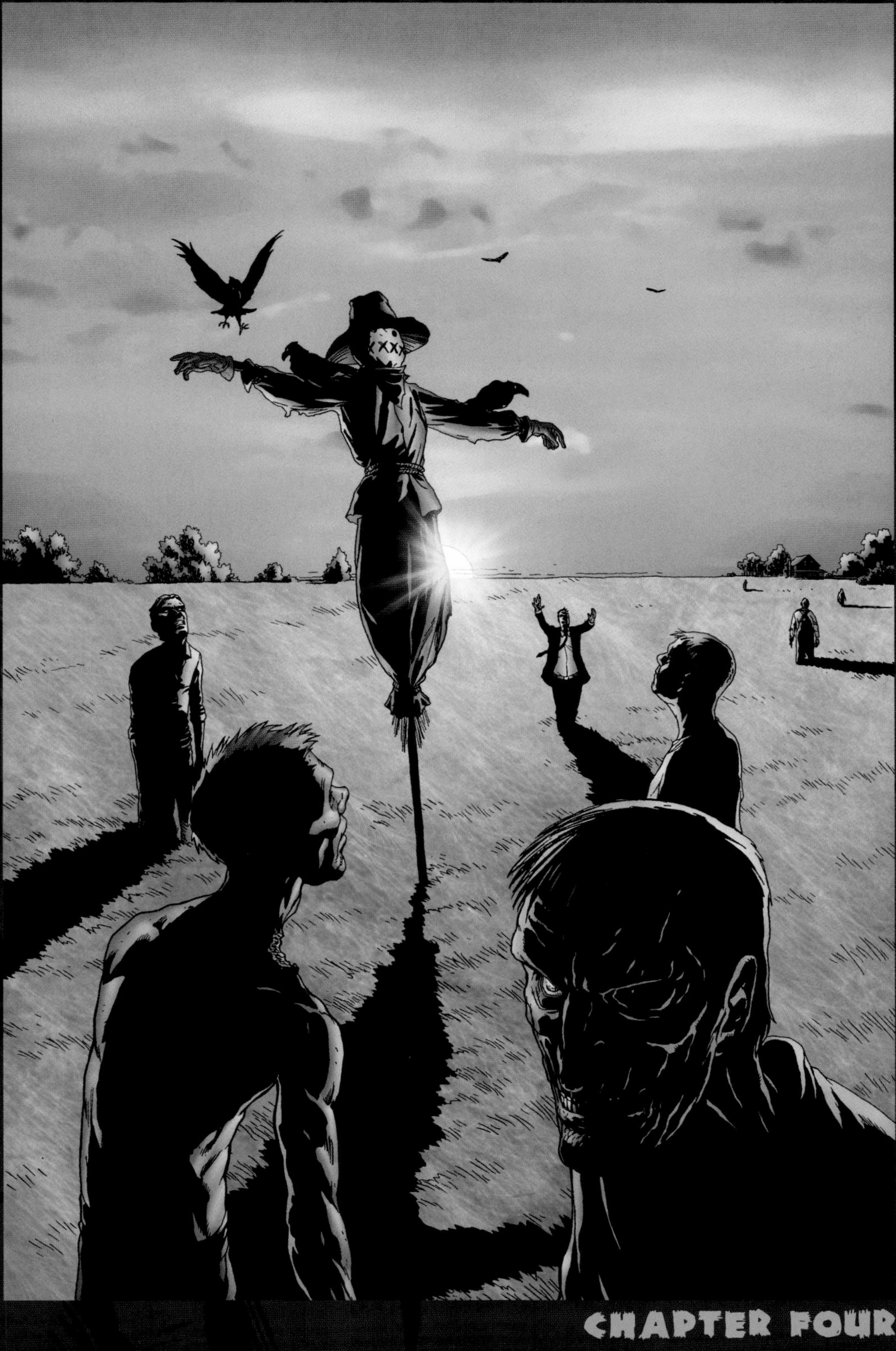

CHAPTER FOUR

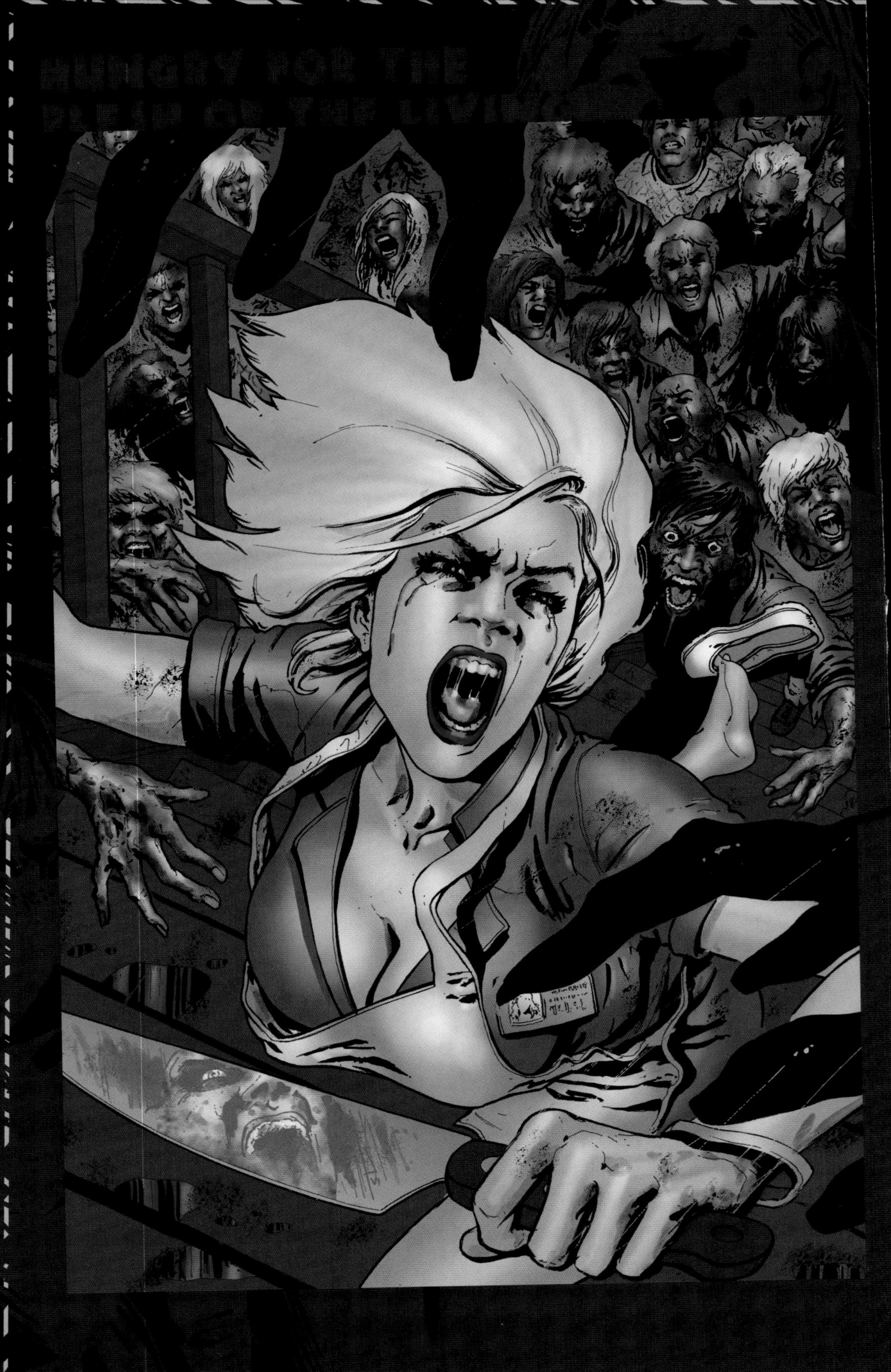
HUNGRY FOR THE
FLESH OF THE LIVI

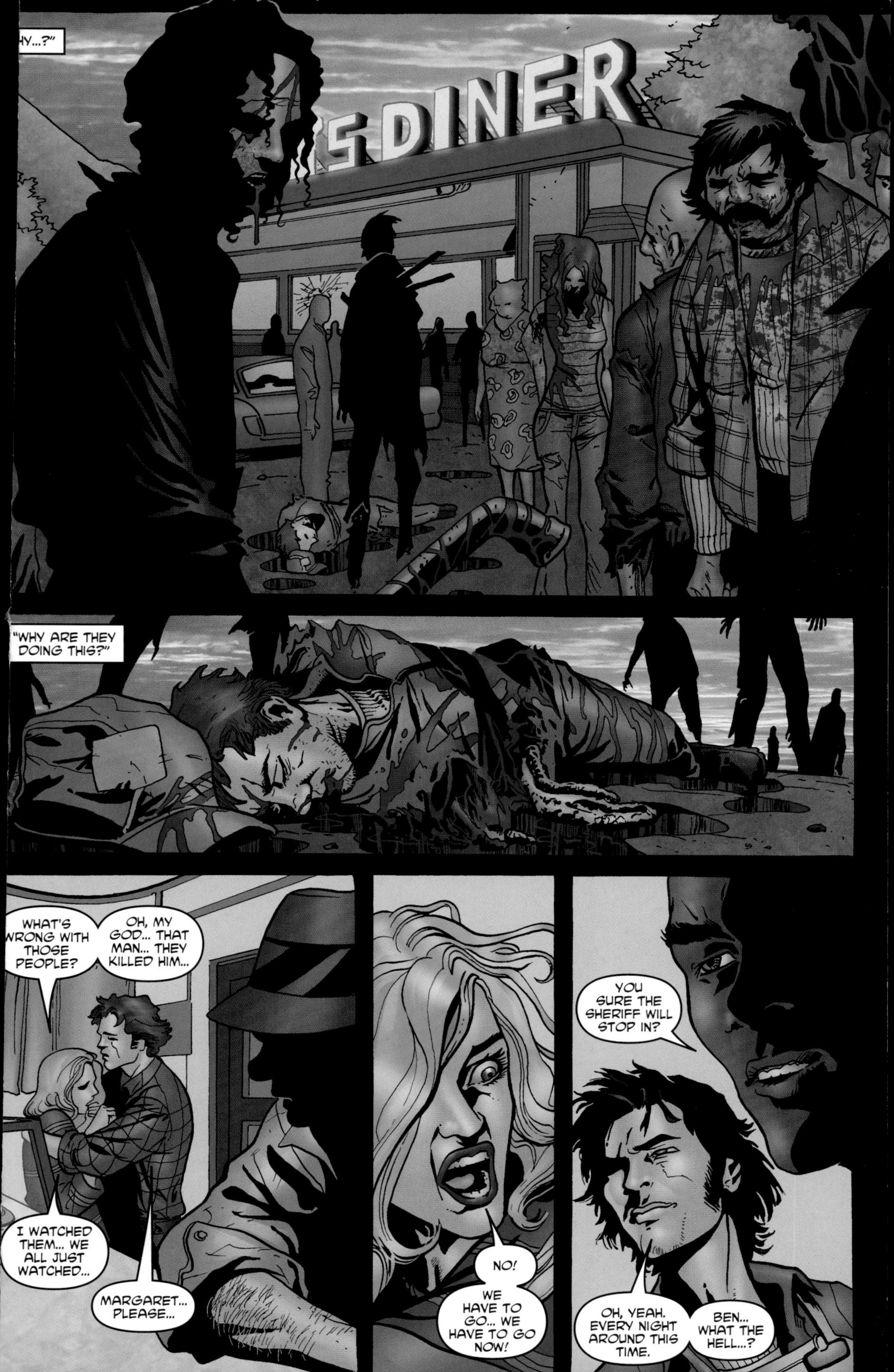
HY...?"
DINER
"WHY ARE THEY DOING THIS?"
WHAT'S WRONG WITH THOSE PEOPLE?
OH, MY GOD... THAT MAN... THEY KILLED HIM...
I WATCHED THEM... WE ALL JUST WATCHED...
MARGARET... PLEASE...
NO!
WE HAVE TO GO... WE HAVE TO GO NOW!
YOU SURE THE SHERIFF WILL STOP IN?
OH, YEAH. EVERY NIGHT AROUND THIS TIME.
BEN... WHAT THE HELL...?

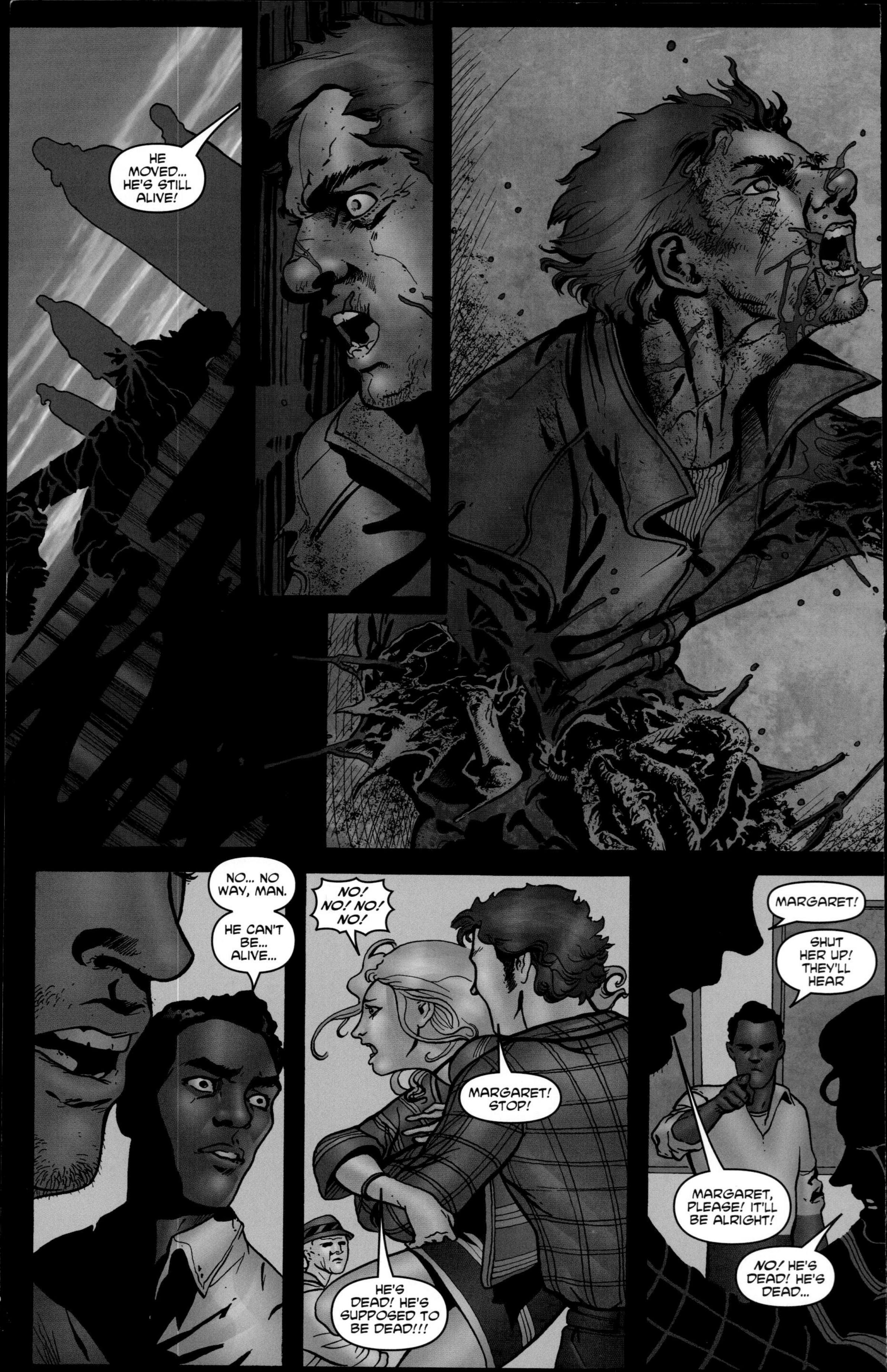
HE MOVED... HE'S STILL ALIVE!
NO... NO WAY, MAN.
HE CAN'T BE... ALIVE...
NO! NO! NO! NO!
MARGARET! STOP!
HE'S DEAD! HE'S SUPPOSED TO BE DEAD!!!
MARGARET!
SHUT HER UP! THEY'LL HEAR
MARGARET, PLEASE! IT'LL BE ALRIGHT!
NO! HE'S DEAD! HE'S DEAD...

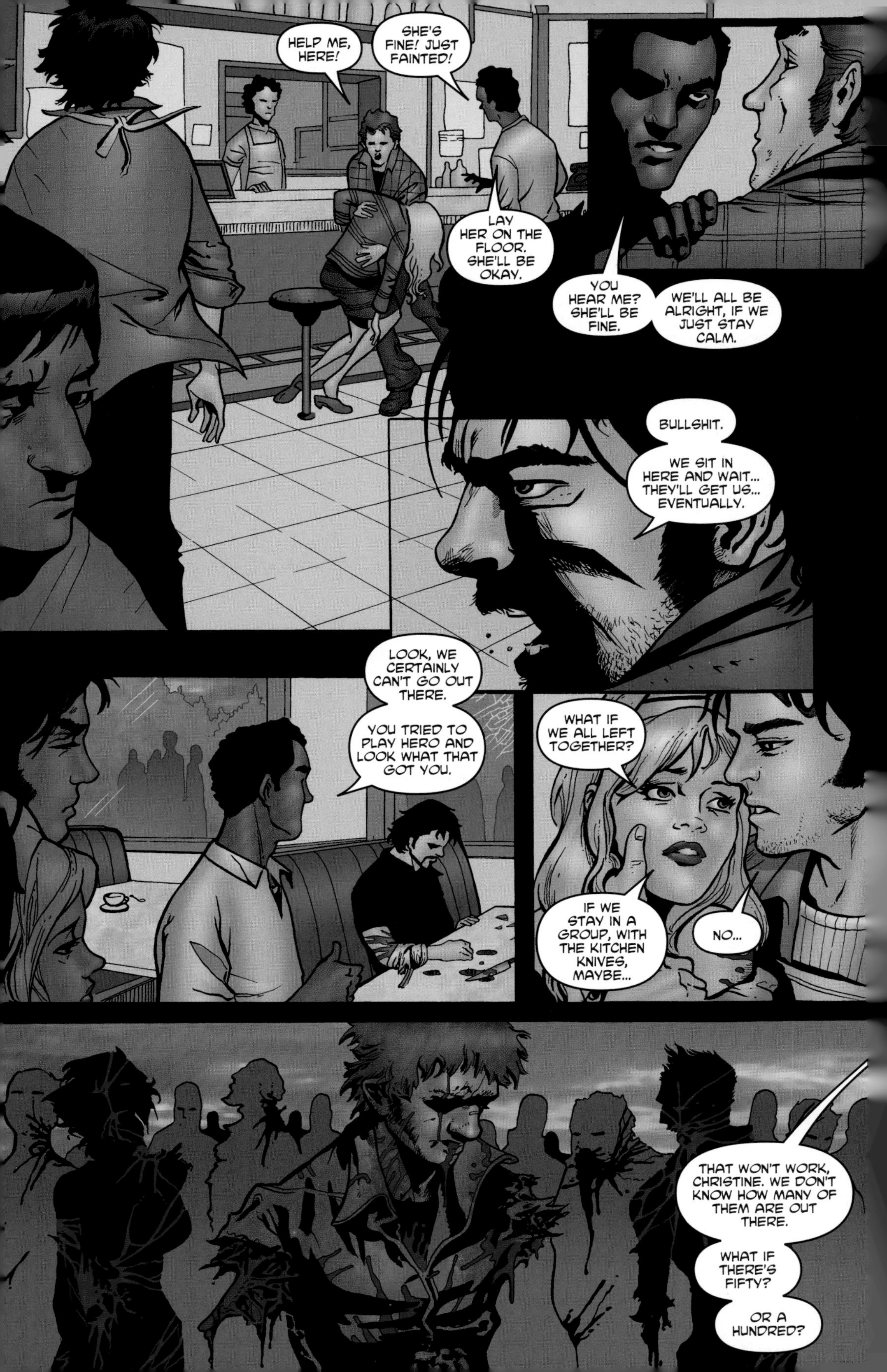
HELP ME, HERE!
SHE'S FINE! JUST FAINTED!
LAY HER ON THE FLOOR. SHE'LL BE OKAY.
YOU HEAR ME? SHE'LL BE FINE.
WE'LL ALL BE ALRIGHT, IF WE JUST STAY CALM.
BULLSHIT.
WE SIT IN HERE AND WAIT... THEY'LL GET US... EVENTUALLY.
LOOK, WE CERTAINLY CAN'T GO OUT THERE.
YOU TRIED TO PLAY HERO AND LOOK WHAT THAT GOT YOU.
WHAT IF WE ALL LEFT TOGETHER?
IF WE STAY IN A GROUP, WITH THE KITCHEN KNIVES, MAYBE...
NO...
THAT WON'T WORK, CHRISTINE. WE DON'T KNOW HOW MANY OF THEM ARE OUT THERE.
WHAT IF THERE'S FIFTY?
OR A HUNDRED?

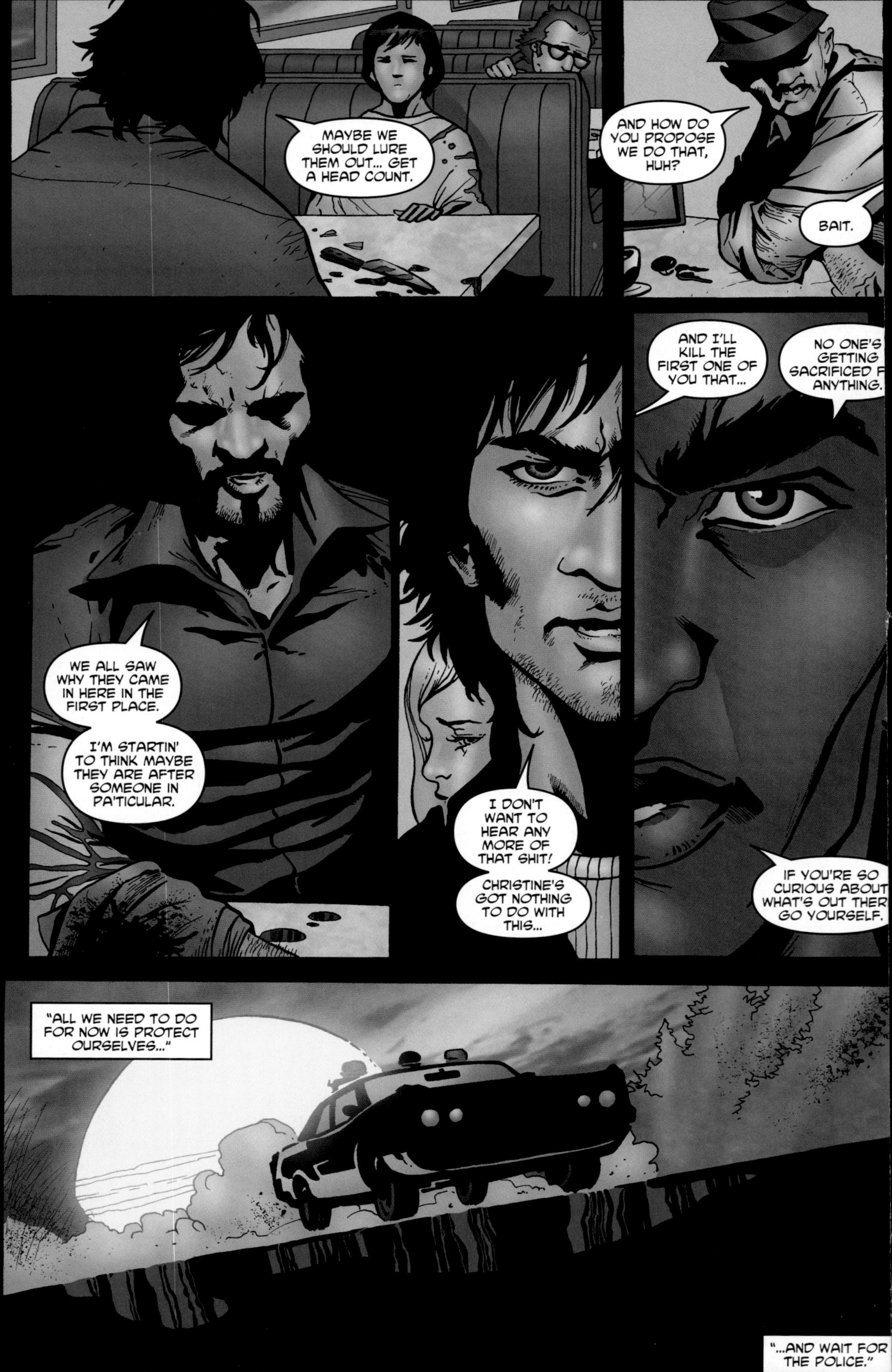
MAYBE WE SHOULD LURE THEM OUT... GET A HEAD COUNT.
AND HOW DO YOU PROPOSE WE DO THAT, HUH?
BAIT.
WE ALL SAW WHY THEY CAME IN HERE IN THE FIRST PLACE.
I'M STARTIN' TO THINK MAYBE THEY ARE AFTER SOMEONE IN PA'TICULAR.
I DON'T WANT TO HEAR ANY MORE OF THAT SHIT!
CHRISTINE'S GOT NOTHING TO DO WITH THIS...
AND I'LL KILL THE FIRST ONE OF YOU THAT...
NO ONE'S GETTING SACRIFICED F ANYTHING.
IF YOU'RE SO CURIOUS ABOUT WHAT'S OUT THER GO YOURSELF.
"ALL WE NEED TO DO FOR NOW IS PROTECT OURSELVES..."
"...AND WAIT FOR THE POLICE."

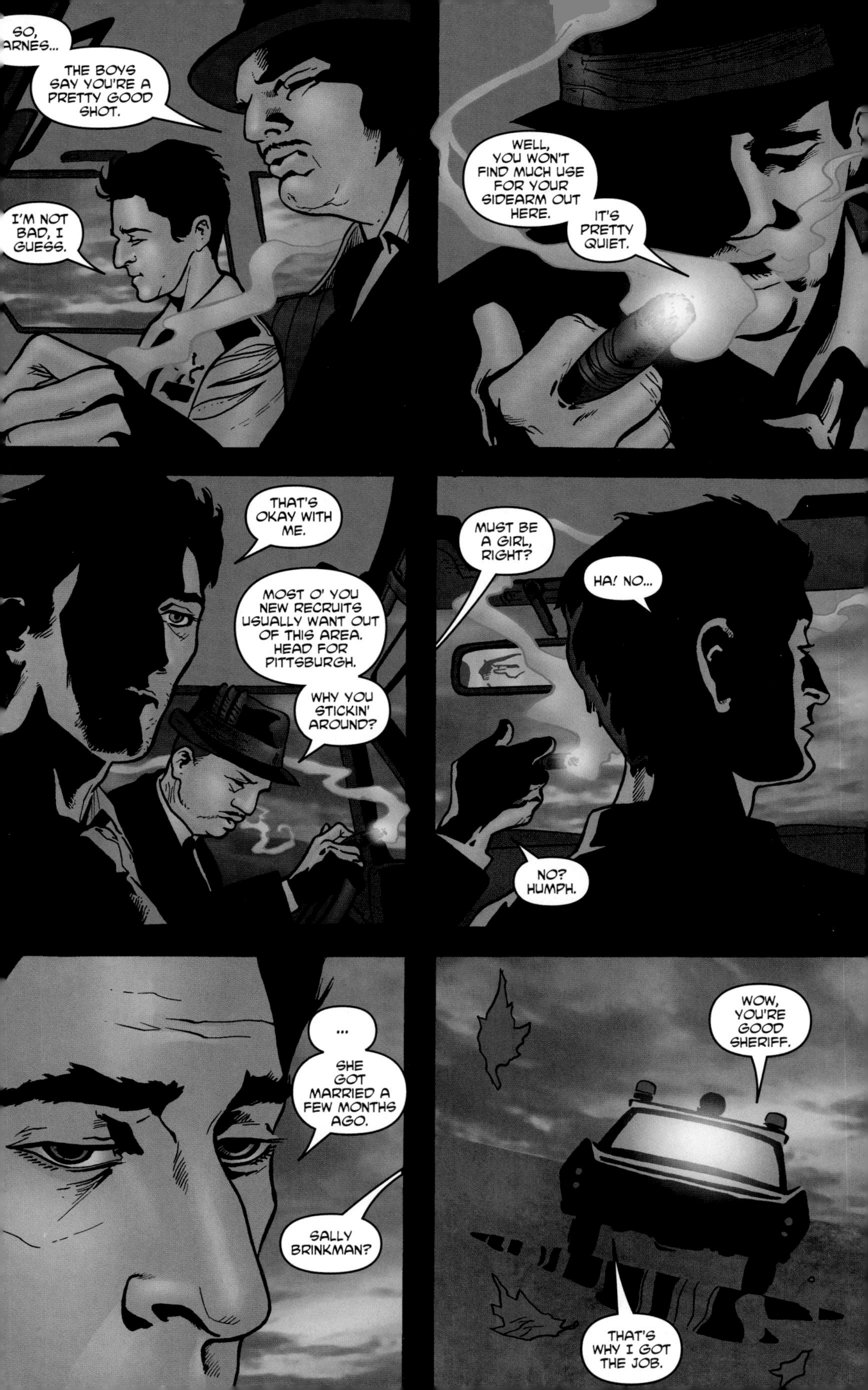
SO, ARNES...
THE BOYS SAY YOU'RE A PRETTY GOOD SHOT.
I'M NOT BAD, I GUESS.
WELL, YOU WON'T FIND MUCH USE FOR YOUR SIDEARM OUT HERE.
IT'S PRETTY QUIET.
THAT'S OKAY WITH ME.
MOST O' YOU NEW RECRUITS USUALLY WANT OUT OF THIS AREA. HEAD FOR PITTSBURGH.
WHY YOU STICKIN' AROUND?
MUST BE A GIRL, RIGHT?
HA! NO...
NO? HUMPH.
...
SHE GOT MARRIED A FEW MONTHS AGO.
SALLY BRINKMAN?
WOW, YOU'RE GOOD SHERIFF.
THAT'S WHY I GOT THE JOB.

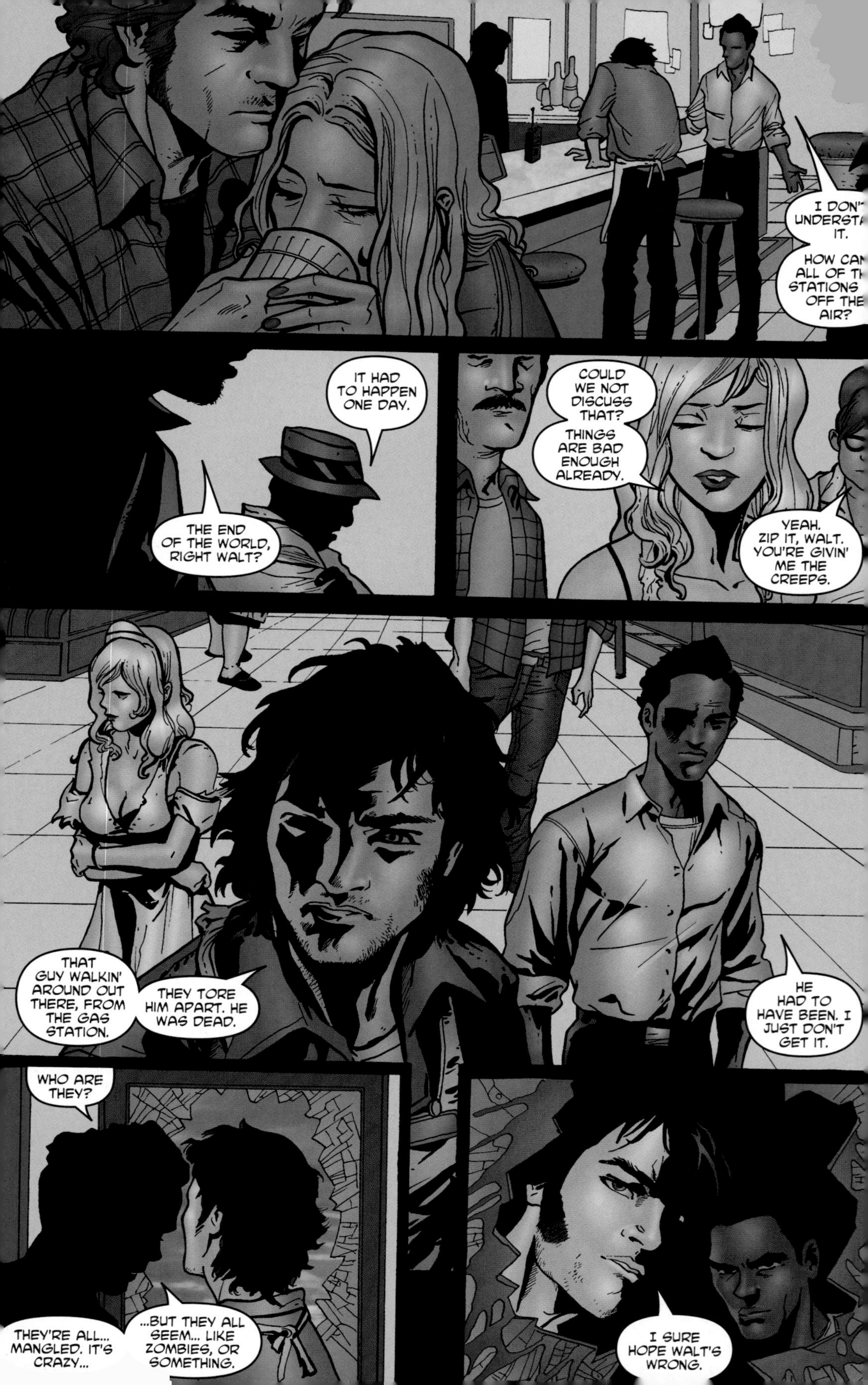
I DON'T UNDERSTA IT.
HOW CAN ALL OF TH STATIONS OFF THE AIR?
IT HAD TO HAPPEN ONE DAY.
THE END OF THE WORLD, RIGHT WALT?
COULD WE NOT DISCUSS THAT?
THINGS ARE BAD ENOUGH ALREADY.
YEAH. ZIP IT, WALT. YOU'RE GIVIN' ME THE CREEPS.
THAT GUY WALKIN' AROUND OUT THERE, FROM THE GAS STATION.
THEY TORE HIM APART. HE WAS DEAD.
HE HAD TO HAVE BEEN. I JUST DON'T GET IT.
WHO ARE THEY?
THEY'RE ALL... MANGLED. IT'S CRAZY...
...BUT THEY ALL SEEM... LIKE ZOMBIES, OR SOMETHING.
I SURE HOPE WALT'S WRONG.

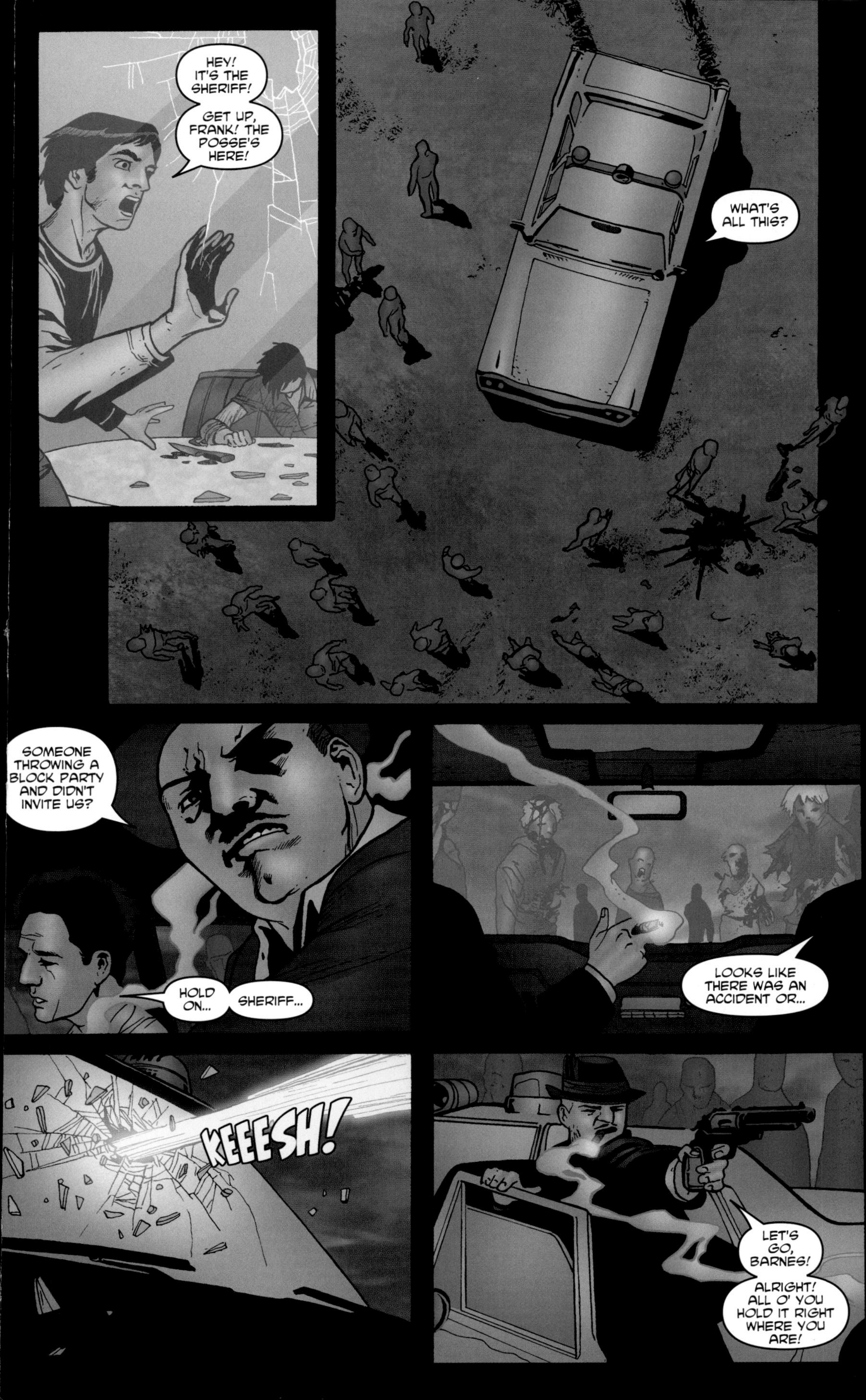
HEY! IT'S THE SHERIFF!
GET UP, FRANK! THE POSSE'S HERE!
WHAT'S ALL THIS?
SOMEONE THROWING A BLOCK PARTY AND DIDN'T INVITE US?
HOLD ON...
SHERIFF...
LOOKS LIKE THERE WAS AN ACCIDENT OR...
KEEESH!
LET'S GO, BARNES!
ALRIGHT! ALL O' YOU HOLD IT RIGHT WHERE YOU ARE!

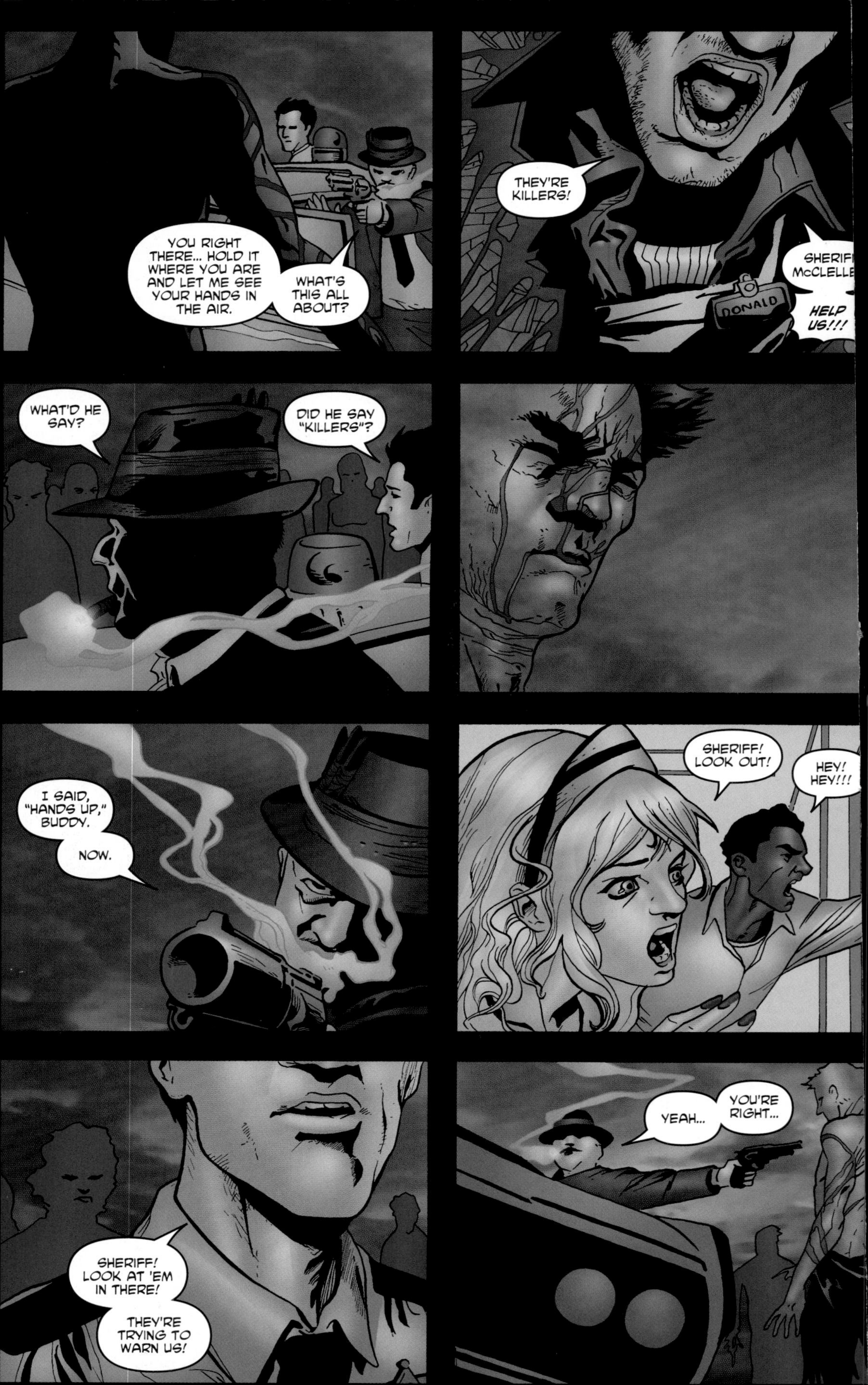
YOU RIGHT THERE... HOLD IT WHERE YOU ARE AND LET ME SEE YOUR HANDS IN THE AIR.
WHAT'S THIS ALL ABOUT?
THEY'RE KILLERS!
DONALD
HELP US!!!
WHAT'D HE SAY?
DID HE SAY "KILLERS"?
I SAID, "HANDS UP," BUDDY.
NOW.
SHERIFF! LOOK OUT!
HEY! HEY!!!
SHERIFF! LOOK AT 'EM IN THERE!
THEY'RE TRYING TO WARN US!
YEAH...
YOU'RE RIGHT...

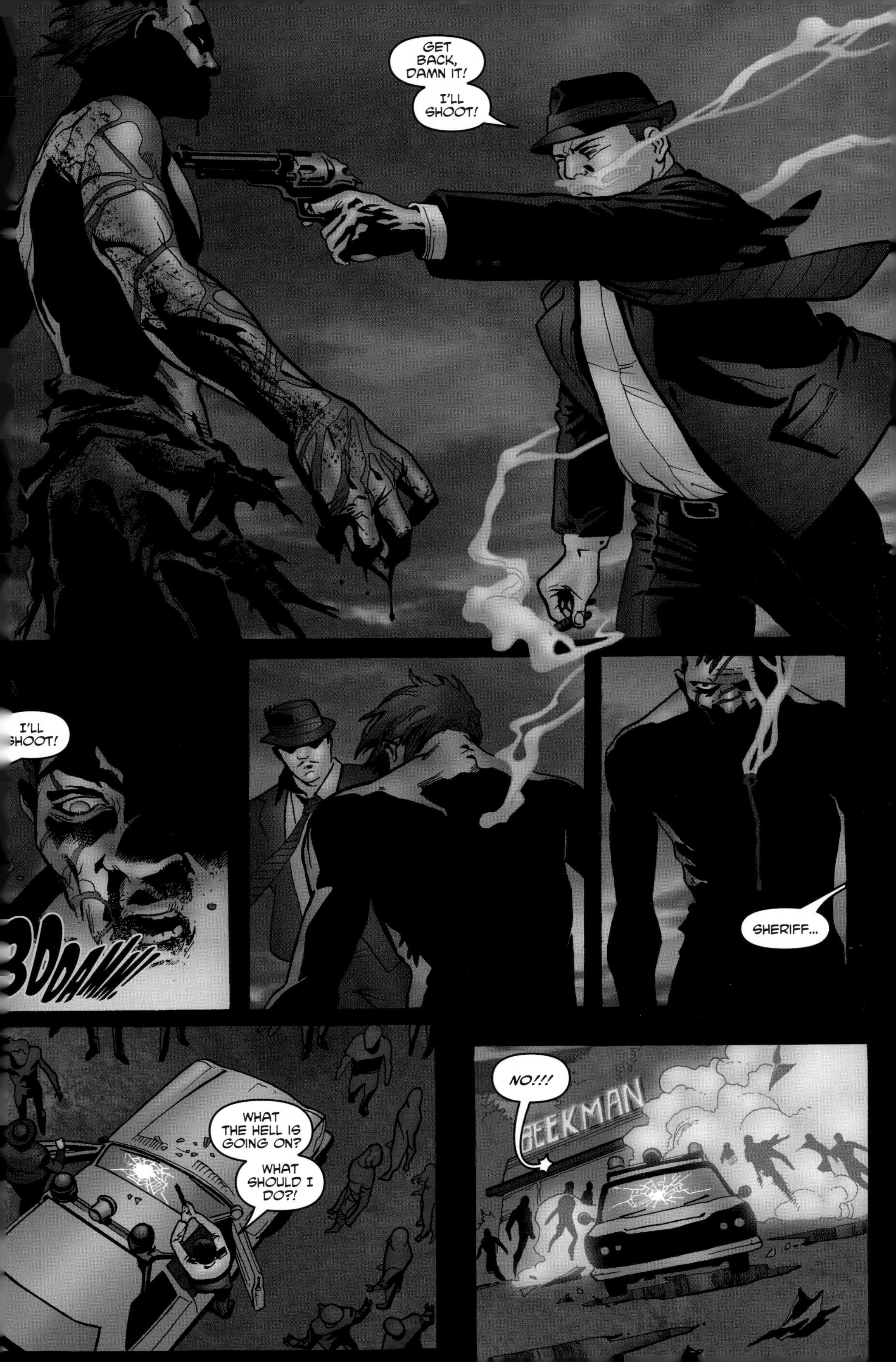
GET BACK, DAMN IT!
I'LL SHOOT!
I'LL SHOOT!
BDDAM!!
SHERIFF...
WHAT THE HELL IS GOING ON?
WHAT SHOULD I DO?!
NO!!!
BEEKMAN

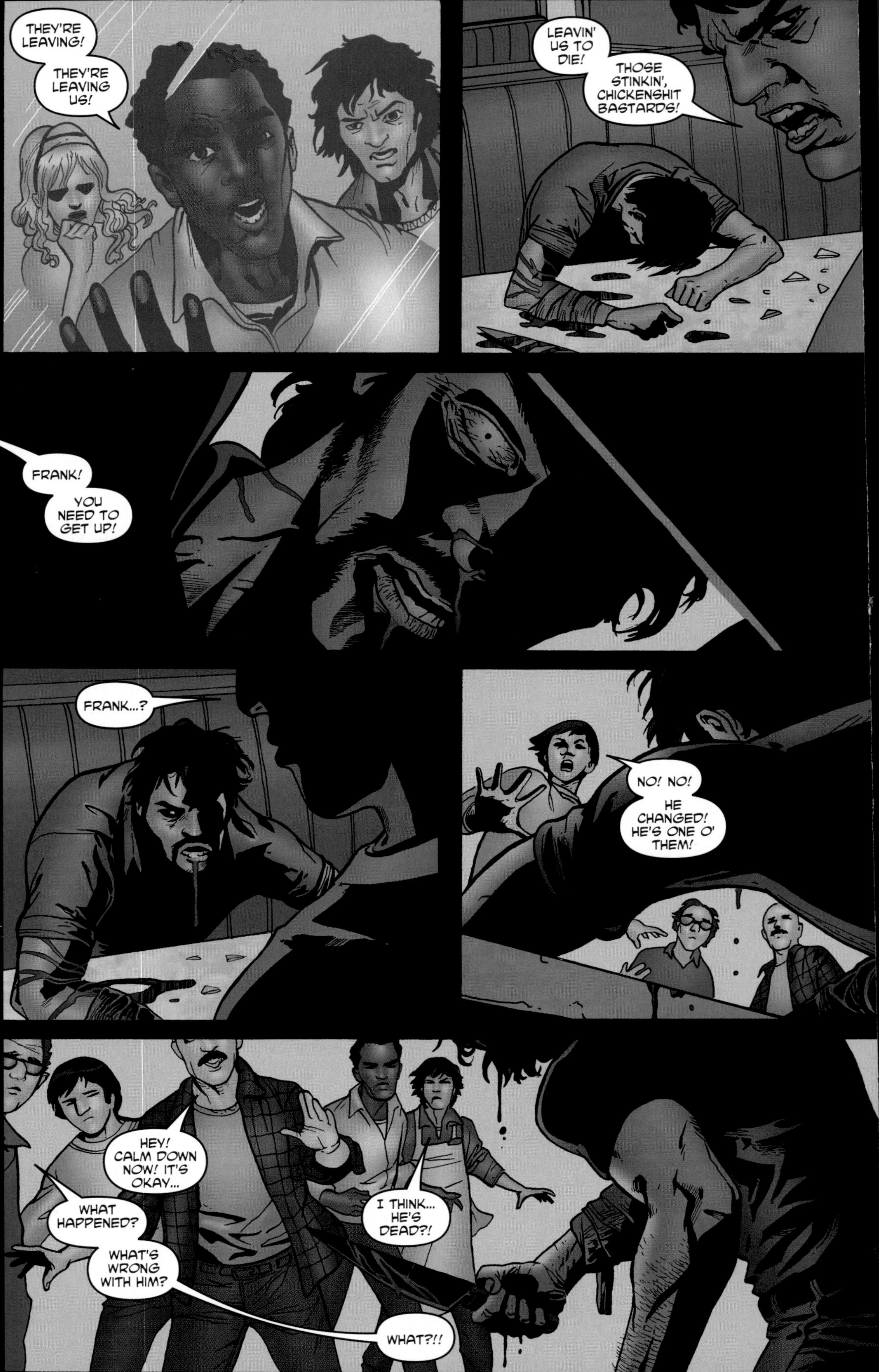
THEY'RE LEAVING!
THEY'RE LEAVING US!
LEAVIN' US TO DIE!
THOSE STINKIN', CHICKENSHIT BASTARDS!
FRANK!
YOU NEED TO GET UP!
FRANK...?
NO! NO!
HE CHANGED! HE'S ONE O' THEM!
HEY! CALM DOWN NOW! IT'S OKAY...
WHAT HAPPENED?
WHAT'S WRONG WITH HIM?
I THINK... HE'S DEAD?!
WHAT?!!

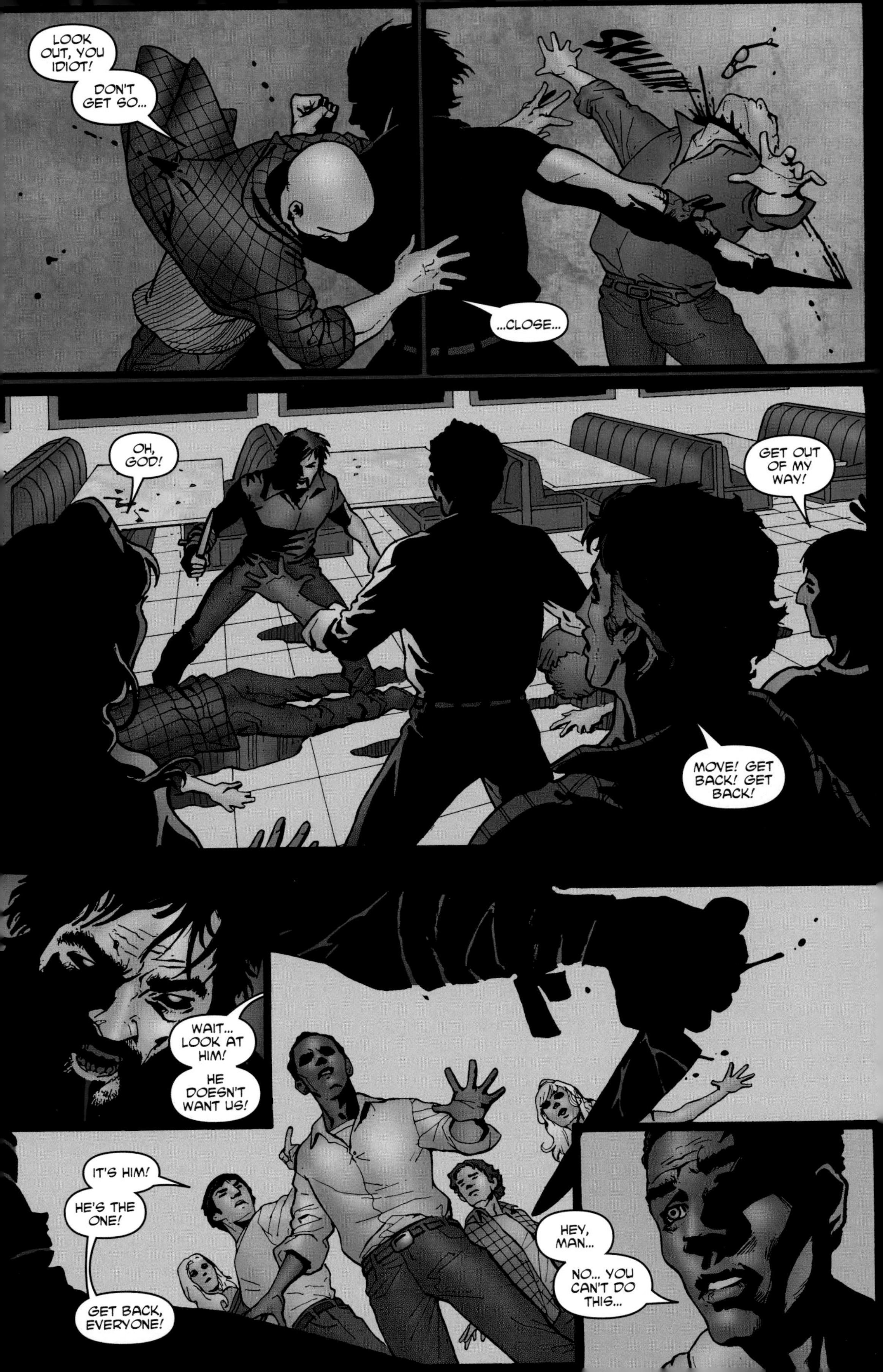
LOOK OUT, YOU IDIOT!
DON'T GET SO...
...CLOSE...
OH, GOD!
GET OUT OF MY WAY!
MOVE! GET BACK! GET BACK!
WAIT... LOOK AT HIM!
HE DOESN'T WANT US!
IT'S HIM!
HE'S THE ONE!
GET BACK, EVERYONE!
HEY, MAN...
NO... YOU CAN'T DO THIS...

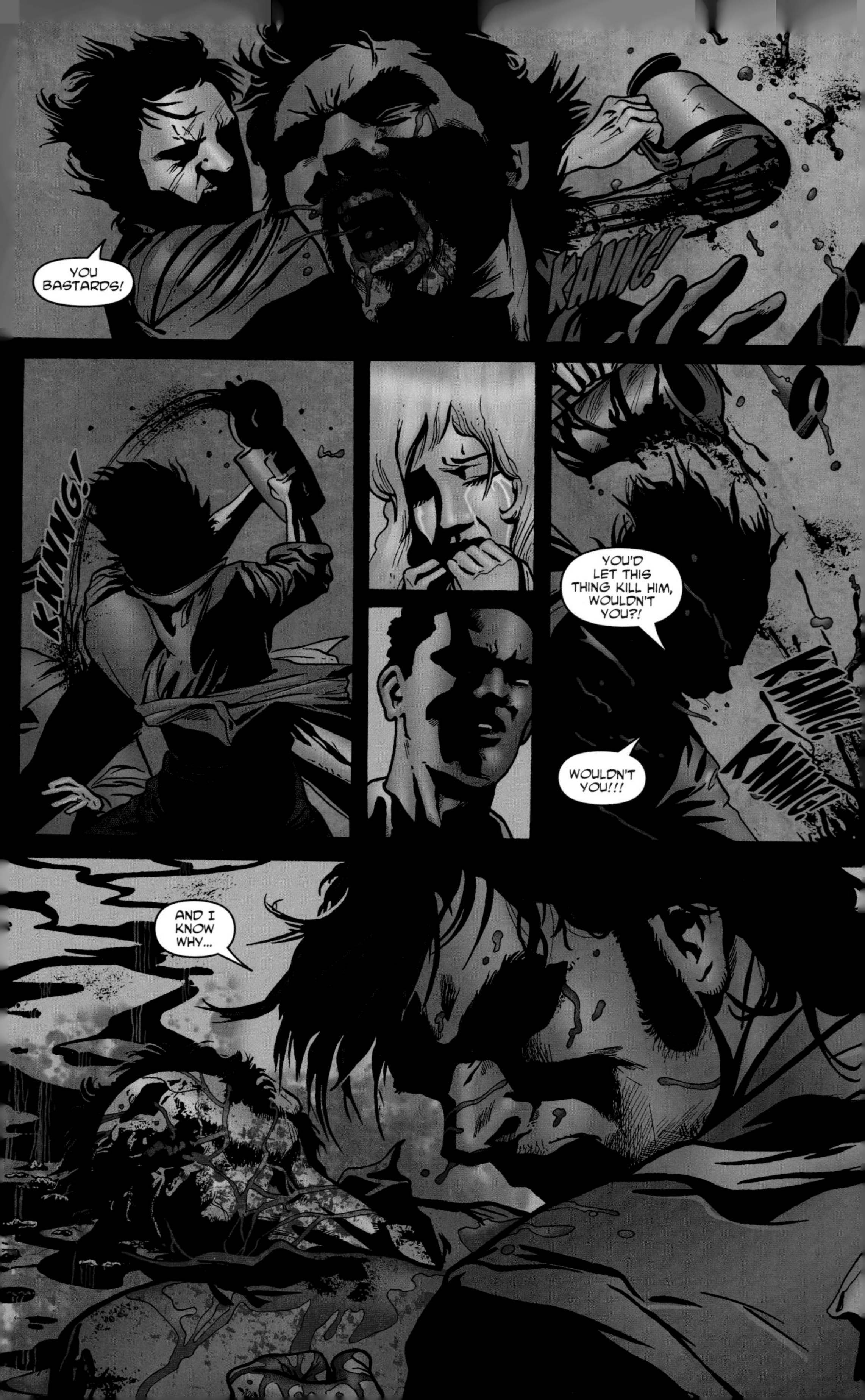
YOU BASTARDS!
KANNG!
KNNNG!
YOU'D LET THIS THING KILL HIM, WOULDN'T YOU?!
WOULDN'T YOU!!!
AND I KNOW WHY...

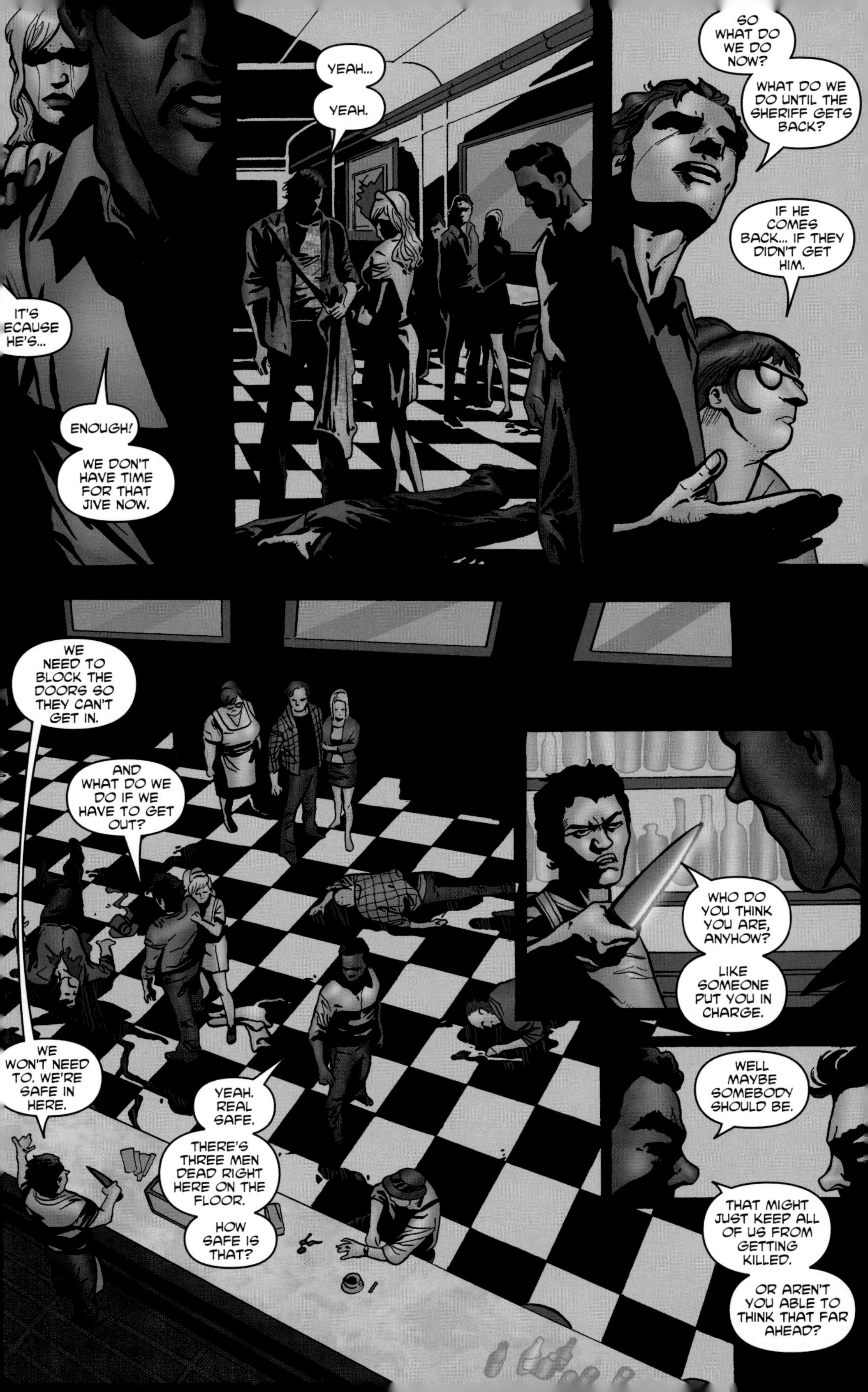
IT'S
ECAUSE HE'S...
ENOUGH!
WE DON'T HAVE TIME FOR THAT JIVE NOW.
YEAH...
YEAH.
SO WHAT DO WE DO NOW?
WHAT DO WE DO UNTIL THE SHERIFF GETS BACK?
IF HE COMES BACK... IF THEY DIDN'T GET HIM.
WE NEED TO BLOCK THE DOORS SO THEY CAN'T GET IN.
AND WHAT DO WE DO IF WE HAVE TO GET OUT?
WE WON'T NEED TO. WE'RE SAFE IN HERE.
YEAH. REAL SAFE.
THERE'S THREE MEN DEAD RIGHT HERE ON THE FLOOR.
HOW SAFE IS THAT?
WHO DO YOU THINK YOU ARE, ANYHOW?
LIKE SOMEONE PUT YOU IN CHARGE.
WELL MAYBE SOMEBODY SHOULD BE.
THAT MIGHT JUST KEEP ALL OF US FROM GETTING KILLED.
OR AREN'T YOU ABLE TO THINK THAT FAR AHEAD?

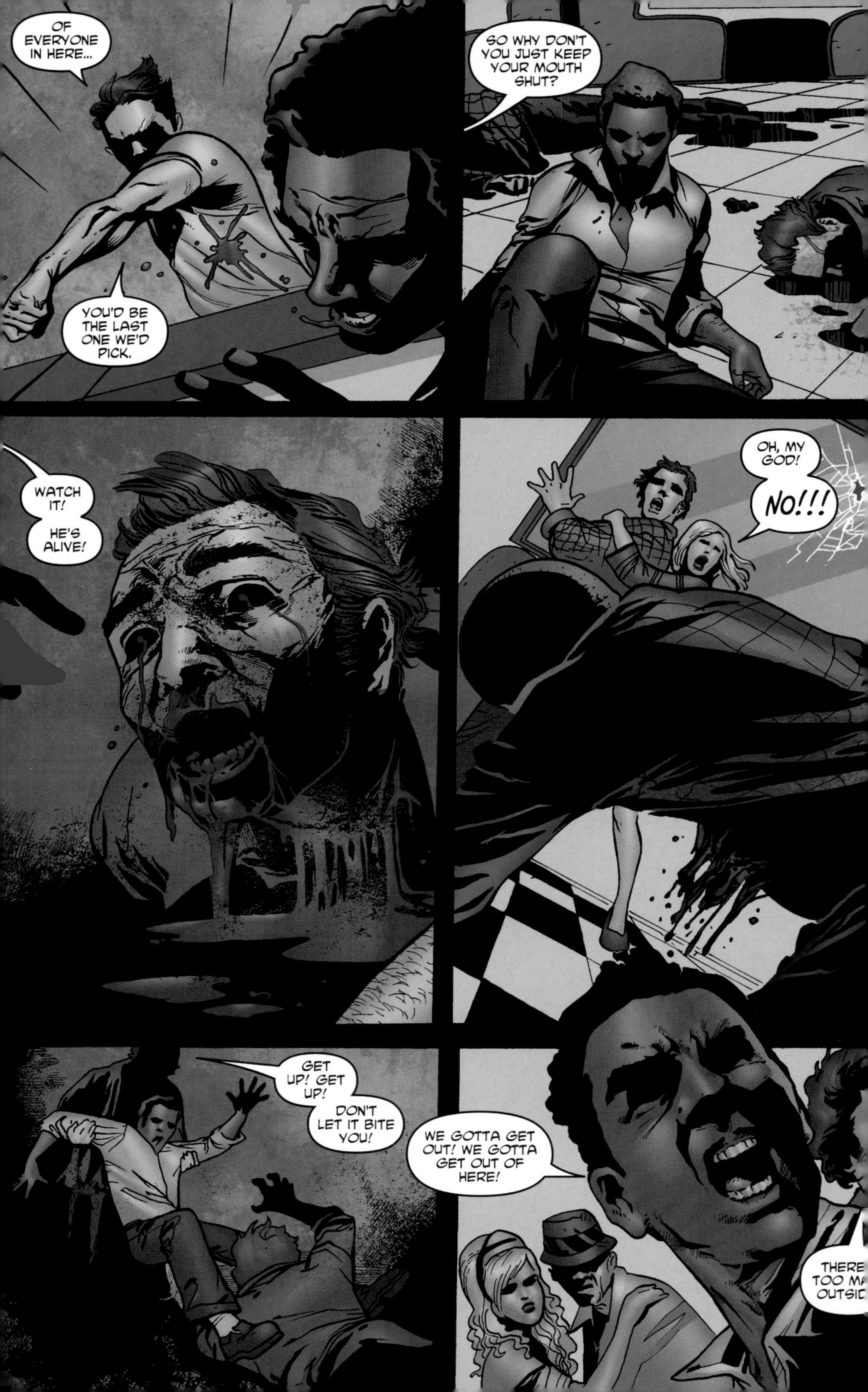
OF EVERYONE IN HERE...
YOU'D BE THE LAST ONE WE'D PICK.
SO WHY DON'T YOU JUST KEEP YOUR MOUTH SHUT?
WATCH IT!
HE'S ALIVE!
OH, MY GOD!
NO!!!
GET UP! GET UP!
DON'T LET IT BITE YOU!
WE GOTTA GET OUT! WE GOTTA GET OUT OF HERE!

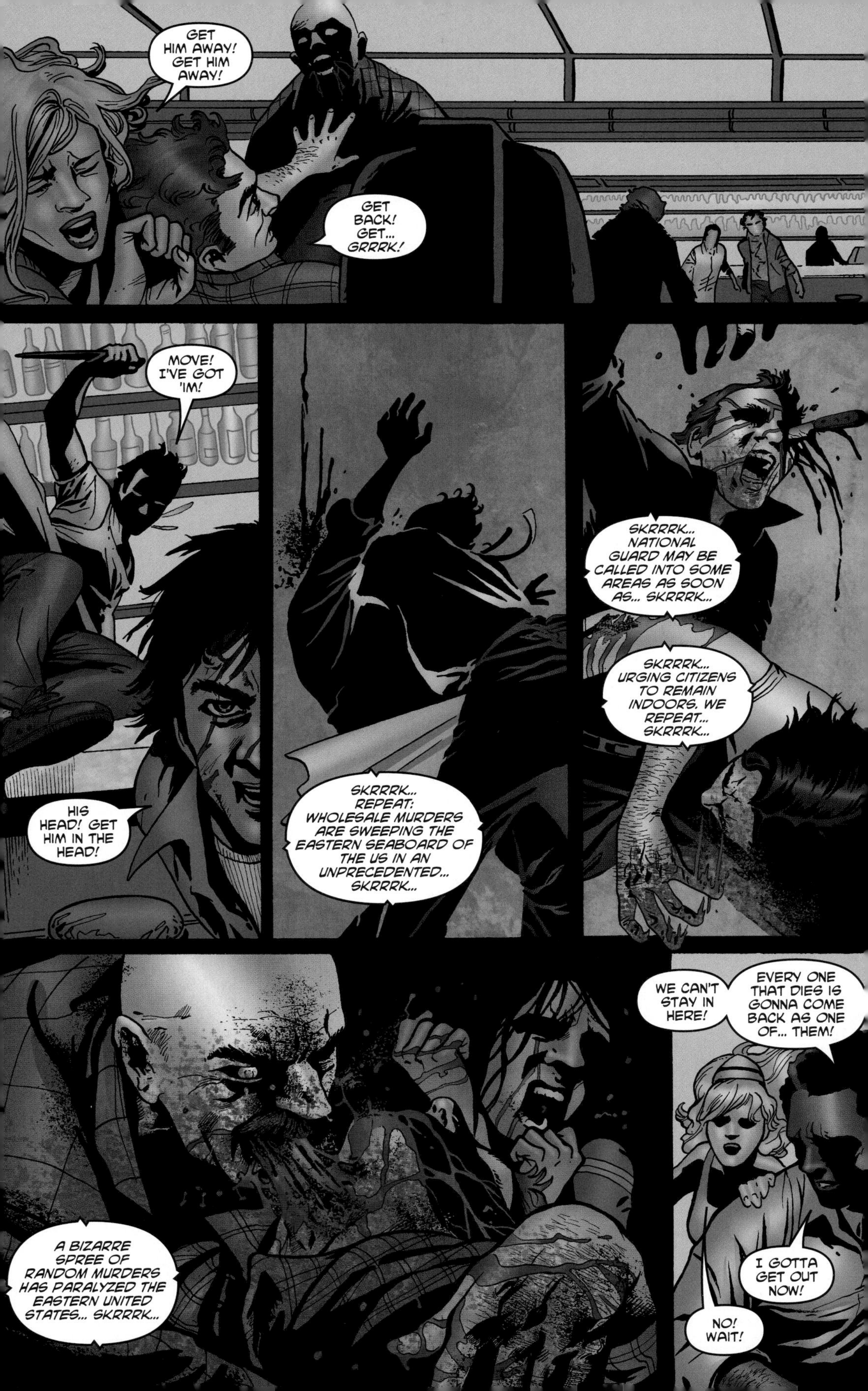
GET HIM AWAY! GET HIM AWAY!
GET BACK! GET... GRRRK!
MOVE! I'VE GOT 'IM!
HIS HEAD! GET HIM IN THE HEAD!
SKRRRK... REPEAT: WHOLESALE MURDERS ARE SWEEPING THE EASTERN SEABOARD OF THE US IN AN UNPRECEDENTED... SKRRRK...
SKRRRK... NATIONAL GUARD MAY BE CALLED INTO SOME AREAS AS SOON AS... SKRRRK...
SKRRRK... URGING CITIZENS TO REMAIN INDOORS. WE REPEAT... SKRRRK...
A BIZARRE SPREE OF RANDOM MURDERS HAS PARALYZED THE EASTERN UNITED STATES... SKRRRK...
WE CAN'T STAY IN HERE!
EVERY ONE THAT DIES IS GONNA COME BACK AS ONE OF... THEM!
I GOTTA GET OUT NOW!
NO! WAIT!

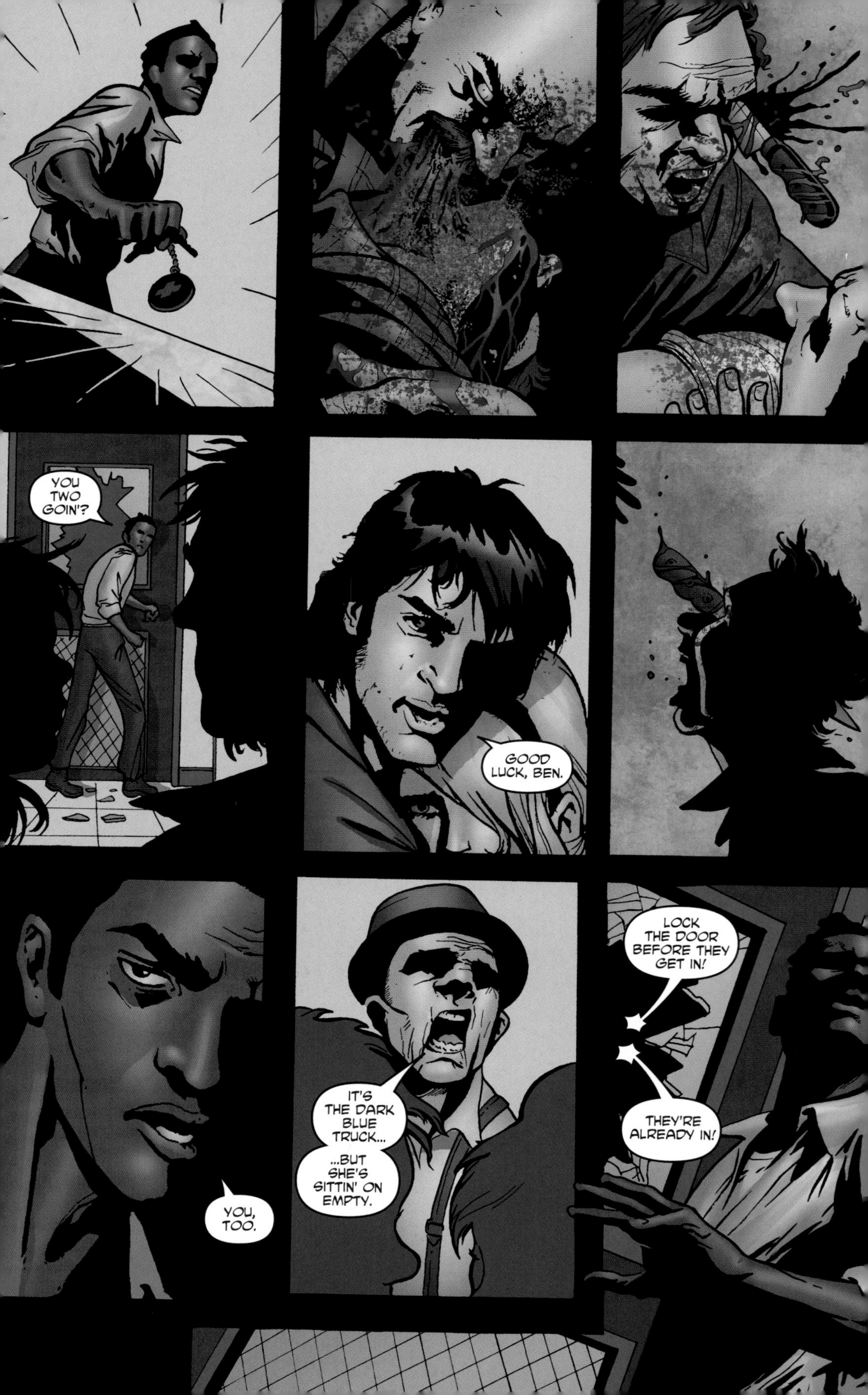
YOU TWO GOIN'?
GOOD LUCK, BEN.
YOU, TOO.
IT'S THE DARK BLUE TRUCK...
...BUT SHE'S SITTIN' ON EMPTY.
LOCK THE DOOR BEFORE THEY GET IN!
THEY'RE ALREADY IN!

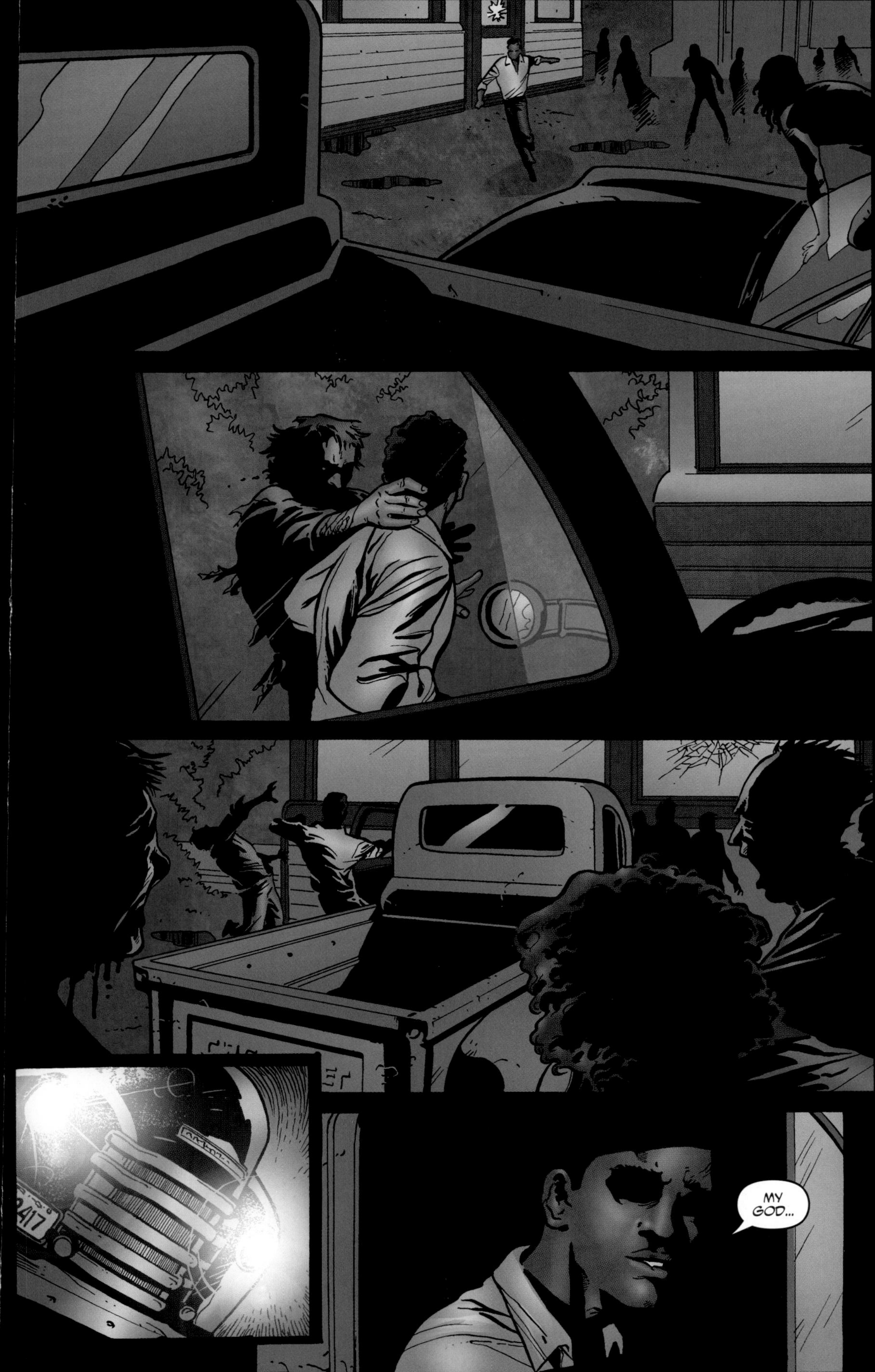
MY GOD...

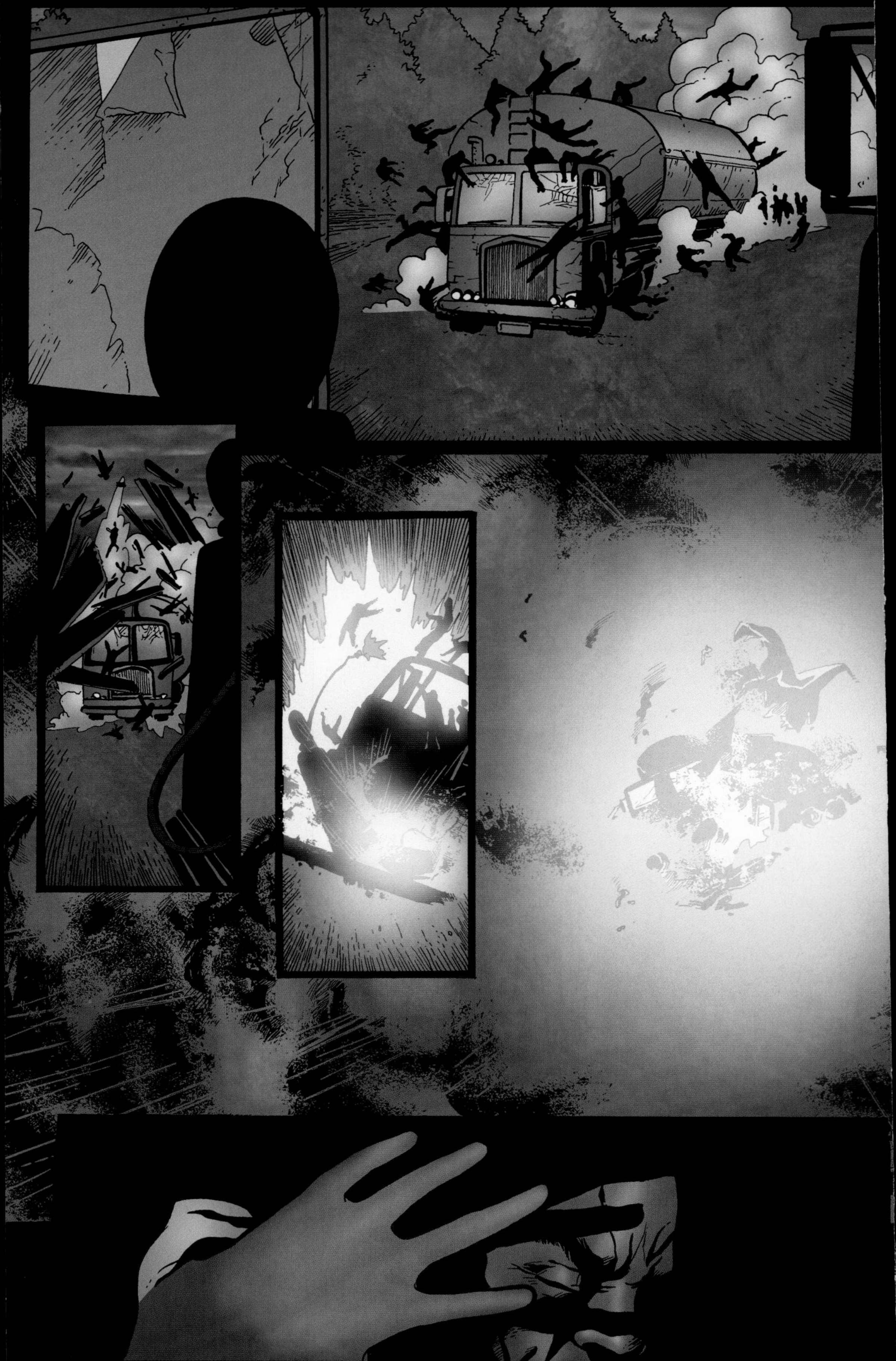

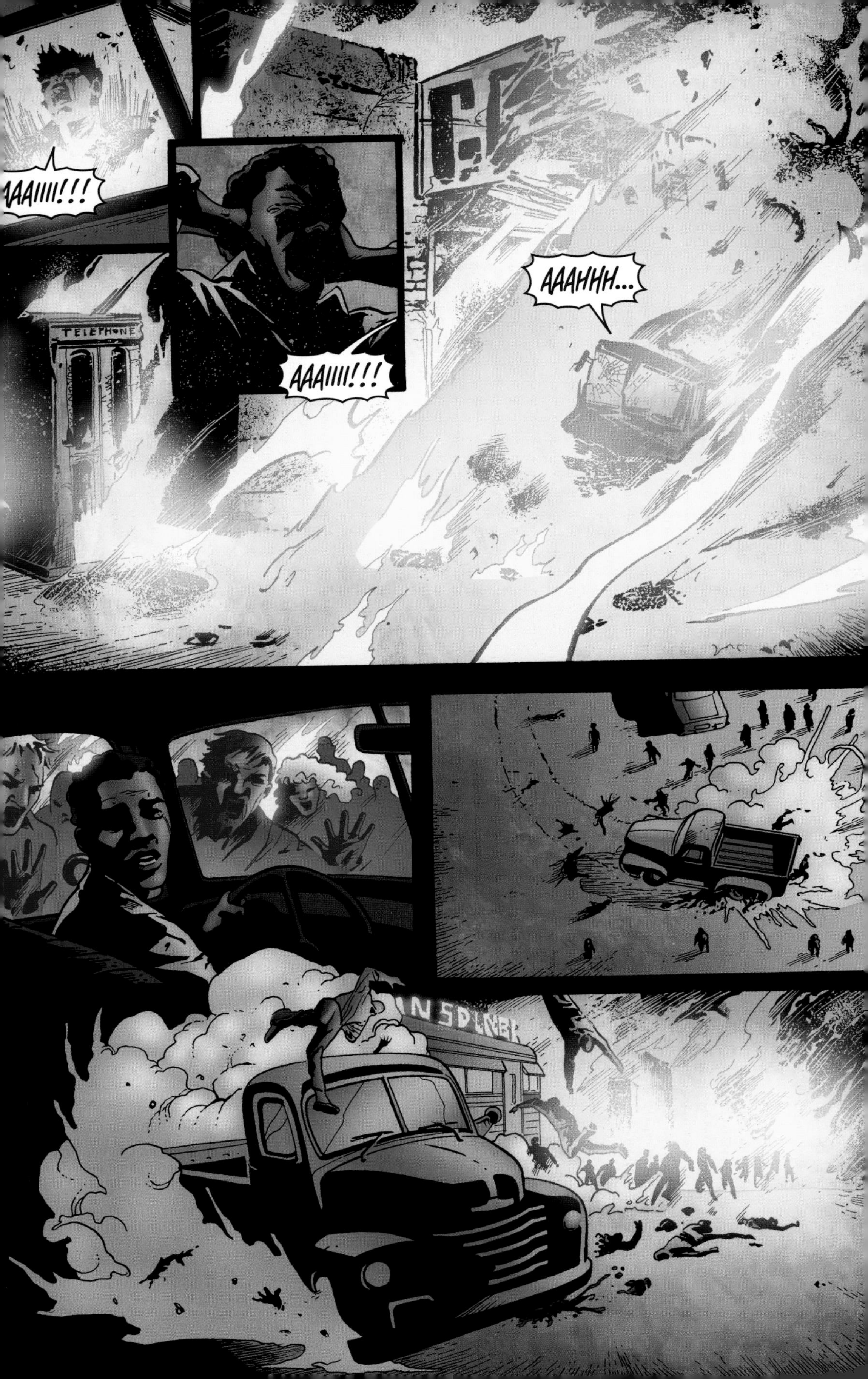
AAAIIII!!!
AAAIIII!!!
AAAHHH...
TELEPHONE

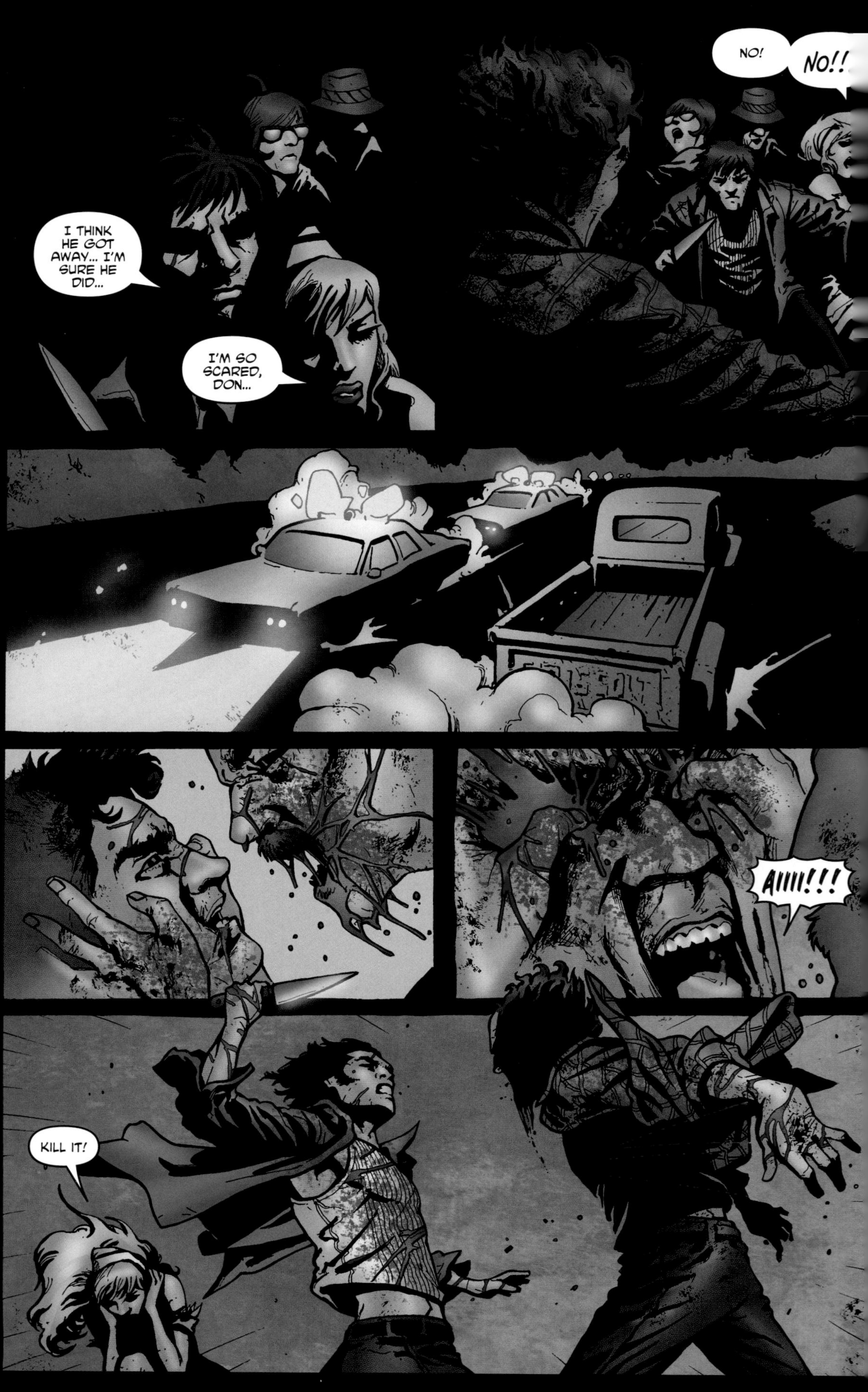
I THINK HE GOT AWAY... I'M SURE HE DID...
I'M SO SCARED, DON...
NO!
NO!!
AIIII!!!
KILL IT!

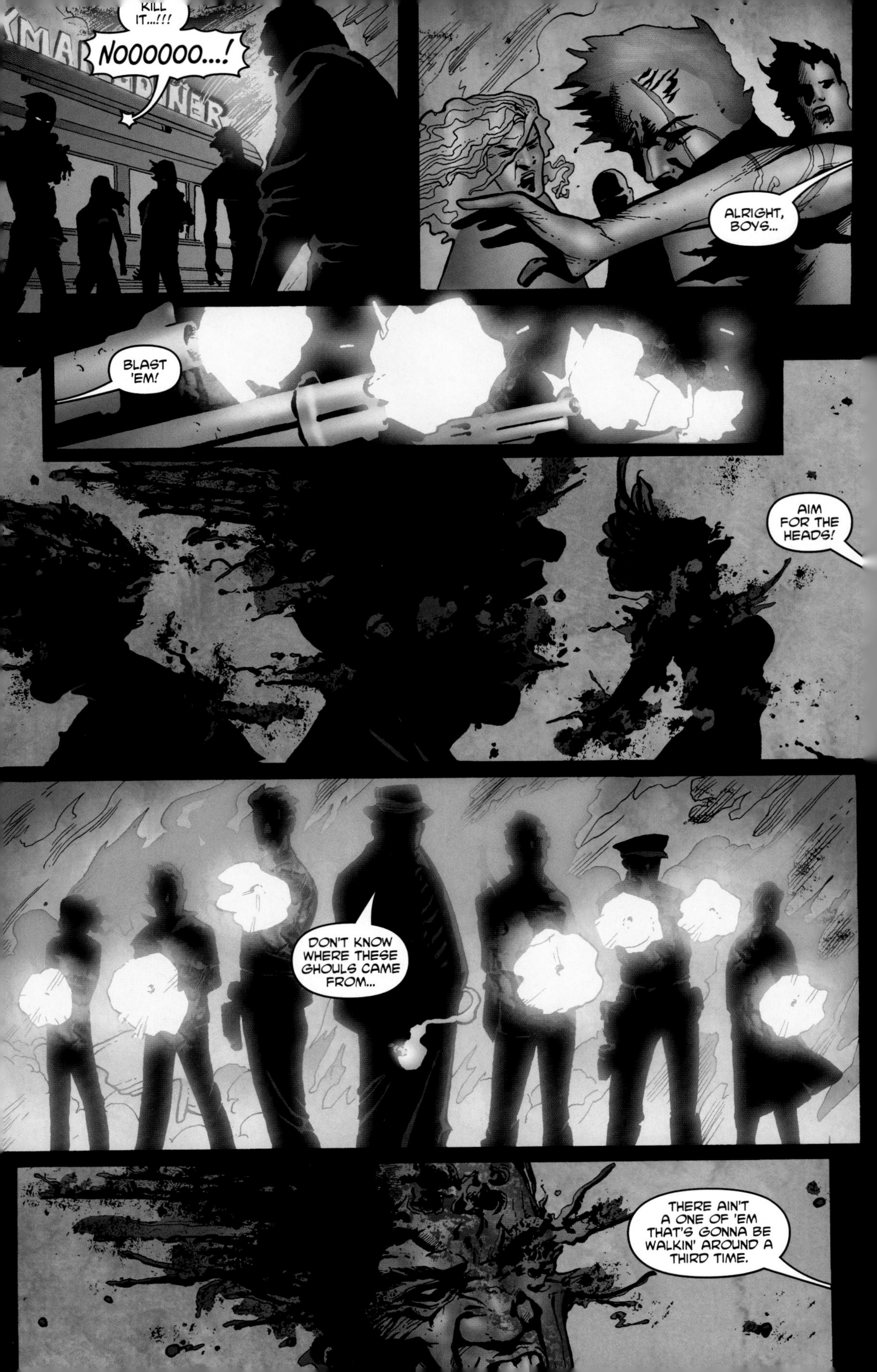
KILL IT...!!!
NOOOOOO...!
ALRIGHT, BOYS...
BLAST 'EM!
AIM FOR THE HEADS!
DON'T KNOW WHERE THESE GHOULS CAME FROM...
THERE AIN'T A ONE OF 'EM THAT'S GONNA BE WALKIN' AROUND A THIRD TIME.

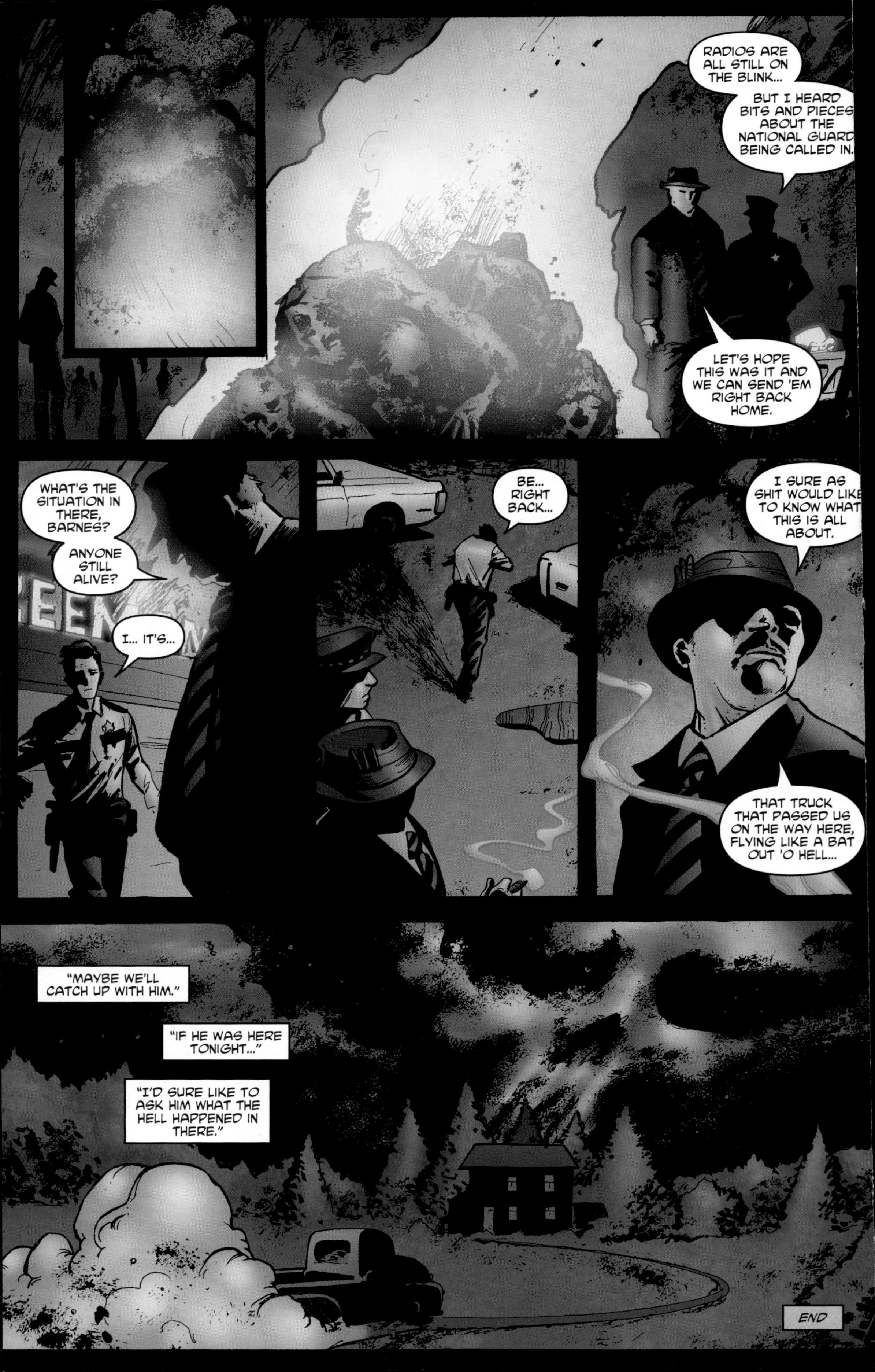
RADIOS ARE ALL STILL ON THE BLINK...
BUT I HEARD BITS AND PIECES ABOUT THE NATIONAL GUARD BEING CALLED IN.
LET'S HOPE THIS WAS IT AND WE CAN SEND 'EM RIGHT BACK HOME.
WHAT'S THE SITUATION IN THERE, BARNES?
ANYONE STILL ALIVE?
I... IT'S...
BE... RIGHT BACK...
I SURE AS SHIT WOULD LIKE TO KNOW WHAT THIS IS ALL ABOUT.
THAT TRUCK THAT PASSED US ON THE WAY HERE, FLYING LIKE A BAT OUT 'O HELL...
"MAYBE WE'LL CATCH UP WITH HIM."
"IF HE WAS HERE TONIGHT..."
"I'D SURE LIKE TO ASK HIM WHAT THE HELL HAPPENED IN THERE."
END

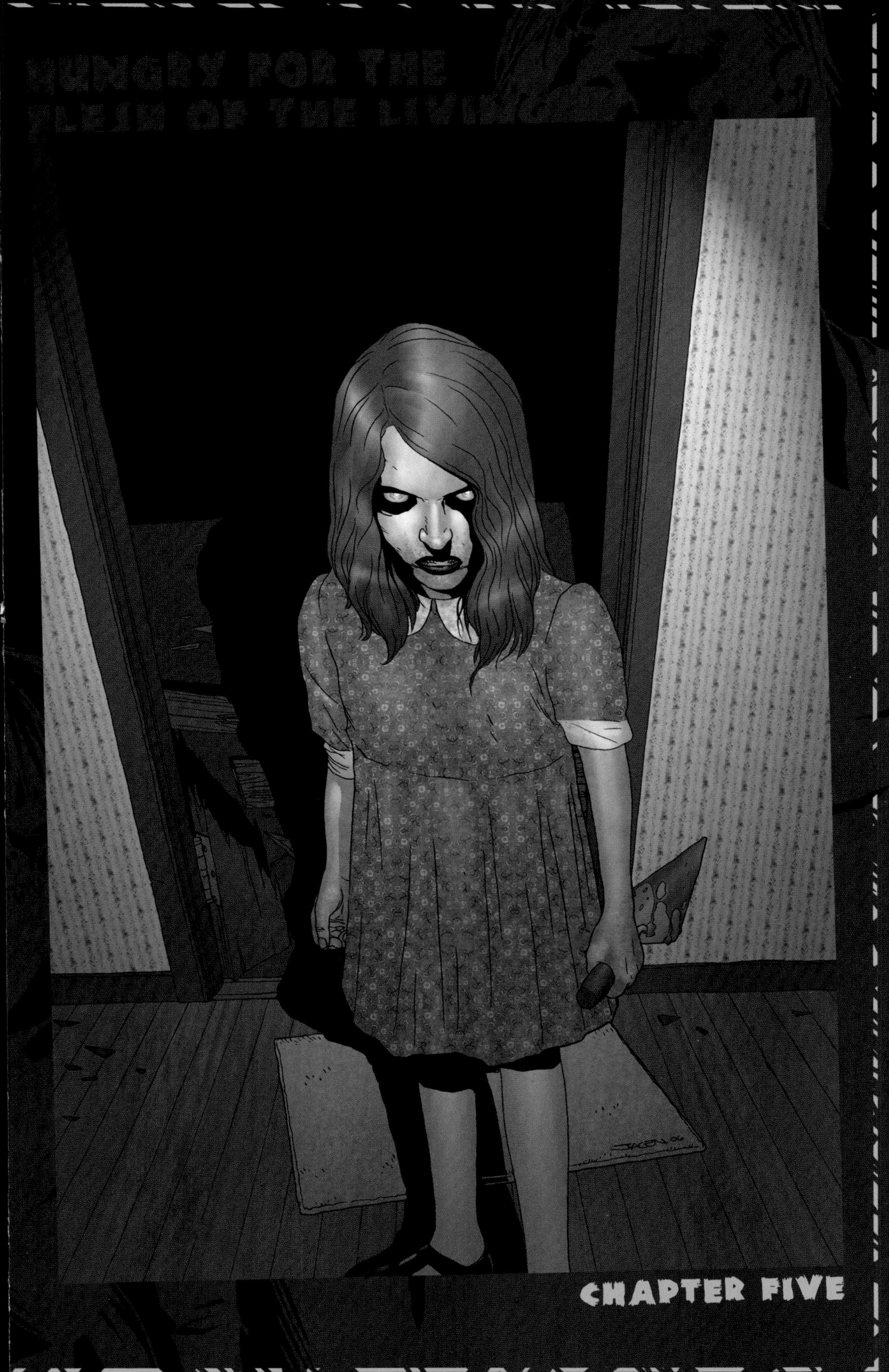
HUNGRY FOR THE
FLESH OF THE
CHAPTER FIVE

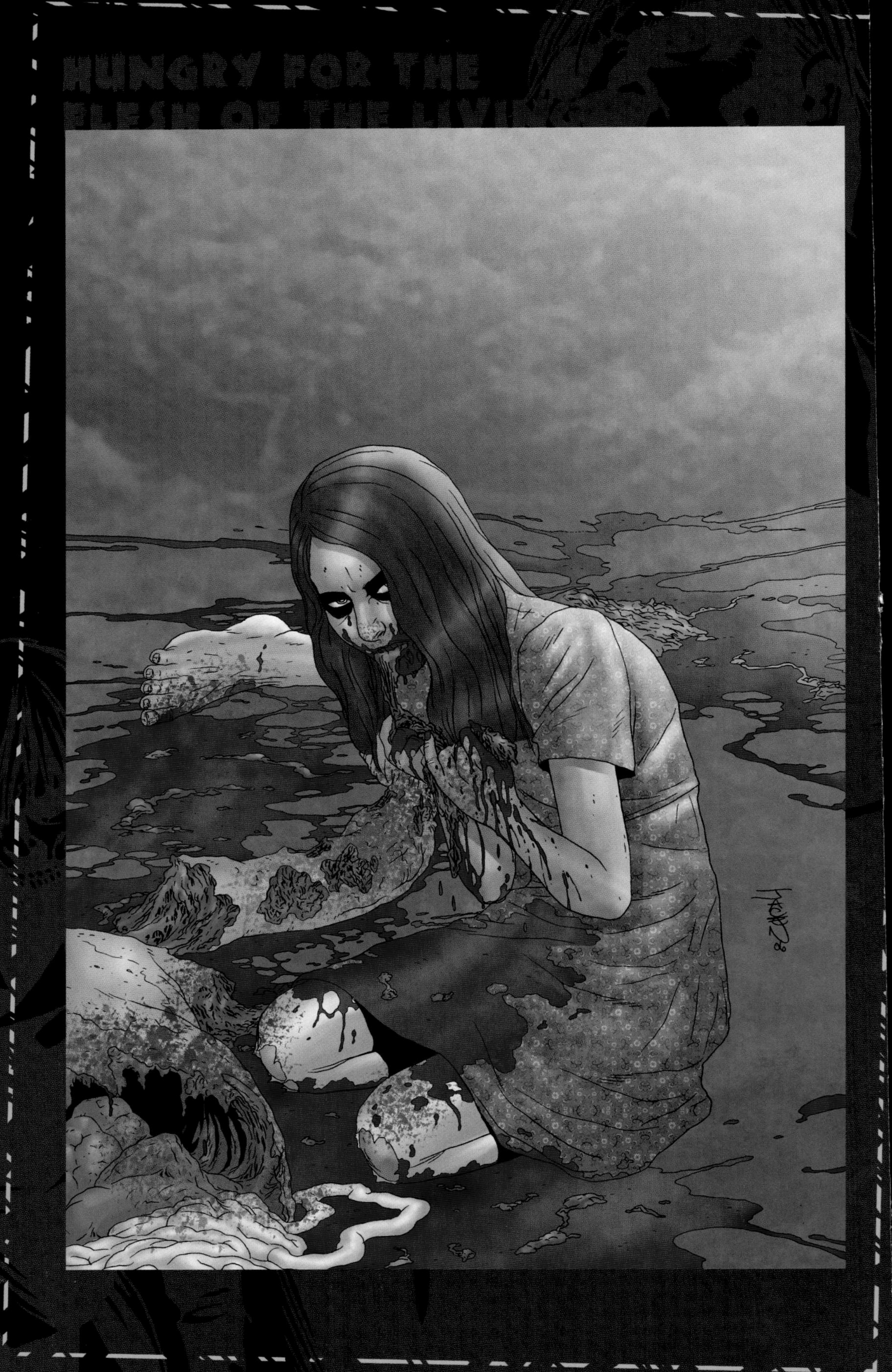
HUNGRY FOR THE
FLESH OF THE

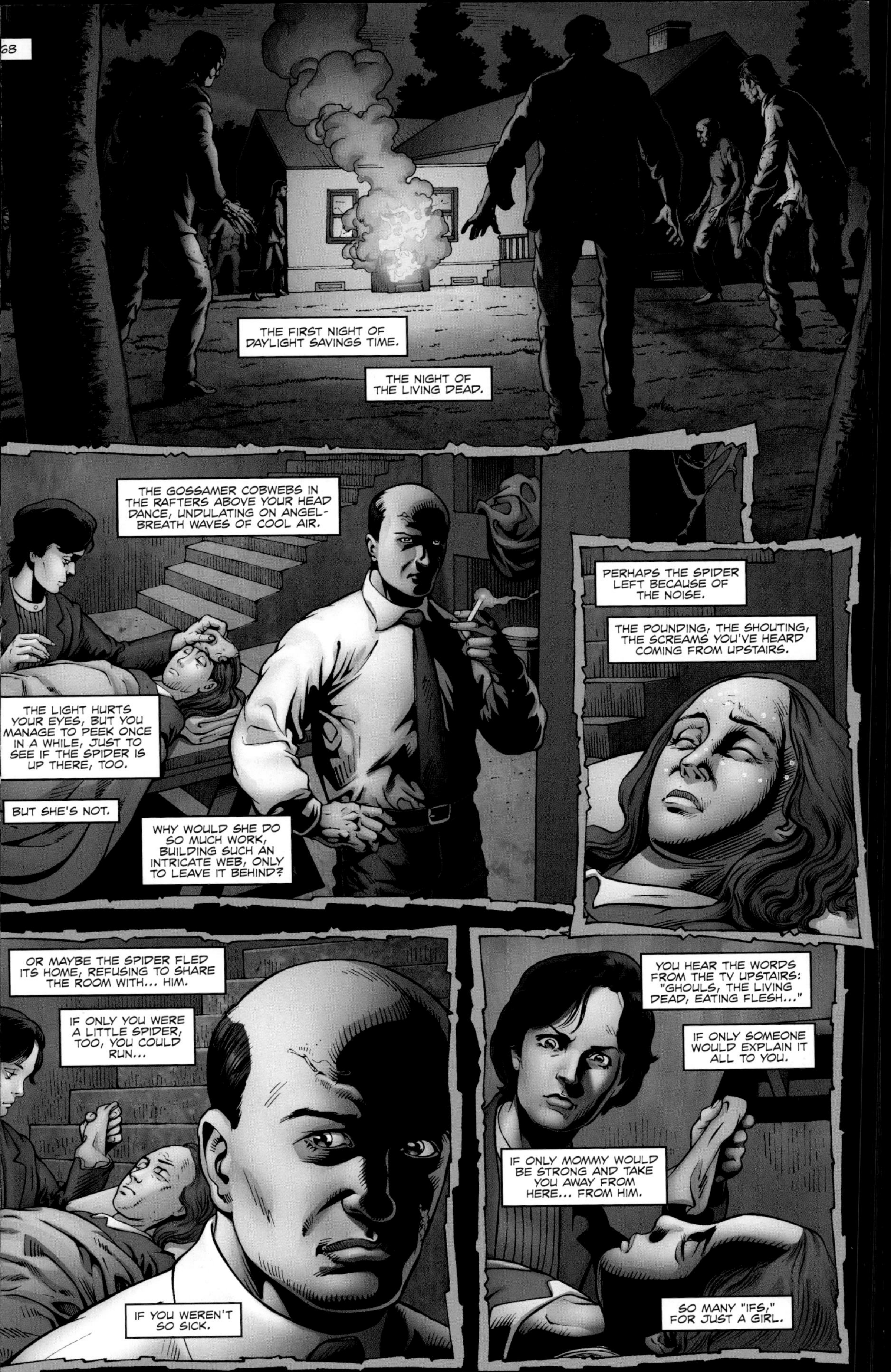
THE FIRST NIGHT OF DAYLIGHT SAVINGS TIME.
THE NIGHT OF THE LIVING DEAD.
THE GOSSAMER COBWEBS IN THE RAFTERS ABOVE YOUR HEAD DANCE, UNDULATING ON ANGEL-BREATH WAVES OF COOL AIR.
THE LIGHT HURTS YOUR EYES, BUT YOU MANAGE TO PEEK ONCE IN A WHILE, JUST TO SEE IF THE SPIDER IS UP THERE, TOO.
BUT SHE'S NOT.
WHY WOULD SHE DO SO MUCH WORK, BUILDING SUCH AN INTRICATE WEB, ONLY TO LEAVE IT BEHIND?
PERHAPS THE SPIDER LEFT BECAUSE OF THE NOISE.
THE POUNDING, THE SHOUTING, THE SCREAMS YOU'VE HEARD COMING FROM UPSTAIRS.
OR MAYBE THE SPIDER FLED ITS HOME, REFUSING TO SHARE THE ROOM WITH... HIM.
IF ONLY YOU WERE A LITTLE SPIDER, TOO, YOU COULD RUN...
IF YOU WEREN'T SO SICK.
YOU HEAR THE WORDS FROM THE TV UPSTAIRS: "GHOULS, THE LIVING DEAD, EATING FLESH..."
IF ONLY SOMEONE WOULD EXPLAIN IT ALL TO YOU.
IF ONLY MOMMY WOULD BE STRONG AND TAKE YOU AWAY FROM HERE... FROM HIM.
SO MANY "IFS," FOR JUST A GIRL.

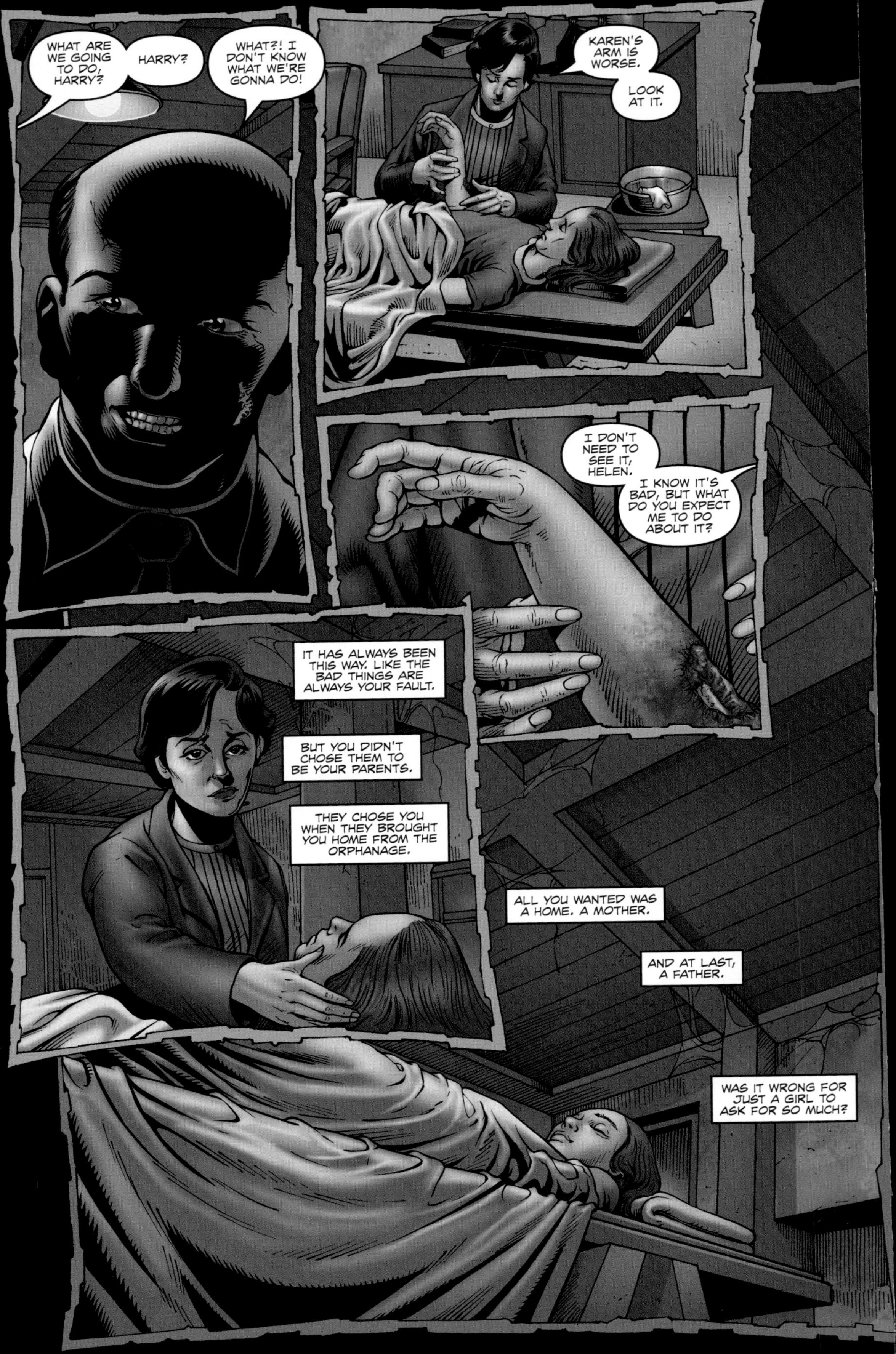
WHAT ARE WE GOING TO DO, HARRY?
HARRY?
WHAT?! I DON'T KNOW WHAT WE'RE GONNA DO!
KAREN'S ARM IS WORSE.
LOOK AT IT.
I DON'T NEED TO SEE IT, HELEN.
I KNOW IT'S BAD, BUT WHAT DO YOU EXPECT ME TO DO ABOUT IT?
IT HAS ALWAYS BEEN THIS WAY. LIKE THE BAD THINGS ARE ALWAYS YOUR FAULT.
BUT YOU DIDN'T CHOSE THEM TO BE YOUR PARENTS.
THEY CHOSE YOU WHEN THEY BROUGHT YOU HOME FROM THE ORPHANAGE.
ALL YOU WANTED WAS A HOME. A MOTHER.
AND AT LAST, A FATHER.
WAS IT WRONG FOR JUST A GIRL TO ASK FOR SO MUCH?

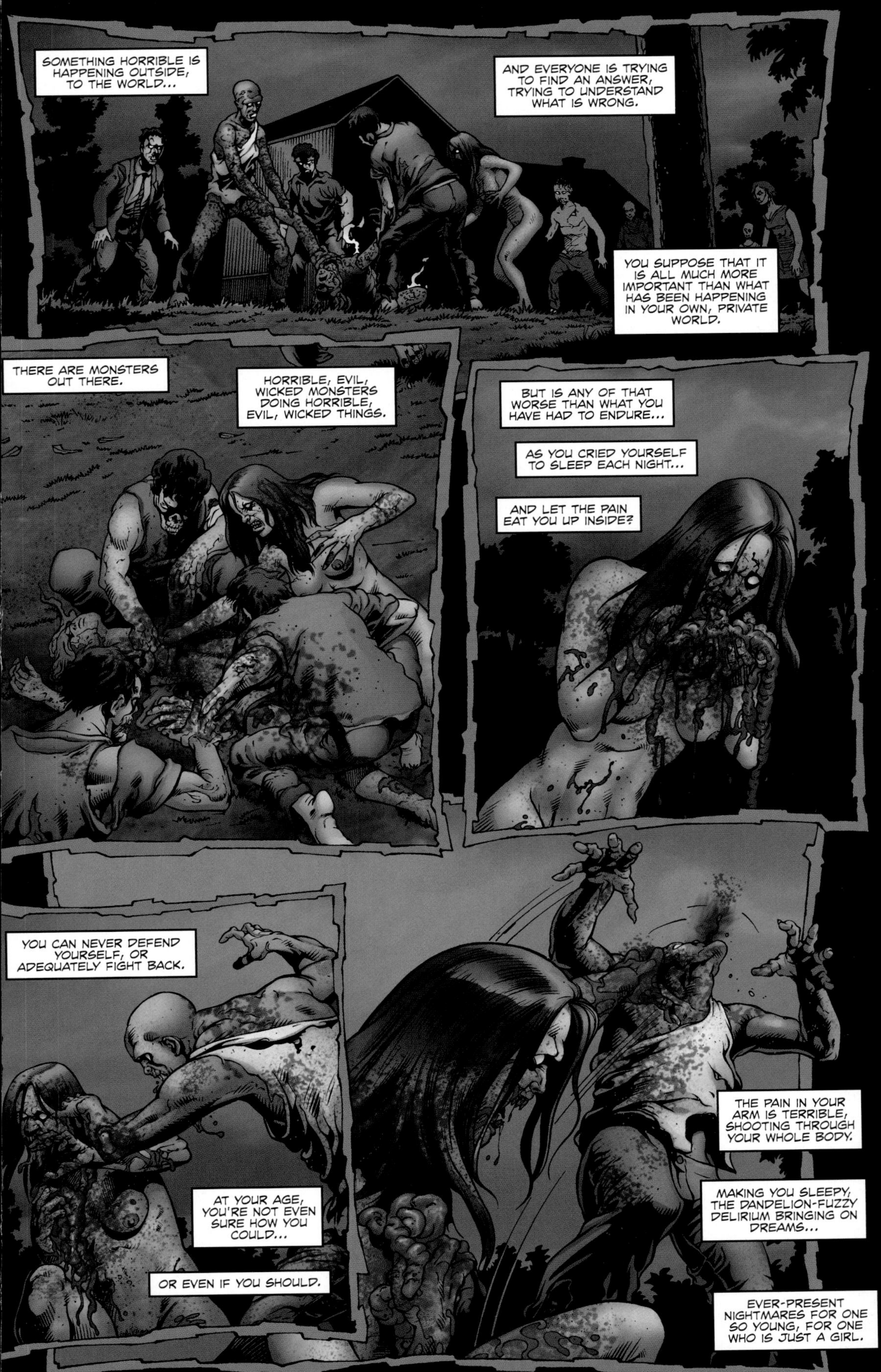
SOMETHING HORRIBLE IS HAPPENING OUTSIDE, TO THE WORLD...
AND EVERYONE IS TRYING TO FIND AN ANSWER, TRYING TO UNDERSTAND WHAT IS WRONG.
YOU SUPPOSE THAT IT IS ALL MUCH MORE IMPORTANT THAN WHAT HAS BEEN HAPPENING IN YOUR OWN, PRIVATE WORLD.
THERE ARE MONSTERS OUT THERE.
HORRIBLE, EVIL, WICKED MONSTERS DOING HORRIBLE, EVIL, WICKED THINGS.
BUT IS ANY OF THAT WORSE THAN WHAT YOU HAVE HAD TO ENDURE...
AS YOU CRIED YOURSELF TO SLEEP EACH NIGHT...
AND LET THE PAIN EAT YOU UP INSIDE?
YOU CAN NEVER DEFEND YOURSELF, OR ADEQUATELY FIGHT BACK.
AT YOUR AGE, YOU'RE NOT EVEN SURE HOW YOU COULD...
OR EVEN IF YOU SHOULD.
THE PAIN IN YOUR ARM IS TERRIBLE, SHOOTING THROUGH YOUR WHOLE BODY.
MAKING YOU SLEEPY, THE DANDELION-FUZZY DELIRIUM BRINGING ON DREAMS...
EVER-PRESENT NIGHTMARES FOR ONE SO YOUNG, FOR ONE WHO IS JUST A GIRL.

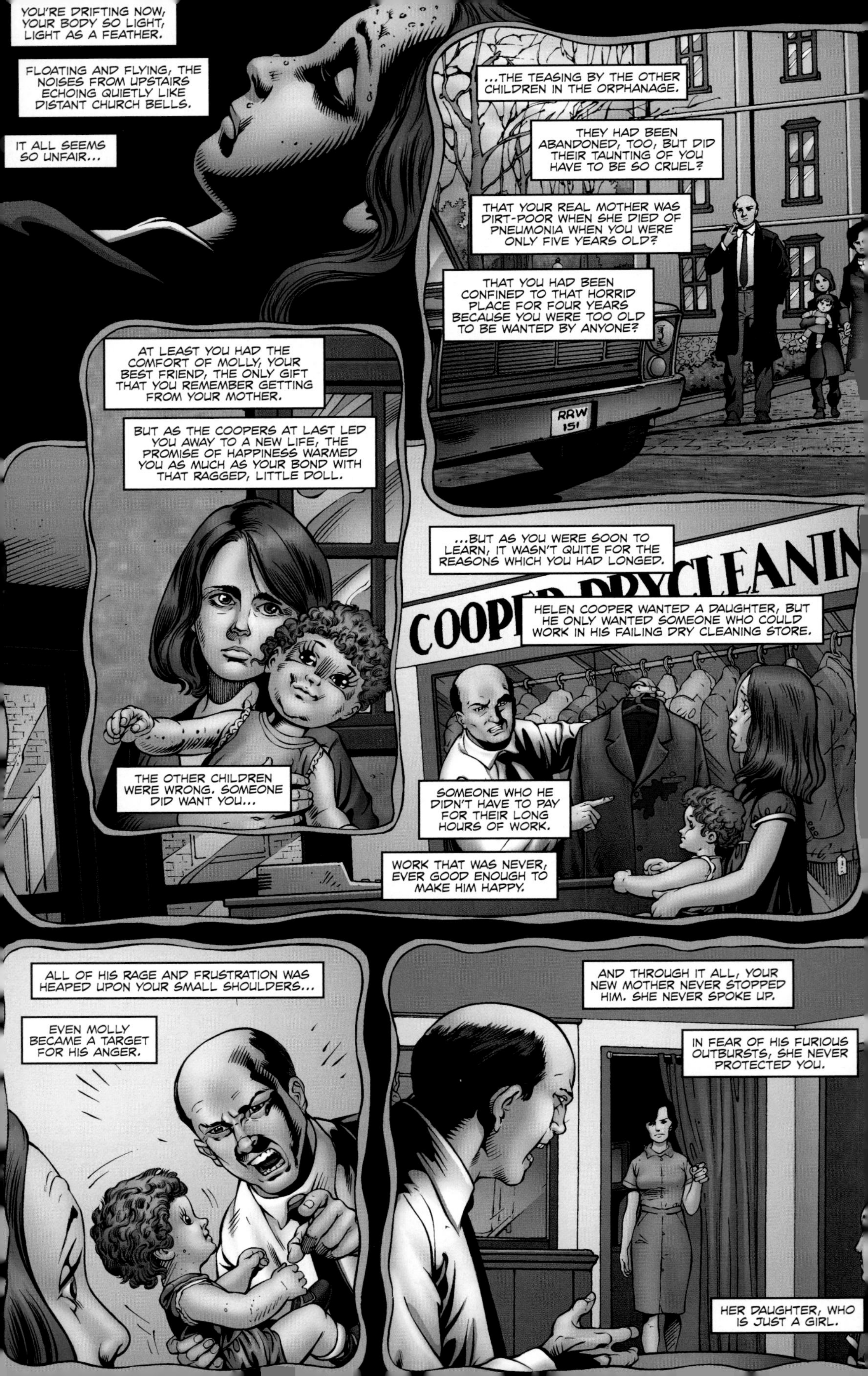
YOU'RE DRIFTING NOW, YOUR BODY SO LIGHT, LIGHT AS A FEATHER.
FLOATING AND FLYING, THE NOISES FROM UPSTAIRS ECHOING QUIETLY LIKE DISTANT CHURCH BELLS.
IT ALL SEEMS SO UNFAIR...
...THE TEASING BY THE OTHER CHILDREN IN THE ORPHANAGE.
THEY HAD BEEN ABANDONED, TOO, BUT DID THEIR TAUNTING OF YOU HAVE TO BE SO CRUEL?
THAT YOUR REAL MOTHER WAS DIRT-POOR WHEN SHE DIED OF PNEUMONIA WHEN YOU WERE ONLY FIVE YEARS OLD?
THAT YOU HAD BEEN CONFINED TO THAT HORRID PLACE FOR FOUR YEARS BECAUSE YOU WERE TOO OLD TO BE WANTED BY ANYONE?
RRW 151
AT LEAST YOU HAD THE COMFORT OF MOLLY, YOUR BEST FRIEND, THE ONLY GIFT THAT YOU REMEMBER GETTING FROM YOUR MOTHER.
BUT AS THE COOPERS AT LAST LED YOU AWAY TO A NEW LIFE, THE PROMISE OF HAPPINESS WARMED YOU AS MUCH AS YOUR BOND WITH THAT RAGGED, LITTLE DOLL.
THE OTHER CHILDREN WERE WRONG. SOMEONE DID WANT YOU...
...BUT AS YOU WERE SOON TO LEARN, IT WASN'T QUITE FOR THE REASONS WHICH YOU HAD LONGED.
COOPER DRYCLEANIN
HELEN COOPER WANTED A DAUGHTER, BUT HE ONLY WANTED SOMEONE WHO COULD WORK IN HIS FAILING DRY CLEANING STORE.
SOMEONE WHO HE DIDN'T HAVE TO PAY FOR THEIR LONG HOURS OF WORK.
WORK THAT WAS NEVER, EVER GOOD ENOUGH TO MAKE HIM HAPPY.
ALL OF HIS RAGE AND FRUSTRATION WAS HEAPED UPON YOUR SMALL SHOULDERS...
EVEN MOLLY BECAME A TARGET FOR HIS ANGER.
AND THROUGH IT ALL, YOUR NEW MOTHER NEVER STOPPED HIM. SHE NEVER SPOKE UP.
IN FEAR OF HIS FURIOUS OUTBURSTS, SHE NEVER PROTECTED YOU.
HER DAUGHTER, WHO IS JUST A GIRL.

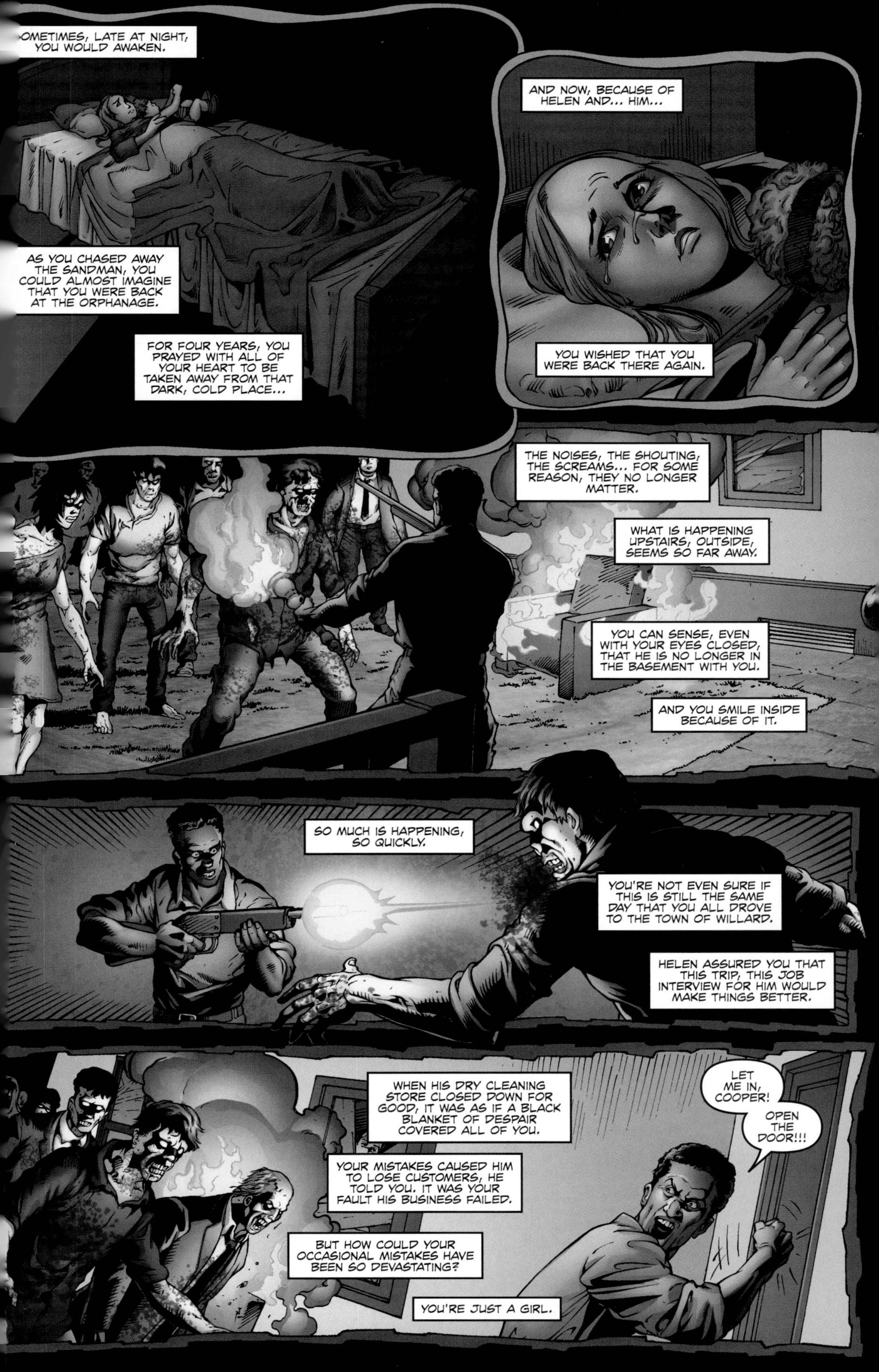
SOMETIMES, LATE AT NIGHT, YOU WOULD AWAKEN.
AS YOU CHASED AWAY THE SANDMAN, YOU COULD ALMOST IMAGINE THAT YOU WERE BACK AT THE ORPHANAGE.
FOR FOUR YEARS, YOU PRAYED WITH ALL OF YOUR HEART TO BE TAKEN AWAY FROM THAT DARK, COLD PLACE...
AND NOW, BECAUSE OF HELEN AND... HIM...
YOU WISHED THAT YOU WERE BACK THERE AGAIN.
THE NOISES, THE SHOUTING, THE SCREAMS... FOR SOME REASON, THEY NO LONGER MATTER.
WHAT IS HAPPENING UPSTAIRS, OUTSIDE, SEEMS SO FAR AWAY.
YOU CAN SENSE, EVEN WITH YOUR EYES CLOSED, THAT HE IS NO LONGER IN THE BASEMENT WITH YOU.
AND YOU SMILE INSIDE BECAUSE OF IT.
SO MUCH IS HAPPENING, SO QUICKLY.
YOU'RE NOT EVEN SURE IF THIS IS STILL THE SAME DAY THAT YOU ALL DROVE TO THE TOWN OF WILLARD.
HELEN ASSURED YOU THAT THIS TRIP, THIS JOB INTERVIEW FOR HIM WOULD MAKE THINGS BETTER.
WHEN HIS DRY CLEANING STORE CLOSED DOWN FOR GOOD, IT WAS AS IF A BLACK BLANKET OF DESPAIR COVERED ALL OF YOU.
LET ME IN, COOPER!
OPEN THE DOOR!!!
YOUR MISTAKES CAUSED HIM TO LOSE CUSTOMERS, HE TOLD YOU. IT WAS YOUR FAULT HIS BUSINESS FAILED.
BUT HOW COULD YOUR OCCASIONAL MISTAKES HAVE BEEN SO DEVASTATING?
YOU'RE JUST A GIRL.

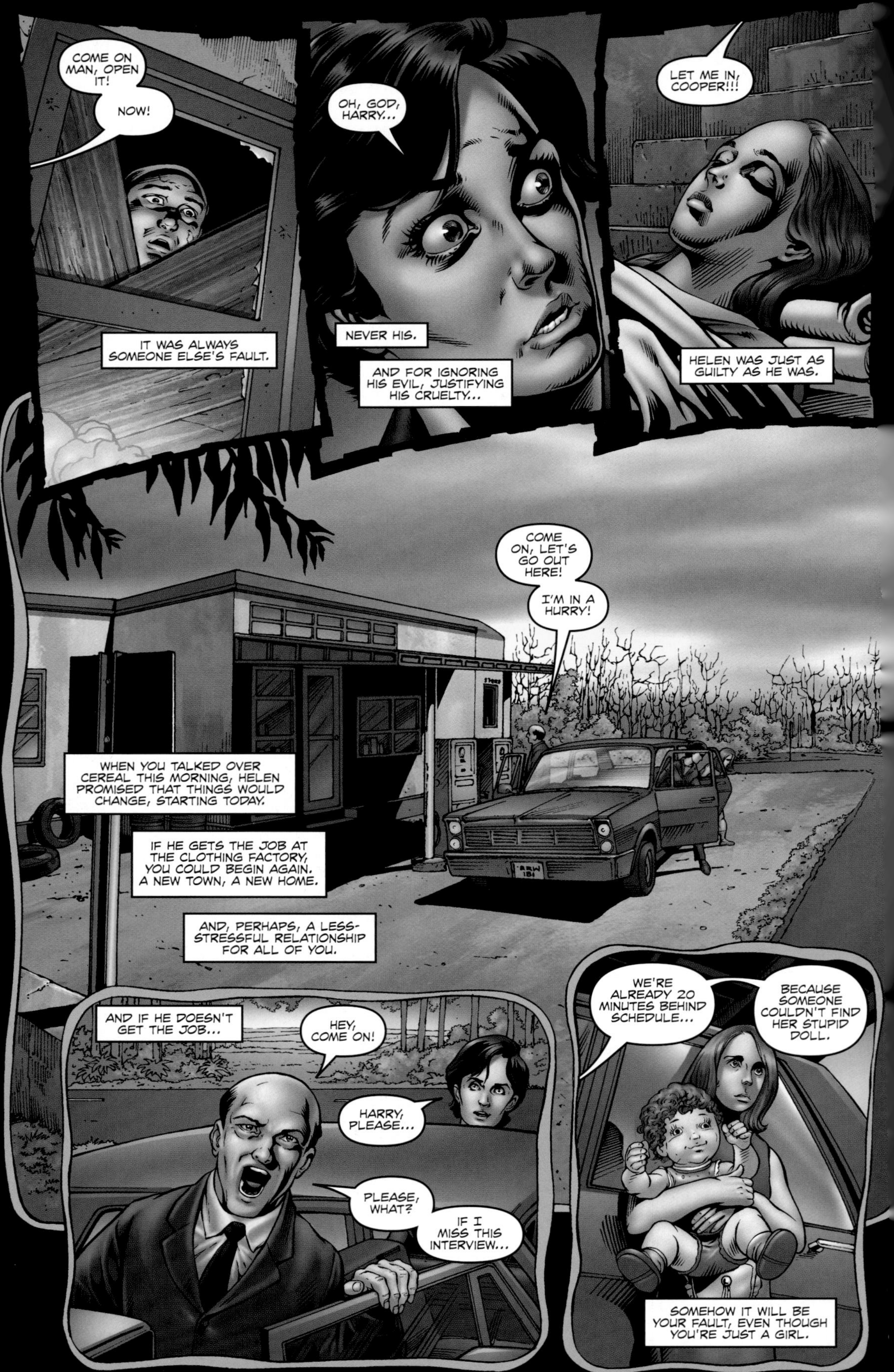
COME ON MAN, OPEN IT!
NOW!
IT WAS ALWAYS SOMEONE ELSE'S FAULT.
OH, GOD, HARRY...
NEVER HIS.
AND FOR IGNORING HIS EVIL, JUSTIFYING HIS CRUELTY...
LET ME IN, COOPER!!!
HELEN WAS JUST AS GUILTY AS HE WAS.
COME ON, LET'S GO OUT HERE!
I'M IN A HURRY!
WHEN YOU TALKED OVER CEREAL THIS MORNING, HELEN PROMISED THAT THINGS WOULD CHANGE, STARTING TODAY.
IF HE GETS THE JOB AT THE CLOTHING FACTORY, YOU COULD BEGIN AGAIN. A NEW TOWN, A NEW HOME.
AND, PERHAPS, A LESS-STRESSFUL RELATIONSHIP FOR ALL OF YOU.
AND IF HE DOESN'T GET THE JOB...
HEY, COME ON!
HARRY, PLEASE...
PLEASE, WHAT?
IF I MISS THIS INTERVIEW...
WE'RE ALREADY 20 MINUTES BEHIND SCHEDULE...
BECAUSE SOMEONE COULDN'T FIND HER STUPID DOLL.
SOMEHOW IT WILL BE YOUR FAULT, EVEN THOUGH YOU'RE JUST A GIRL.

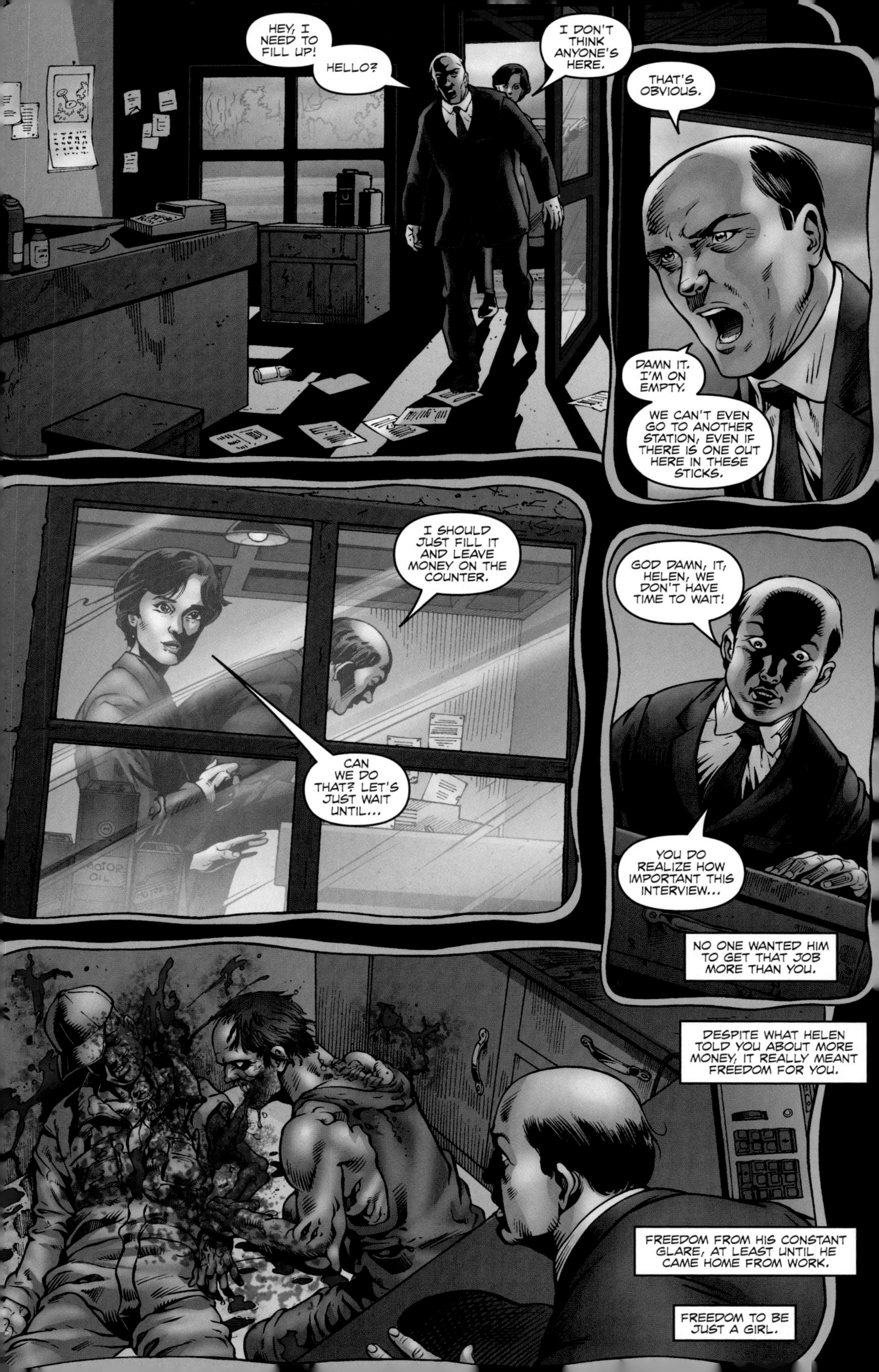
HEY, I NEED TO FILL UP!
HELLO?
I DON'T THINK ANYONE'S HERE.
THAT'S OBVIOUS.
DAMN IT. I'M ON EMPTY.
WE CAN'T EVEN GO TO ANOTHER STATION, EVEN IF THERE IS ONE OUT HERE IN THESE STICKS.
I SHOULD JUST FILL IT AND LEAVE MONEY ON THE COUNTER.
CAN WE DO THAT? LET'S JUST WAIT UNTIL...
GOD DAMN, IT, HELEN, WE DON'T HAVE TIME TO WAIT!
YOU DO REALIZE HOW IMPORTANT THIS INTERVIEW...
NO ONE WANTED HIM TO GET THAT JOB MORE THAN YOU.
DESPITE WHAT HELEN TOLD YOU ABOUT MORE MONEY, IT REALLY MEANT FREEDOM FOR YOU.
FREEDOM FROM HIS CONSTANT GLARE, AT LEAST UNTIL HE CAME HOME FROM WORK.
FREEDOM TO BE JUST A GIRL.
MOTOR OIL

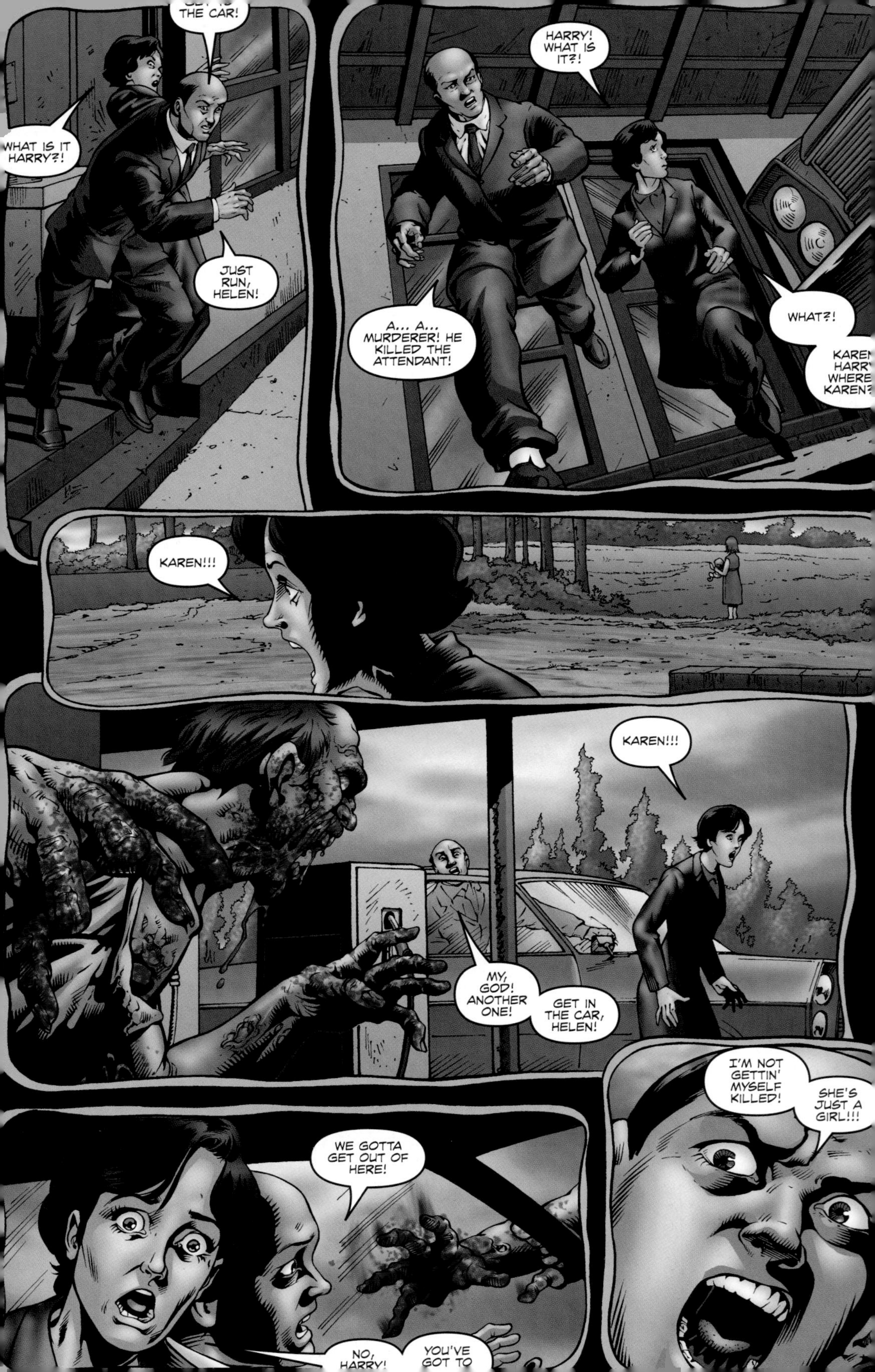
THE CAR!
WHAT IS IT HARRY?!
JUST RUN, HELEN!
HARRY! WHAT IS IT?!
A... A... MURDERER! HE KILLED THE ATTENDANT!
WHAT?!
KAREN HARR WHERE KAREN?
KAREN!!!
KAREN!!!
MY, GOD! ANOTHER ONE!
GET IN THE CAR, HELEN!
WE GOTTA GET OUT OF HERE!
I'M NOT GETTIN' MYSELF KILLED!
SHE'S JUST A GIRL!!!
NO, HARRY!
YOU'VE GOT TO

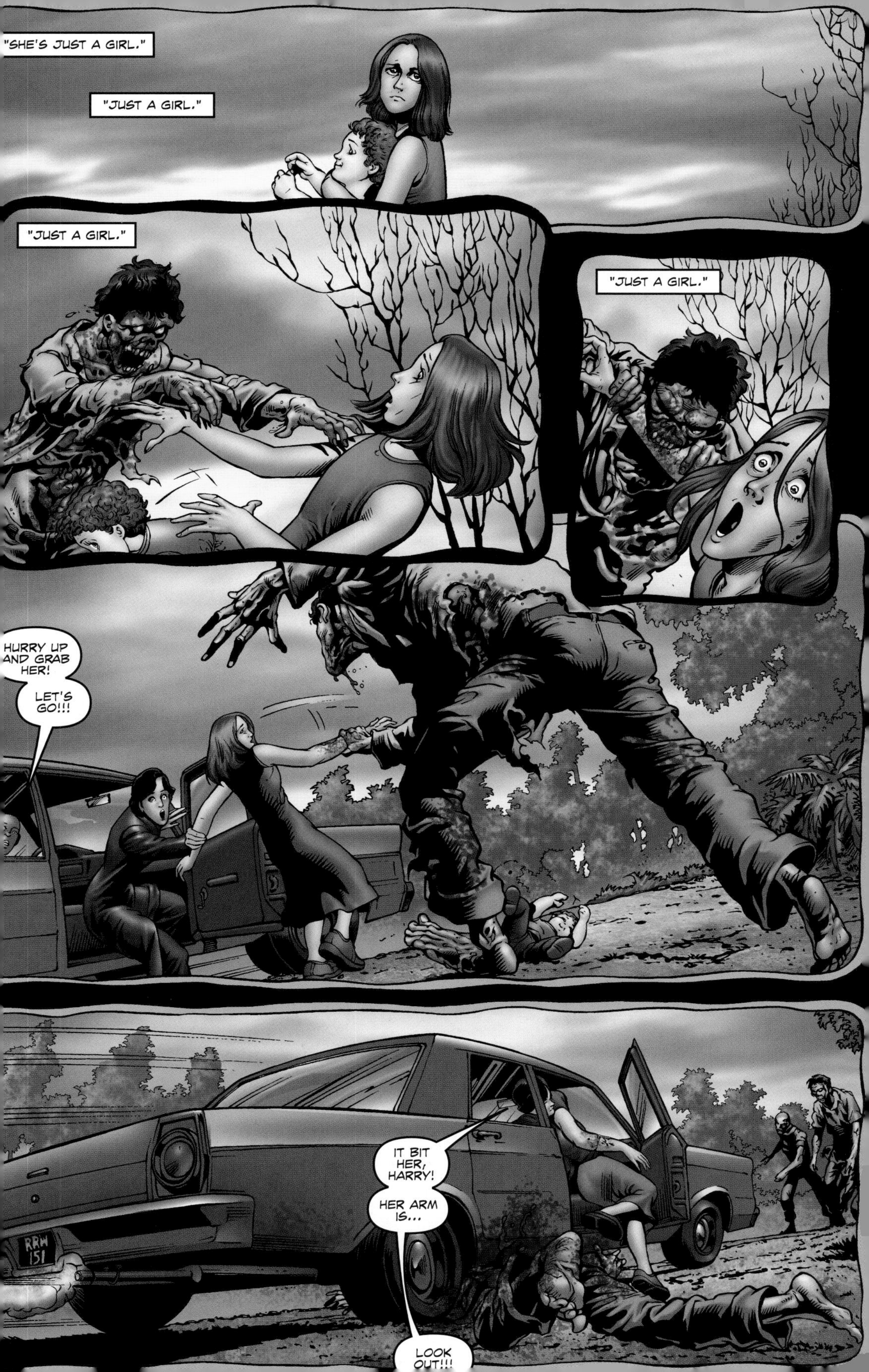
"SHE'S JUST A GIRL."
"JUST A GIRL."
"JUST A GIRL."
"JUST A GIRL."
HURRY UP AND GRAB HER!
LET'S GO!!!
RRW 151
IT BIT HER, HARRY!
HER ARM IS...
LOOK OUT!!!

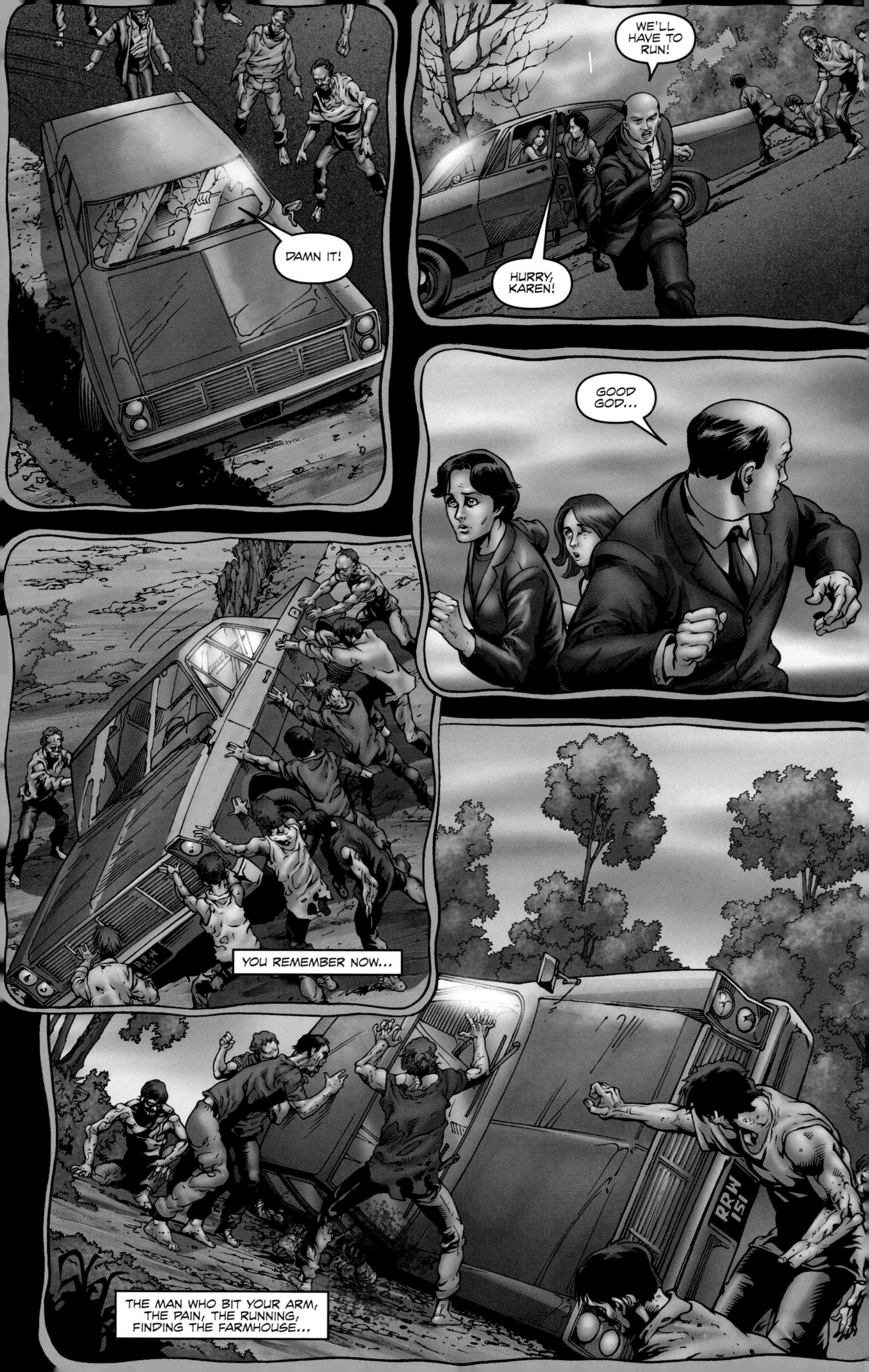
DAMN IT!
WE'LL HAVE TO RUN!
HURRY, KAREN!
GOOD GOD...
YOU REMEMBER NOW...
RRW 151
THE MAN WHO BIT YOUR ARM, THE PAIN, THE RUNNING, FINDING THE FARMHOUSE...

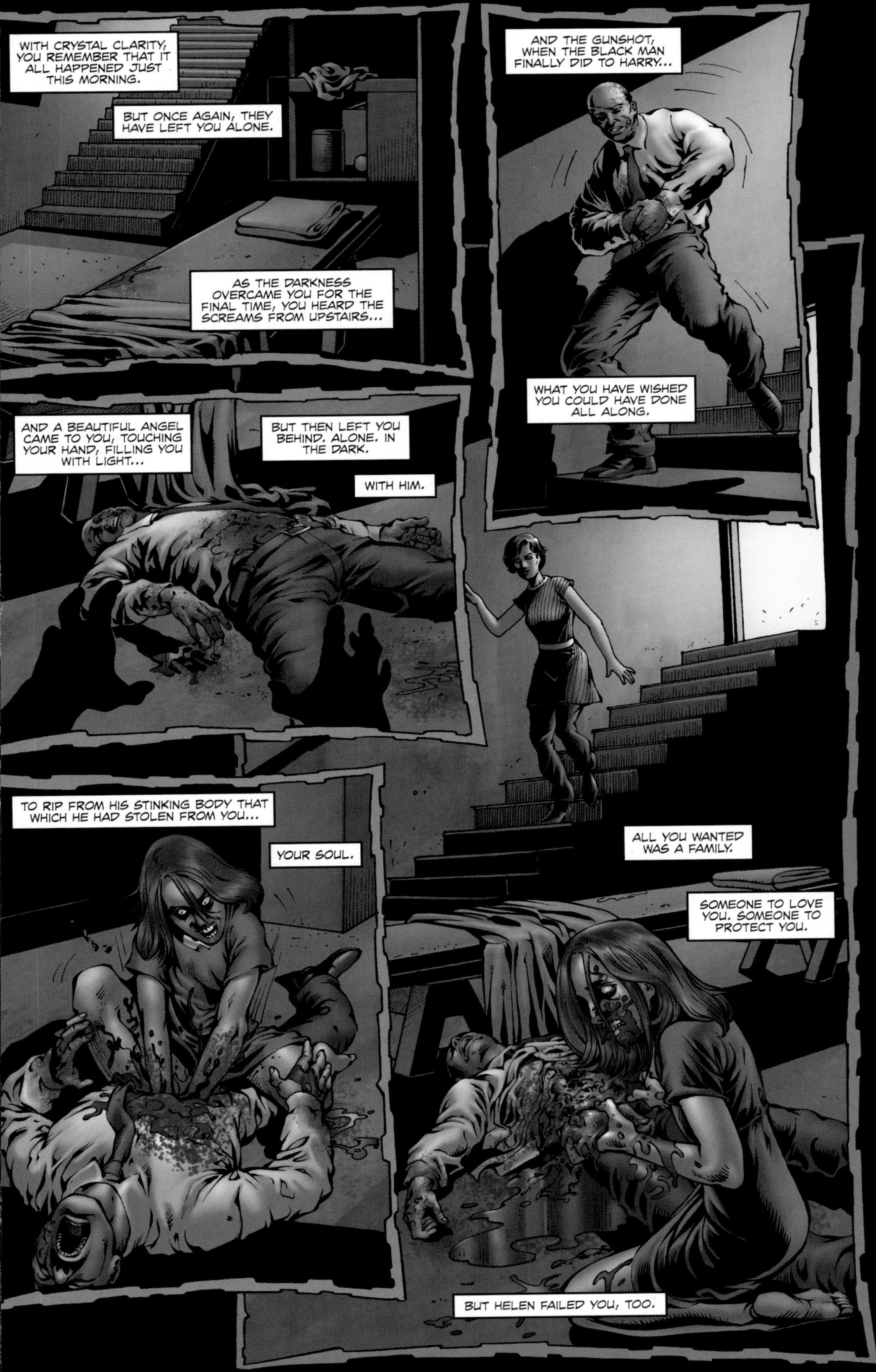
WITH CRYSTAL CLARITY, YOU REMEMBER THAT IT ALL HAPPENED JUST THIS MORNING.
BUT ONCE AGAIN, THEY HAVE LEFT YOU ALONE.
AS THE DARKNESS OVERCAME YOU FOR THE FINAL TIME, YOU HEARD THE SCREAMS FROM UPSTAIRS...
AND THE GUNSHOT, WHEN THE BLACK MAN FINALLY DID TO HARRY...
WHAT YOU HAVE WISHED YOU COULD HAVE DONE ALL ALONG.
AND A BEAUTIFUL ANGEL CAME TO YOU, TOUCHING YOUR HAND, FILLING YOU WITH LIGHT...
BUT THEN LEFT YOU BEHIND. ALONE. IN THE DARK.
WITH HIM.
TO RIP FROM HIS STINKING BODY THAT WHICH HE HAD STOLEN FROM YOU...
YOUR SOUL.
ALL YOU WANTED WAS A FAMILY.
SOMEONE TO LOVE YOU. SOMEONE TO PROTECT YOU.
BUT HELEN FAILED YOU, TOO.

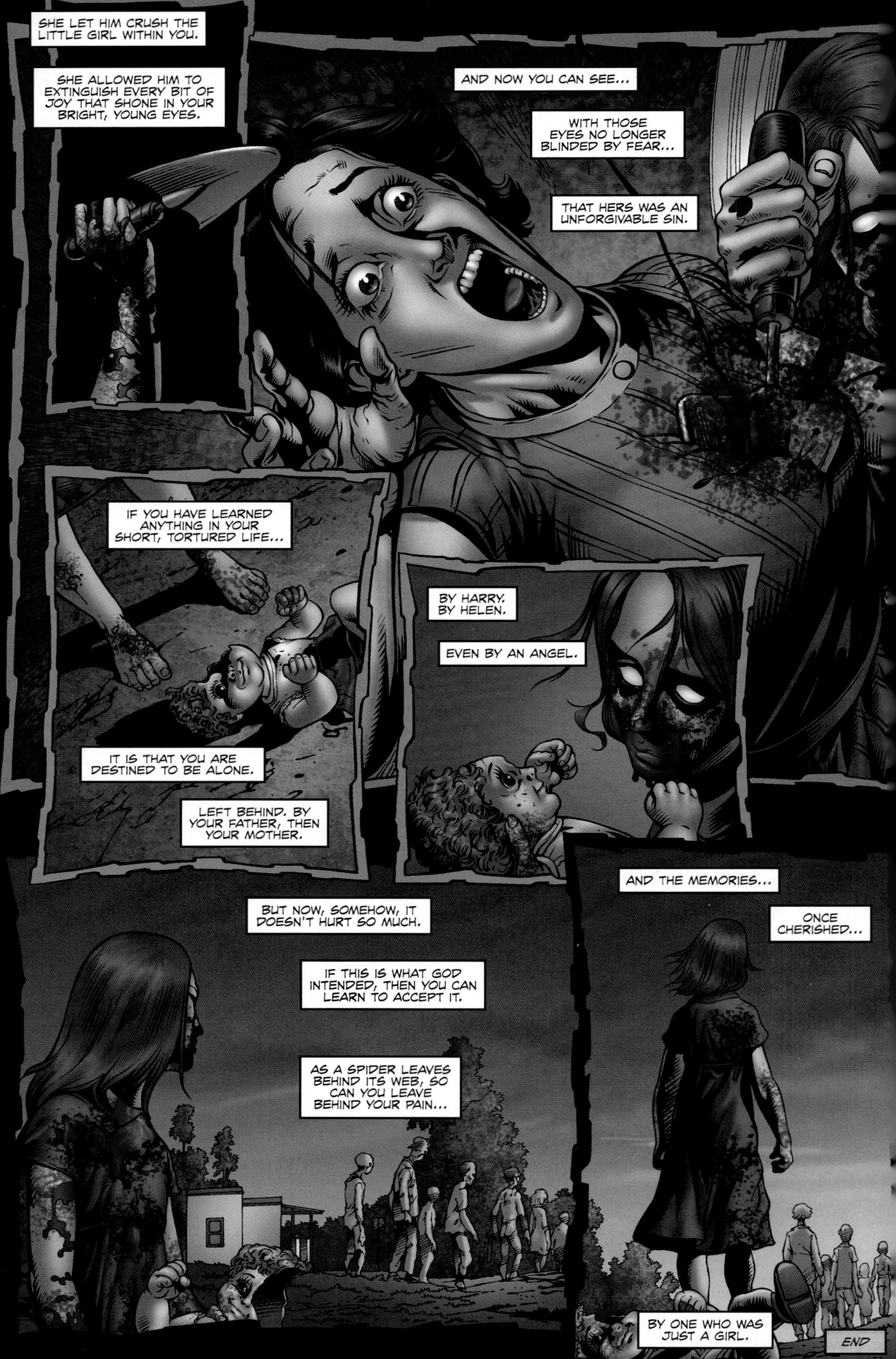
SHE LET HIM CRUSH THE LITTLE GIRL WITHIN YOU.
SHE ALLOWED HIM TO EXTINGUISH EVERY BIT OF JOY THAT SHONE IN YOUR BRIGHT, YOUNG EYES.
AND NOW YOU CAN SEE...
WITH THOSE EYES NO LONGER BLINDED BY FEAR...
THAT HERS WAS AN UNFORGIVABLE SIN.
IF YOU HAVE LEARNED ANYTHING IN YOUR SHORT, TORTURED LIFE...
IT IS THAT YOU ARE DESTINED TO BE ALONE.
LEFT BEHIND. BY YOUR FATHER, THEN YOUR MOTHER.
BY HARRY. BY HELEN.
EVEN BY AN ANGEL.
BUT NOW, SOMEHOW, IT DOESN'T HURT SO MUCH.
IF THIS IS WHAT GOD INTENDED, THEN YOU CAN LEARN TO ACCEPT IT.
AS A SPIDER LEAVES BEHIND ITS WEB, SO CAN YOU LEAVE BEHIND YOUR PAIN...
AND THE MEMORIES...
ONCE CHERISHED...
BY ONE WHO WAS JUST A GIRL.
END

CHAPTER SIX

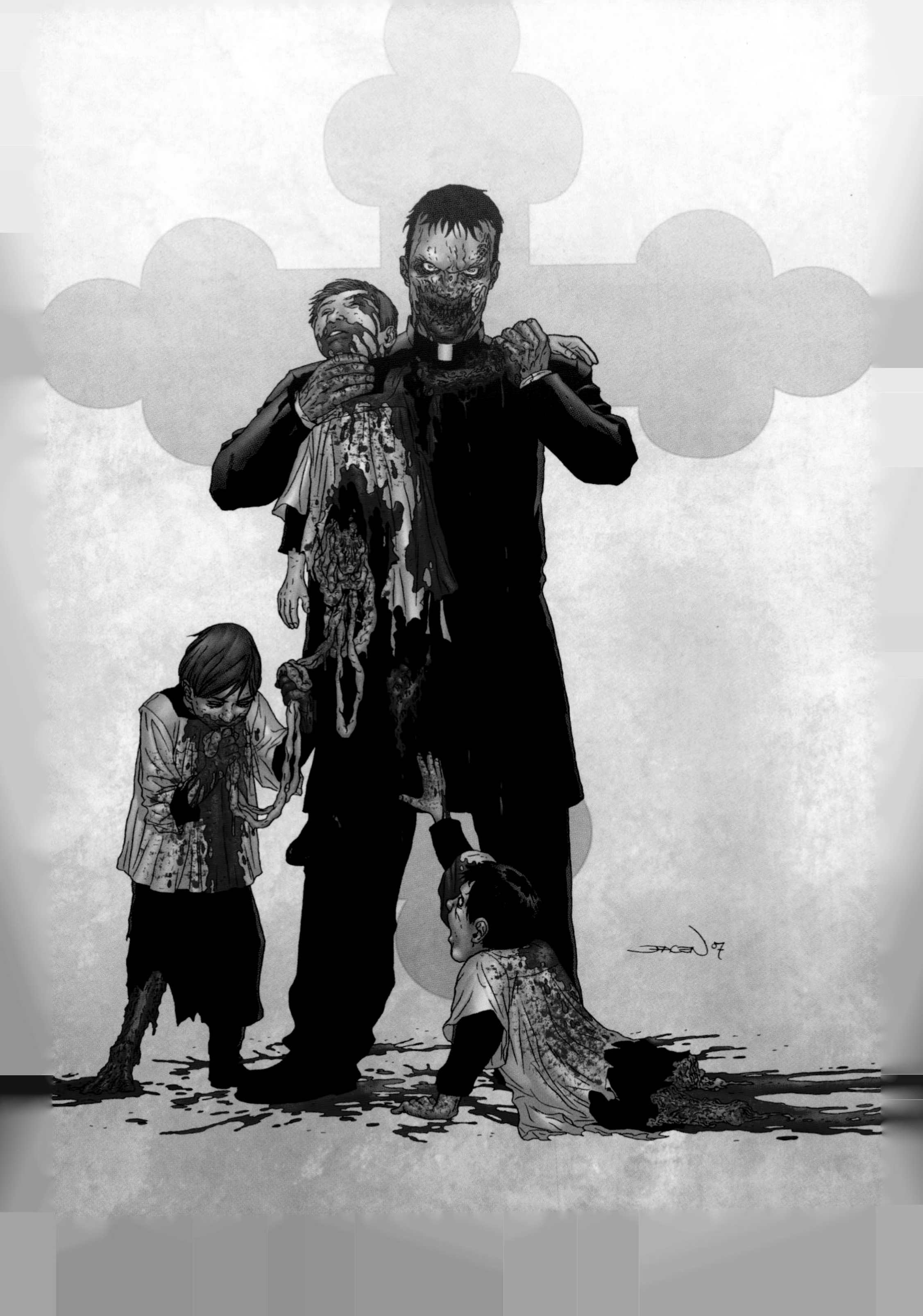

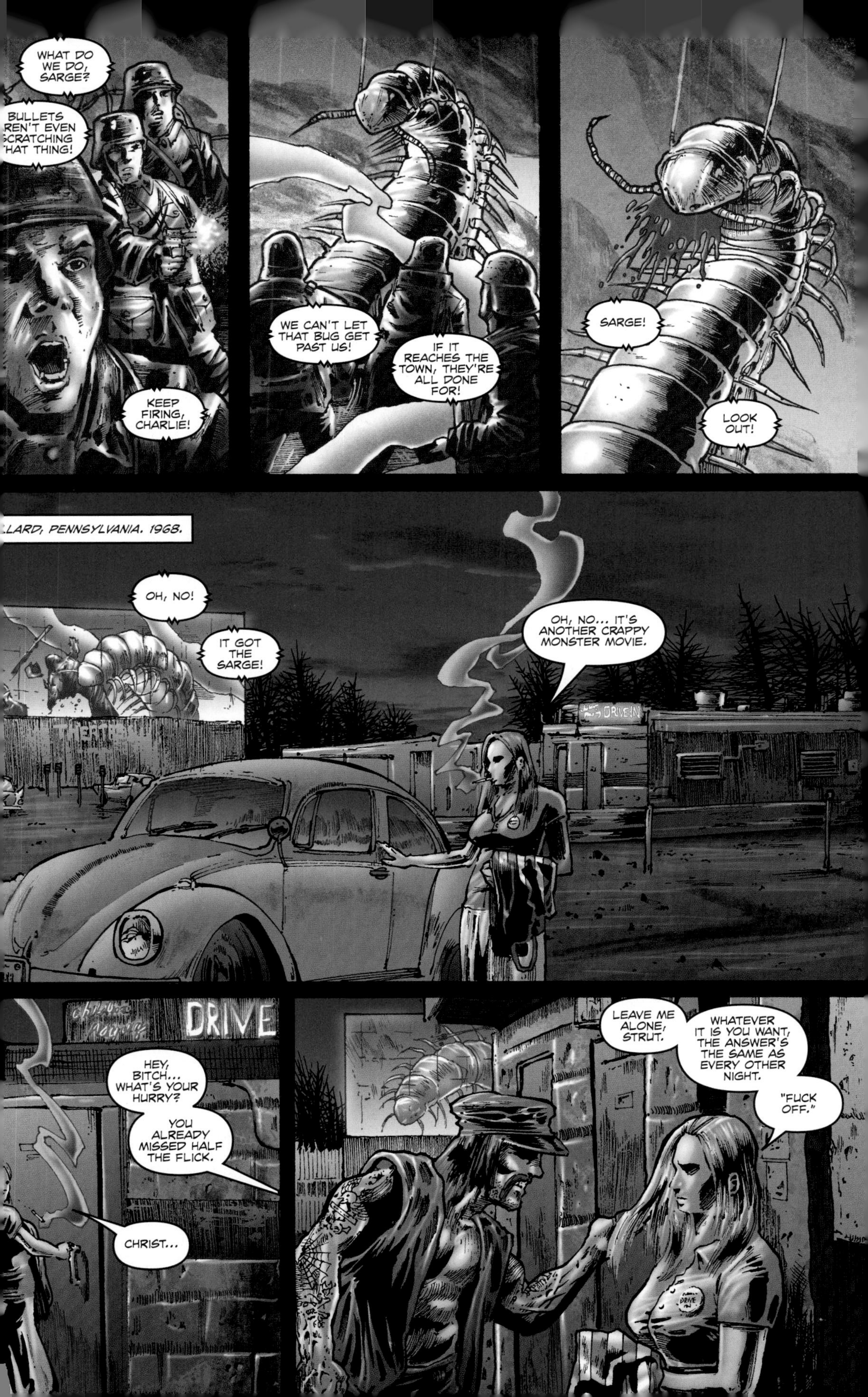
WHAT DO WE DO, SARGE?
BULLETS REN'T EVEN SCRATCHING THAT THING!
KEEP FIRING, CHARLIE!
WE CAN'T LET THAT BUG GET PAST US!
IF IT REACHES THE TOWN, THEY'RE ALL DONE FOR!
SARGE!
LOOK OUT!
LLARD, PENNSYLVANIA. 1968.
OH, NO!
IT GOT THE SARGE!
OH, NO... IT'S ANOTHER CRAPPY MONSTER MOVIE.
DRIVE-IN
DRIVE
HEY, BITCH... WHAT'S YOUR HURRY?
YOU ALREADY MISSED HALF THE FLICK.
CHRIST...
LEAVE ME ALONE, STRUT.
WHATEVER IT IS YOU WANT, THE ANSWER'S THE SAME AS EVERY OTHER NIGHT.
"FUCK OFF."

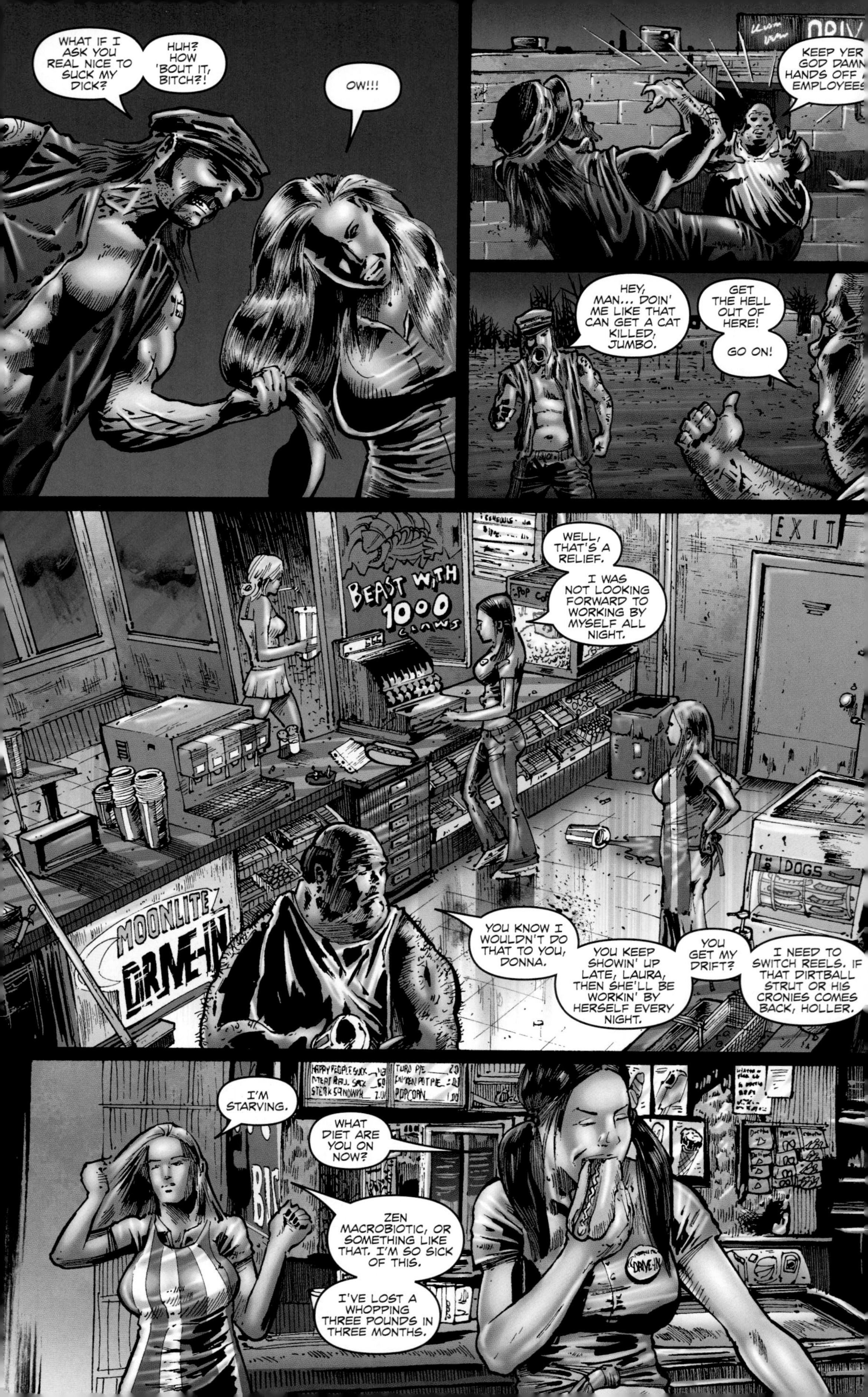
WHAT IF I ASK YOU REAL NICE TO SUCK MY DICK?
HUH? HOW 'BOUT IT, BITCH?!
OW!!!
KEEP YER GOD DAMN HANDS OFF MY EMPLOYEES
HEY, MAN... DOIN' ME LIKE THAT CAN GET A CAT KILLED, JUMBO.
GET THE HELL OUT OF HERE!
GO ON!
EXIT
BEAST WITH 1000 CLAWS
WELL, THAT'S A RELIEF.
I WAS NOT LOOKING FORWARD TO WORKING BY MYSELF ALL NIGHT.
MOONLITE DRIVE-IN
DOGS
YOU KNOW I WOULDN'T DO THAT TO YOU, DONNA.
YOU KEEP SHOWIN' UP LATE, LAURA, THEN SHE'LL BE WORKIN' BY HERSELF EVERY NIGHT.
YOU GET MY DRIFT?
I NEED TO SWITCH REELS. IF THAT DIRTBALL STRUT OR HIS CRONIES COMES BACK, HOLLER.
I'M STARVING.
WHAT DIET ARE YOU ON NOW?
ZEN MACROBIOTIC, OR SOMETHING LIKE THAT. I'M SO SICK OF THIS.
I'VE LOST A WHOPPING THREE POUNDS IN THREE MONTHS.

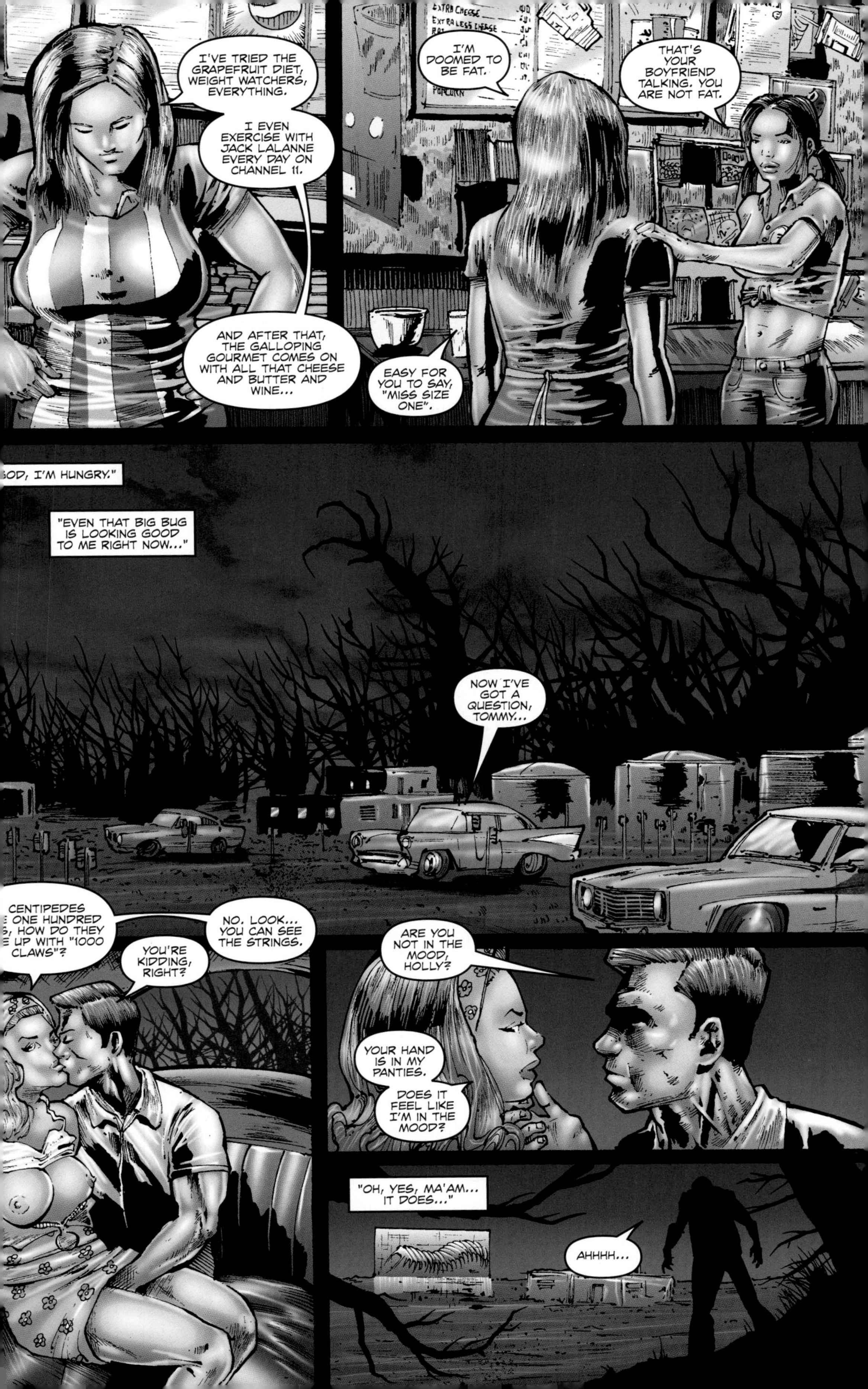
I'VE TRIED THE GRAPEFRUIT DIET, WEIGHT WATCHERS, EVERYTHING.
I EVEN EXERCISE WITH JACK LALANNE EVERY DAY ON CHANNEL 11.
AND AFTER THAT, THE GALLOPING GOURMET COMES ON WITH ALL THAT CHEESE AND BUTTER AND WINE...
I'M DOOMED TO BE FAT.
EASY FOR YOU TO SAY, "MISS SIZE ONE".
THAT'S YOUR BOYFRIEND TALKING. YOU ARE NOT FAT.
OD, I'M HUNGRY."
"EVEN THAT BIG BUG IS LOOKING GOOD TO ME RIGHT NOW..."
NOW I'VE GOT A QUESTION, TOMMY...
CENTIPEDES ONE HUNDRED , HOW DO THEY UP WITH "1000 CLAWS"?
YOU'RE KIDDING, RIGHT?
NO. LOOK... YOU CAN SEE THE STRINGS.
ARE YOU NOT IN THE MOOD, HOLLY?
YOUR HAND IS IN MY PANTIES.
DOES IT FEEL LIKE I'M IN THE MOOD?
"OH, YES, MA'AM... IT DOES..."
AHHHH...

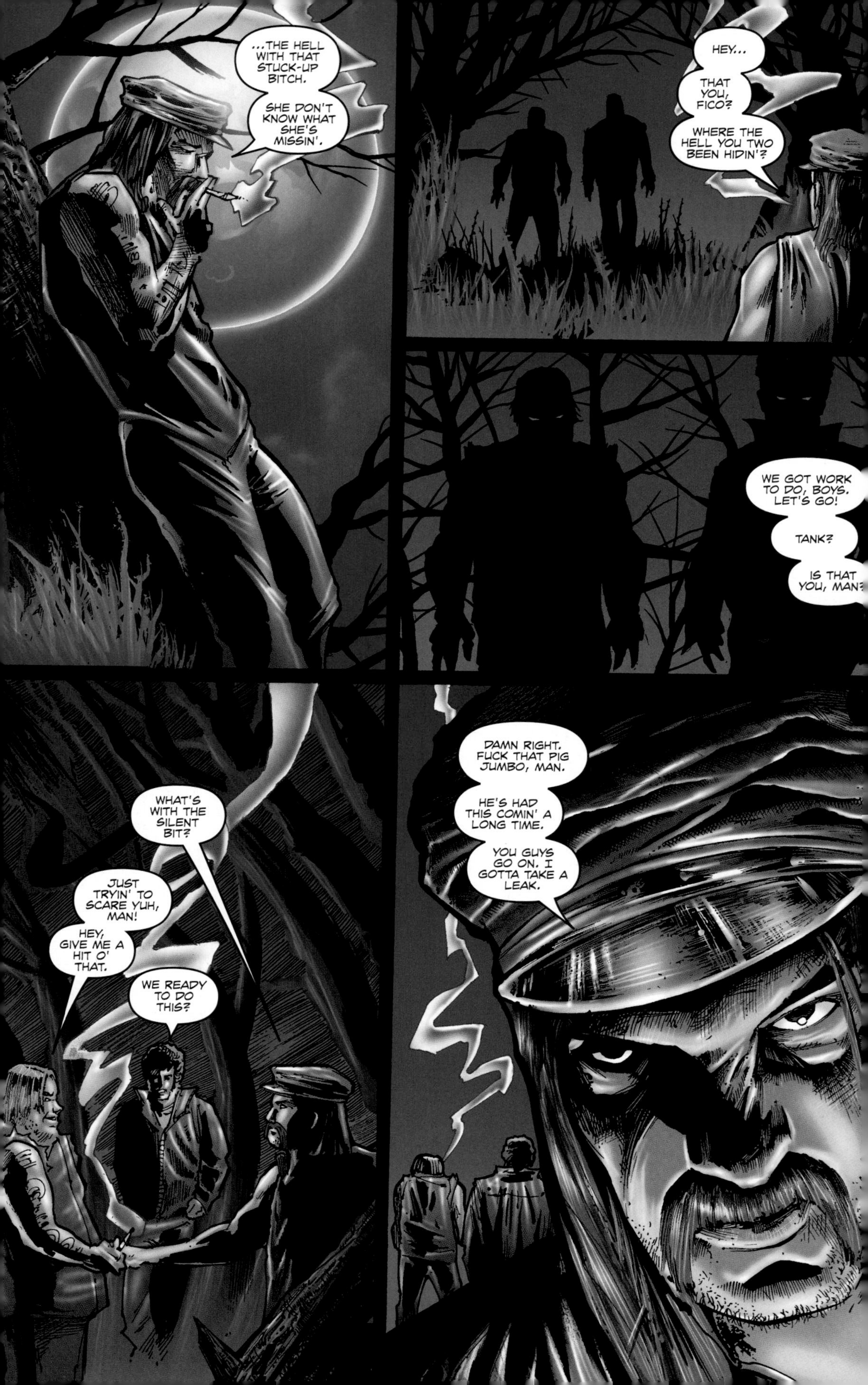
...THE HELL WITH THAT STUCK-UP BITCH.
SHE DON'T KNOW WHAT SHE'S MISSIN'.
HEY...
THAT YOU, FICO?
WHERE THE HELL YOU TWO BEEN HIDIN'?
WE GOT WORK TO DO, BOYS. LET'S GO!
TANK?
IS THAT YOU, MAN?
WHAT'S WITH THE SILENT BIT?
JUST TRYIN' TO SCARE YUH, MAN!
HEY, GIVE ME A HIT O' THAT.
WE READY TO DO THIS?
DAMN RIGHT. FUCK THAT PIG JUMBO, MAN.
HE'S HAD THIS COMIN' A LONG TIME.
YOU GUYS GO ON. I GOTTA TAKE A LEAK.

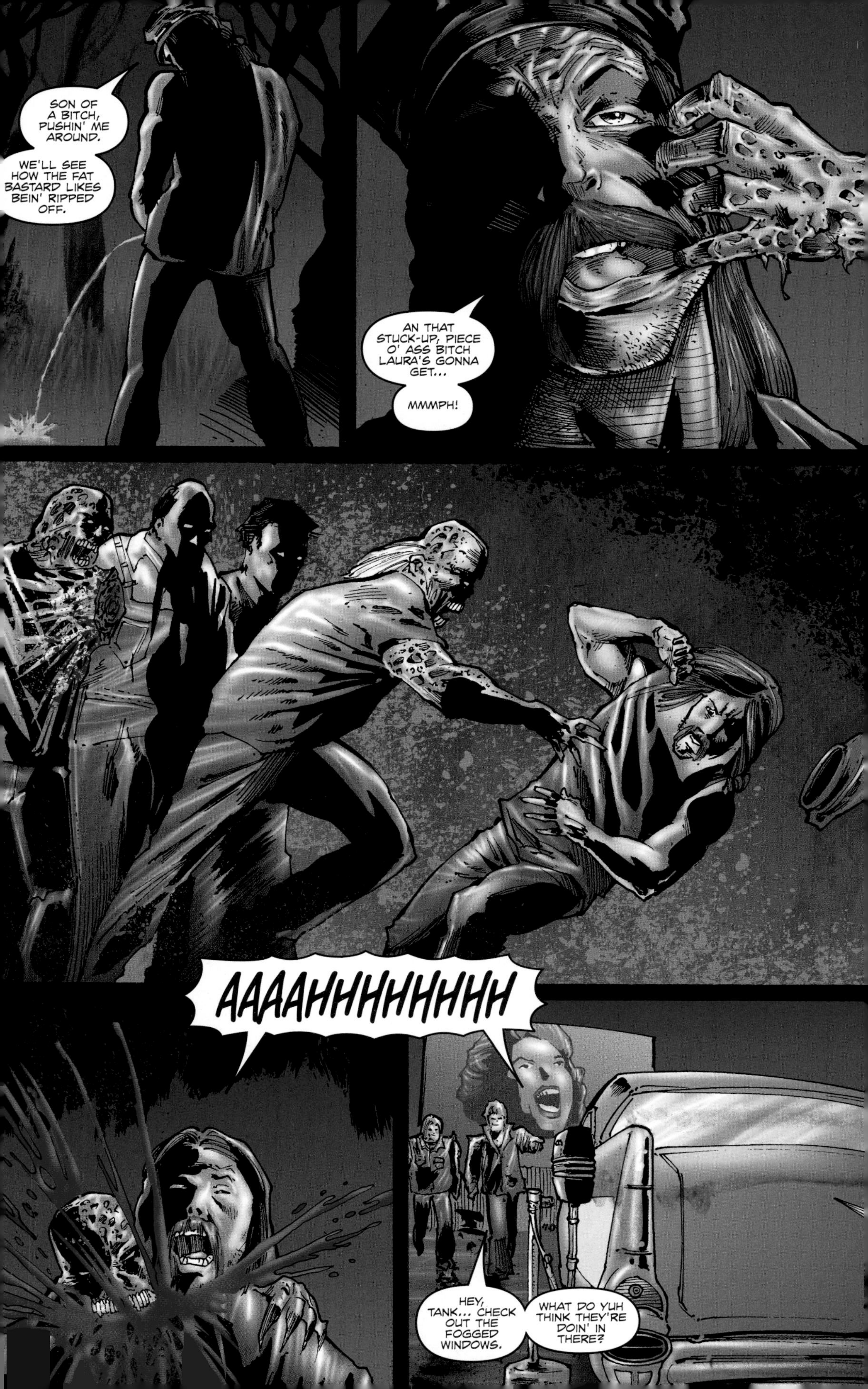
SON OF A BITCH, PUSHIN' ME AROUND.
WE'LL SEE HOW THE FAT BASTARD LIKES BEIN' RIPPED OFF.
AN THAT STUCK-UP, PIECE O' ASS BITCH LAURA'S GONNA GET...
MMMPH!
AAAAHHHHHHHH
HEY, TANK... CHECK OUT THE FOGGED WINDOWS.
WHAT DO YUH THINK THEY'RE DOIN' IN THERE?

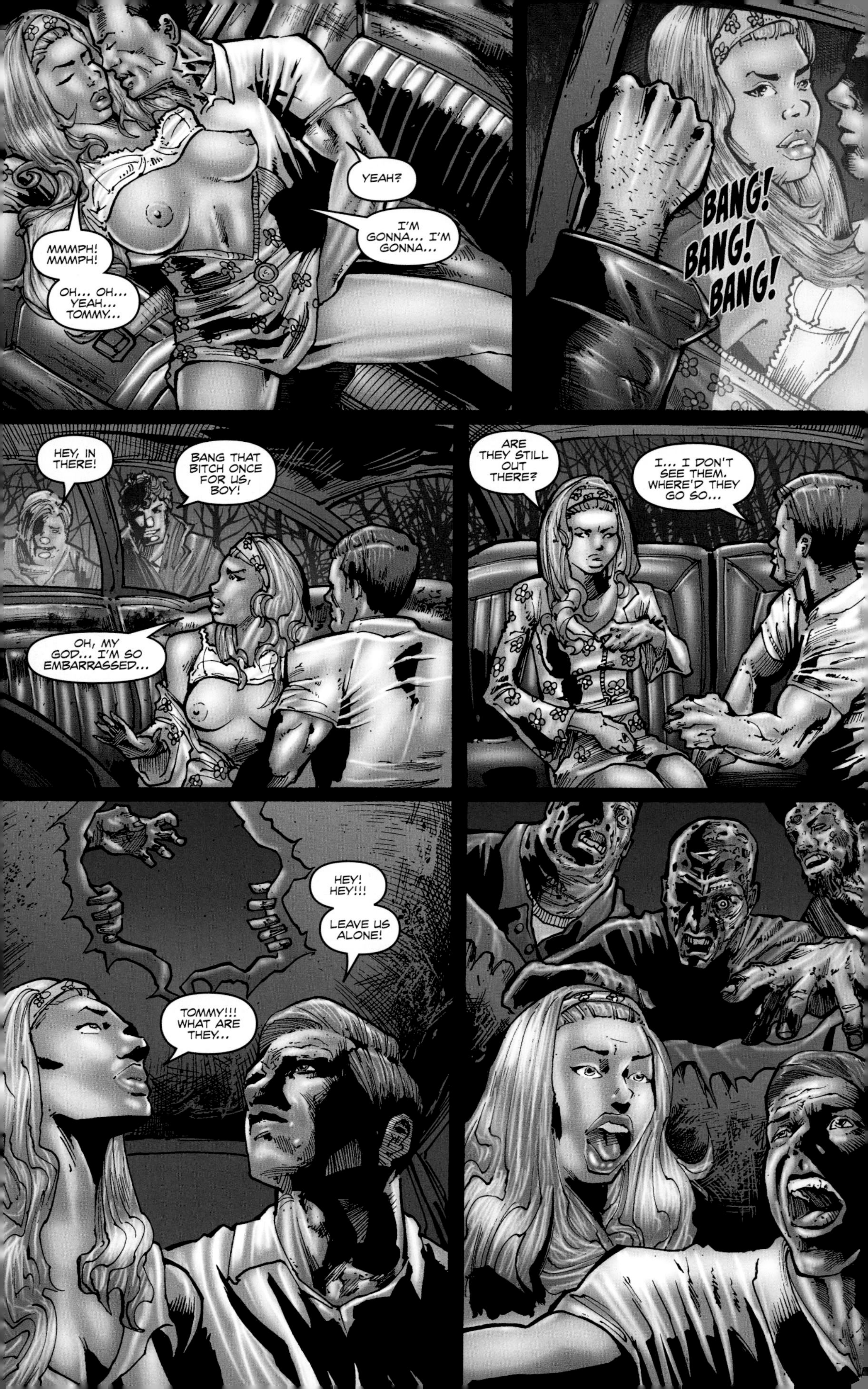

YEAH?
MMMPH! MMMPH!
I'M GONNA... I'M GONNA...
OH... OH... YEAH... TOMMY...
BANG! BANG! BANG!
HEY, IN THERE!
BANG THAT BITCH ONCE FOR US, BOY!
OH, MY GOD... I'M SO EMBARRASSED...
ARE THEY STILL OUT THERE?
I... I DON'T SEE THEM. WHERE'D THEY GO SO...
HEY! HEY!!!
LEAVE US ALONE!
TOMMY!!! WHAT ARE THEY...

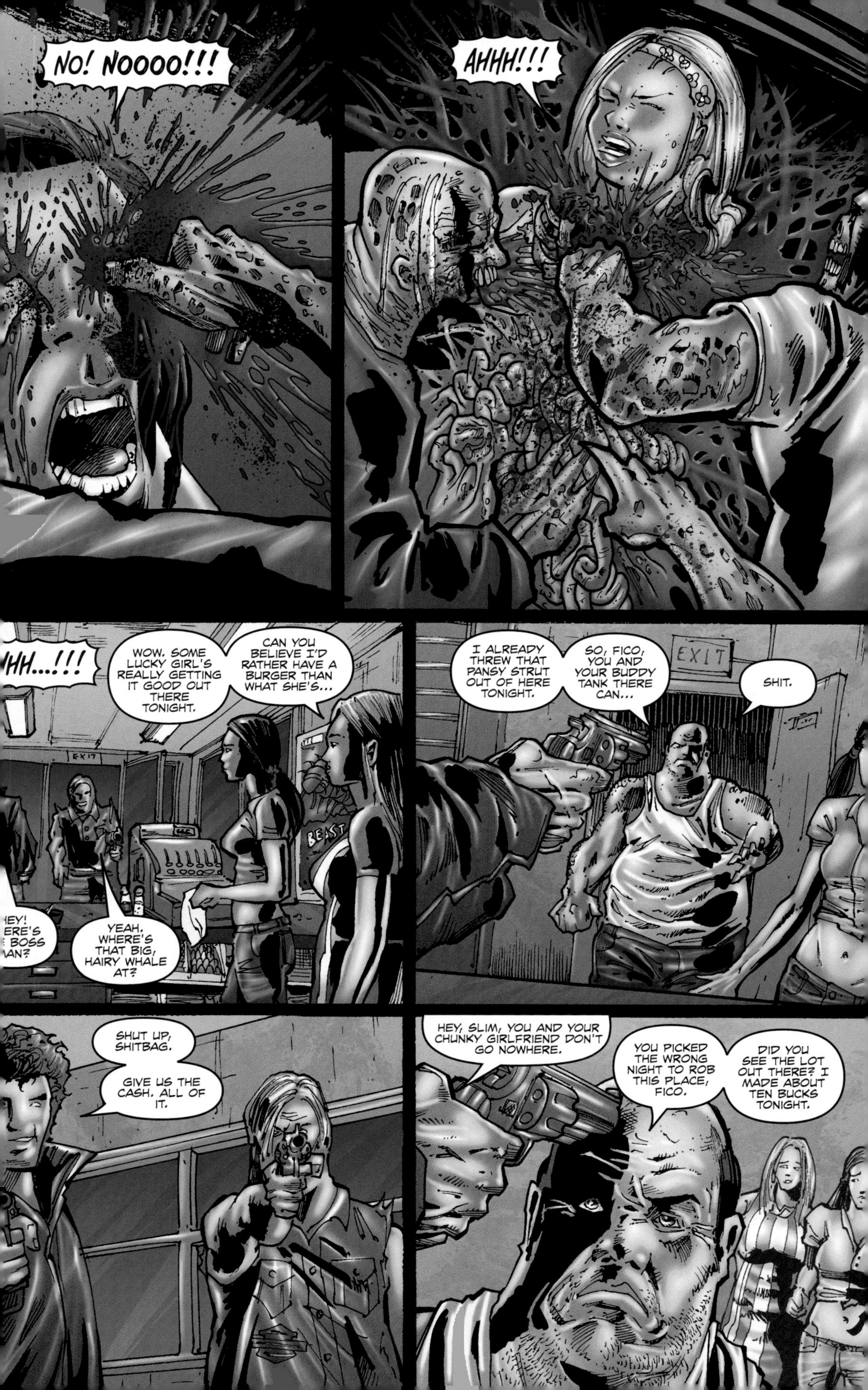
NO! NOOOO!!!
AHHH!!!
HH...!!!
WOW. SOME LUCKY GIRL'S REALLY GETTING IT GOOD OUT THERE TONIGHT.
CAN YOU BELIEVE I'D RATHER HAVE A BURGER THAN WHAT SHE'S...
EXIT
BEAST
HEY! ERE'S BOSS AN?
YEAH. WHERE'S THAT BIG, HAIRY WHALE AT?
I ALREADY THREW THAT PANSY STRUT OUT OF HERE TONIGHT.
SO, FICO, YOU AND YOUR BUDDY TANK THERE CAN...
EXIT
SHIT.
SHUT UP, SHITBAG.
GIVE US THE CASH. ALL OF IT.
HEY, SLIM, YOU AND YOUR CHUNKY GIRLFRIEND DON'T GO NOWHERE.
YOU PICKED THE WRONG NIGHT TO ROB THIS PLACE, FICO.
DID YOU SEE THE LOT OUT THERE? I MADE ABOUT TEN BUCKS TONIGHT.

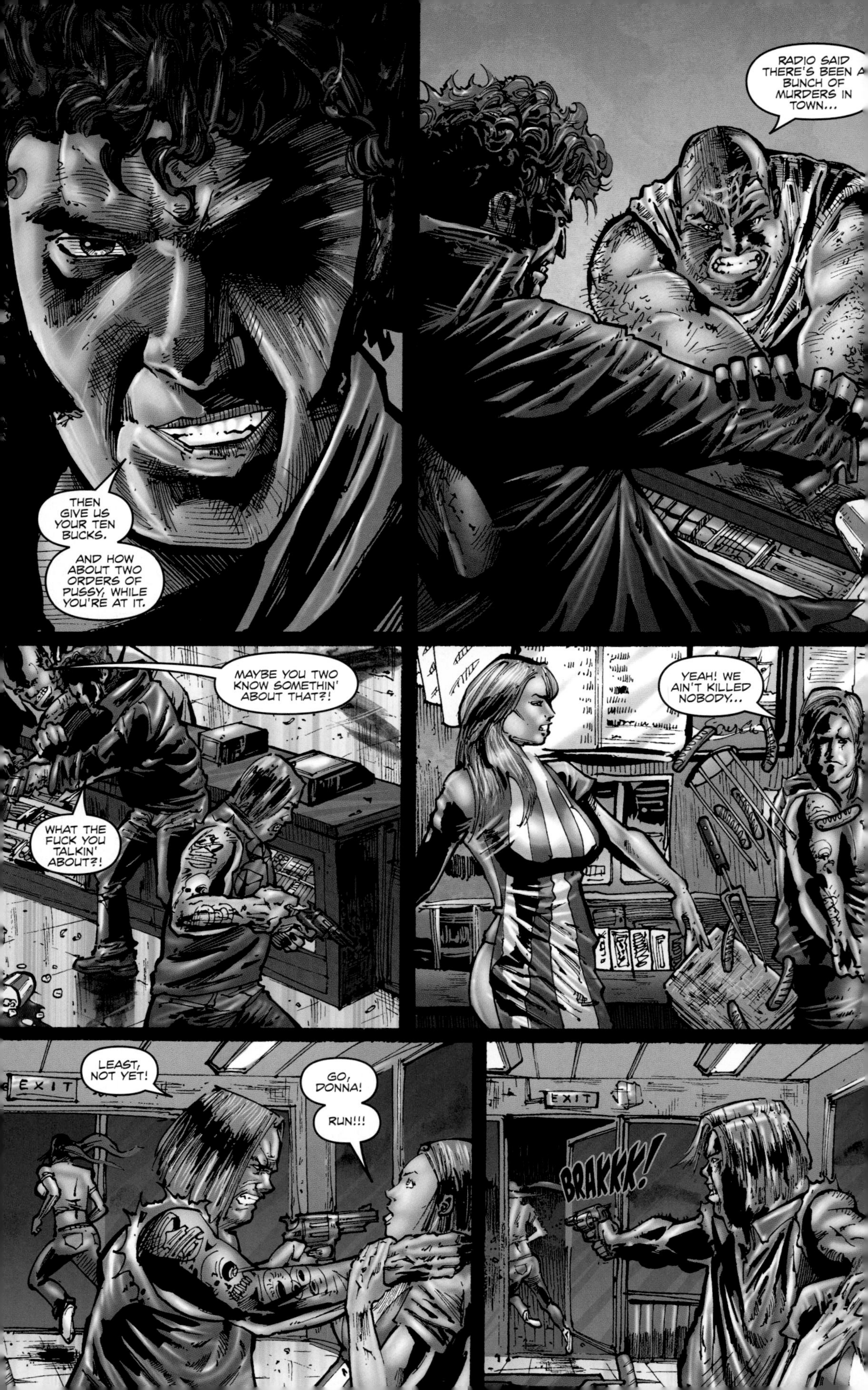
THEN GIVE US YOUR TEN BUCKS.
AND HOW ABOUT TWO ORDERS OF PUSSY, WHILE YOU'RE AT IT.
RADIO SAID THERE'S BEEN A BUNCH OF MURDERS IN TOWN...
MAYBE YOU TWO KNOW SOMETHIN' ABOUT THAT?!
WHAT THE FUCK YOU TALKIN' ABOUT?!
YEAH! WE AIN'T KILLED NOBODY...
LEAST, NOT YET!
EXIT
GO, DONNA!
RUN!!!
EXIT
BRAKKK!

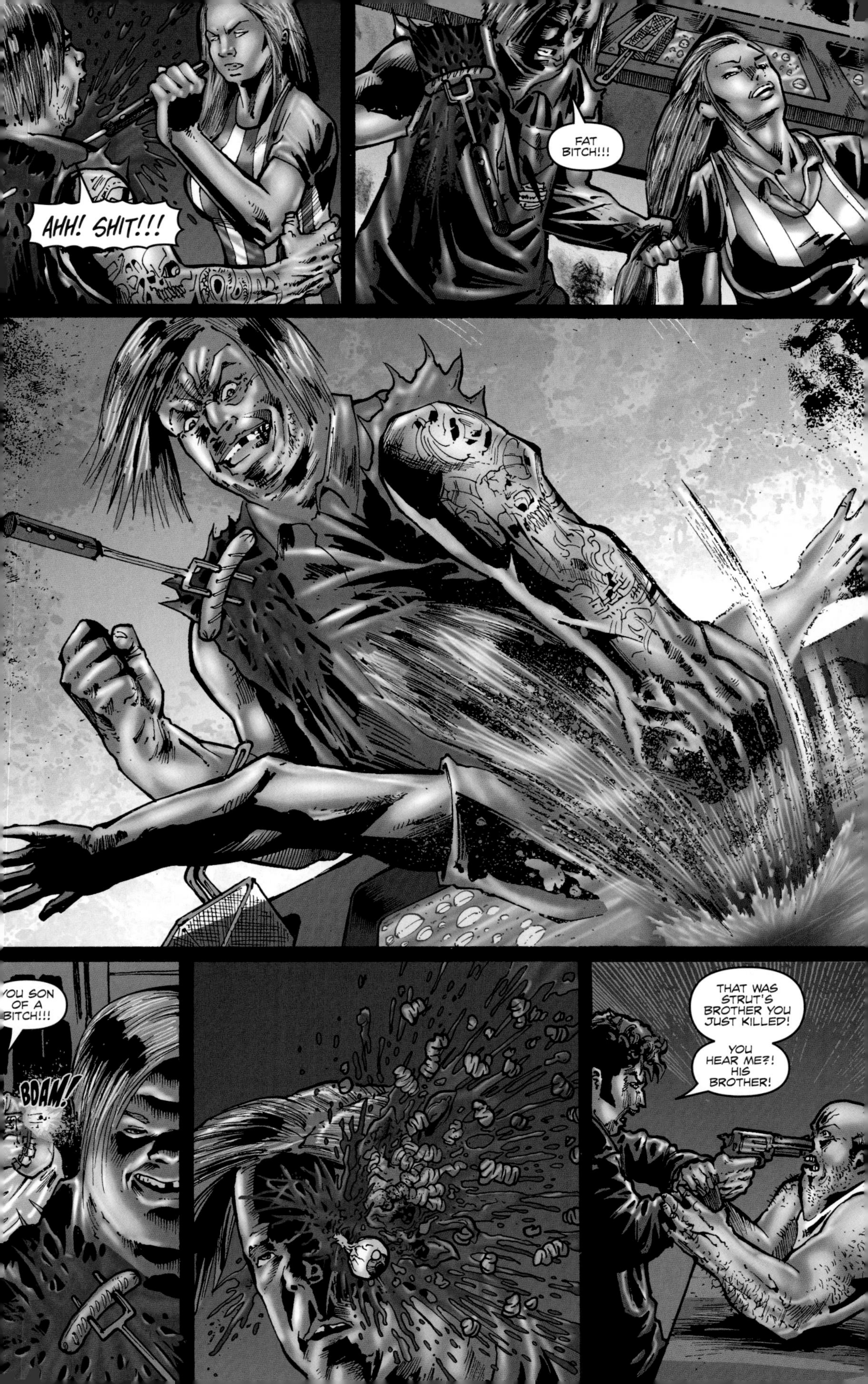
AHH! SHIT!!!
FAT BITCH!!!
YOU SON OF A BITCH!!!
BOAM!
THAT WAS STRUT'S BROTHER YOU JUST KILLED!
YOU HEAR ME?! HIS BROTHER!

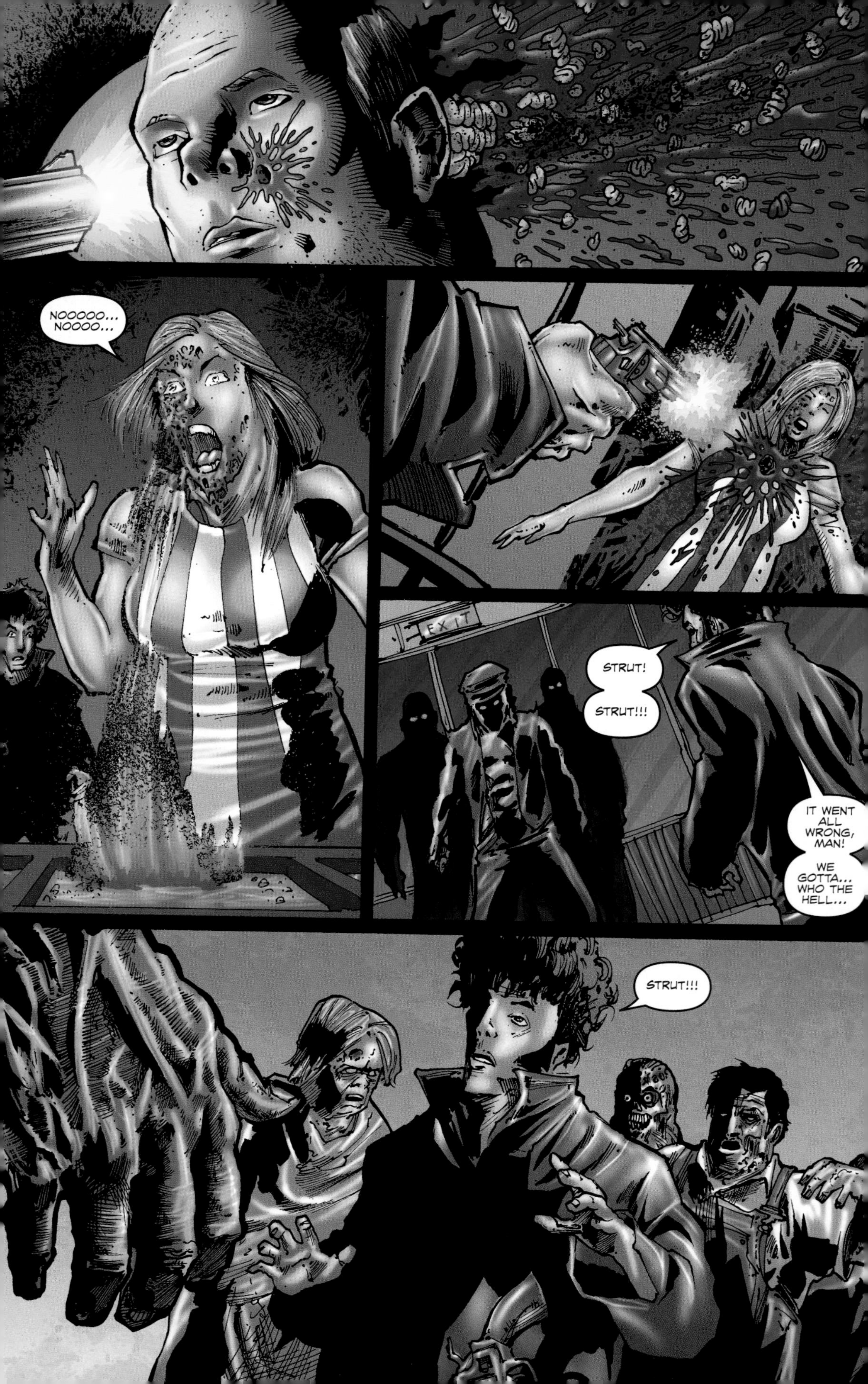
NOOOOO...
NOOOO...
STRUT!
STRUT!!!
IT WENT ALL WRONG, MAN!
WE GOTTA... WHO THE HELL...
STRUT!!!

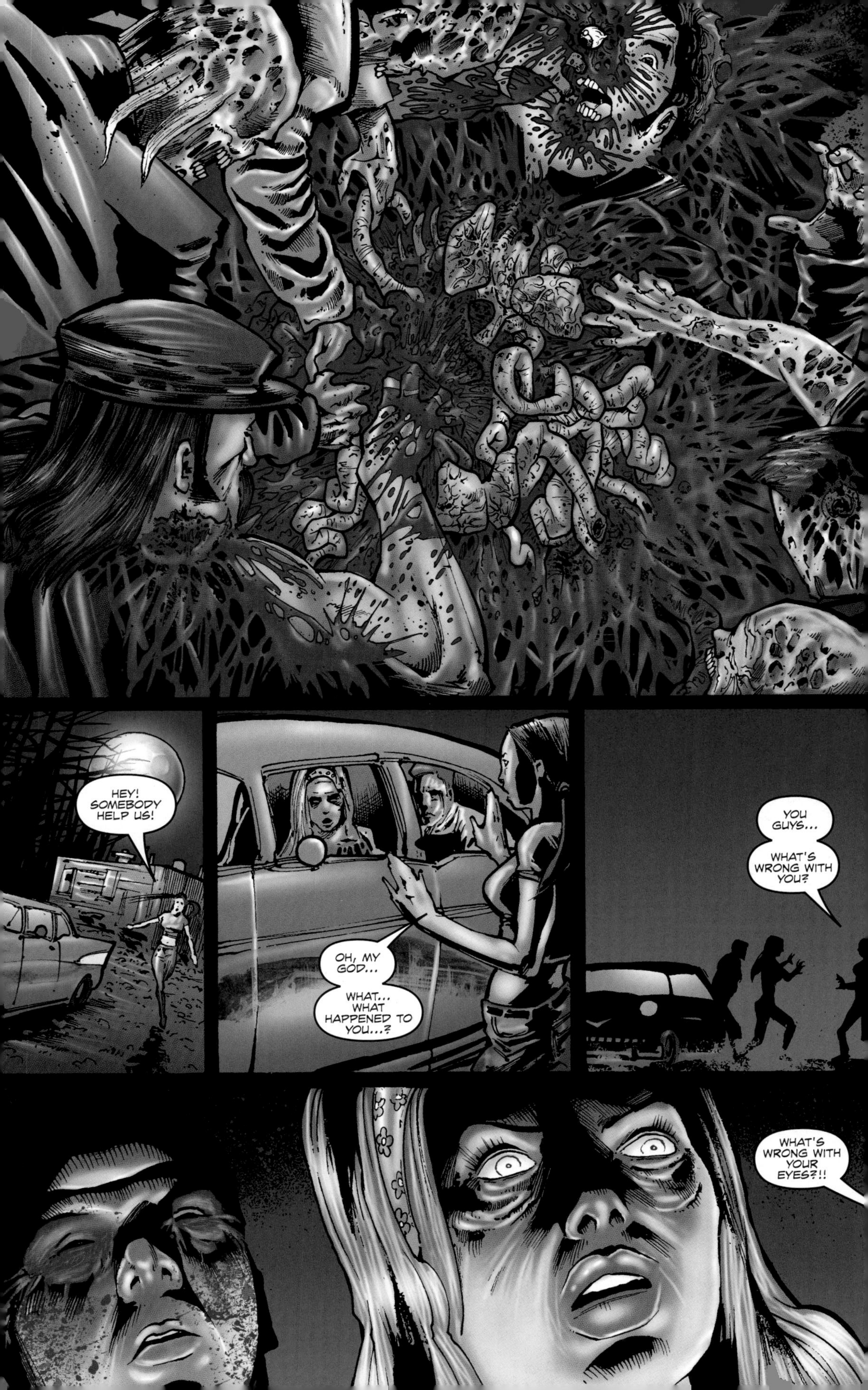
HEY! SOMEBODY HELP US!
OH, MY GOD...
WHAT... WHAT HAPPENED TO YOU...?
YOU GUYS...
WHAT'S WRONG WITH YOU?
WHAT'S WRONG WITH YOUR EYES?!!

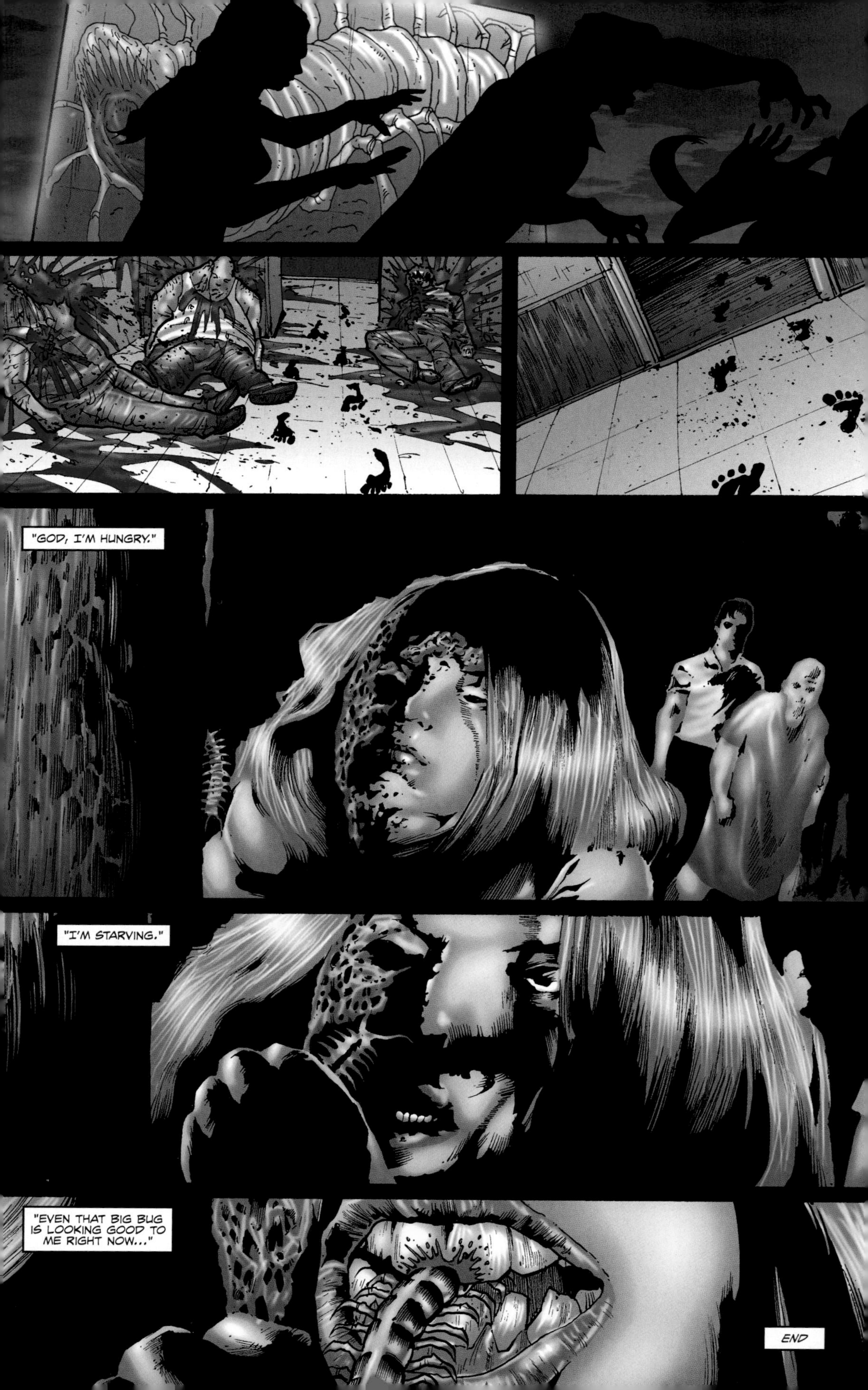
"GOD, I'M HUNGRY."
"I'M STARVING."
"EVEN THAT BIG BUG IS LOOKING GOOD TO ME RIGHT NOW..."
END

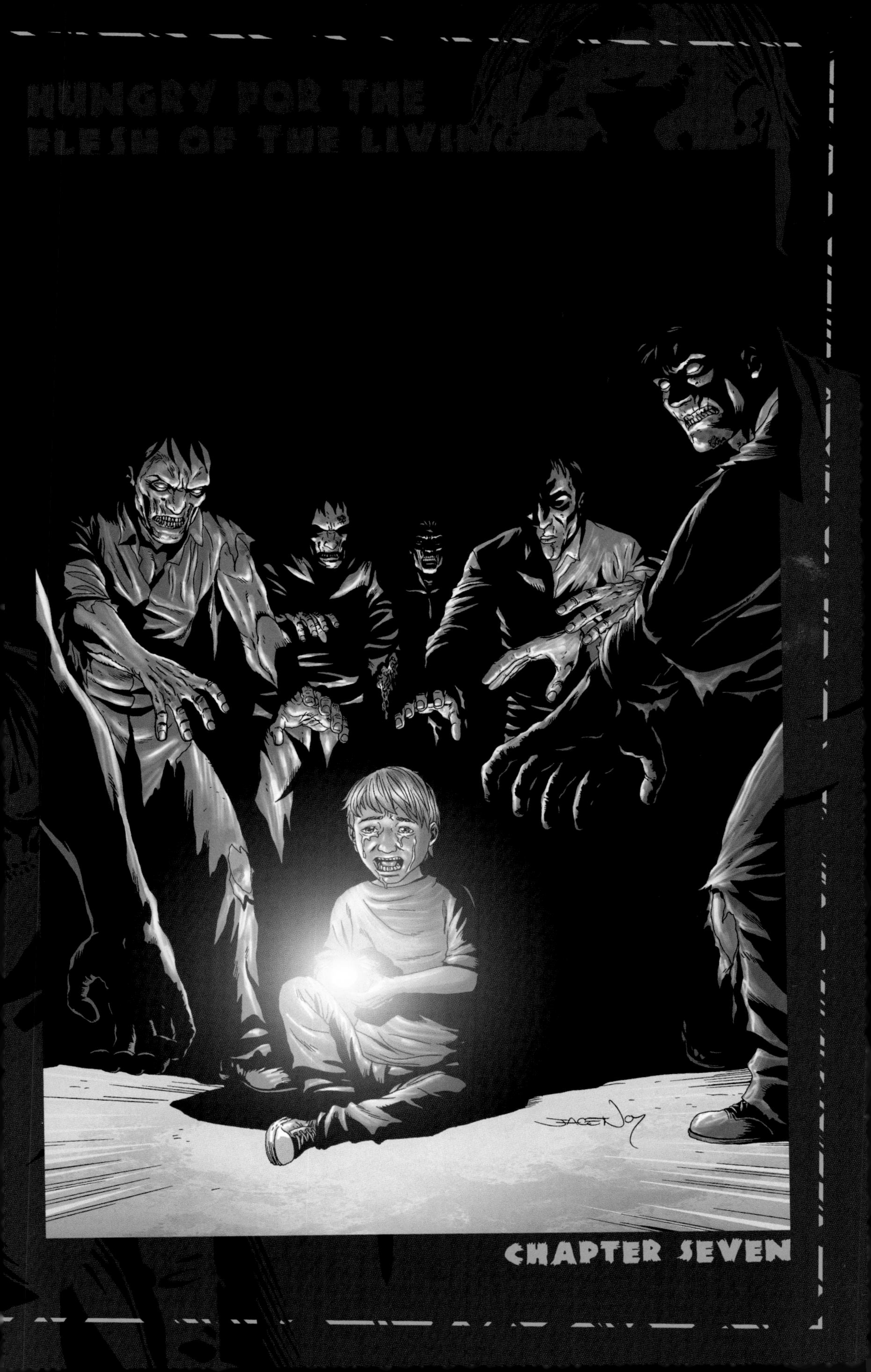
HUNGRY FOR THE
FLESH OF THE LIVING
CHAPTER SEVEN

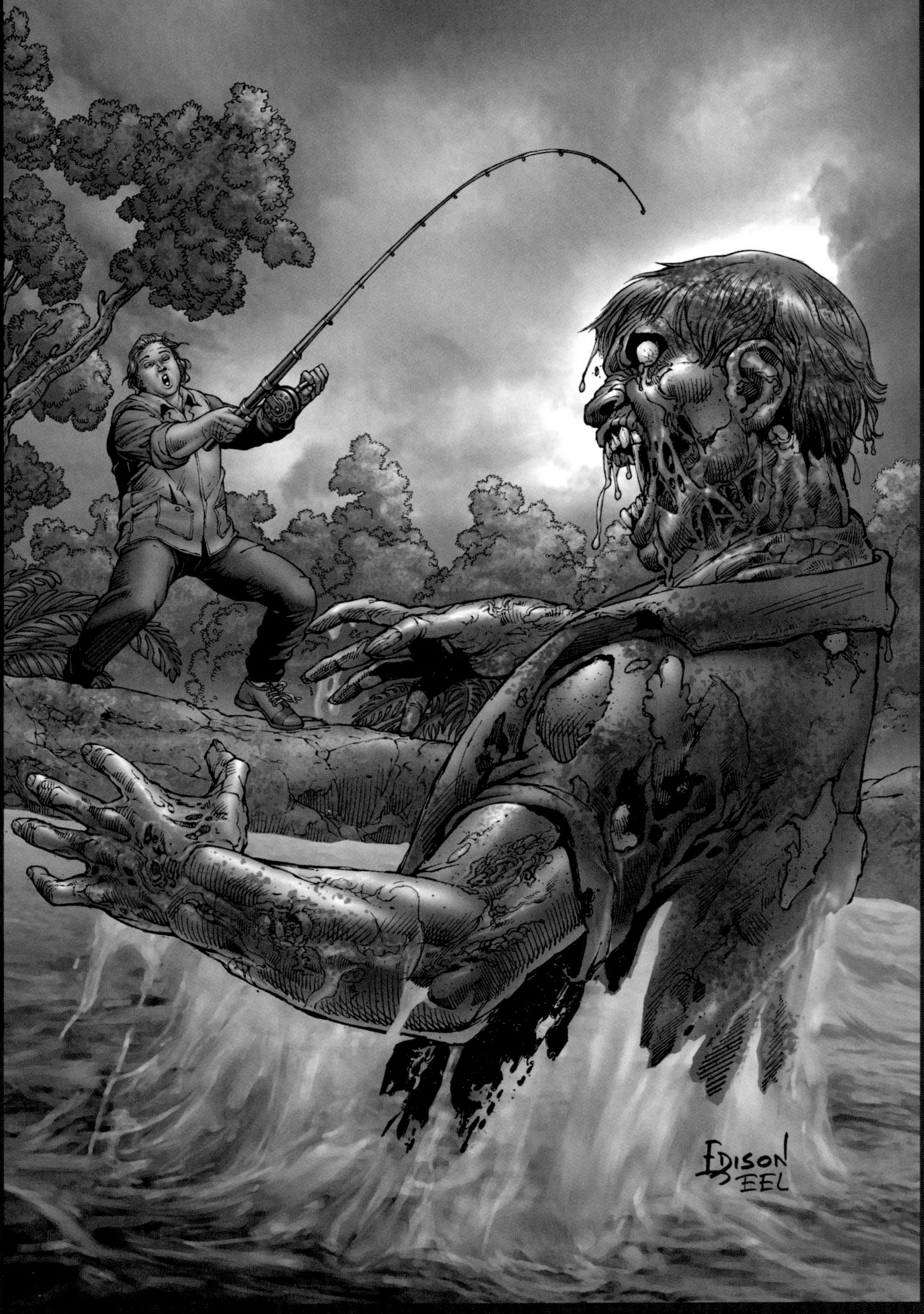

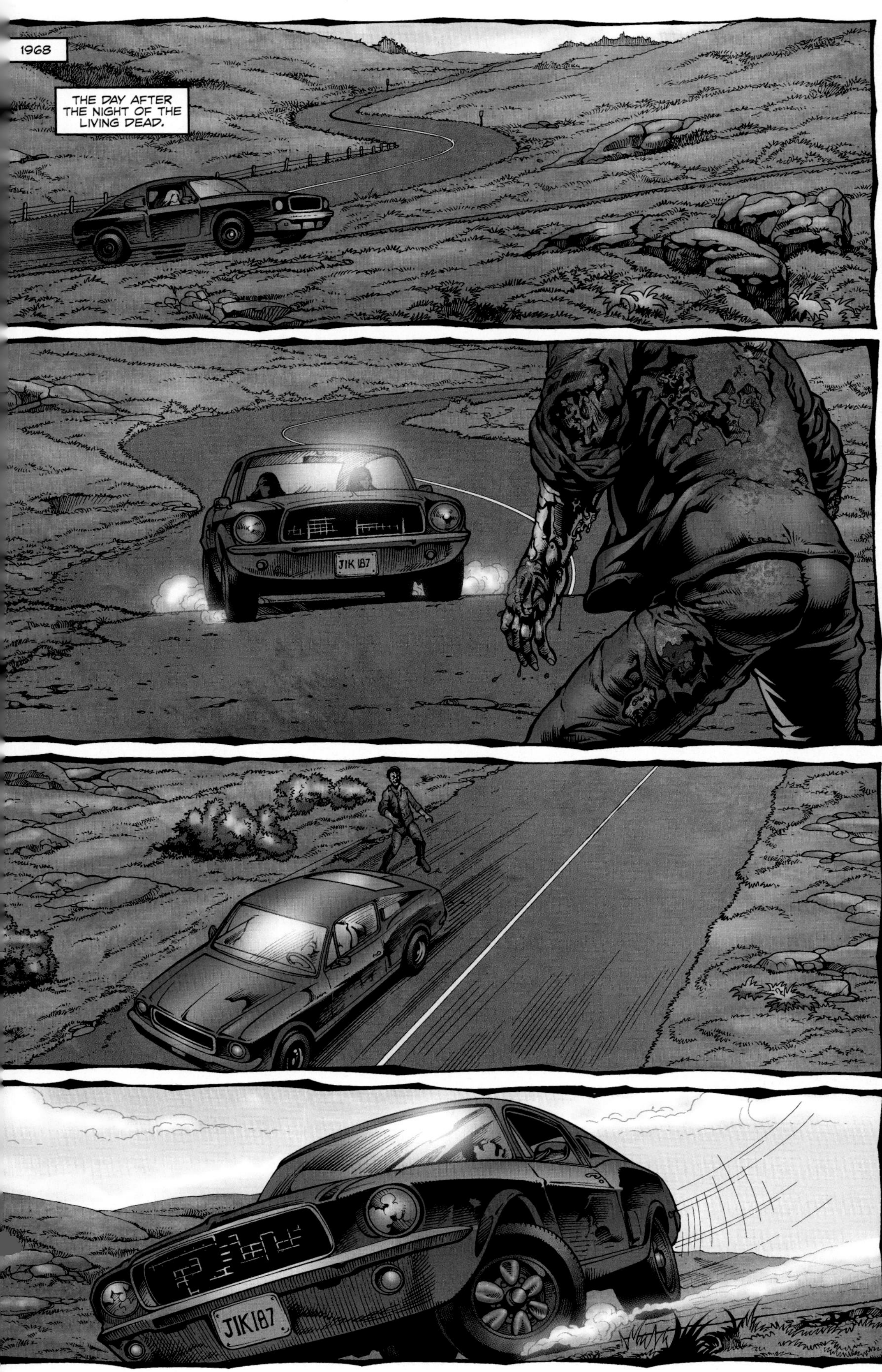
1968
THE DAY AFTER THE NIGHT OF THE LIVING DEAD.
JIK 187
JIK187

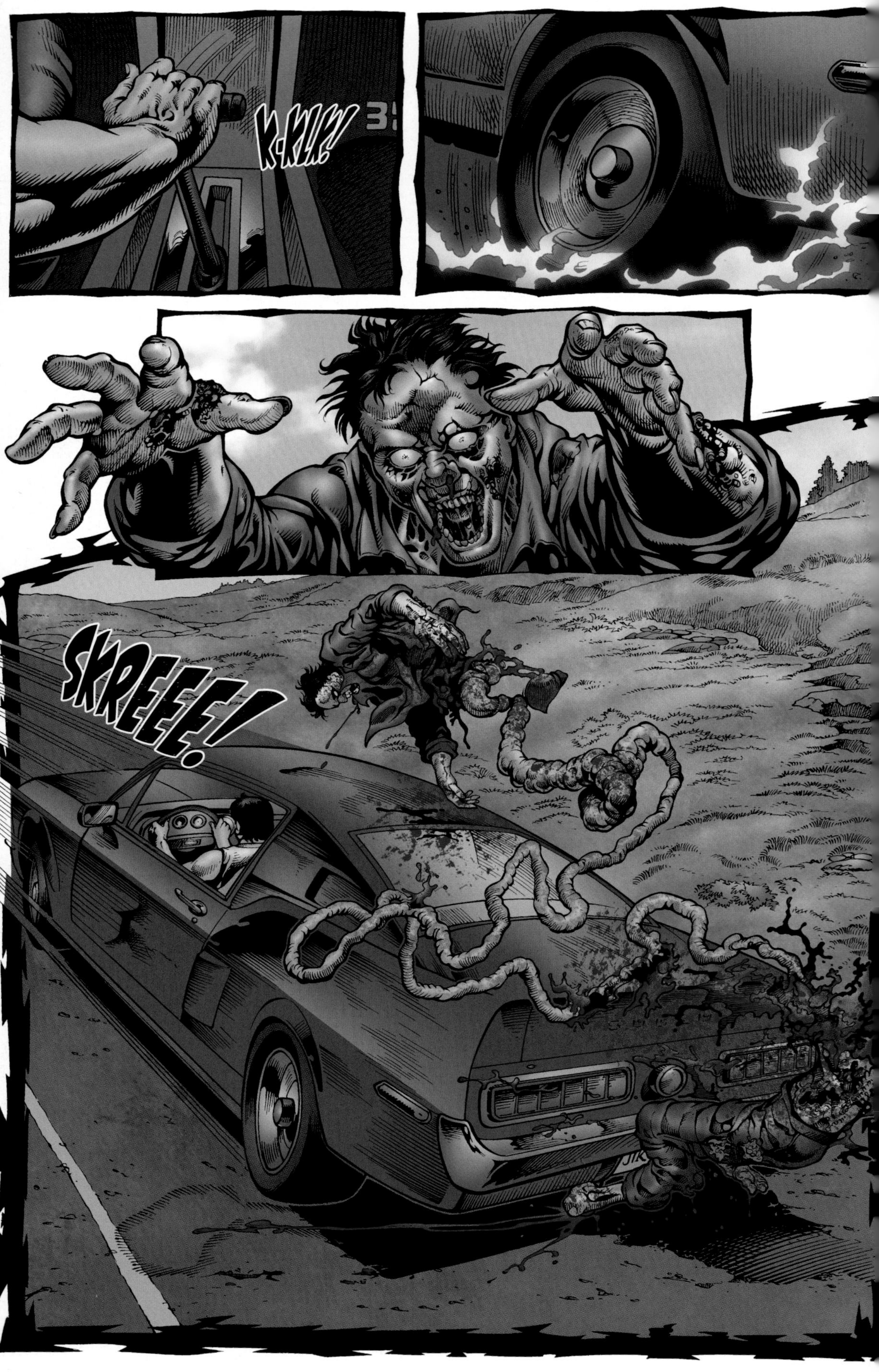
K-KLIK!
SKREEE!

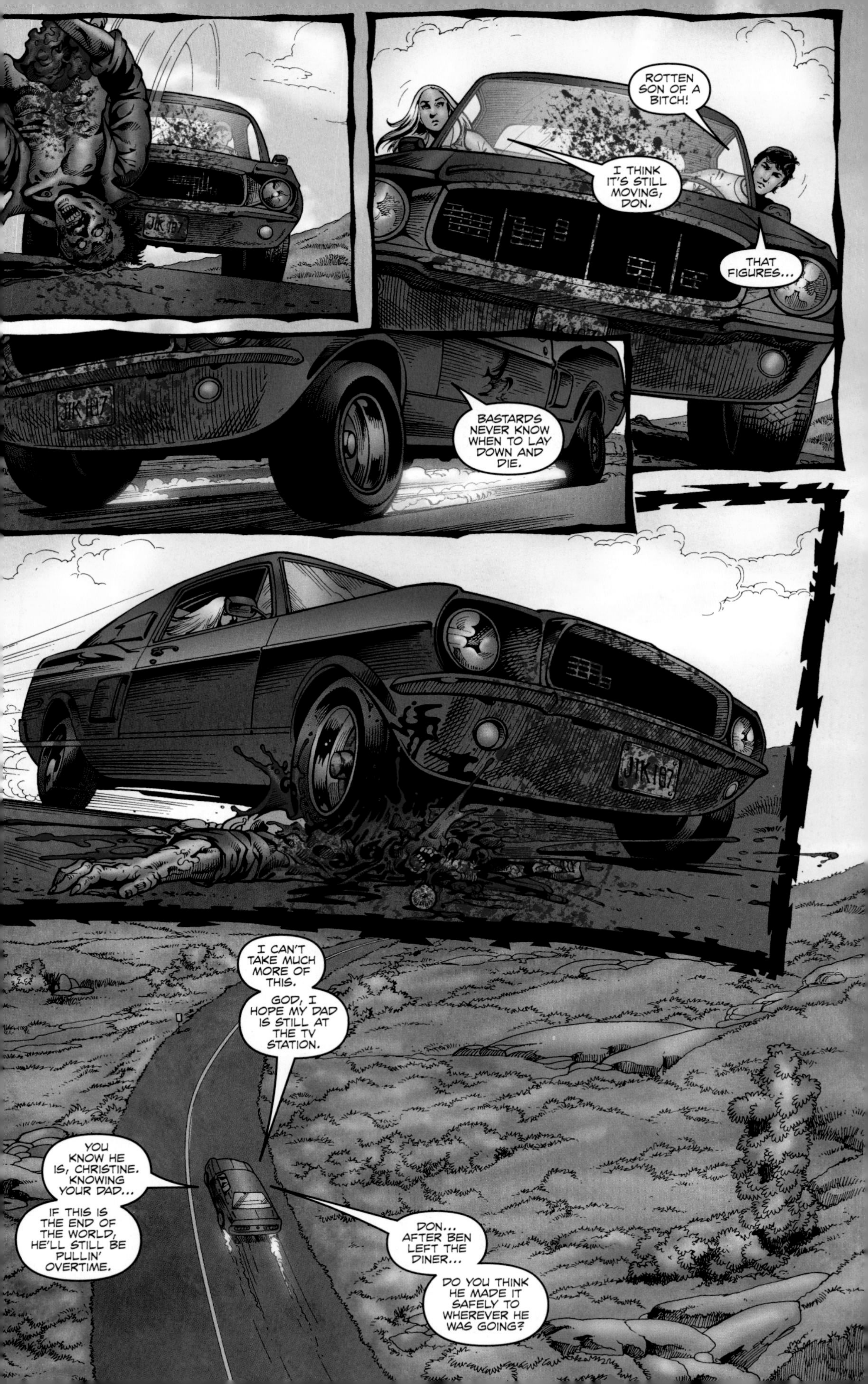
ROTTEN SON OF A BITCH!
I THINK IT'S STILL MOVING, DON.
THAT FIGURES...
BASTARDS NEVER KNOW WHEN TO LAY DOWN AND DIE.
JJK 107
I CAN'T TAKE MUCH MORE OF THIS.
GOD, I HOPE MY DAD IS STILL AT THE TV STATION.
YOU KNOW HE IS, CHRISTINE. KNOWING YOUR DAD...
IF THIS IS THE END OF THE WORLD, HE'LL STILL BE PULLIN' OVERTIME.
DON... AFTER BEN LEFT THE DINER...
DO YOU THINK HE MADE IT SAFELY TO WHEREVER HE WAS GOING?

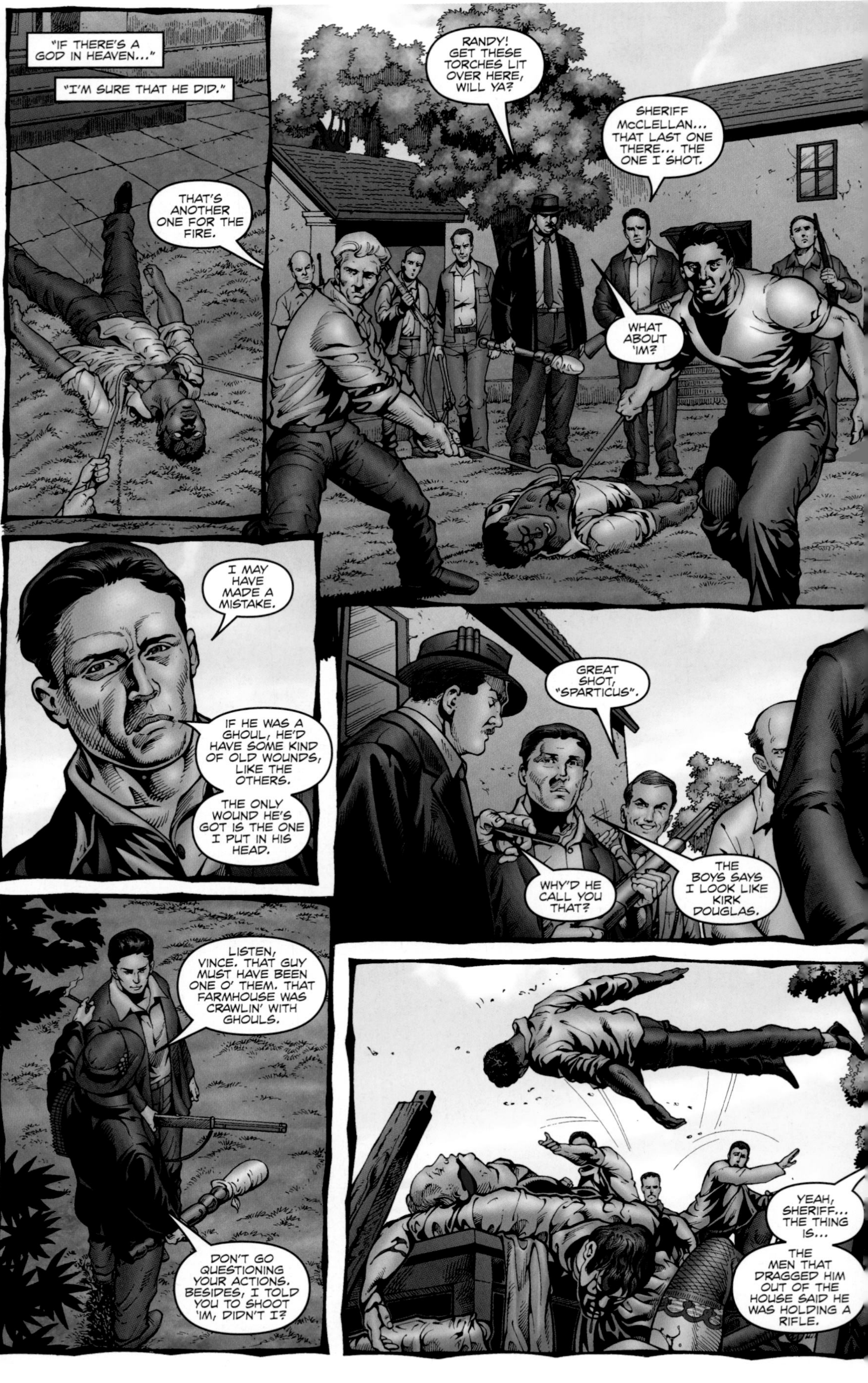
"IF THERE'S A GOD IN HEAVEN..."
"I'M SURE THAT HE DID."
THAT'S ANOTHER ONE FOR THE FIRE.
RANDY! GET THESE TORCHES LIT OVER HERE, WILL YA?
SHERIFF McCLELLAN... THAT LAST ONE THERE... THE ONE I SHOT.
WHAT ABOUT 'IM?
I MAY HAVE MADE A MISTAKE.
IF HE WAS A GHOUL, HE'D HAVE SOME KIND OF OLD WOUNDS, LIKE THE OTHERS.
THE ONLY WOUND HE'S GOT IS THE ONE I PUT IN HIS HEAD.
GREAT SHOT, "SPARTICUS".
WHY'D HE CALL YOU THAT?
THE BOYS SAYS I LOOK LIKE KIRK DOUGLAS.
LISTEN, VINCE. THAT GUY MUST HAVE BEEN ONE O' THEM. THAT FARMHOUSE WAS CRAWLIN' WITH GHOULS.
DON'T GO QUESTIONING YOUR ACTIONS. BESIDES, I TOLD YOU TO SHOOT 'IM, DIDN'T I?
YEAH, SHERIFF... THE THING IS...
THE MEN THAT DRAGGED HIM OUT OF THE HOUSE SAID HE WAS HOLDING A RIFLE.

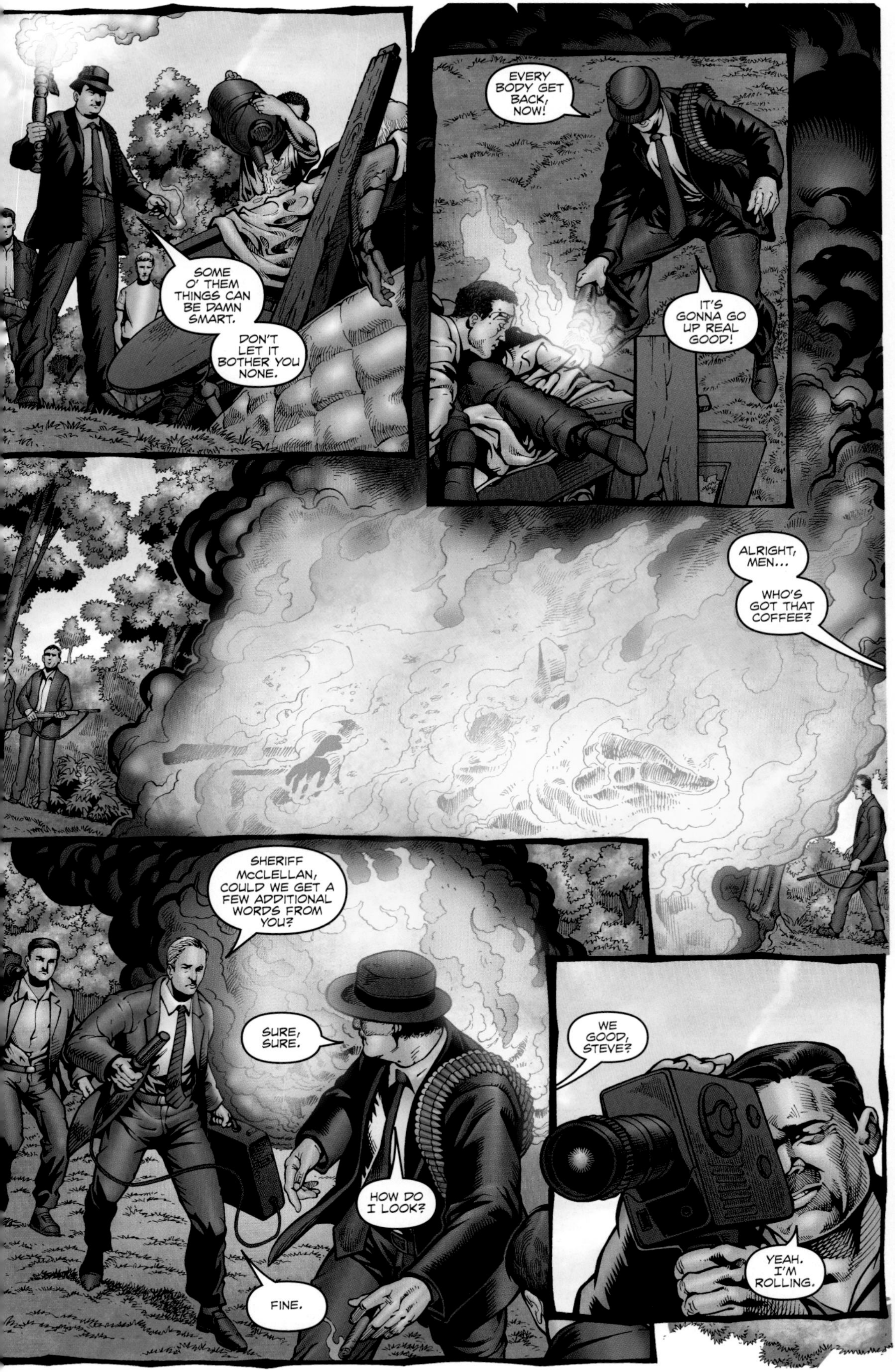
SOME O' THEM THINGS CAN BE DAMN SMART.
DON'T LET IT BOTHER YOU NONE.
EVERY BODY GET BACK, NOW!
IT'S GONNA GO UP REAL GOOD!
ALRIGHT, MEN...
WHO'S GOT THAT COFFEE?
SHERIFF McCLELLAN, COULD WE GET A FEW ADDITIONAL WORDS FROM YOU?
SURE, SURE.
HOW DO I LOOK?
FINE.
WE GOOD, STEVE?
YEAH. I'M ROLLING.

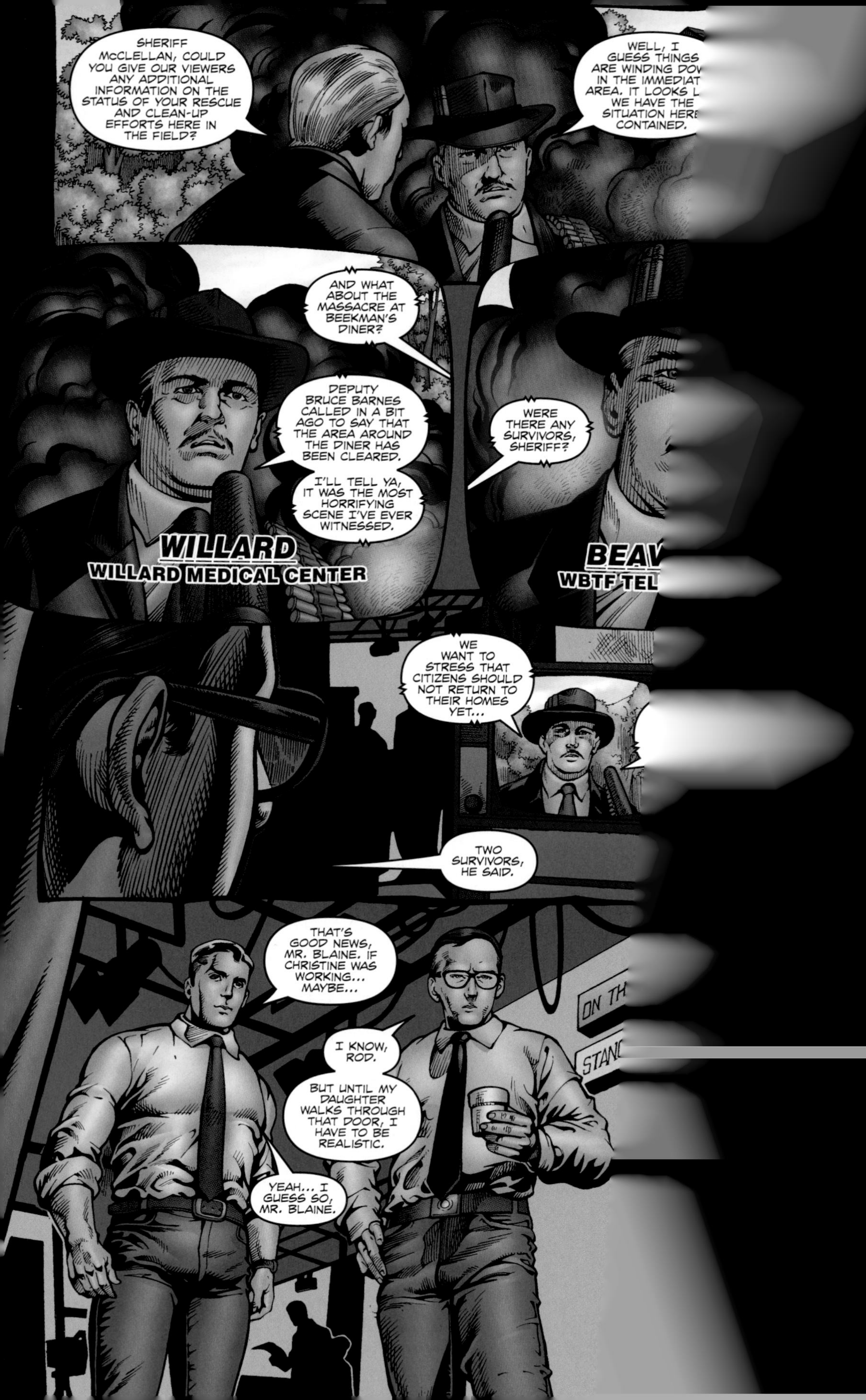
SHERIFF McCLELLAN, COULD YOU GIVE OUR VIEWERS ANY ADDITIONAL INFORMATION ON THE STATUS OF YOUR RESCUE AND CLEAN-UP EFFORTS HERE IN THE FIELD?
WELL, I GUESS THINGS ARE WINDING DOW IN THE IMMEDIAT AREA. IT LOOKS L WE HAVE THE SITUATION HERE CONTAINED.
AND WHAT ABOUT THE MASSACRE AT BEEKMAN'S DINER?
DEPUTY BRUCE BARNES CALLED IN A BIT AGO TO SAY THAT THE AREA AROUND THE DINER HAS BEEN CLEARED.
I'LL TELL YA, IT WAS THE MOST HORRIFYING SCENE I'VE EVER WITNESSED.
WILLARD
WILLARD MEDICAL CENTER
WERE THERE ANY SURVIVORS, SHERIFF?
BEAV
WBTF TEL
WE WANT TO STRESS THAT CITIZENS SHOULD NOT RETURN TO THEIR HOMES YET...
TWO SURVIVORS, HE SAID.
THAT'S GOOD NEWS, MR. BLAINE. IF CHRISTINE WAS WORKING... MAYBE...
I KNOW, ROD.
BUT UNTIL MY DAUGHTER WALKS THROUGH THAT DOOR, I HAVE TO BE REALISTIC.
YEAH... I GUESS SO, MR. BLAINE.
ON TH
STANC

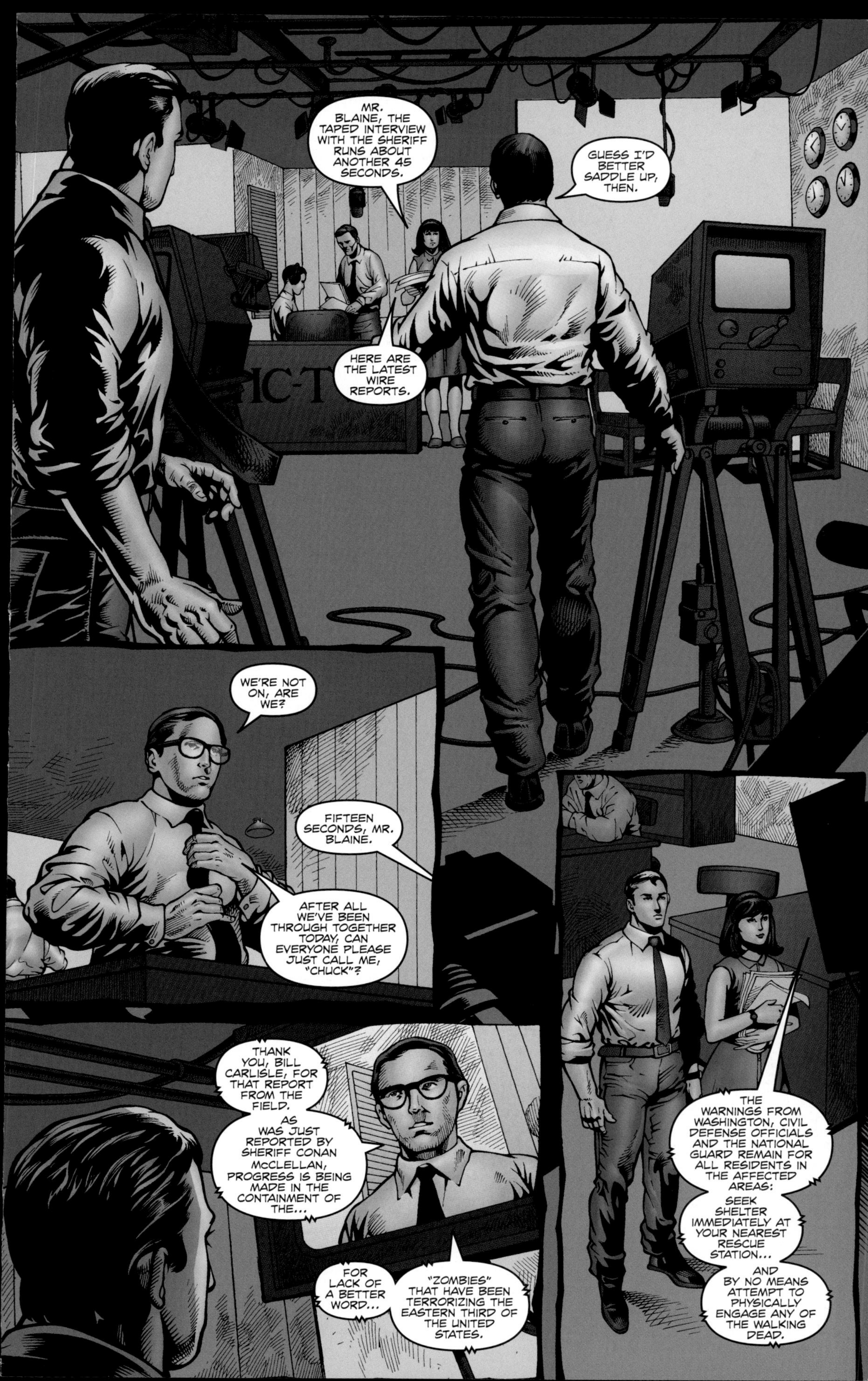
MR. BLAINE, THE TAPED INTERVIEW WITH THE SHERIFF RUNS ABOUT ANOTHER 45 SECONDS.
GUESS I'D BETTER SADDLE UP, THEN.
HERE ARE THE LATEST WIRE REPORTS.
WE'RE NOT ON, ARE WE?
FIFTEEN SECONDS, MR. BLAINE.
AFTER ALL WE'VE BEEN THROUGH TOGETHER TODAY, CAN EVERYONE PLEASE JUST CALL ME, "CHUCK"?
THANK YOU, BILL CARLISLE, FOR THAT REPORT FROM THE FIELD.
AS WAS JUST REPORTED BY SHERIFF CONAN McCLELLAN, PROGRESS IS BEING MADE IN THE CONTAINMENT OF THE...
FOR LACK OF A BETTER WORD...
"ZOMBIES" THAT HAVE BEEN TERRORIZING THE EASTERN THIRD OF THE UNITED STATES.
THE WARNINGS FROM WASHINGTON, CIVIL DEFENSE OFFICIALS AND THE NATIONAL GUARD REMAIN FOR ALL RESIDENTS IN THE AFFECTED AREAS:
SEEK SHELTER IMMEDIATELY AT YOUR NEAREST RESCUE STATION...
AND BY NO MEANS ATTEMPT TO PHYSICALLY ENGAGE ANY OF THE WALKING DEAD.

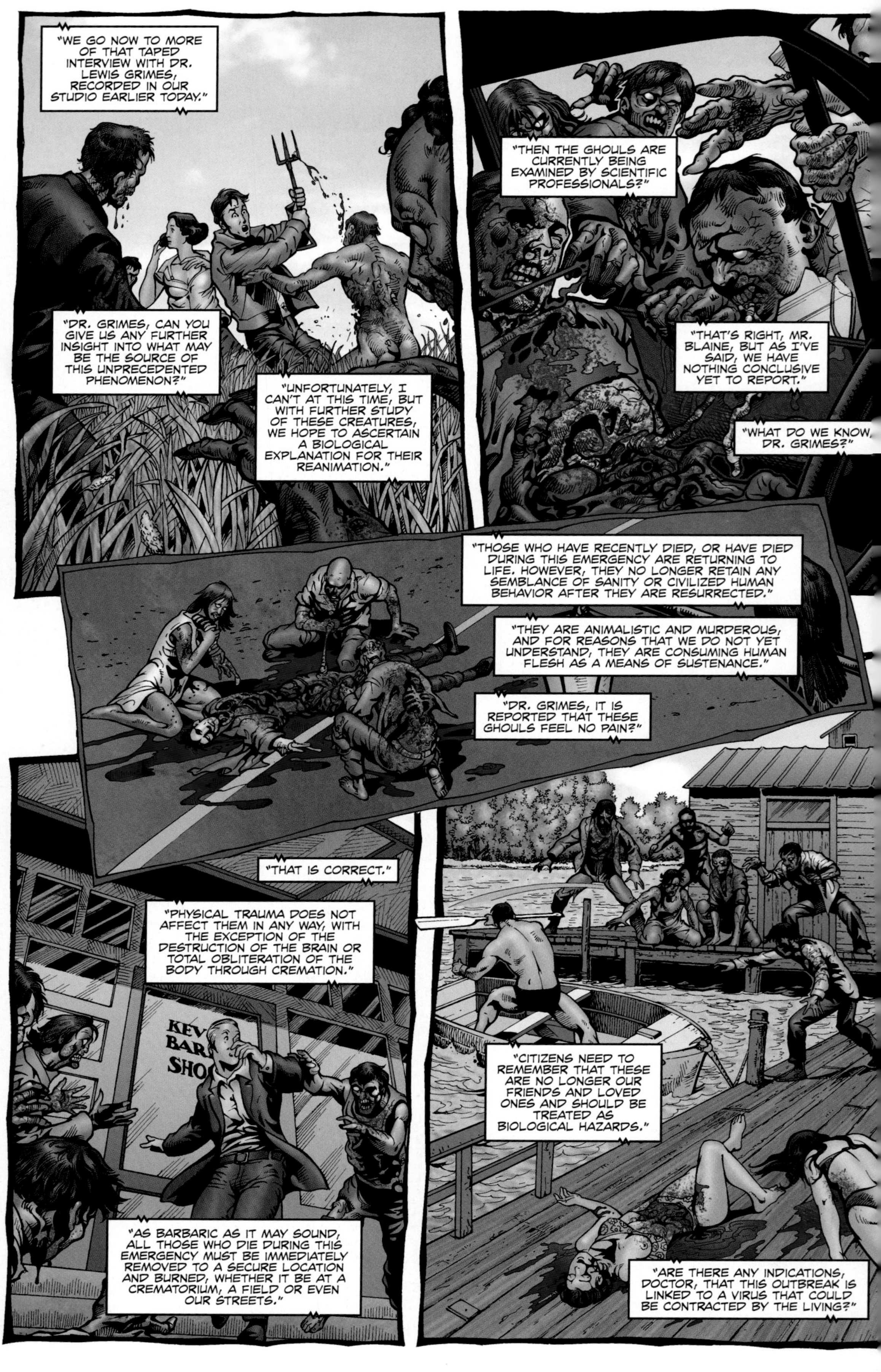
"WE GO NOW TO MORE OF THAT TAPED INTERVIEW WITH DR. LEWIS GRIMES, RECORDED IN OUR STUDIO EARLIER TODAY."
"DR. GRIMES, CAN YOU GIVE US ANY FURTHER INSIGHT INTO WHAT MAY BE THE SOURCE OF THIS UNPRECEDENTED PHENOMENON?"
"UNFORTUNATELY, I CAN'T AT THIS TIME, BUT WITH FURTHER STUDY OF THESE CREATURES, WE HOPE TO ASCERTAIN A BIOLOGICAL EXPLANATION FOR THEIR REANIMATION."
"THEN THE GHOULS ARE CURRENTLY BEING EXAMINED BY SCIENTIFIC PROFESSIONALS?"
"THAT'S RIGHT, MR. BLAINE, BUT AS I'VE SAID, WE HAVE NOTHING CONCLUSIVE YET TO REPORT."
"WHAT DO WE KNOW, DR. GRIMES?"
"THOSE WHO HAVE RECENTLY DIED, OR HAVE DIED DURING THIS EMERGENCY ARE RETURNING TO LIFE. HOWEVER, THEY NO LONGER RETAIN ANY SEMBLANCE OF SANITY OR CIVILIZED HUMAN BEHAVIOR AFTER THEY ARE RESURRECTED."
"THEY ARE ANIMALISTIC AND MURDEROUS, AND FOR REASONS THAT WE DO NOT YET UNDERSTAND, THEY ARE CONSUMING HUMAN FLESH AS A MEANS OF SUSTENANCE."
"DR. GRIMES, IT IS REPORTED THAT THESE GHOULS FEEL NO PAIN?"
"THAT IS CORRECT."
"PHYSICAL TRAUMA DOES NOT AFFECT THEM IN ANY WAY, WITH THE EXCEPTION OF THE DESTRUCTION OF THE BRAIN OR TOTAL OBLITERATION OF THE BODY THROUGH CREMATION."
"AS BARBARIC AS IT MAY SOUND, ALL THOSE WHO DIE DURING THIS EMERGENCY MUST BE IMMEDIATELY REMOVED TO A SECURE LOCATION AND BURNED, WHETHER IT BE AT A CREMATORIUM, A FIELD OR EVEN OUR STREETS."
"CITIZENS NEED TO REMEMBER THAT THESE ARE NO LONGER OUR FRIENDS AND LOVED ONES AND SHOULD BE TREATED AS BIOLOGICAL HAZARDS."
"ARE THERE ANY INDICATIONS, DOCTOR, THAT THIS OUTBREAK IS LINKED TO A VIRUS THAT COULD BE CONTRACTED BY THE LIVING?"

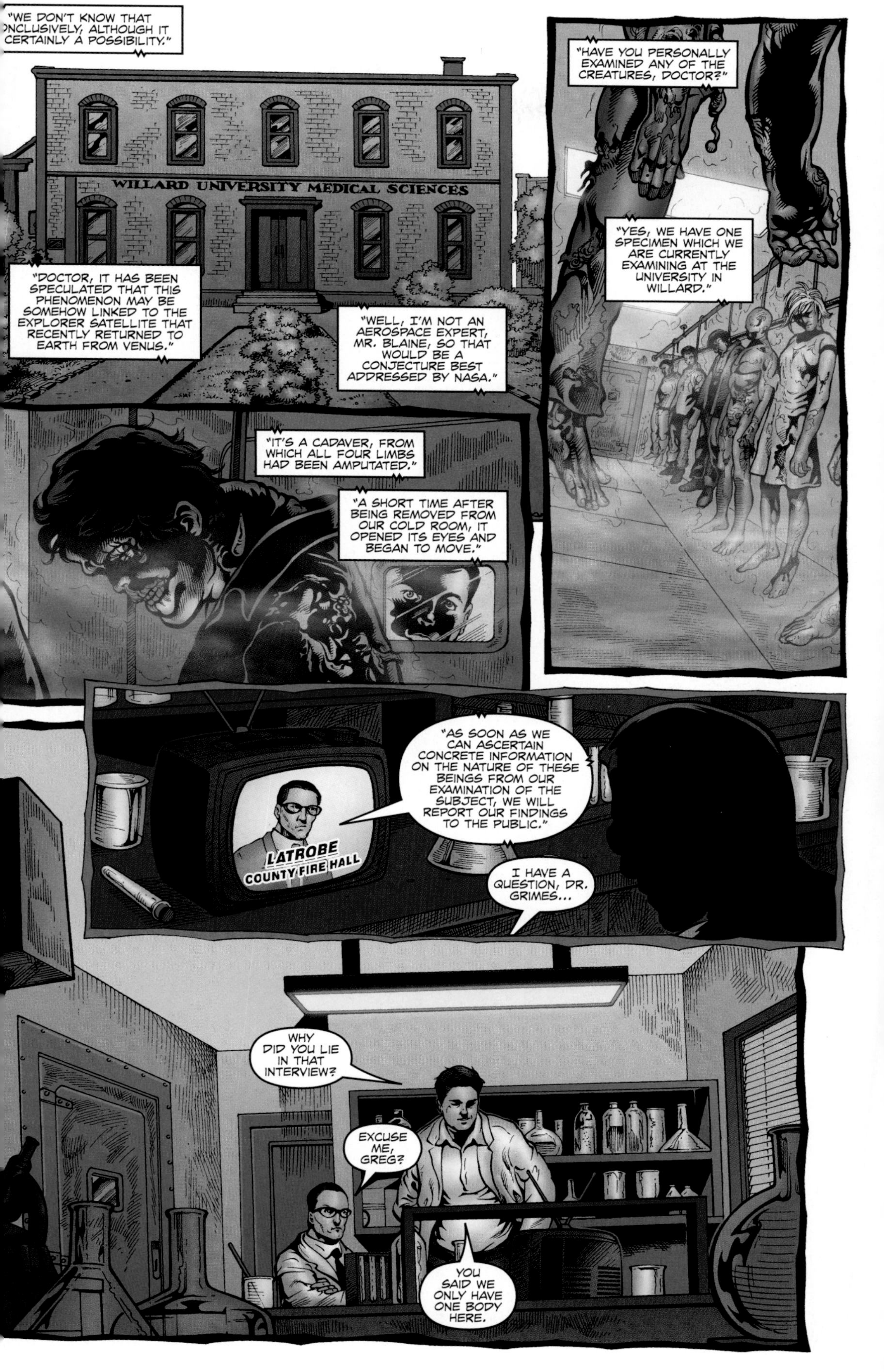
"WE DON'T KNOW THAT ONCLUSIVELY, ALTHOUGH IT CERTAINLY A POSSIBILITY."
WILLARD UNIVERSITY MEDICAL SCIENCES
"DOCTOR, IT HAS BEEN SPECULATED THAT THIS PHENOMENON MAY BE SOMEHOW LINKED TO THE EXPLORER SATELLITE THAT RECENTLY RETURNED TO EARTH FROM VENUS."
"WELL, I'M NOT AN AEROSPACE EXPERT, MR. BLAINE, SO THAT WOULD BE A CONJECTURE BEST ADDRESSED BY NASA."
"HAVE YOU PERSONALLY EXAMINED ANY OF THE CREATURES, DOCTOR?"
"YES, WE HAVE ONE SPECIMEN WHICH WE ARE CURRENTLY EXAMINING AT THE UNIVERSITY IN WILLARD."
"IT'S A CADAVER, FROM WHICH ALL FOUR LIMBS HAD BEEN AMPUTATED."
"A SHORT TIME AFTER BEING REMOVED FROM OUR COLD ROOM, IT OPENED ITS EYES AND BEGAN TO MOVE."
"AS SOON AS WE CAN ASCERTAIN CONCRETE INFORMATION ON THE NATURE OF THESE BEINGS FROM OUR EXAMINATION OF THE SUBJECT, WE WILL REPORT OUR FINDINGS TO THE PUBLIC."
LATROBE COUNTY FIRE HALL
I HAVE A QUESTION, DR. GRIMES...
WHY DID YOU LIE IN THAT INTERVIEW?
EXCUSE ME, GREG?
YOU SAID WE ONLY HAVE ONE BODY HERE.

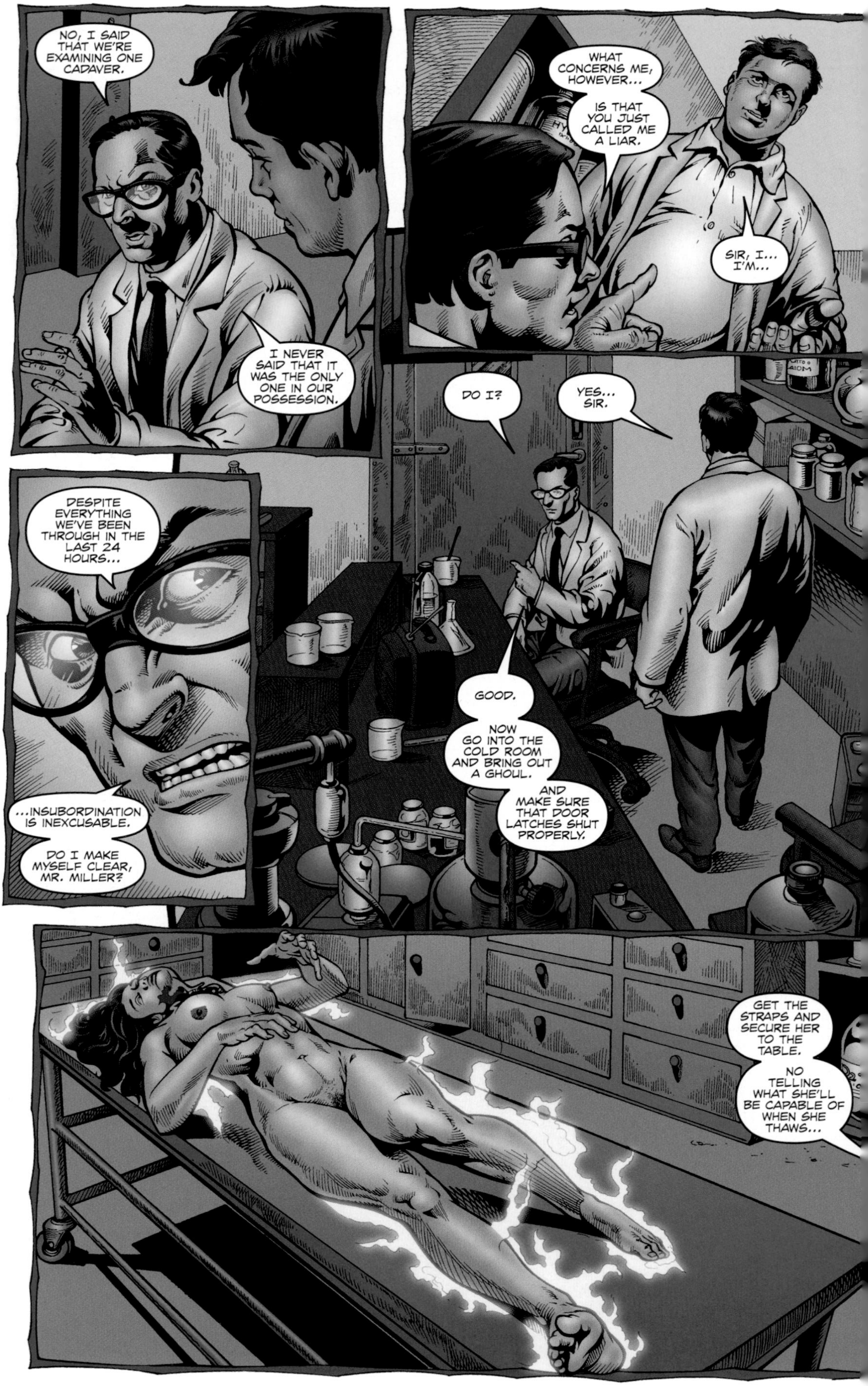
NO, I SAID THAT WE'RE EXAMINING ONE CADAVER.
I NEVER SAID THAT IT WAS THE ONLY ONE IN OUR POSSESSION.
WHAT CONCERNS ME, HOWEVER...
IS THAT YOU JUST CALLED ME A LIAR.
SIR, I... I'M...
DESPITE EVERYTHING WE'VE BEEN THROUGH IN THE LAST 24 HOURS...
...INSUBORDINATION IS INEXCUSABLE.
DO I MAKE MYSELF CLEAR, MR. MILLER?
DO I?
YES... SIR.
GOOD.
NOW GO INTO THE COLD ROOM AND BRING OUT A GHOUL.
AND MAKE SURE THAT DOOR LATCHES SHUT PROPERLY.
GET THE STRAPS AND SECURE HER TO THE TABLE.
NO TELLING WHAT SHE'LL BE CAPABLE OF WHEN SHE THAWS...

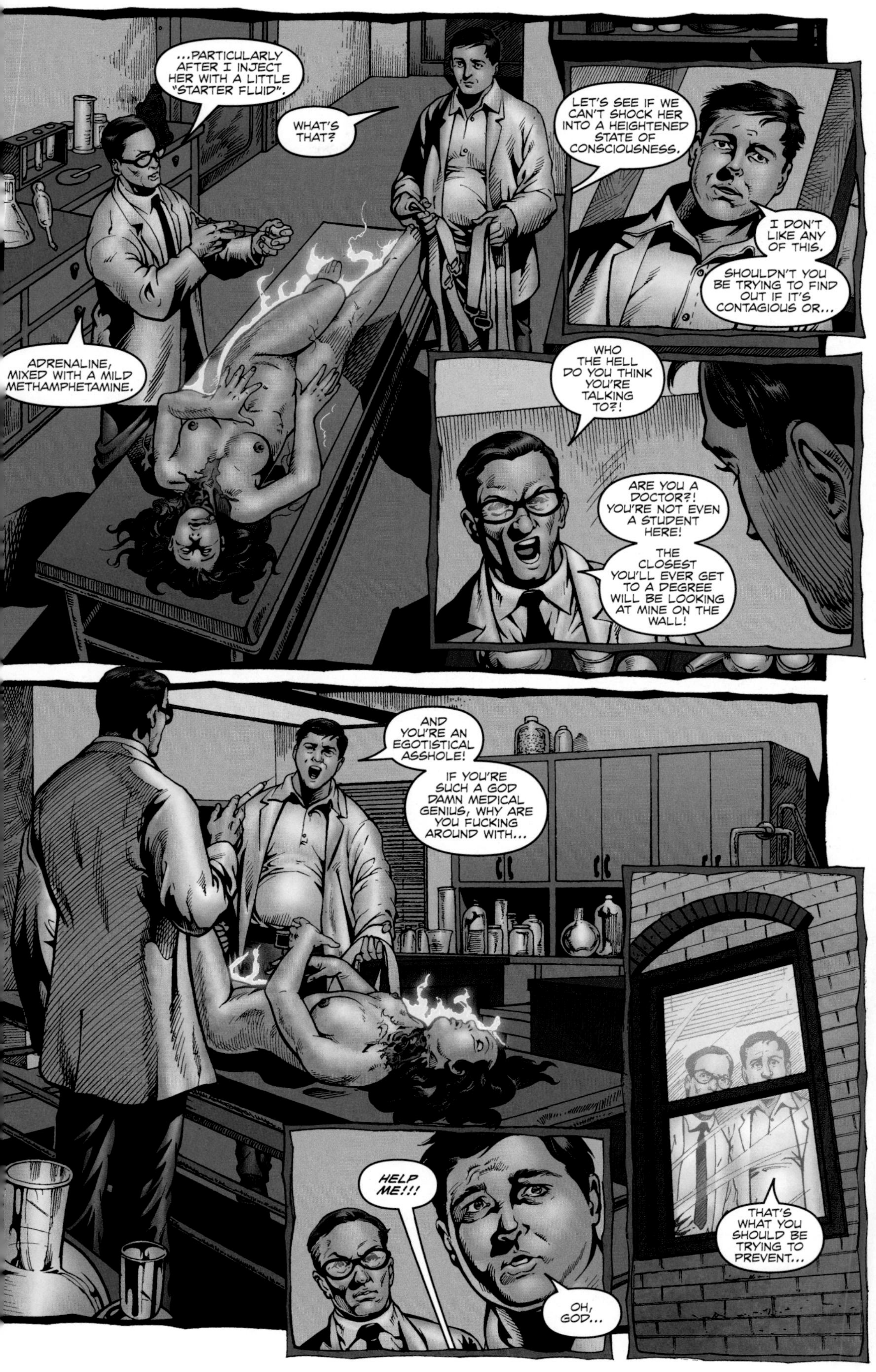
...PARTICULARLY AFTER I INJECT HER WITH A LITTLE "STARTER FLUID".
WHAT'S THAT?
ADRENALINE, MIXED WITH A MILD METHAMPHETAMINE.
LET'S SEE IF WE CAN'T SHOCK HER INTO A HEIGHTENED STATE OF CONSCIOUSNESS.
I DON'T LIKE ANY OF THIS.
SHOULDN'T YOU BE TRYING TO FIND OUT IF IT'S CONTAGIOUS OR...
WHO THE HELL DO YOU THINK YOU'RE TALKING TO?!
ARE YOU A DOCTOR?! YOU'RE NOT EVEN A STUDENT HERE!
THE CLOSEST YOU'LL EVER GET TO A DEGREE WILL BE LOOKING AT MINE ON THE WALL!
AND YOU'RE AN EGOTISTICAL ASSHOLE!
IF YOU'RE SUCH A GOD DAMN MEDICAL GENIUS, WHY ARE YOU FUCKING AROUND WITH...
HELP ME!!!
OH, GOD...
THAT'S WHAT YOU SHOULD BE TRYING TO PREVENT...

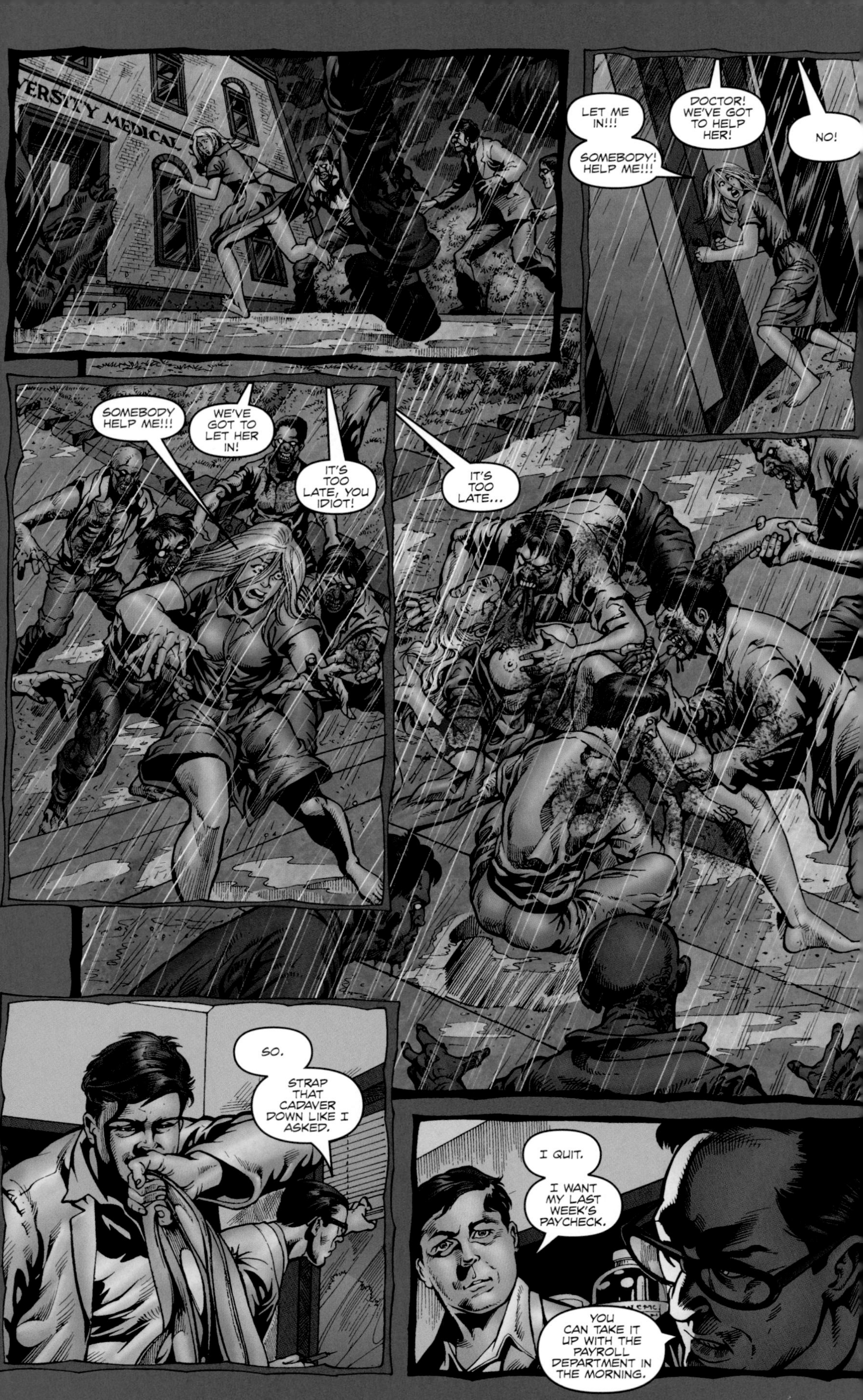
VERSITY MEDICAL
LET ME IN!!!
SOMEBODY! HELP ME!!!
DOCTOR! WE'VE GOT TO HELP HER!
NO!
SOMEBODY HELP ME!!!
WE'VE GOT TO LET HER IN!
IT'S TOO LATE, YOU IDIOT!
IT'S TOO LATE...
SO.
STRAP THAT CADAVER DOWN LIKE I ASKED.
I QUIT.
I WANT MY LAST WEEK'S PAYCHECK.
YOU CAN TAKE IT UP WITH THE PAYROLL DEPARTMENT IN THE MORNING.

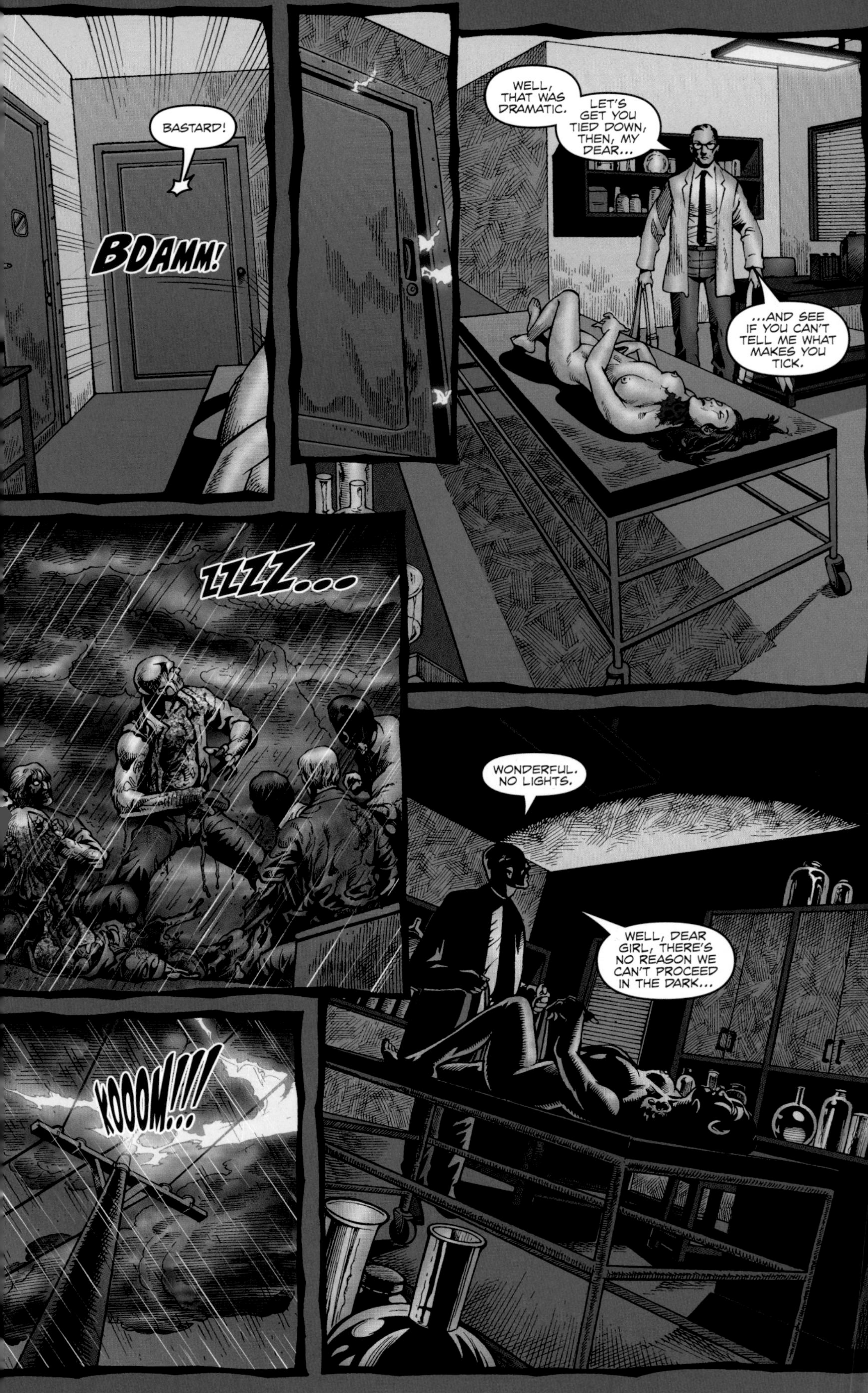
BASTARD!
BDAMM!
WELL, THAT WAS DRAMATIC.
LET'S GET YOU TIED DOWN, THEN, MY DEAR...
...AND SEE IF YOU CAN'T TELL ME WHAT MAKES YOU TICK.
ZZZZ...
WONDERFUL. NO LIGHTS.
WELL, DEAR GIRL, THERE'S NO REASON WE CAN'T PROCEED IN THE DARK...
KOOOM!!!

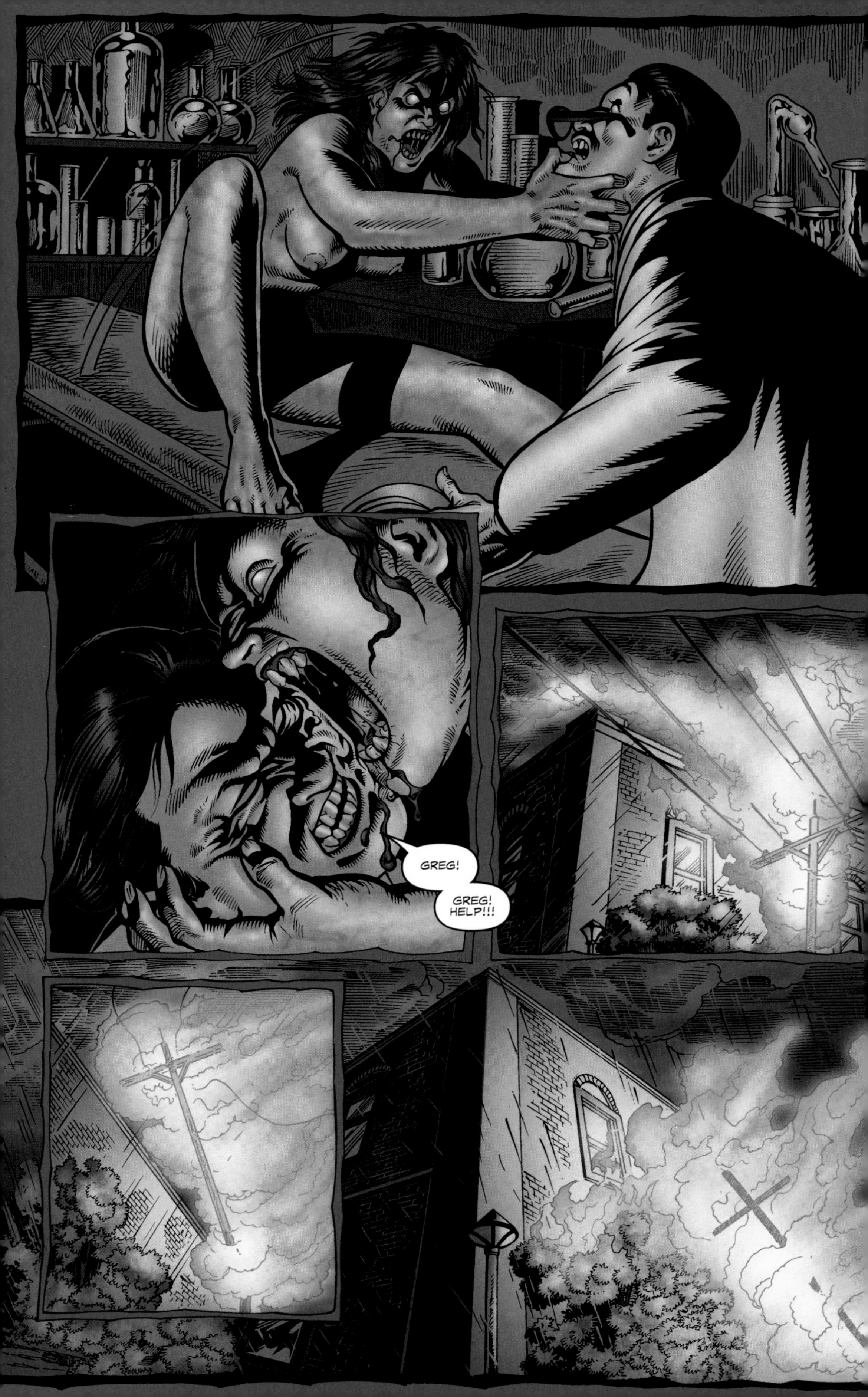
GREG!
GREG! HELP!!!

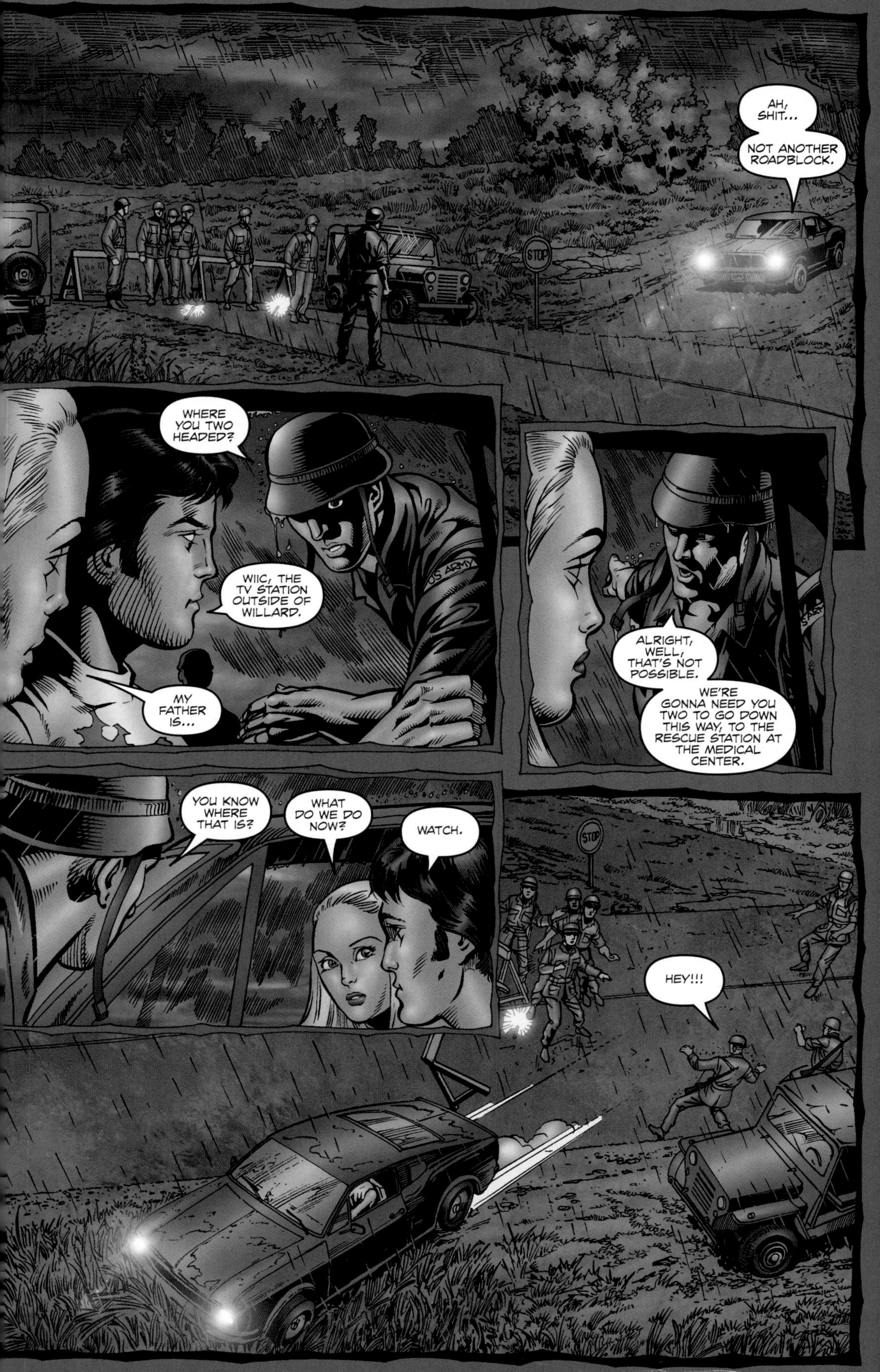
AH, SHIT...
NOT ANOTHER ROADBLOCK.
STOP
WHERE YOU TWO HEADED?
WIIC, THE TV STATION OUTSIDE OF WILLARD.
MY FATHER IS...
US ARMY
ALRIGHT, WELL, THAT'S NOT POSSIBLE.
WE'RE GONNA NEED YOU TWO TO GO DOWN THIS WAY, TO THE RESCUE STATION AT THE MEDICAL CENTER.
YOU KNOW WHERE THAT IS?
WHAT DO WE DO NOW?
WATCH.
STOP
HEY!!!

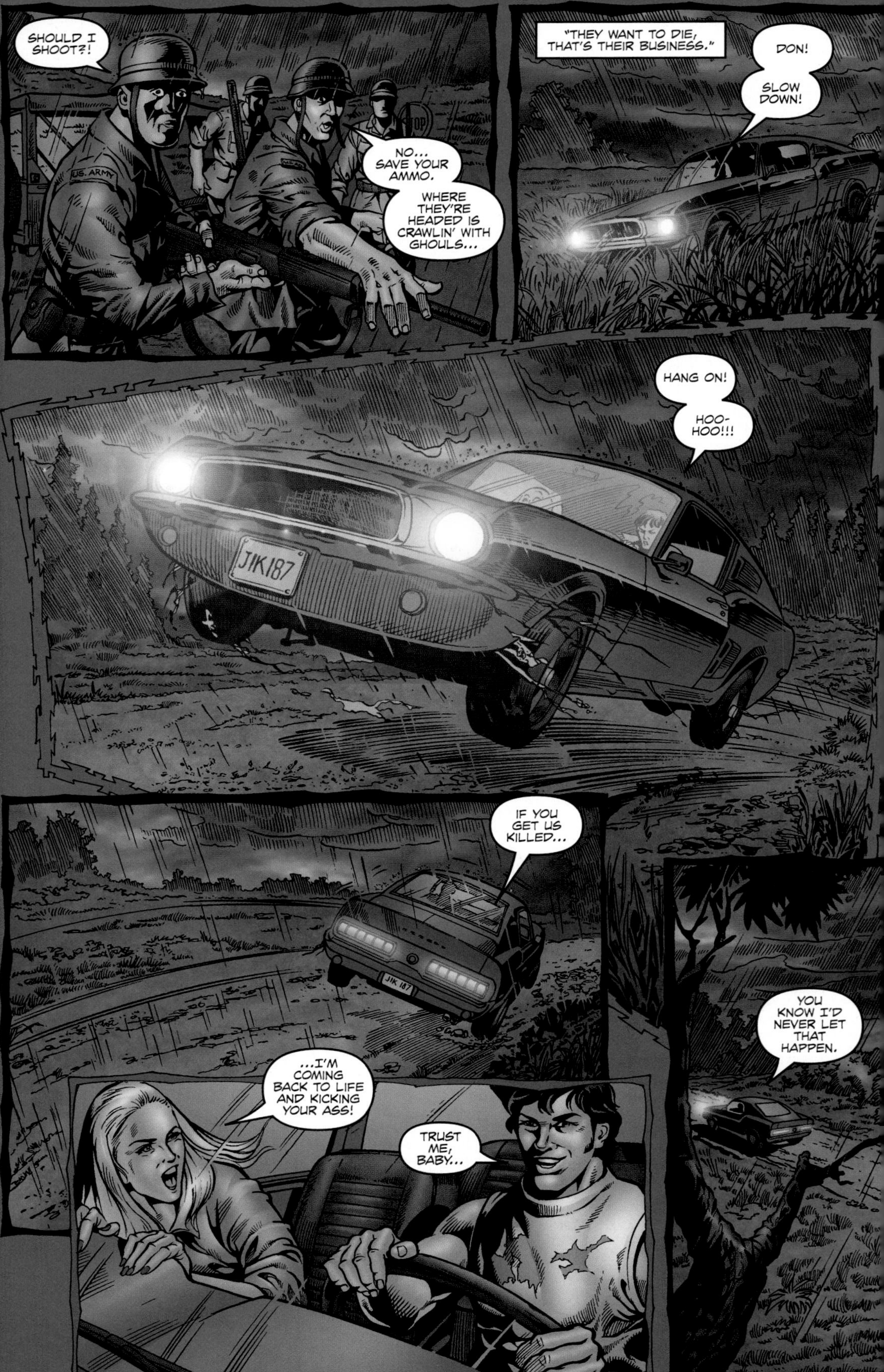
SHOULD I SHOOT?!
NO... SAVE YOUR AMMO.
WHERE THEY'RE HEADED IS CRAWLIN' WITH GHOULS...
"THEY WANT TO DIE, THAT'S THEIR BUSINESS."
DON!
SLOW DOWN!
HANG ON!
HOO-HOO!!!
JIK 187
IF YOU GET US KILLED...
...I'M COMING BACK TO LIFE AND KICKING YOUR ASS!
TRUST ME, BABY...
YOU KNOW I'D NEVER LET THAT HAPPEN.

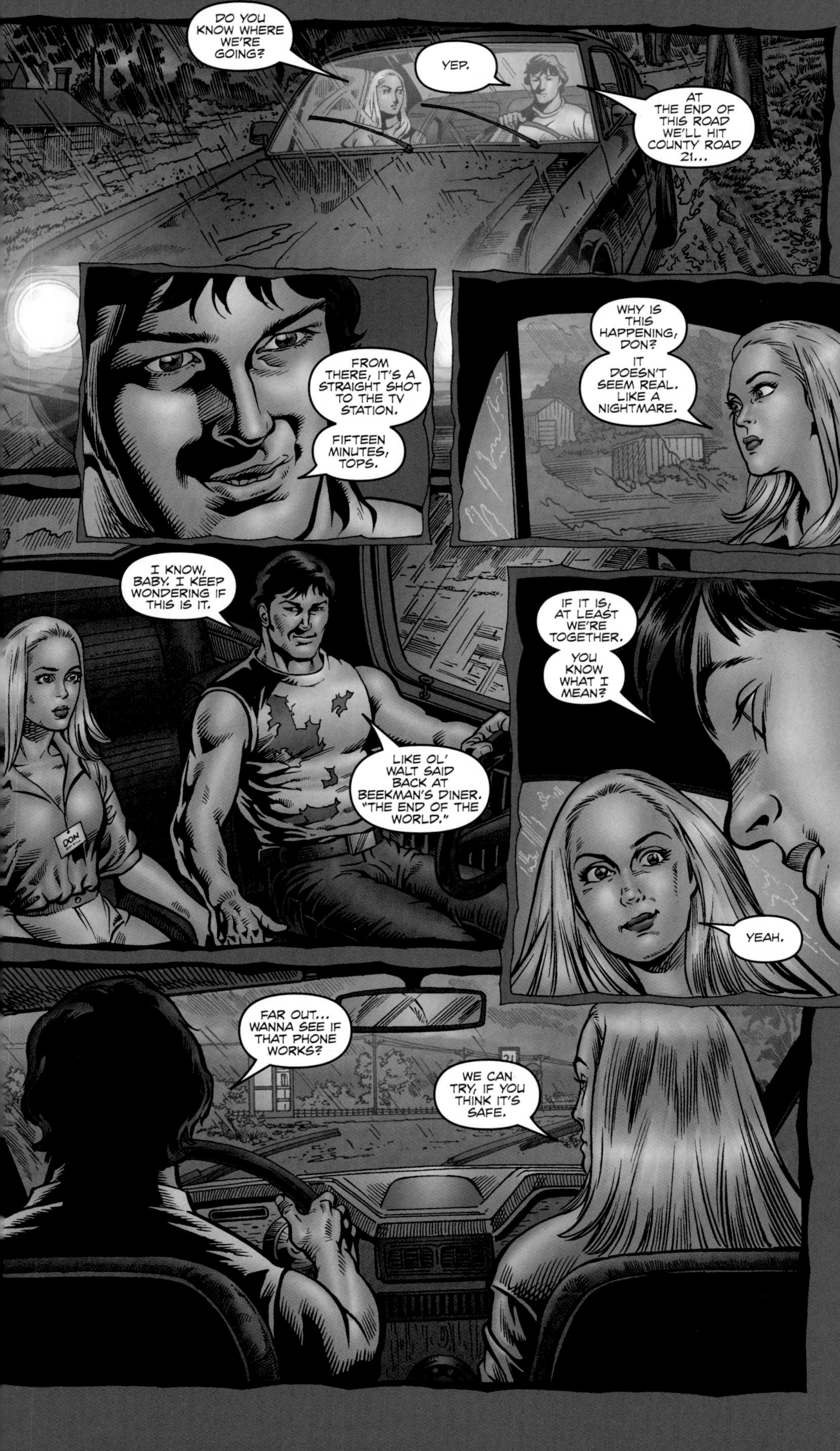
DO YOU KNOW WHERE WE'RE GOING?
YEP.
AT THE END OF THIS ROAD WE'LL HIT COUNTY ROAD 21...
FROM THERE, IT'S A STRAIGHT SHOT TO THE TV STATION.
FIFTEEN MINUTES, TOPS.
WHY IS THIS HAPPENING, DON?
IT DOESN'T SEEM REAL. LIKE A NIGHTMARE.
I KNOW, BABY. I KEEP WONDERING IF THIS IS IT.
LIKE OL' WALT SAID BACK AT BEEKMAN'S DINER. "THE END OF THE WORLD."
DON
IF IT IS, AT LEAST WE'RE TOGETHER.
YOU KNOW WHAT I MEAN?
YEAH.
FAR OUT... WANNA SEE IF THAT PHONE WORKS?
21
WE CAN TRY, IF YOU THINK IT'S SAFE.

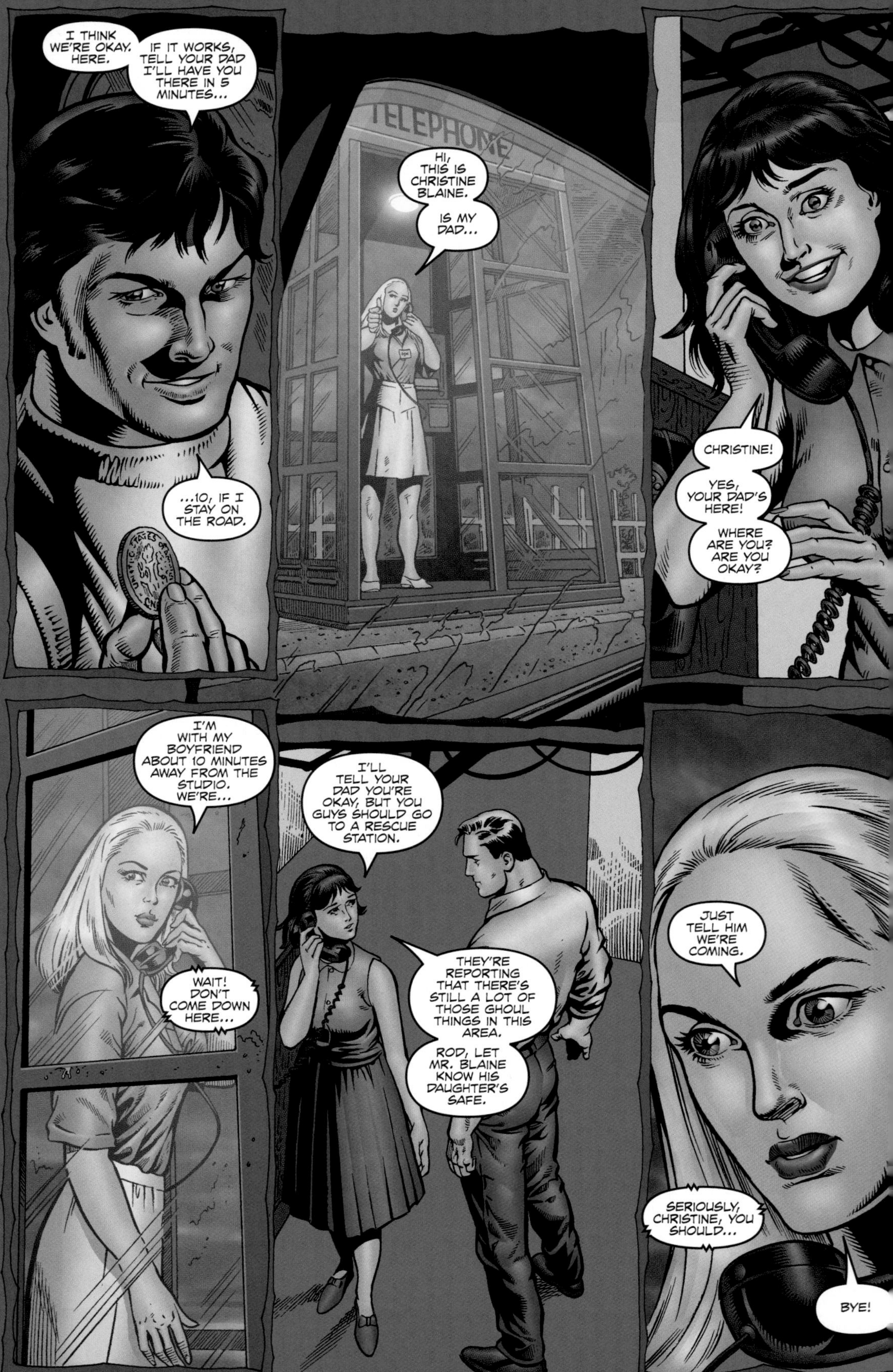
I THINK WE'RE OKAY. HERE.
IF IT WORKS, TELL YOUR DAD I'LL HAVE YOU THERE IN 5 MINUTES...
...10, IF I STAY ON THE ROAD.
TELEPHONE
HI, THIS IS CHRISTINE BLAINE.
IS MY DAD...
CHRISTINE!
YES, YOUR DAD'S HERE!
WHERE ARE YOU? ARE YOU OKAY?
I'M WITH MY BOYFRIEND ABOUT 10 MINUTES AWAY FROM THE STUDIO. WE'RE...
WAIT! DON'T COME DOWN HERE...
I'LL TELL YOUR DAD YOU'RE OKAY, BUT YOU GUYS SHOULD GO TO A RESCUE STATION.
THEY'RE REPORTING THAT THERE'S STILL A LOT OF THOSE GHOUL THINGS IN THIS AREA.
ROD, LET MR. BLAINE KNOW HIS DAUGHTER'S SAFE.
JUST TELL HIM WE'RE COMING.
SERIOUSLY, CHRISTINE, YOU SHOULD...
BYE!

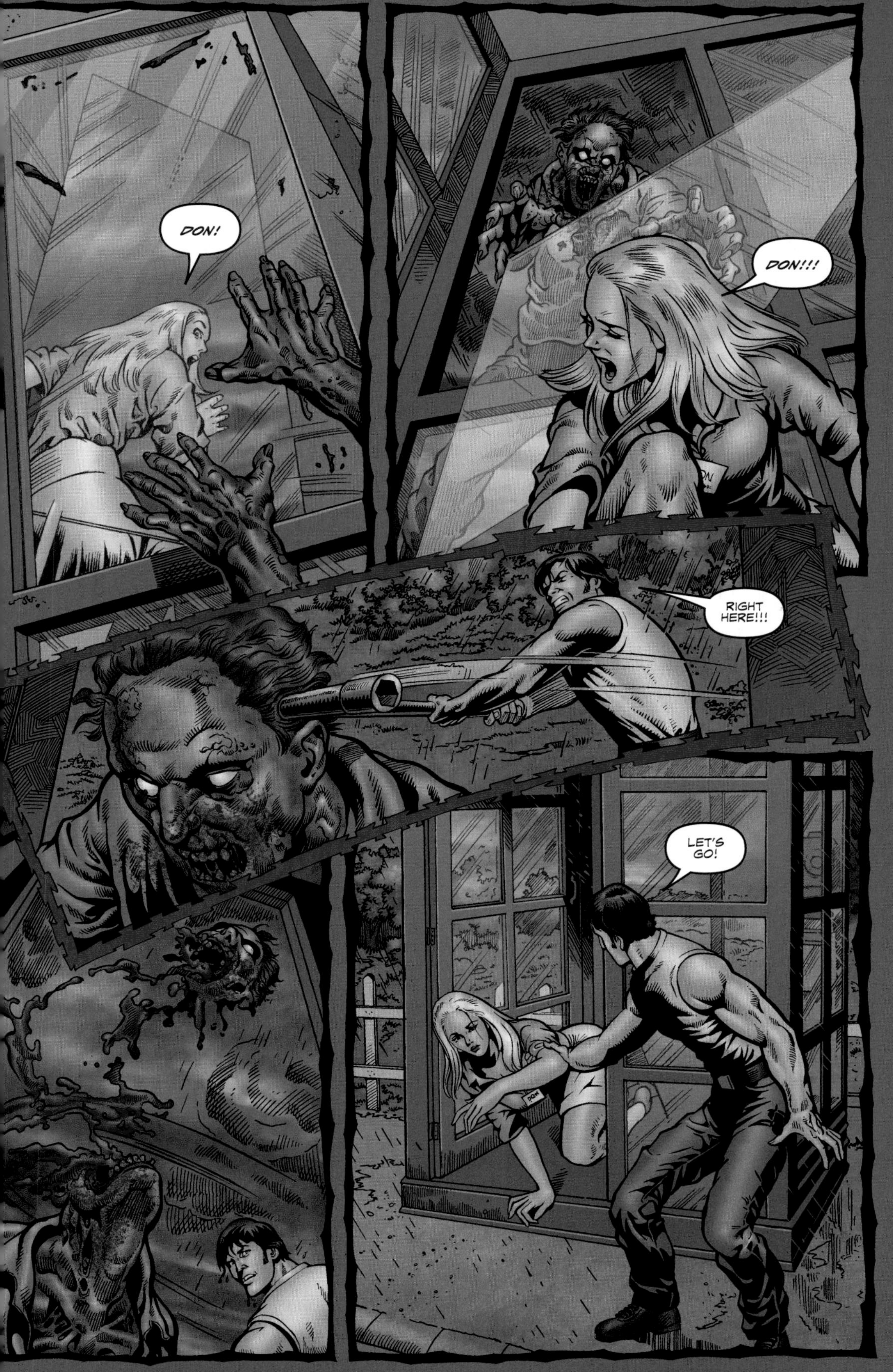
DON!
DON!!!
RIGHT HERE!!!
LET'S GO!

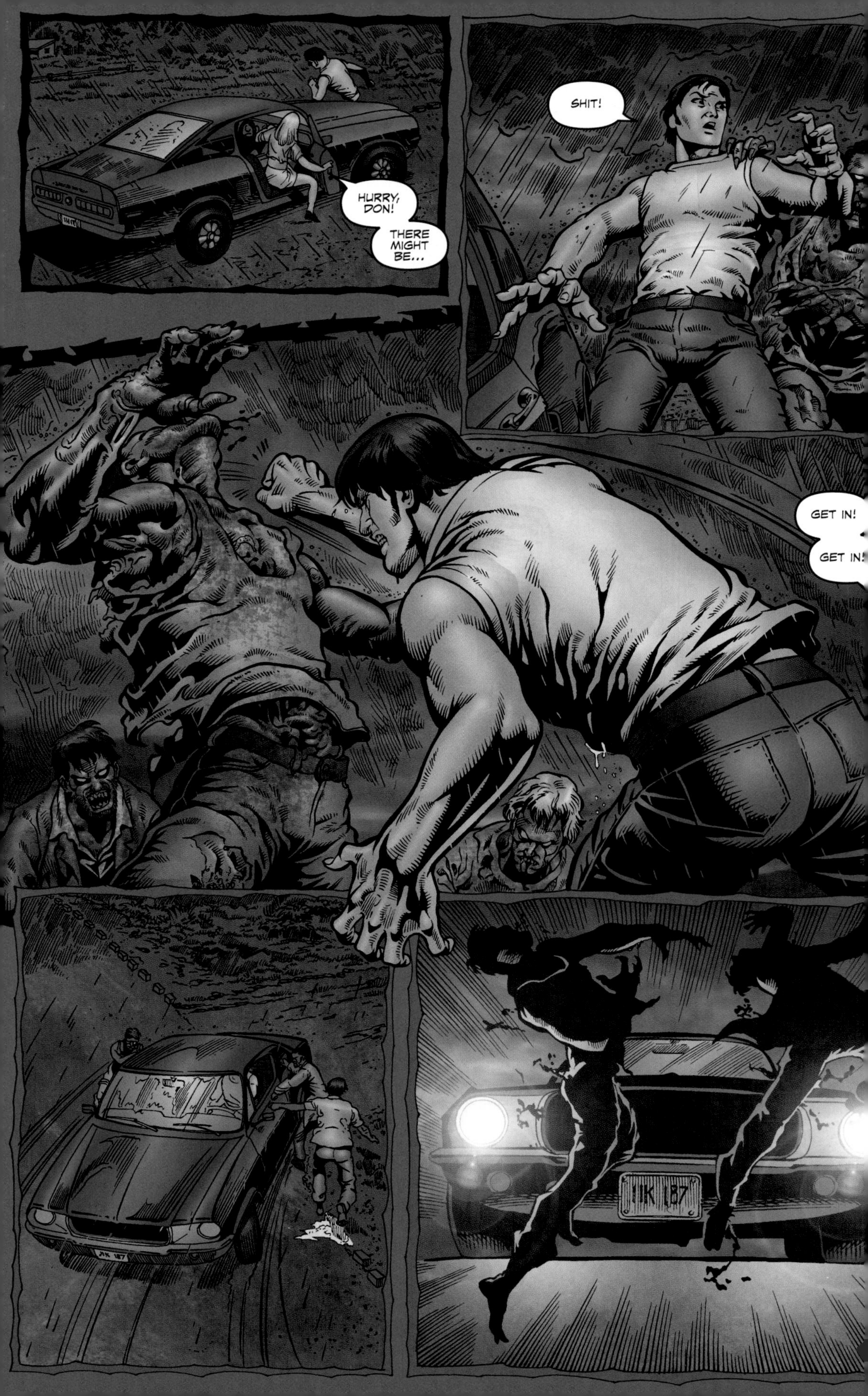
HURRY, DON!
THERE MIGHT BE...
SHIT!
GET IN!
GET IN!

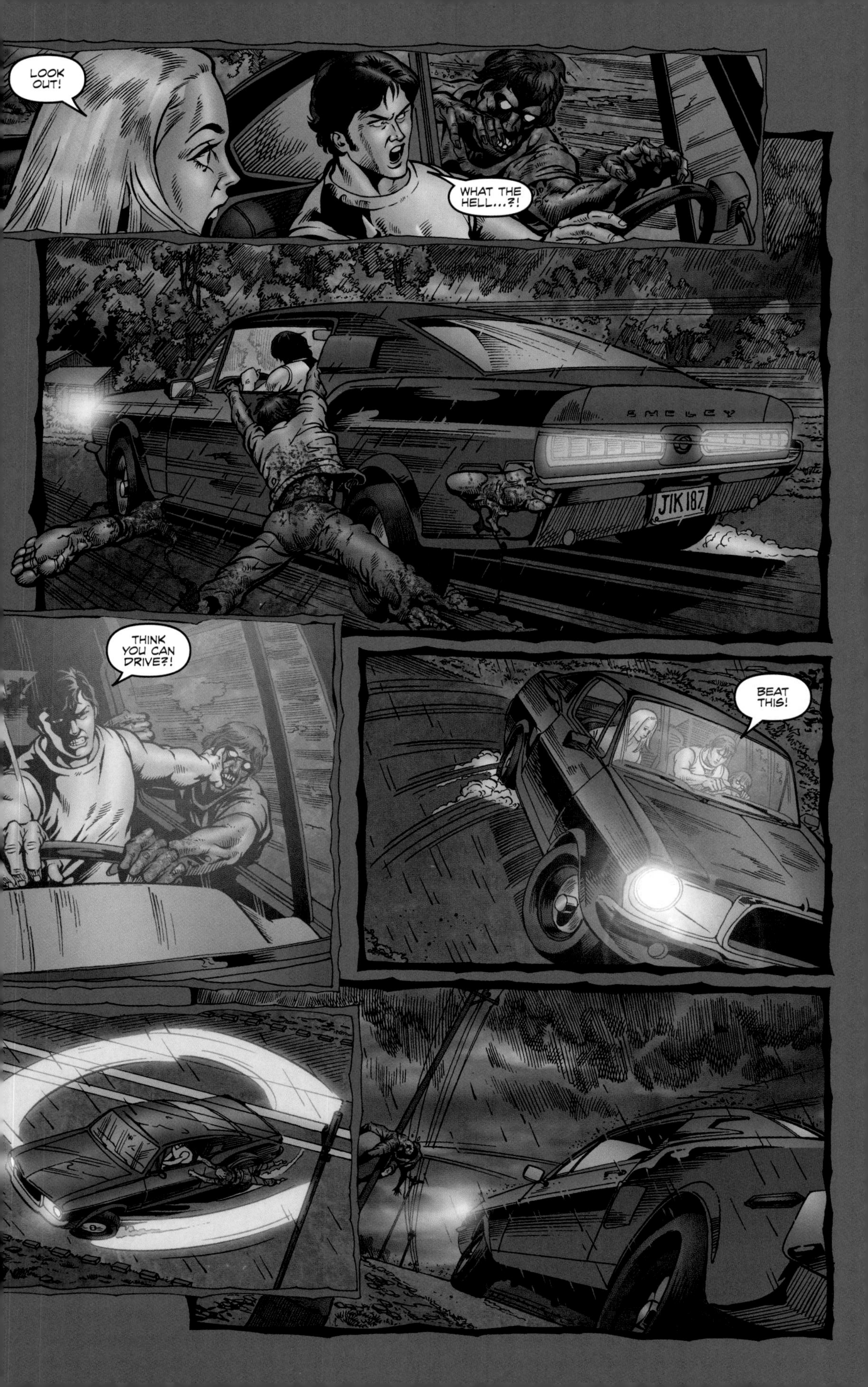
LOOK OUT!
WHAT THE HELL...?!
THINK YOU CAN DRIVE?!
BEAT THIS!
JIK 187

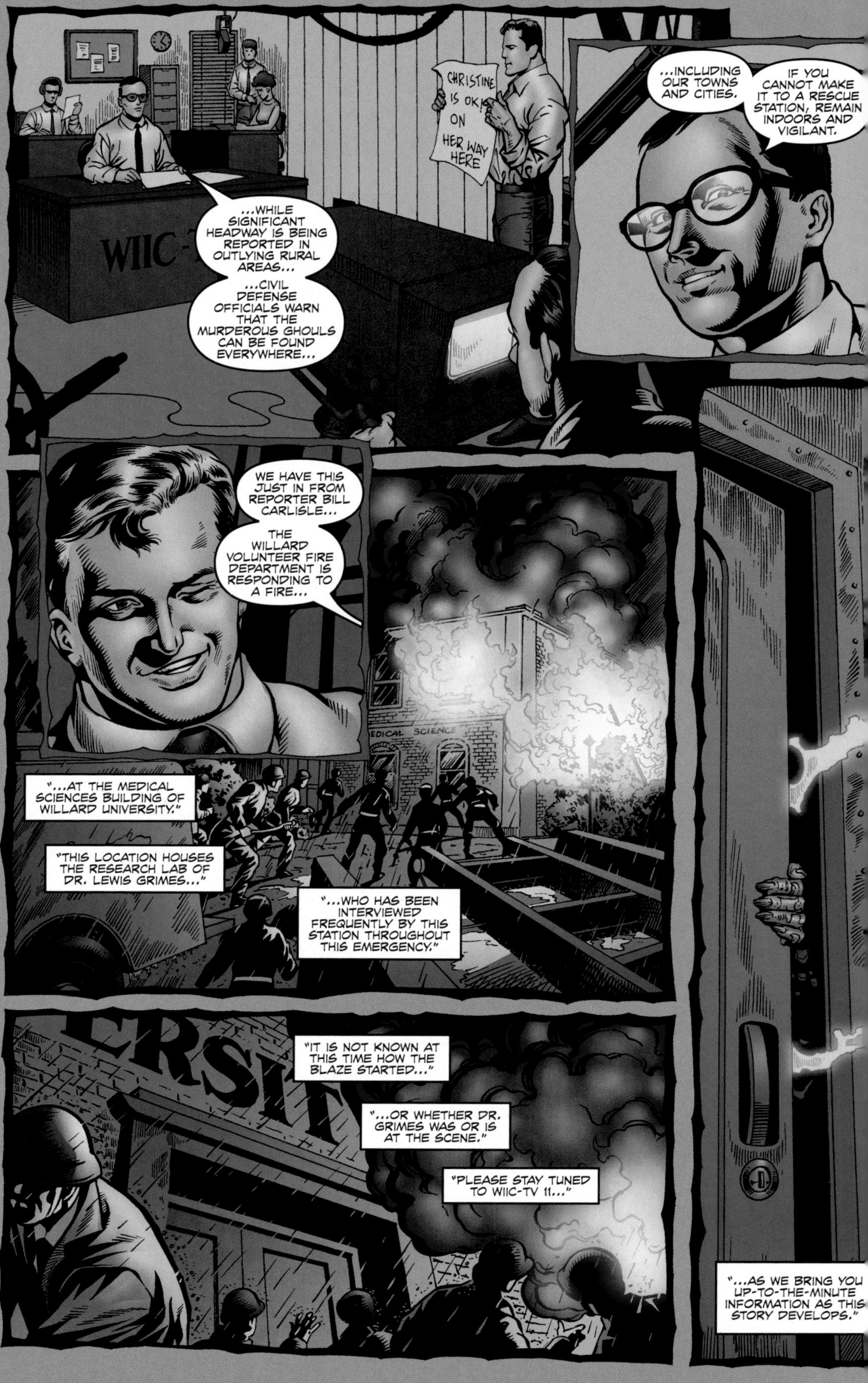
CHRISTINE IS OK! ON HER WAY HERE
WIIC-
...WHILE SIGNIFICANT HEADWAY IS BEING REPORTED IN OUTLYING RURAL AREAS...
...CIVIL DEFENSE OFFICIALS WARN THAT THE MURDEROUS GHOULS CAN BE FOUND EVERYWHERE...
...INCLUDING OUR TOWNS AND CITIES.
IF YOU CANNOT MAKE IT TO A RESCUE STATION, REMAIN INDOORS AND VIGILANT.
WE HAVE THIS JUST IN FROM REPORTER BILL CARLISLE...
THE WILLARD VOLUNTEER FIRE DEPARTMENT IS RESPONDING TO A FIRE...
"...AT THE MEDICAL SCIENCES BUILDING OF WILLARD UNIVERSITY."
"THIS LOCATION HOUSES THE RESEARCH LAB OF DR. LEWIS GRIMES..."
"...WHO HAS BEEN INTERVIEWED FREQUENTLY BY THIS STATION THROUGHOUT THIS EMERGENCY."
"IT IS NOT KNOWN AT THIS TIME HOW THE BLAZE STARTED..."
"...OR WHETHER DR. GRIMES WAS OR IS AT THE SCENE."
"PLEASE STAY TUNED TO WIIC-TV 11..."
"...AS WE BRING YOU UP-TO-THE-MINUTE INFORMATION AS THIS STORY DEVELOPS."

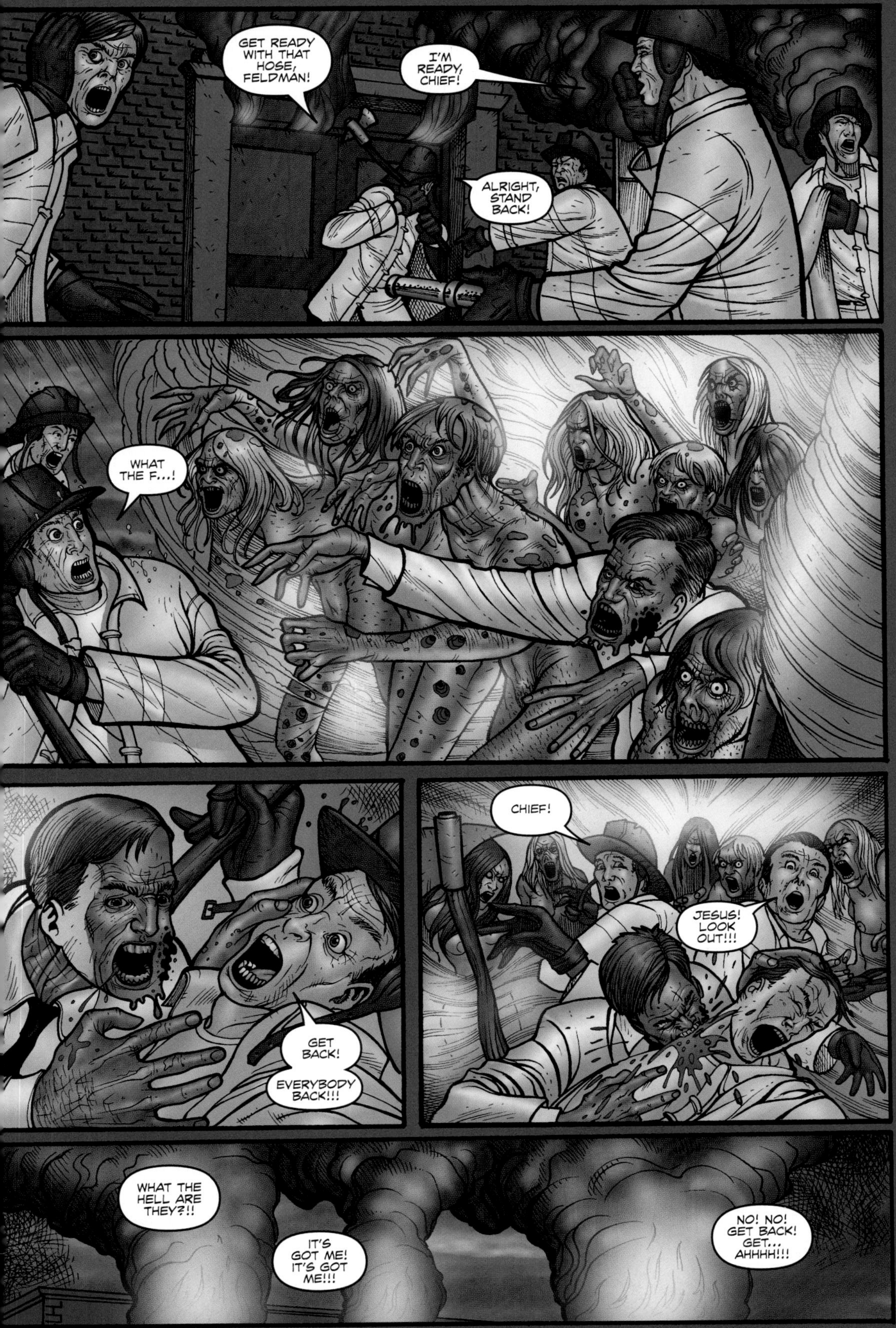
GET READY WITH THAT HOSE, FELDMAN!
I'M READY, CHIEF!
ALRIGHT, STAND BACK!
WHAT THE F...!
GET BACK!
EVERYBODY BACK!!!
CHIEF!
JESUS! LOOK OUT!!!
WHAT THE HELL ARE THEY?!!
IT'S GOT ME! IT'S GOT ME!!!
NO! NO! GET BACK! GET... AHHHH!!!

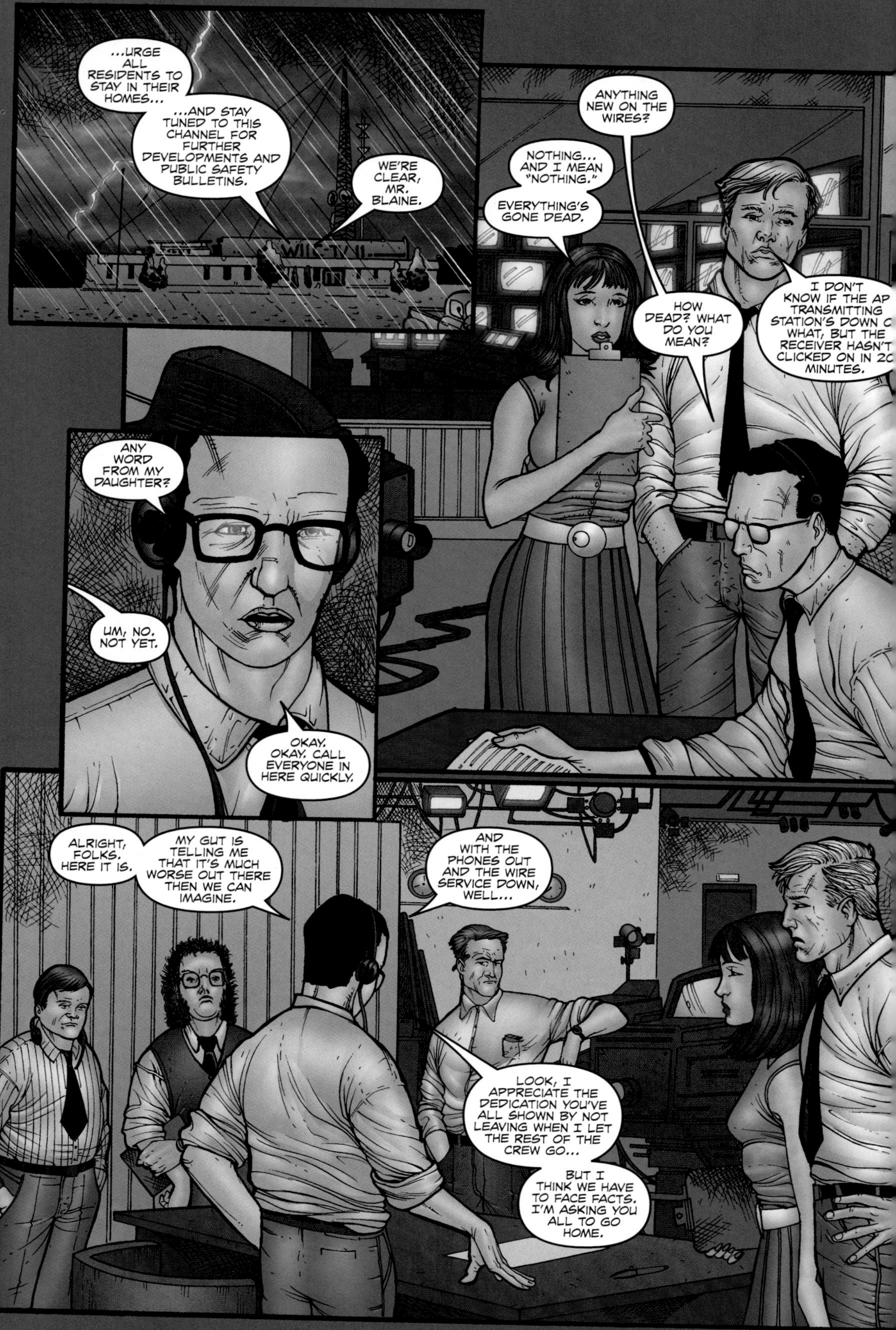
...URGE ALL RESIDENTS TO STAY IN THEIR HOMES...
...AND STAY TUNED TO THIS CHANNEL FOR FURTHER DEVELOPMENTS AND PUBLIC SAFETY BULLETINS.
WE'RE CLEAR, MR. BLAINE.
ANYTHING NEW ON THE WIRES?
NOTHING... AND I MEAN "NOTHING."
EVERYTHING'S GONE DEAD.
HOW DEAD? WHAT DO YOU MEAN?
I DON'T KNOW IF THE AP TRANSMITTING STATION'S DOWN O WHAT, BUT THE RECEIVER HASN'T CLICKED ON IN 20 MINUTES.
ANY WORD FROM MY DAUGHTER?
UM, NO. NOT YET.
OKAY. OKAY. CALL EVERYONE IN HERE QUICKLY.
ALRIGHT, FOLKS. HERE IT IS.
MY GUT IS TELLING ME THAT IT'S MUCH WORSE OUT THERE THEN WE CAN IMAGINE.
AND WITH THE PHONES OUT AND THE WIRE SERVICE DOWN, WELL...
LOOK, I APPRECIATE THE DEDICATION YOU'VE ALL SHOWN BY NOT LEAVING WHEN I LET THE REST OF THE CREW GO...
BUT I THINK WE HAVE TO FACE FACTS. I'M ASKING YOU ALL TO GO HOME.

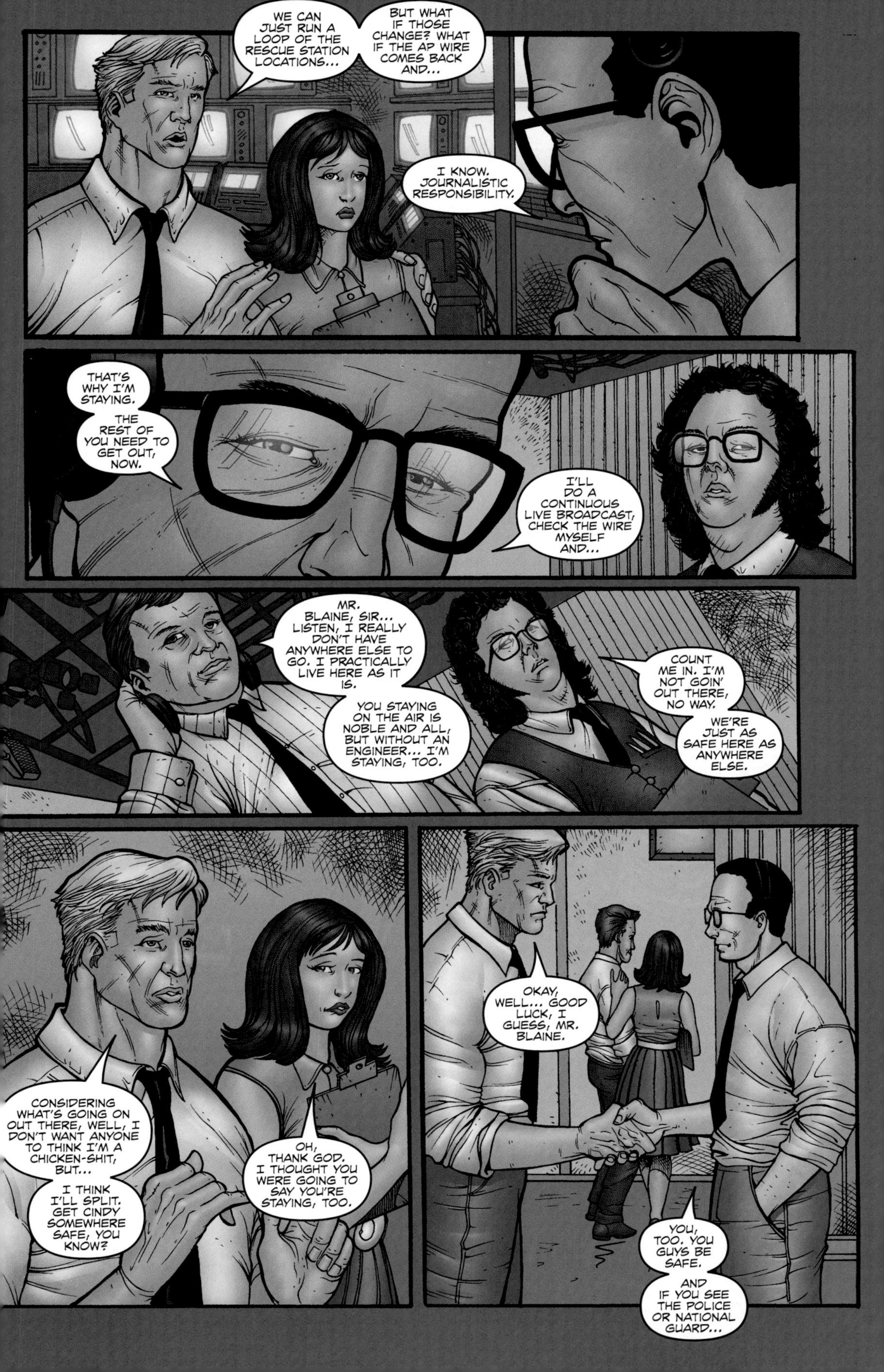
WE CAN JUST RUN A LOOP OF THE RESCUE STATION LOCATIONS...
BUT WHAT IF THOSE CHANGE? WHAT IF THE AP WIRE COMES BACK AND...
I KNOW. JOURNALISTIC RESPONSIBILITY.
THAT'S WHY I'M STAYING.
THE REST OF YOU NEED TO GET OUT, NOW.
I'LL DO A CONTINUOUS LIVE BROADCAST, CHECK THE WIRE MYSELF AND...
MR. BLAINE, SIR... LISTEN, I REALLY DON'T HAVE ANYWHERE ELSE TO GO. I PRACTICALLY LIVE HERE AS IT IS.
YOU STAYING ON THE AIR IS NOBLE AND ALL, BUT WITHOUT AN ENGINEER... I'M STAYING, TOO.
COUNT ME IN. I'M NOT GOIN' OUT THERE, NO WAY.
WE'RE JUST AS SAFE HERE AS ANYWHERE ELSE.
CONSIDERING WHAT'S GOING ON OUT THERE, WELL, I DON'T WANT ANYONE TO THINK I'M A CHICKEN-SHIT, BUT...
I THINK I'LL SPLIT. GET CINDY SOMEWHERE SAFE, YOU KNOW?
OH, THANK GOD. I THOUGHT YOU WERE GOING TO SAY YOU'RE STAYING, TOO.
OKAY, WELL... GOOD LUCK, I GUESS, MR. BLAINE.
YOU, TOO. YOU GUYS BE SAFE.
AND IF YOU SEE THE POLICE OR NATIONAL GUARD...

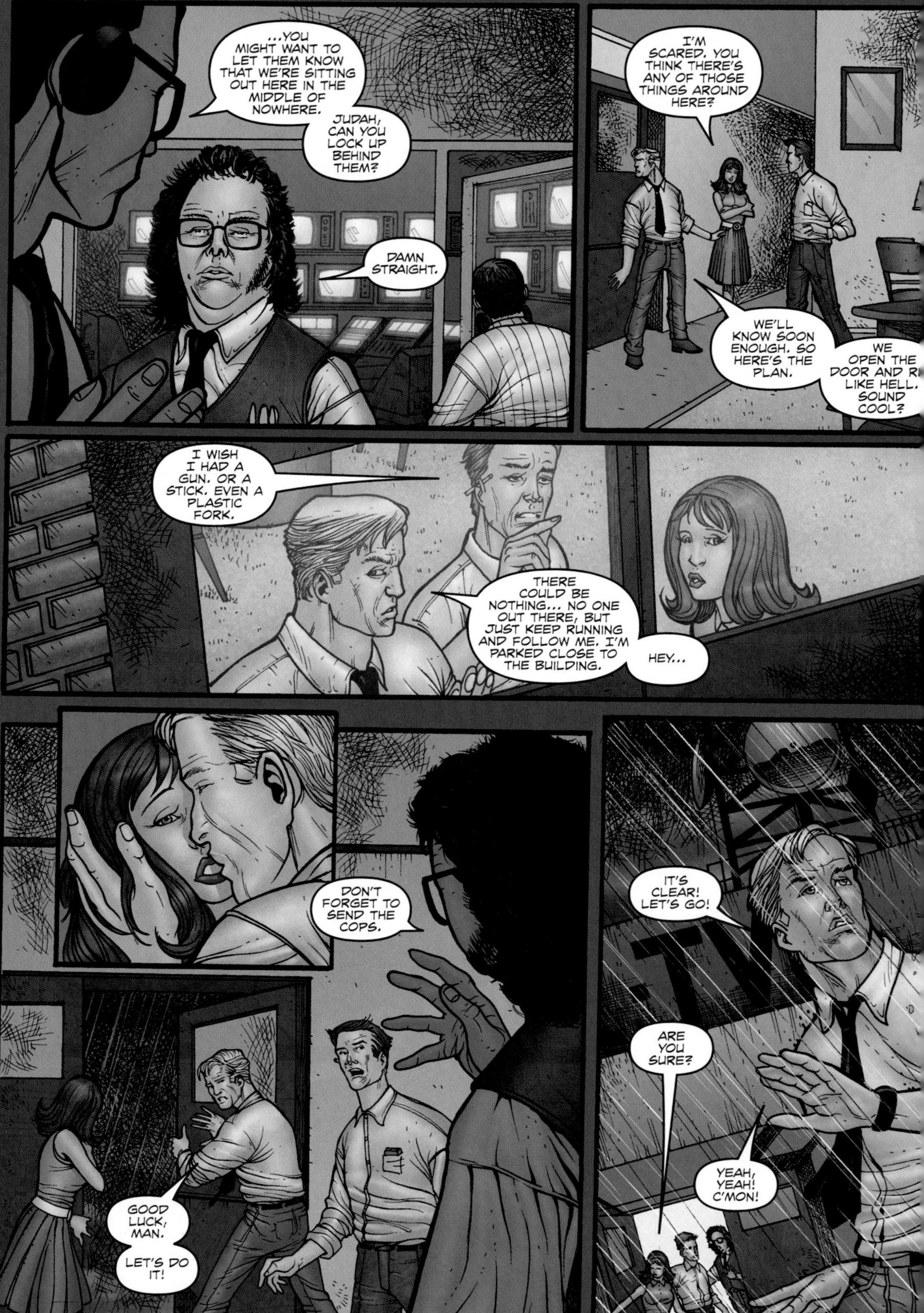
...YOU MIGHT WANT TO LET THEM KNOW THAT WE'RE SITTING OUT HERE IN THE MIDDLE OF NOWHERE.
JUDAH, CAN YOU LOCK UP BEHIND THEM?
DAMN STRAIGHT.
I'M SCARED. YOU THINK THERE'S ANY OF THOSE THINGS AROUND HERE?
WE'LL KNOW SOON ENOUGH. SO HERE'S THE PLAN.
WE OPEN THE DOOR AND R LIKE HELL. SOUND COOL?
I WISH I HAD A GUN. OR A STICK. EVEN A PLASTIC FORK.
THERE COULD BE NOTHING... NO ONE OUT THERE, BUT JUST KEEP RUNNING AND FOLLOW ME. I'M PARKED CLOSE TO THE BUILDING.
HEY...
DON'T FORGET TO SEND THE COPS.
GOOD LUCK, MAN.
LET'S DO IT!
IT'S CLEAR! LET'S GO!
ARE YOU SURE?
YEAH, YEAH! C'MON!

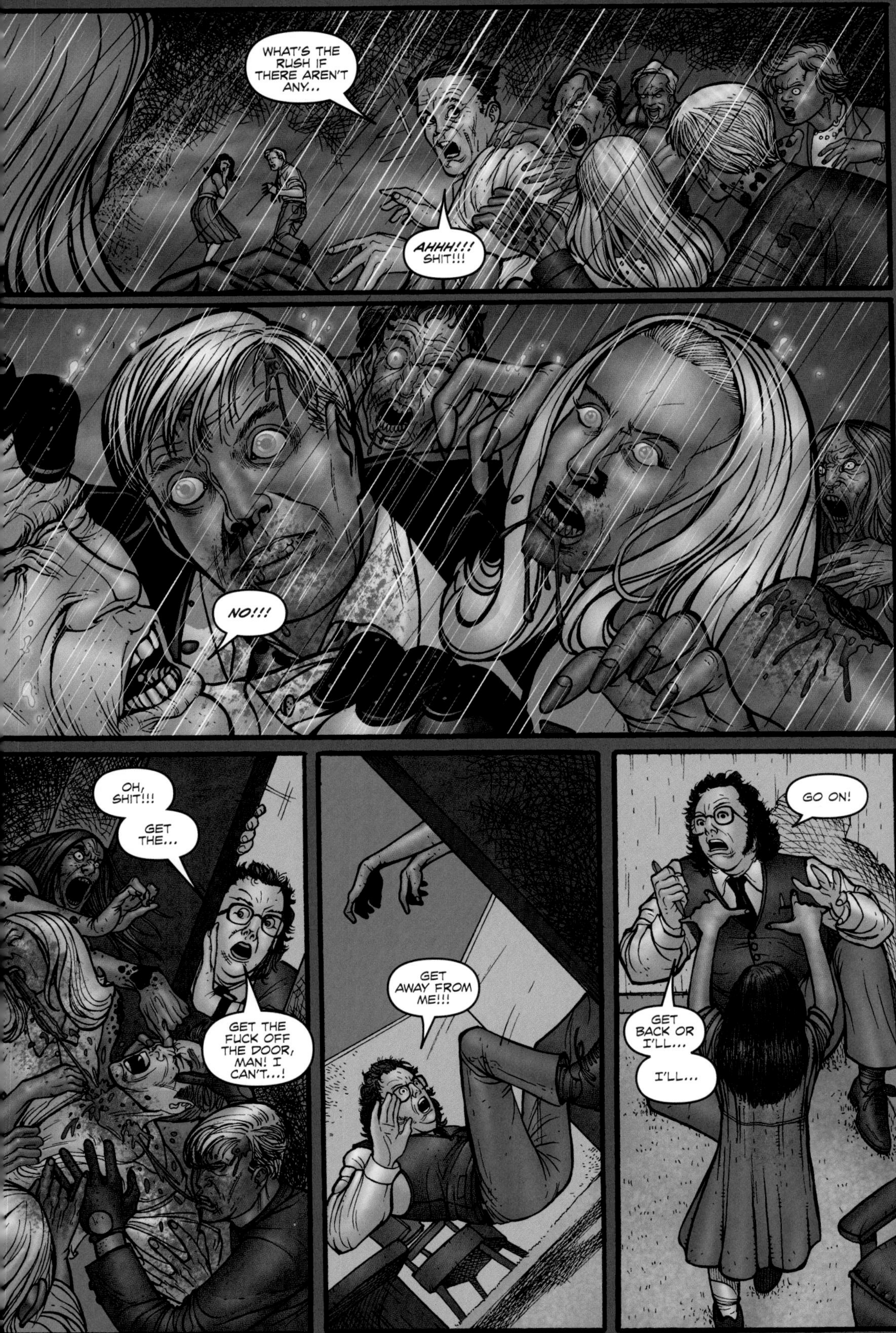
WHAT'S THE RUSH IF THERE AREN'T ANY...
AHHH!!! SHIT!!!
NO!!!
OH, SHIT!!!
GET THE...
GET THE FUCK OFF THE DOOR, MAN! I CAN'T...!
GET AWAY FROM ME!!!
GO ON!
GET BACK OR I'LL...
I'LL...

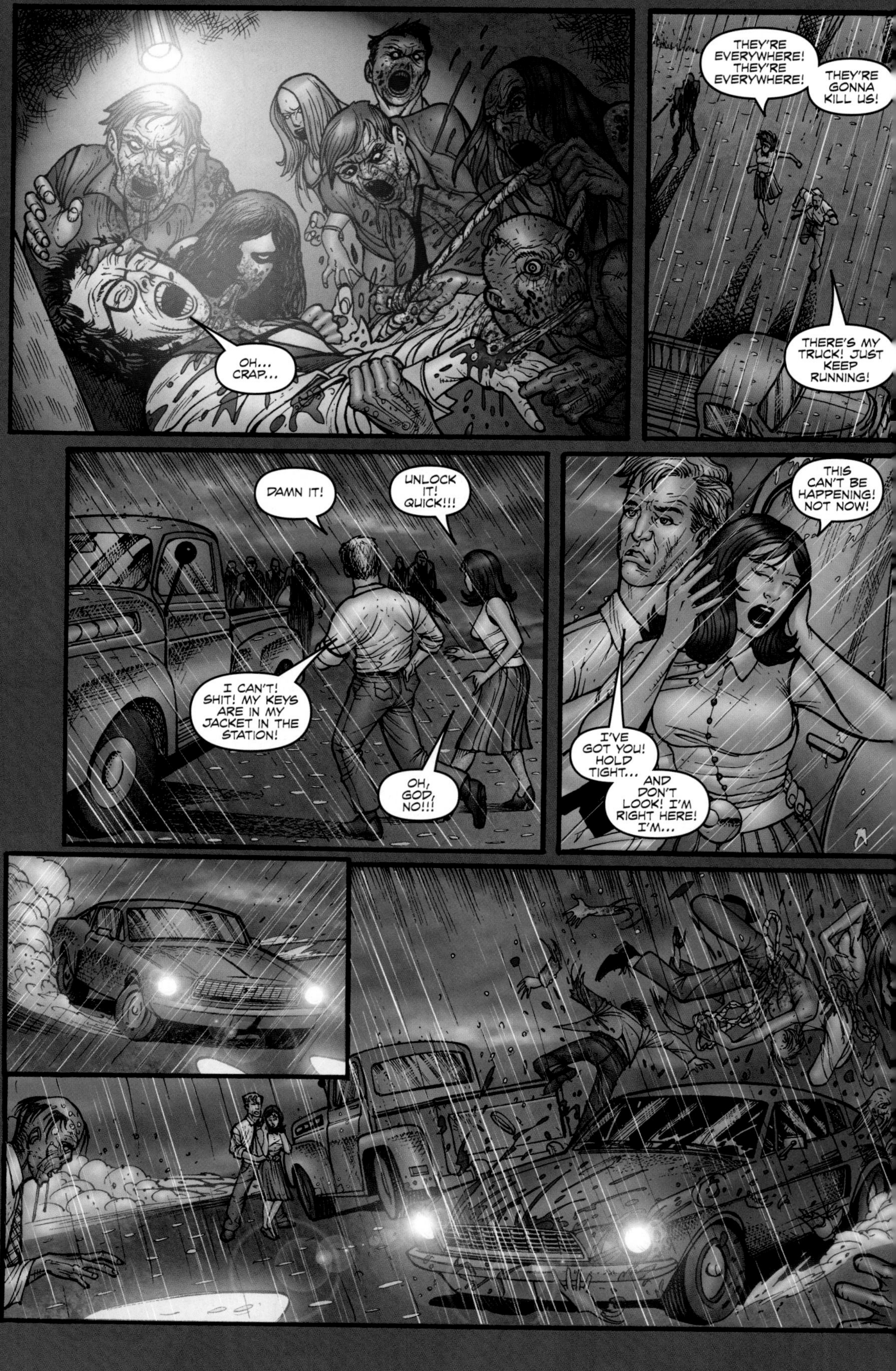
OH... CRAP...
THEY'RE EVERYWHERE! THEY'RE EVERYWHERE!
THEY'RE GONNA KILL US!
THERE'S MY TRUCK! JUST KEEP RUNNING!
DAMN IT!
UNLOCK IT! QUICK!!!
I CAN'T! SHIT! MY KEYS ARE IN MY JACKET IN THE STATION!
OH, GOD, NO!!!
THIS CAN'T BE HAPPENING! NOT NOW!
I'VE GOT YOU! HOLD TIGHT...
AND DON'T LOOK! I'M RIGHT HERE! I'M...

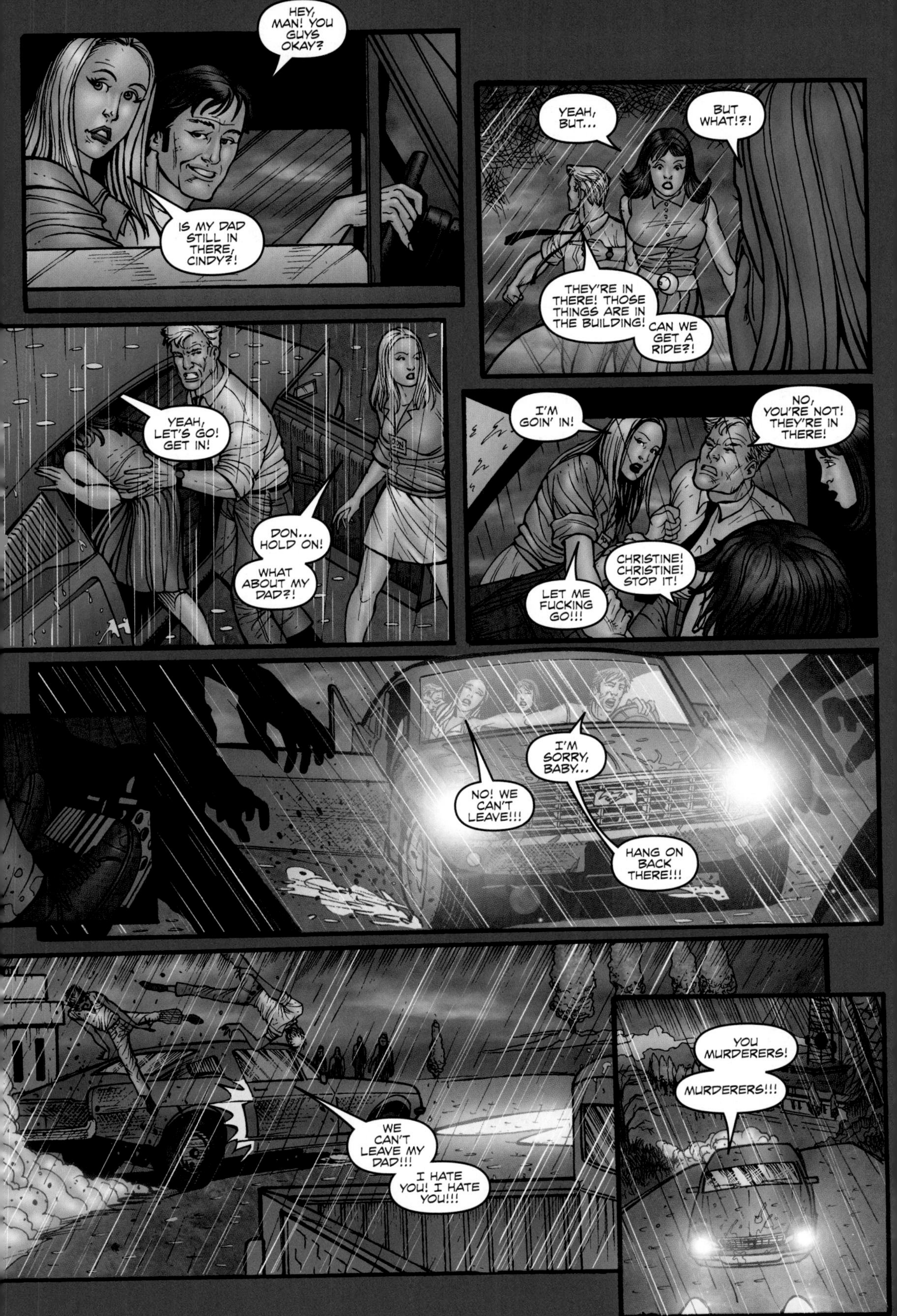
HEY, MAN! YOU GUYS OKAY?
IS MY DAD STILL IN THERE, CINDY?!
YEAH, BUT...
BUT WHAT!?!
THEY'RE IN THERE! THOSE THINGS ARE IN THE BUILDING!
CAN WE GET A RIDE?!
YEAH, LET'S GO! GET IN!
DON... HOLD ON!
WHAT ABOUT MY DAD?!
I'M GOIN' IN!
NO, YOU'RE NOT! THEY'RE IN THERE!
CHRISTINE! CHRISTINE! STOP IT!
LET ME FUCKING GO!!!
I'M SORRY, BABY...
NO! WE CAN'T LEAVE!!!
HANG ON BACK THERE!!!
WE CAN'T LEAVE MY DAD!!!
I HATE YOU! I HATE YOU!!!
YOU MURDERERS!
MURDERERS!!!

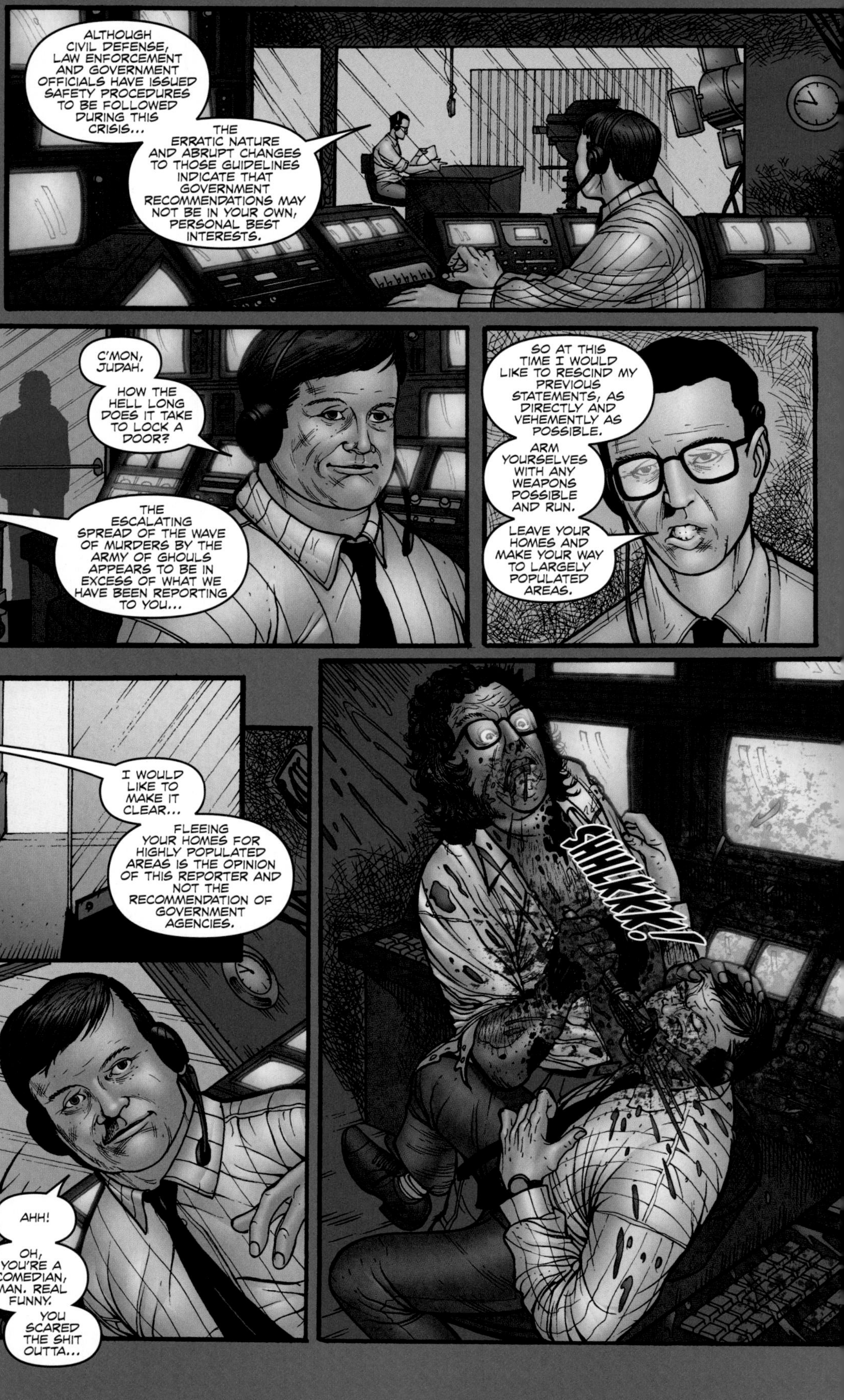
ALTHOUGH CIVIL DEFENSE, LAW ENFORCEMENT AND GOVERNMENT OFFICIALS HAVE ISSUED SAFETY PROCEDURES TO BE FOLLOWED DURING THIS CRISIS...
THE ERRATIC NATURE AND ABRUPT CHANGES TO THOSE GUIDELINES INDICATE THAT GOVERNMENT RECOMMENDATIONS MAY NOT BE IN YOUR OWN, PERSONAL BEST INTERESTS.
C'MON, JUDAH.
HOW THE HELL LONG DOES IT TAKE TO LOCK A DOOR?
THE ESCALATING SPREAD OF THE WAVE OF MURDERS BY THE ARMY OF GHOULS APPEARS TO BE IN EXCESS OF WHAT WE HAVE BEEN REPORTING TO YOU...
SO AT THIS TIME I WOULD LIKE TO RESCIND MY PREVIOUS STATEMENTS, AS DIRECTLY AND VEHEMENTLY AS POSSIBLE.
ARM YOURSELVES WITH ANY WEAPONS POSSIBLE AND RUN.
LEAVE YOUR HOMES AND MAKE YOUR WAY TO LARGELY POPULATED AREAS.
I WOULD LIKE TO MAKE IT CLEAR...
FLEEING YOUR HOMES FOR HIGHLY POPULATED AREAS IS THE OPINION OF THIS REPORTER AND NOT THE RECOMMENDATION OF GOVERNMENT AGENCIES.
AHH!
OH, YOU'RE A COMEDIAN, MAN. REAL FUNNY.
YOU SCARED THE SHIT OUTTA...
SHHLKKK!

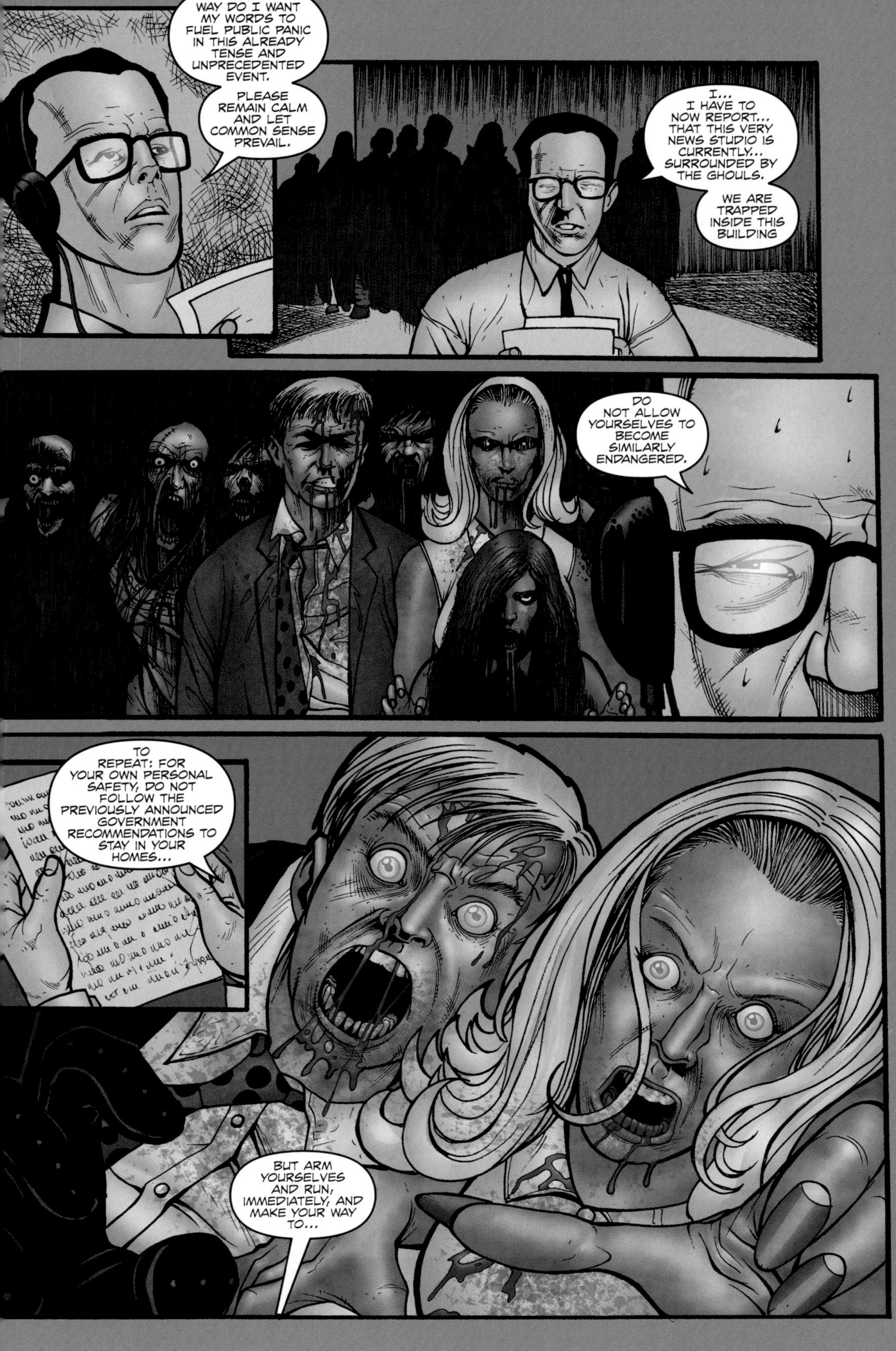
IN NO WAY DO I WANT MY WORDS TO FUEL PUBLIC PANIC IN THIS ALREADY TENSE AND UNPRECEDENTED EVENT.
PLEASE REMAIN CALM AND LET COMMON SENSE PREVAIL.
I... I HAVE TO NOW REPORT... THAT THIS VERY NEWS STUDIO IS CURRENTLY... SURROUNDED BY THE GHOULS.
WE ARE TRAPPED INSIDE THIS BUILDING
DO NOT ALLOW YOURSELVES TO BECOME SIMILARLY ENDANGERED.
TO REPEAT: FOR YOUR OWN PERSONAL SAFETY, DO NOT FOLLOW THE PREVIOUSLY ANNOUNCED GOVERNMENT RECOMMENDATIONS TO STAY IN YOUR HOMES...
BUT ARM YOURSELVES AND RUN, IMMEDIATELY, AND MAKE YOUR WAY TO...

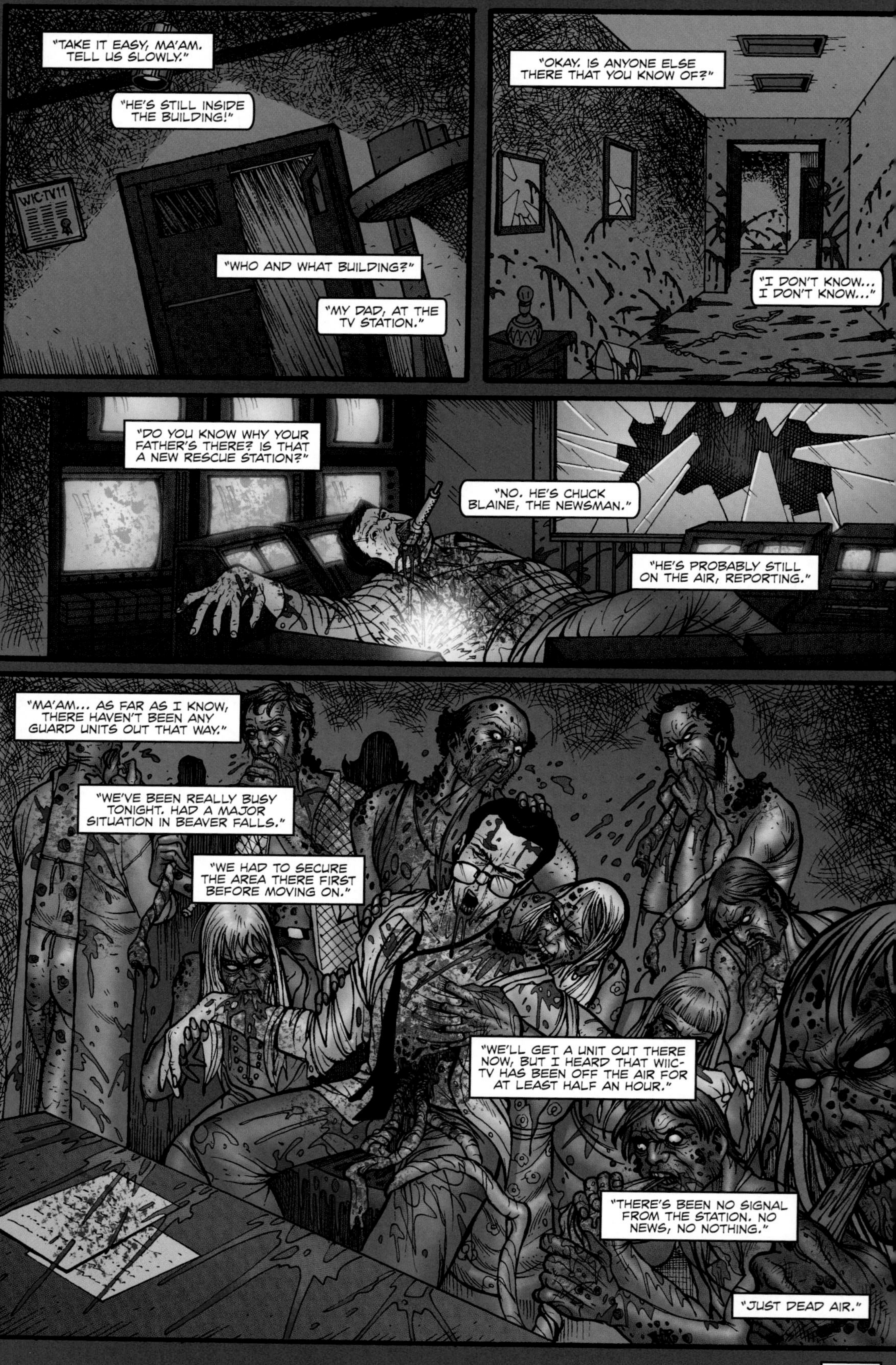
"TAKE IT EASY, MA'AM. TELL US SLOWLY."
"HE'S STILL INSIDE THE BUILDING!"
WIC-TV11
"WHO AND WHAT BUILDING?"
"MY DAD, AT THE TV STATION."
"OKAY. IS ANYONE ELSE THERE THAT YOU KNOW OF?"
"I DON'T KNOW... I DON'T KNOW..."
"DO YOU KNOW WHY YOUR FATHER'S THERE? IS THAT A NEW RESCUE STATION?"
"NO. HE'S CHUCK BLAINE, THE NEWSMAN."
"HE'S PROBABLY STILL ON THE AIR, REPORTING."
"MA'AM... AS FAR AS I KNOW, THERE HAVEN'T BEEN ANY GUARD UNITS OUT THAT WAY."
"WE'VE BEEN REALLY BUSY TONIGHT. HAD A MAJOR SITUATION IN BEAVER FALLS."
"WE HAD TO SECURE THE AREA THERE FIRST BEFORE MOVING ON."
"WE'LL GET A UNIT OUT THERE NOW, BUT I HEARD THAT WIIC-TV HAS BEEN OFF THE AIR FOR AT LEAST HALF AN HOUR."
"THERE'S BEEN NO SIGNAL FROM THE STATION. NO NEWS, NO NOTHING."
"JUST DEAD AIR."

END.

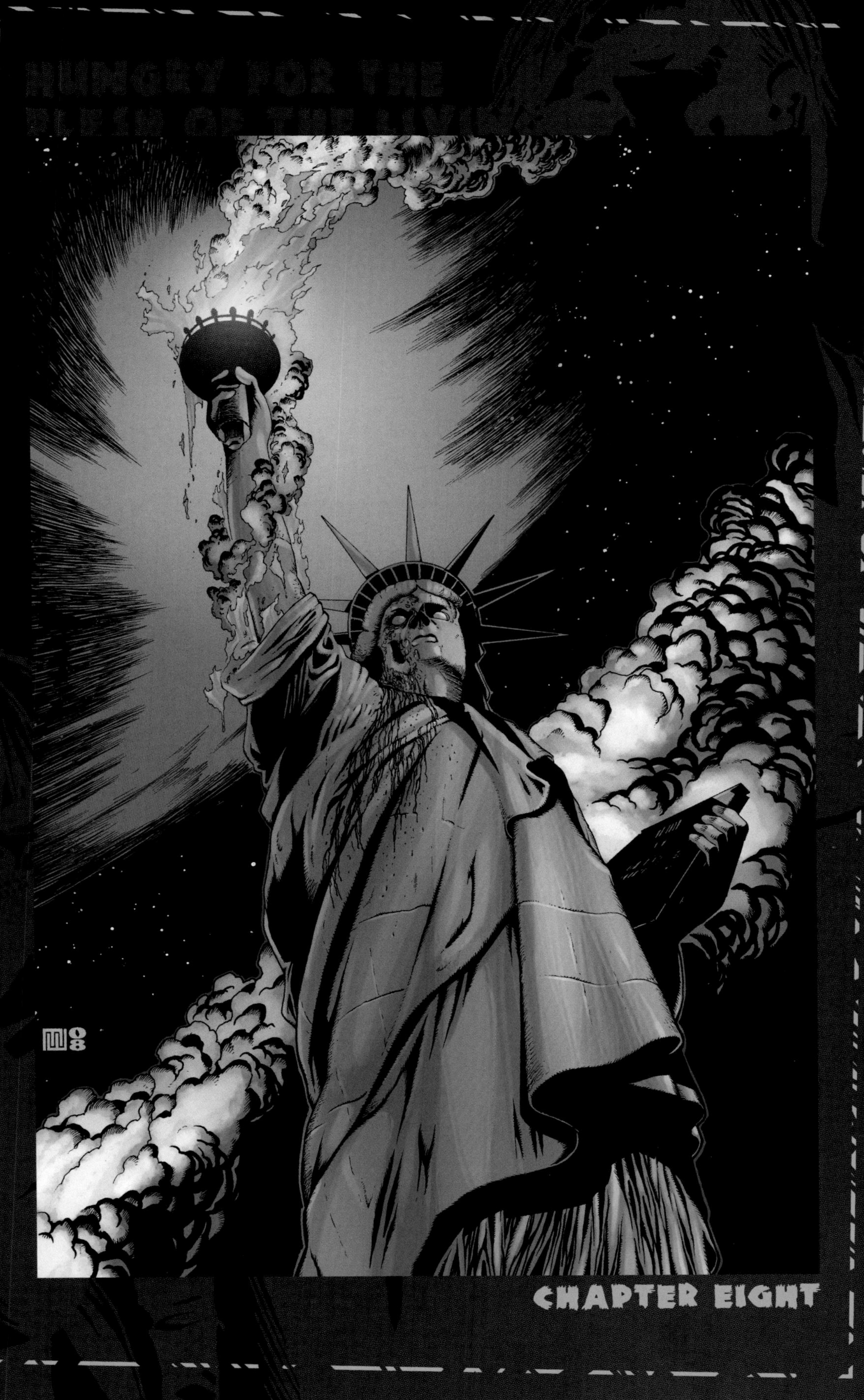
HUNGRY FOR THE
FLESH OF THE
CHAPTER EIGHT

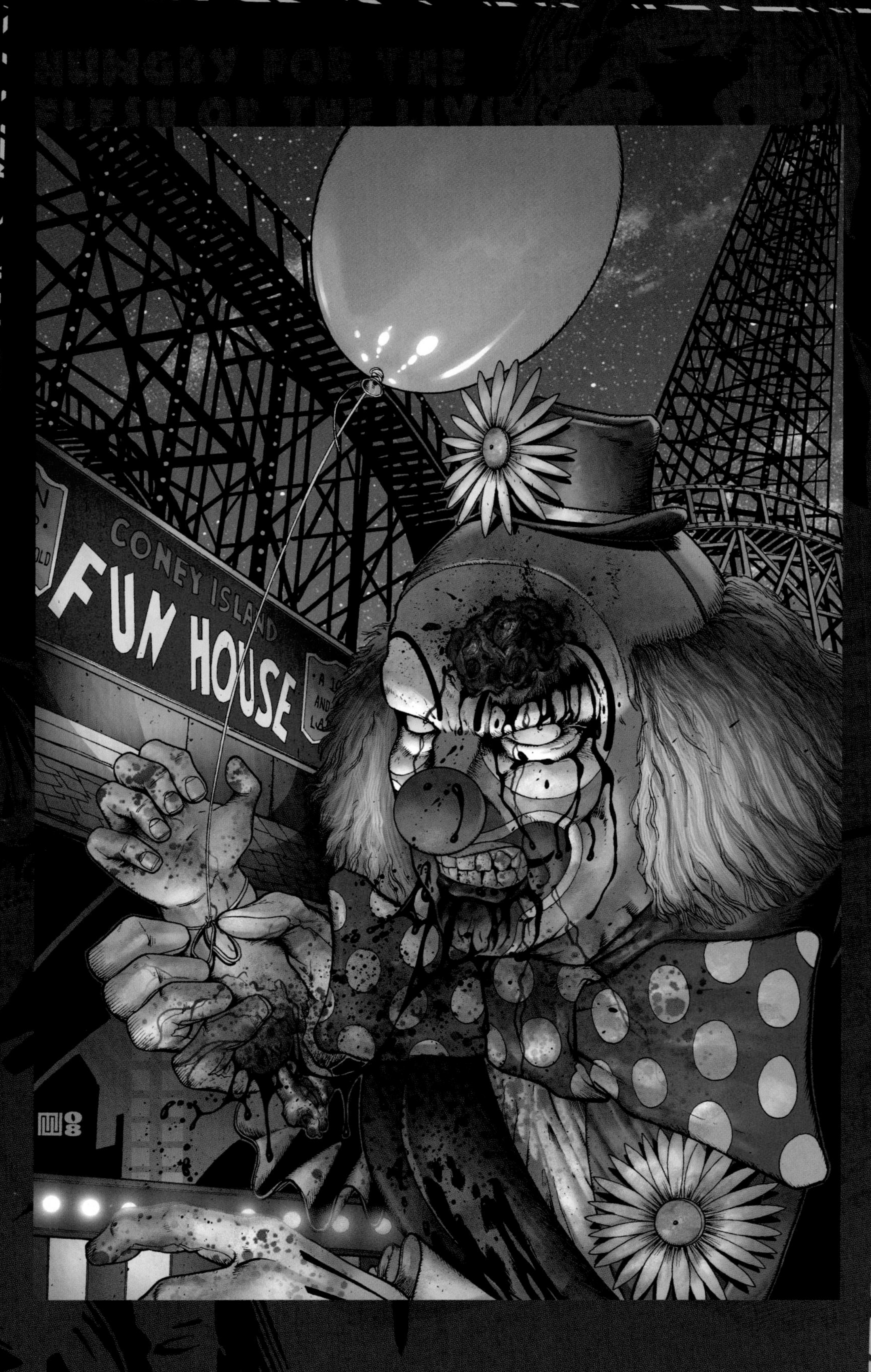
HUNGRY FOR THE
FLESH OF THE
CONEY ISLAND
FUN HOUSE

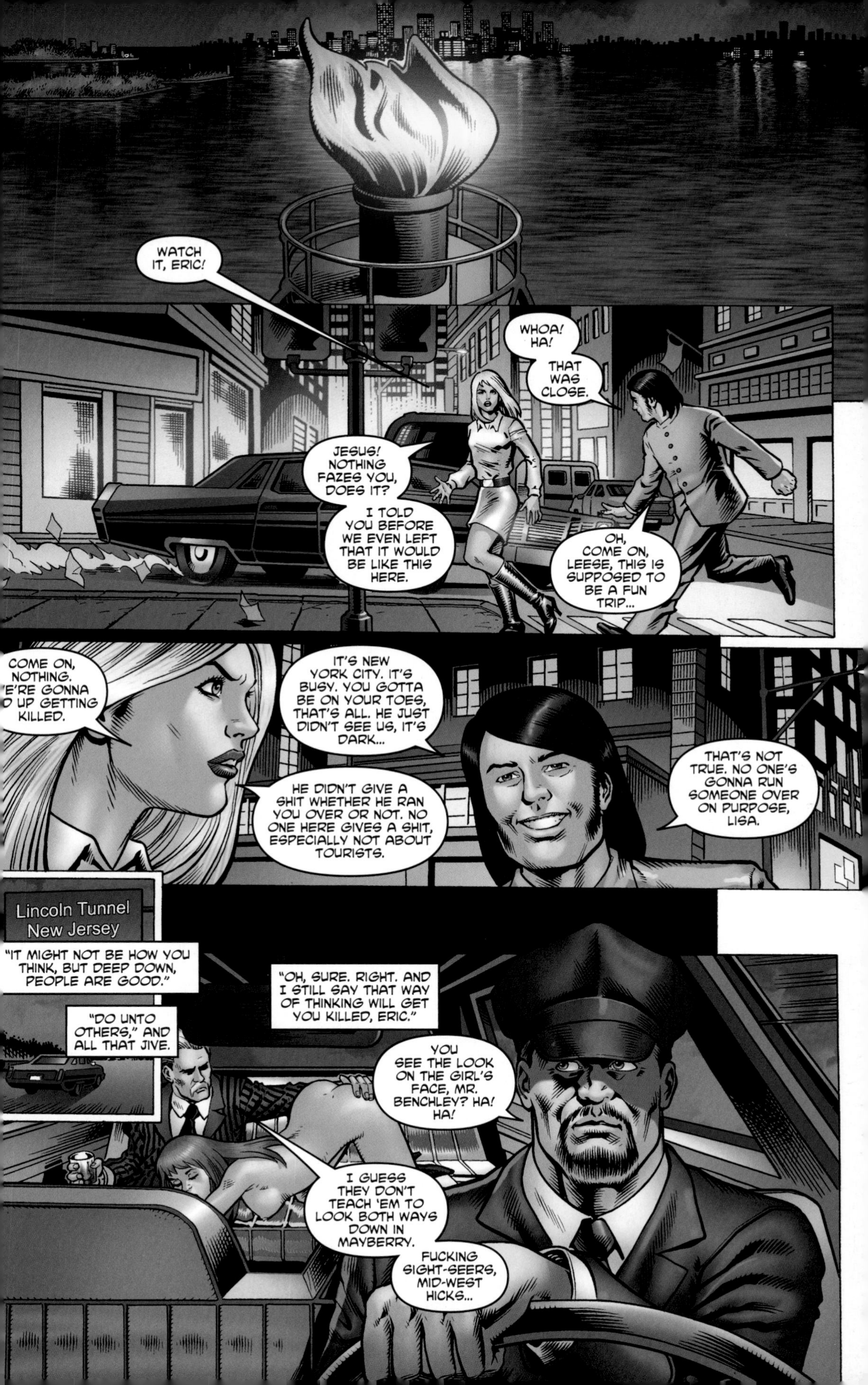
WATCH IT, ERIC!
WHOA! HA!
THAT WAS CLOSE.
JESUS! NOTHING FAZES YOU, DOES IT?
I TOLD YOU BEFORE WE EVEN LEFT THAT IT WOULD BE LIKE THIS HERE.
OH, COME ON, LEESE, THIS IS SUPPOSED TO BE A FUN TRIP...
COME ON, NOTHING. 'E'RE GONNA D UP GETTING KILLED.
IT'S NEW YORK CITY. IT'S BUSY. YOU GOTTA BE ON YOUR TOES, THAT'S ALL. HE JUST DIDN'T SEE US, IT'S DARK...
HE DIDN'T GIVE A SHIT WHETHER HE RAN YOU OVER OR NOT. NO ONE HERE GIVES A SHIT, ESPECIALLY NOT ABOUT TOURISTS.
THAT'S NOT TRUE. NO ONE'S GONNA RUN SOMEONE OVER ON PURPOSE, LISA.
Lincoln Tunnel New Jersey
"IT MIGHT NOT BE HOW YOU THINK, BUT DEEP DOWN, PEOPLE ARE GOOD."
"DO UNTO OTHERS," AND ALL THAT JIVE.
"OH, SURE. RIGHT. AND I STILL SAY THAT WAY OF THINKING WILL GET YOU KILLED, ERIC."
YOU SEE THE LOOK ON THE GIRL'S FACE, MR. BENCHLEY? HA! HA!
I GUESS THEY DON'T TEACH 'EM TO LOOK BOTH WAYS DOWN IN MAYBERRY.
FUCKING SIGHT-SEERS, MID-WEST HICKS...

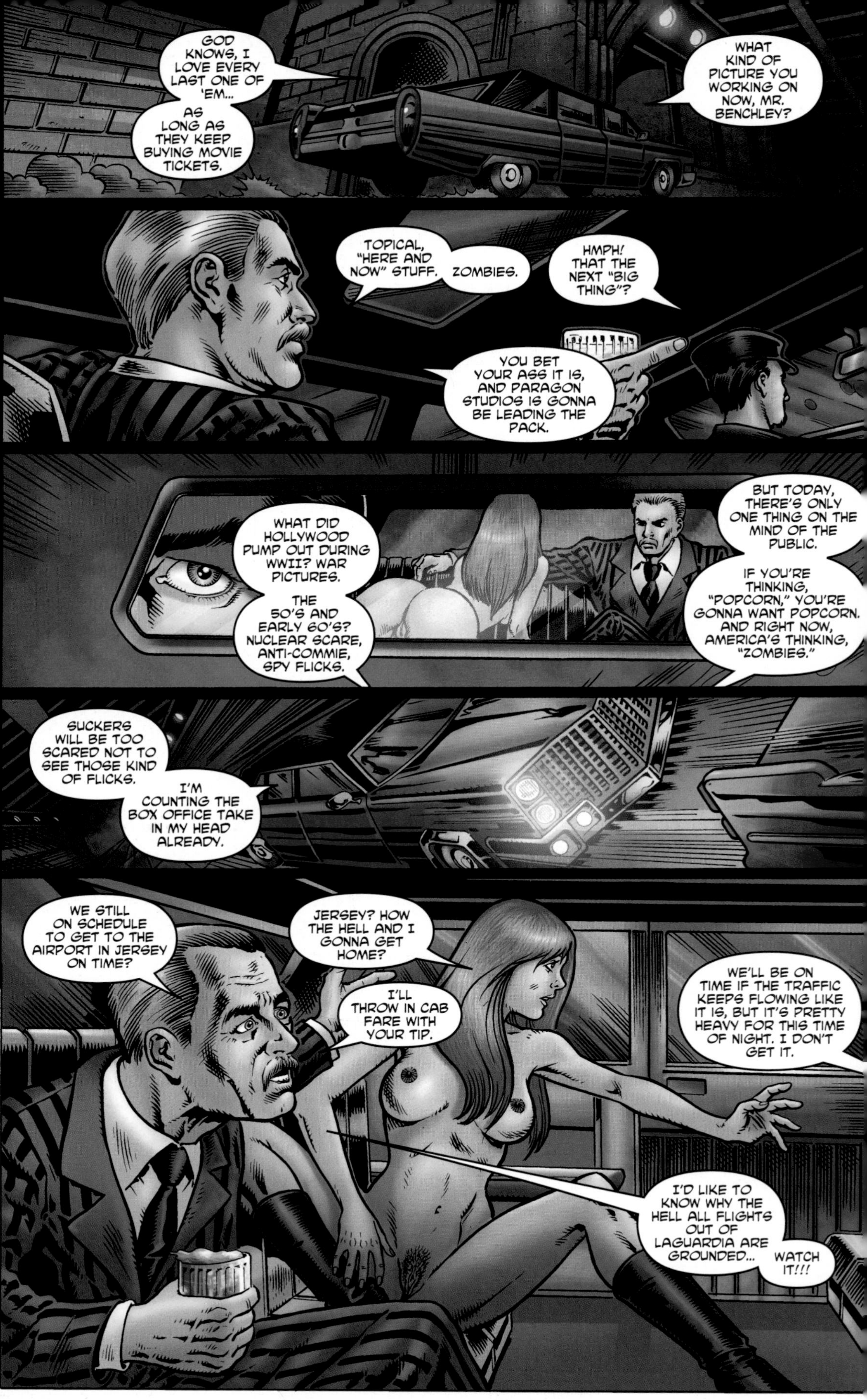
GOD KNOWS, I LOVE EVERY LAST ONE OF 'EM...
AS LONG AS THEY KEEP BUYING MOVIE TICKETS.
WHAT KIND OF PICTURE YOU WORKING ON NOW, MR. BENCHLEY?
TOPICAL, "HERE AND NOW" STUFF.
ZOMBIES.
HMPH! THAT THE NEXT "BIG THING"?
YOU BET YOUR ASS IT IS, AND PARAGON STUDIOS IS GONNA BE LEADING THE PACK.
WHAT DID HOLLYWOOD PUMP OUT DURING WWII? WAR PICTURES.
THE 50'S AND EARLY 60'S? NUCLEAR SCARE, ANTI-COMMIE, SPY FLICKS.
BUT TODAY, THERE'S ONLY ONE THING ON THE MIND OF THE PUBLIC.
IF YOU'RE THINKING, "POPCORN," YOU'RE GONNA WANT POPCORN. AND RIGHT NOW, AMERICA'S THINKING, "ZOMBIES."
SUCKERS WILL BE TOO SCARED NOT TO SEE THOSE KIND OF FLICKS.
I'M COUNTING THE BOX OFFICE TAKE IN MY HEAD ALREADY.
WE STILL ON SCHEDULE TO GET TO THE AIRPORT IN JERSEY ON TIME?
JERSEY? HOW THE HELL AND I GONNA GET HOME?
I'LL THROW IN CAB FARE WITH YOUR TIP.
WE'LL BE ON TIME IF THE TRAFFIC KEEPS FLOWING LIKE IT IS, BUT IT'S PRETTY HEAVY FOR THIS TIME OF NIGHT. I DON'T GET IT.
I'D LIKE TO KNOW WHY THE HELL ALL FLIGHTS OUT OF LAGUARDIA ARE GROUNDED...
WATCH IT!!!

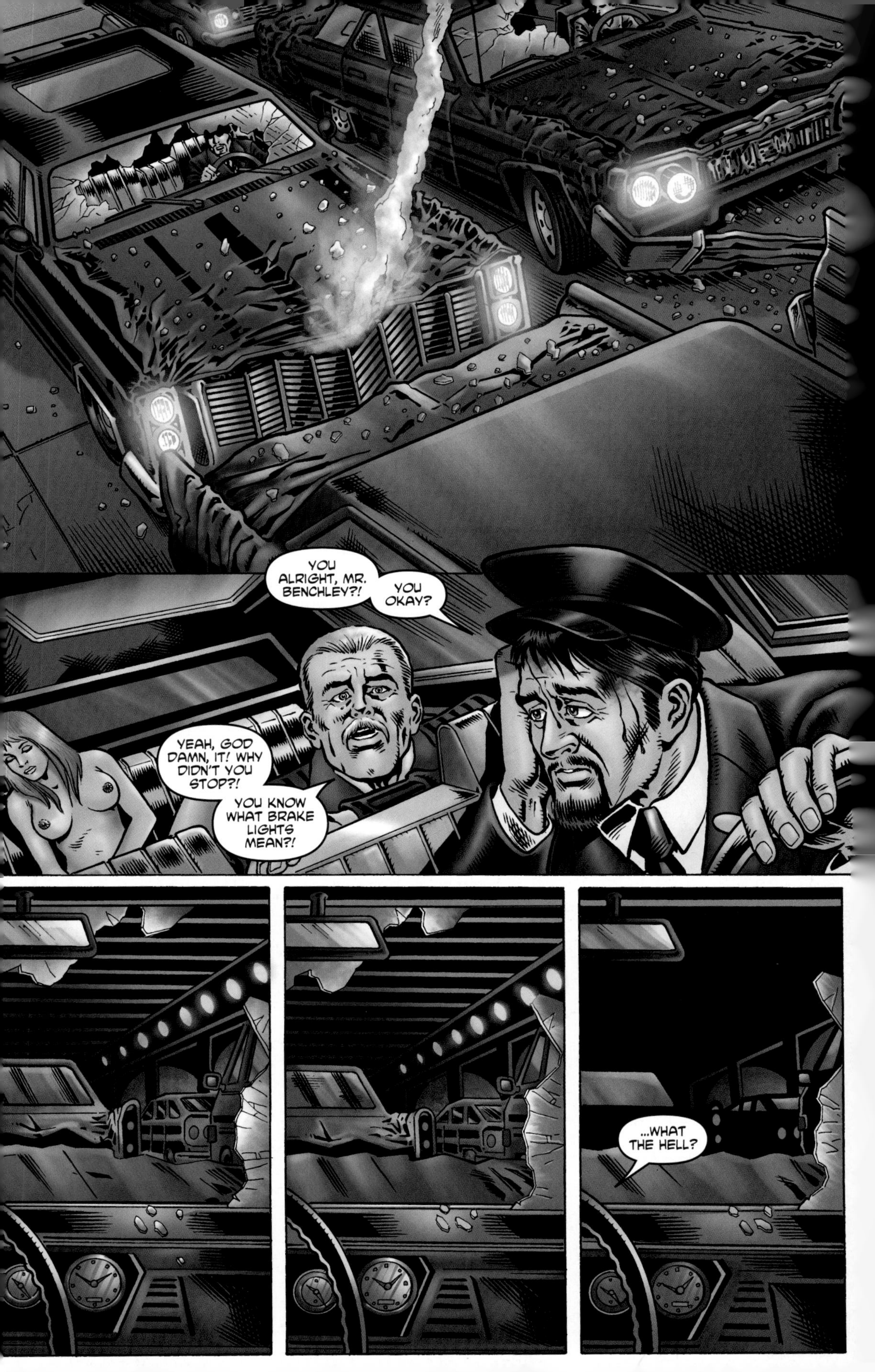
YOU ALRIGHT, MR. BENCHLEY?!
YOU OKAY?
YEAH, GOD DAMN, IT! WHY DIDN'T YOU STOP?!
YOU KNOW WHAT BRAKE LIGHTS MEAN?!
...WHAT THE HELL?

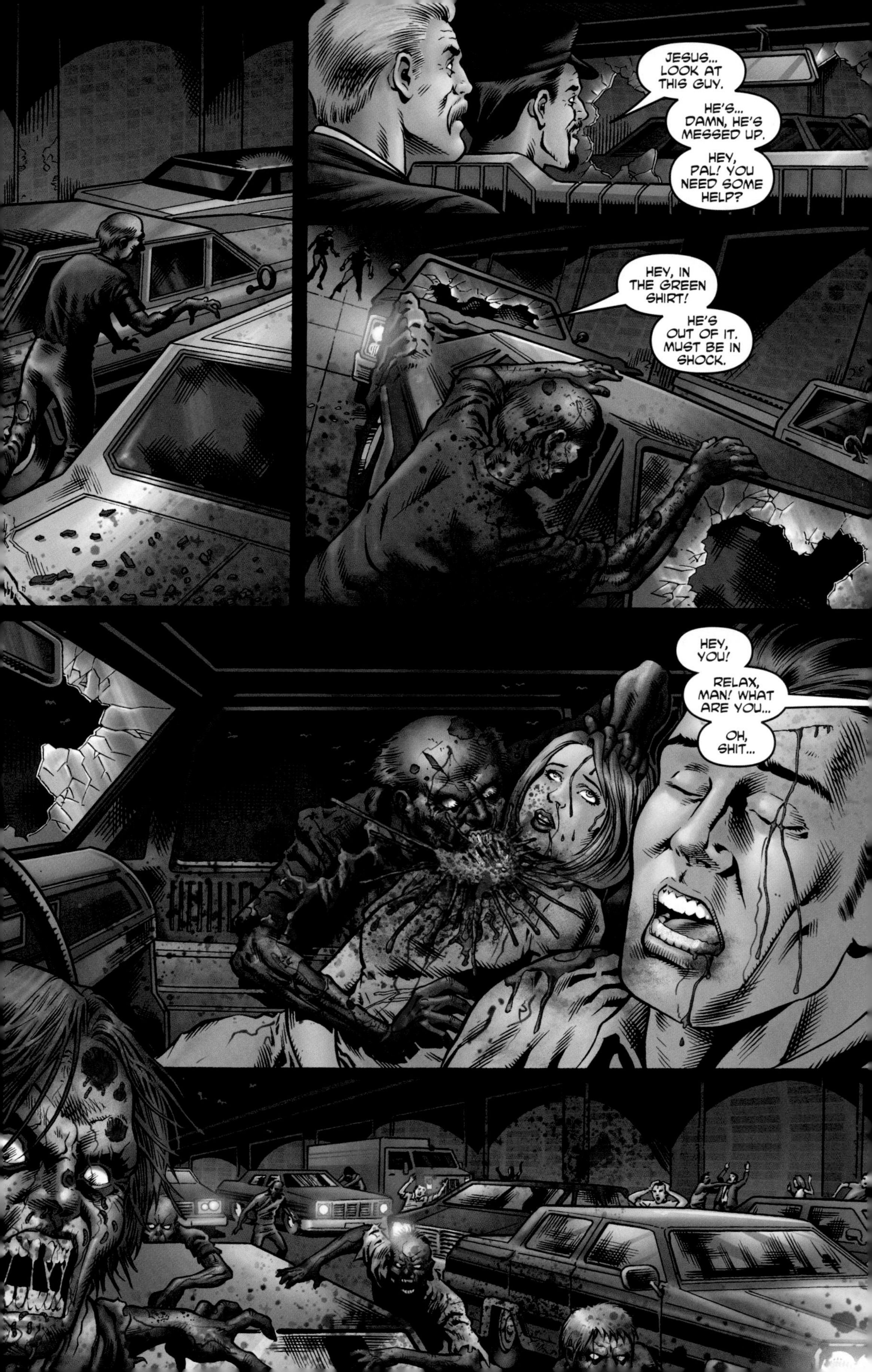
JESUS... LOOK AT THIS GUY.
HE'S... DAMN, HE'S MESSED UP.
HEY, PAL! YOU NEED SOME HELP?
HEY, IN THE GREEN SHIRT!
HE'S OUT OF IT. MUST BE IN SHOCK.
HEY, YOU!
RELAX, MAN! WHAT ARE YOU...
OH, SHIT...

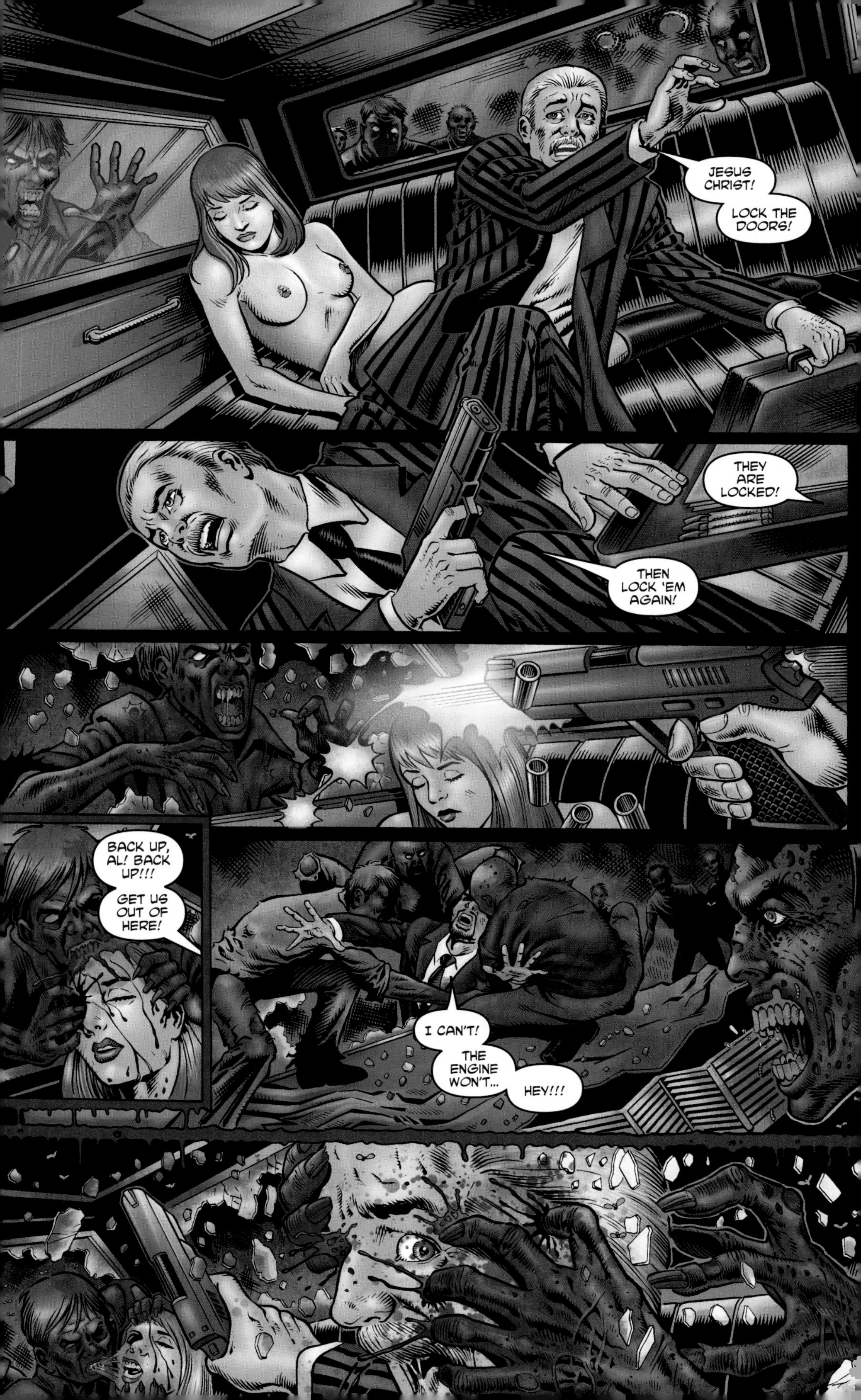
JESUS CHRIST!
LOCK THE DOORS!
THEY ARE LOCKED!
THEN LOCK 'EM AGAIN!
BACK UP, AL! BACK UP!!!
GET US OUT OF HERE!
I CAN'T!
THE ENGINE WON'T...
HEY!!!

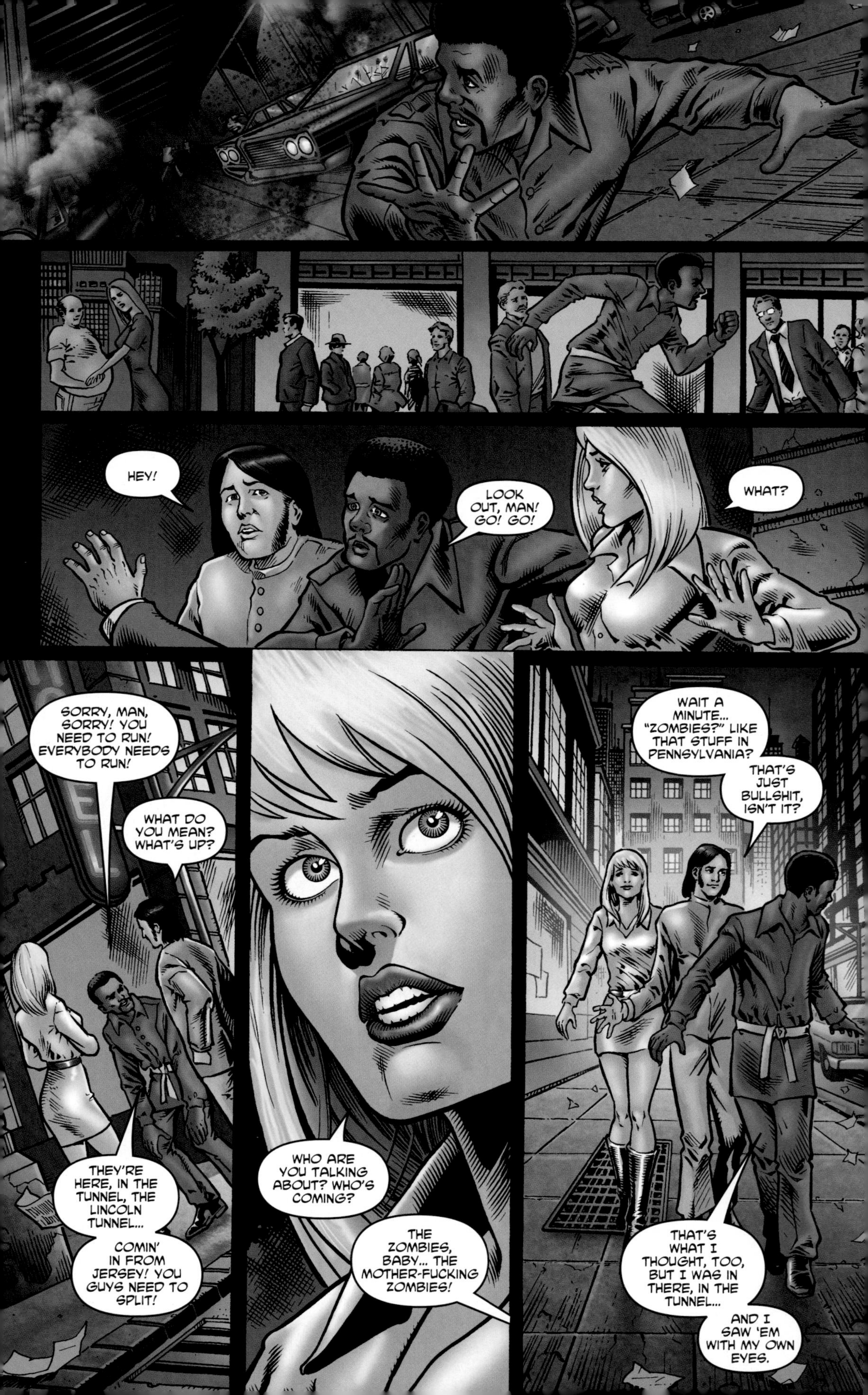
HEY!
LOOK OUT, MAN! GO! GO!
WHAT?
SORRY, MAN, SORRY! YOU NEED TO RUN! EVERYBODY NEEDS TO RUN!
WHAT DO YOU MEAN? WHAT'S UP?
THEY'RE HERE, IN THE TUNNEL, THE LINCOLN TUNNEL...
COMIN' IN FROM JERSEY! YOU GUYS NEED TO SPLIT!
WHO ARE YOU TALKING ABOUT? WHO'S COMING?
THE ZOMBIES, BABY... THE MOTHER-FUCKING ZOMBIES!
WAIT A MINUTE... "ZOMBIES?" LIKE THAT STUFF IN PENNSYLVANIA?
THAT'S JUST BULLSHIT, ISN'T IT?
THAT'S WHAT I THOUGHT, TOO, BUT I WAS IN THERE, IN THE TUNNEL...
AND I SAW 'EM WITH MY OWN EYES.

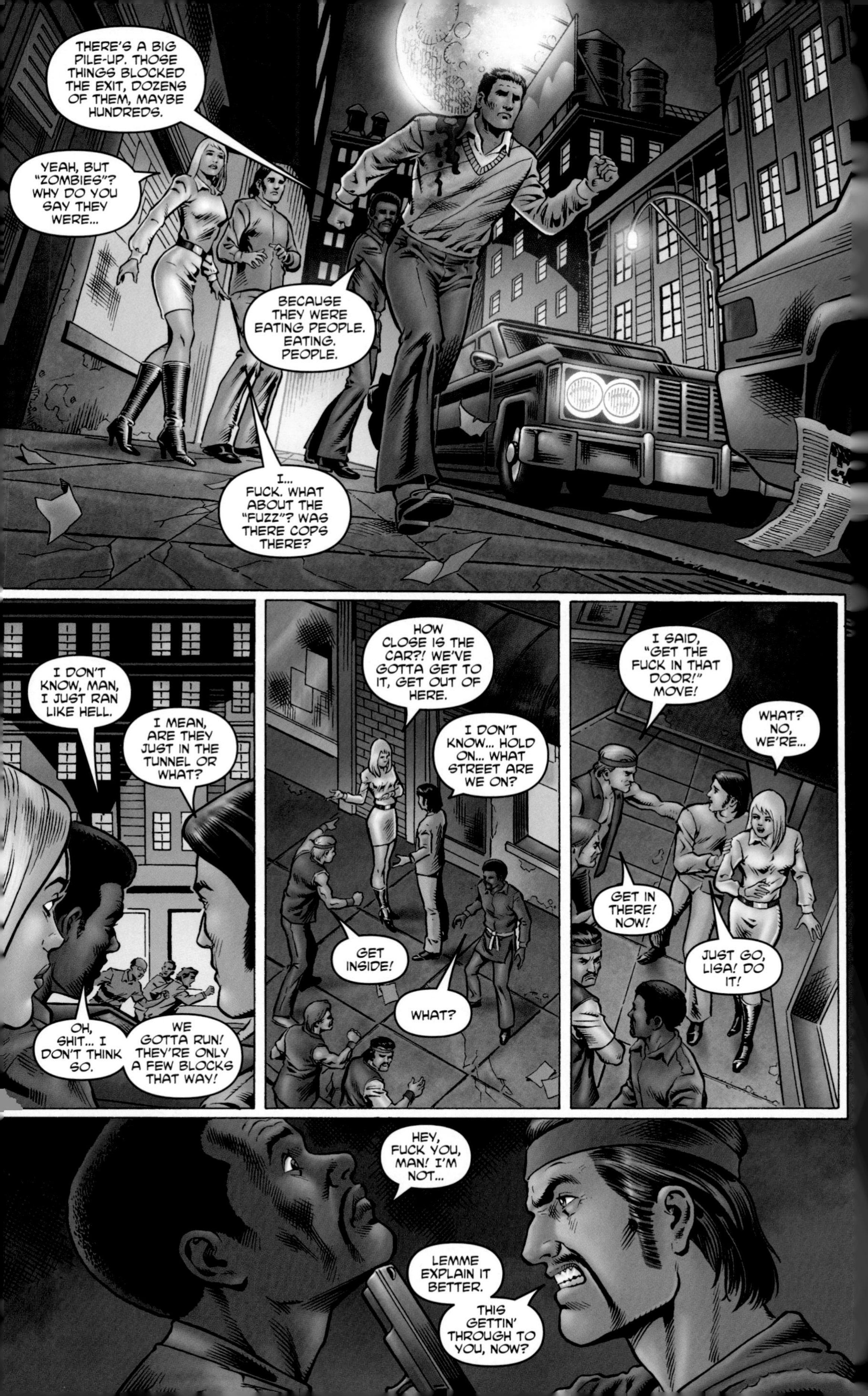
THERE'S A BIG PILE-UP. THOSE THINGS BLOCKED THE EXIT, DOZENS OF THEM, MAYBE HUNDREDS.
YEAH, BUT "ZOMBIES"? WHY DO YOU SAY THEY WERE...
BECAUSE THEY WERE EATING PEOPLE. EATING. PEOPLE.
I... FUCK. WHAT ABOUT THE "FUZZ"? WAS THERE COPS THERE?
I DON'T KNOW, MAN, I JUST RAN LIKE HELL.
I MEAN, ARE THEY JUST IN THE TUNNEL OR WHAT?
OH, SHIT... I DON'T THINK SO.
WE GOTTA RUN! THEY'RE ONLY A FEW BLOCKS THAT WAY!
HOW CLOSE IS THE CAR?! WE'VE GOTTA GET TO IT, GET OUT OF HERE.
I DON'T KNOW... HOLD ON... WHAT STREET ARE WE ON?
GET INSIDE!
WHAT?
I SAID, "GET THE FUCK IN THAT DOOR!" MOVE!
WHAT? NO, WE'RE...
GET IN THERE! NOW!
JUST GO, LISA! DO IT!
HEY, FUCK YOU, MAN! I'M NOT...
LEMME EXPLAIN IT BETTER.
THIS GETTIN' THROUGH TO YOU, NOW?

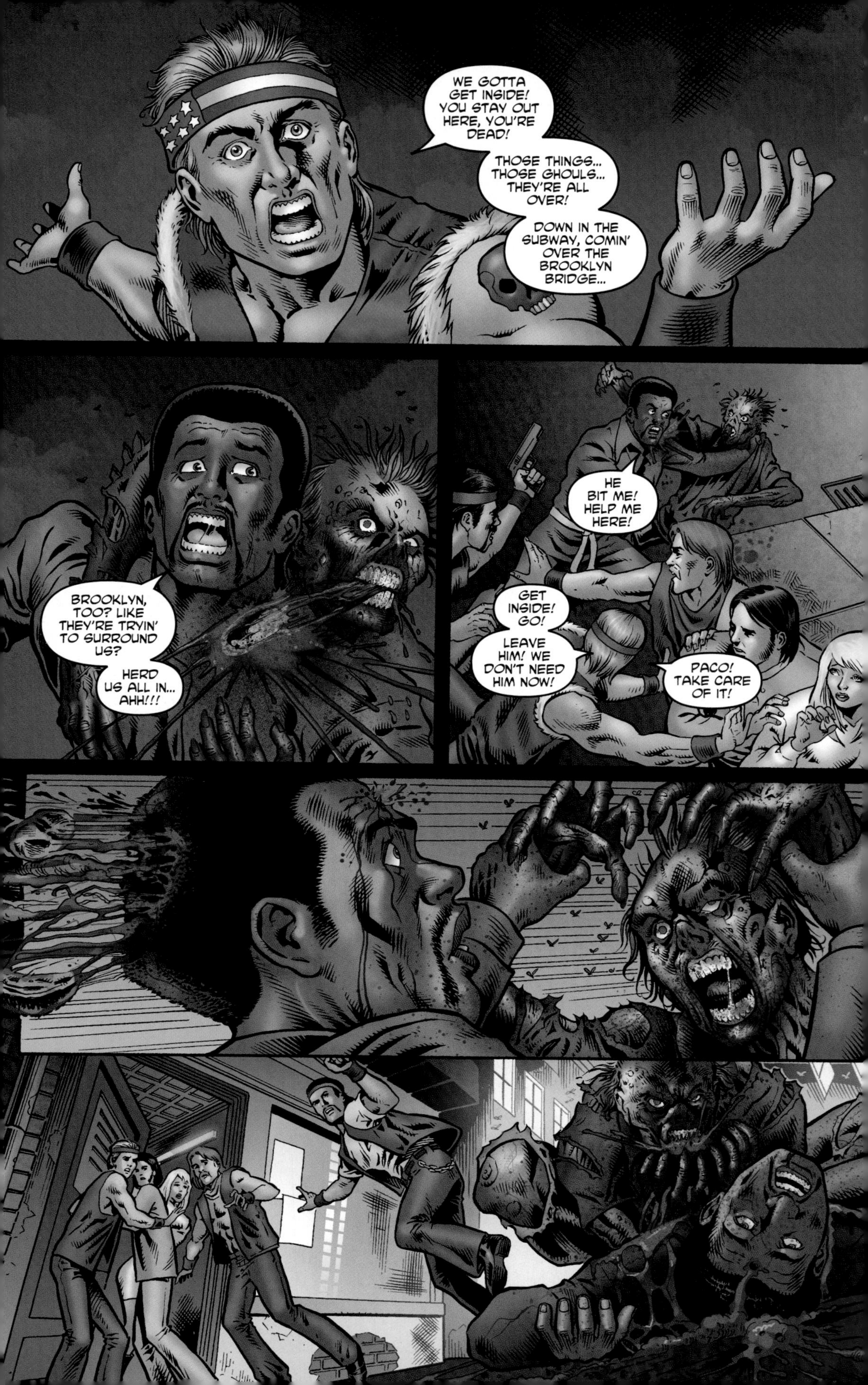
WE GOTTA GET INSIDE! YOU STAY OUT HERE, YOU'RE DEAD!
THOSE THINGS... THOSE GHOULS... THEY'RE ALL OVER!
DOWN IN THE SUBWAY, COMIN' OVER THE BROOKLYN BRIDGE...
BROOKLYN, TOO? LIKE THEY'RE TRYIN' TO SURROUND US?
HERD US ALL IN... AHH!!!
HE BIT ME! HELP ME HERE!
GET INSIDE! GO!
LEAVE HIM! WE DON'T NEED HIM NOW!
PACO! TAKE CARE OF IT!

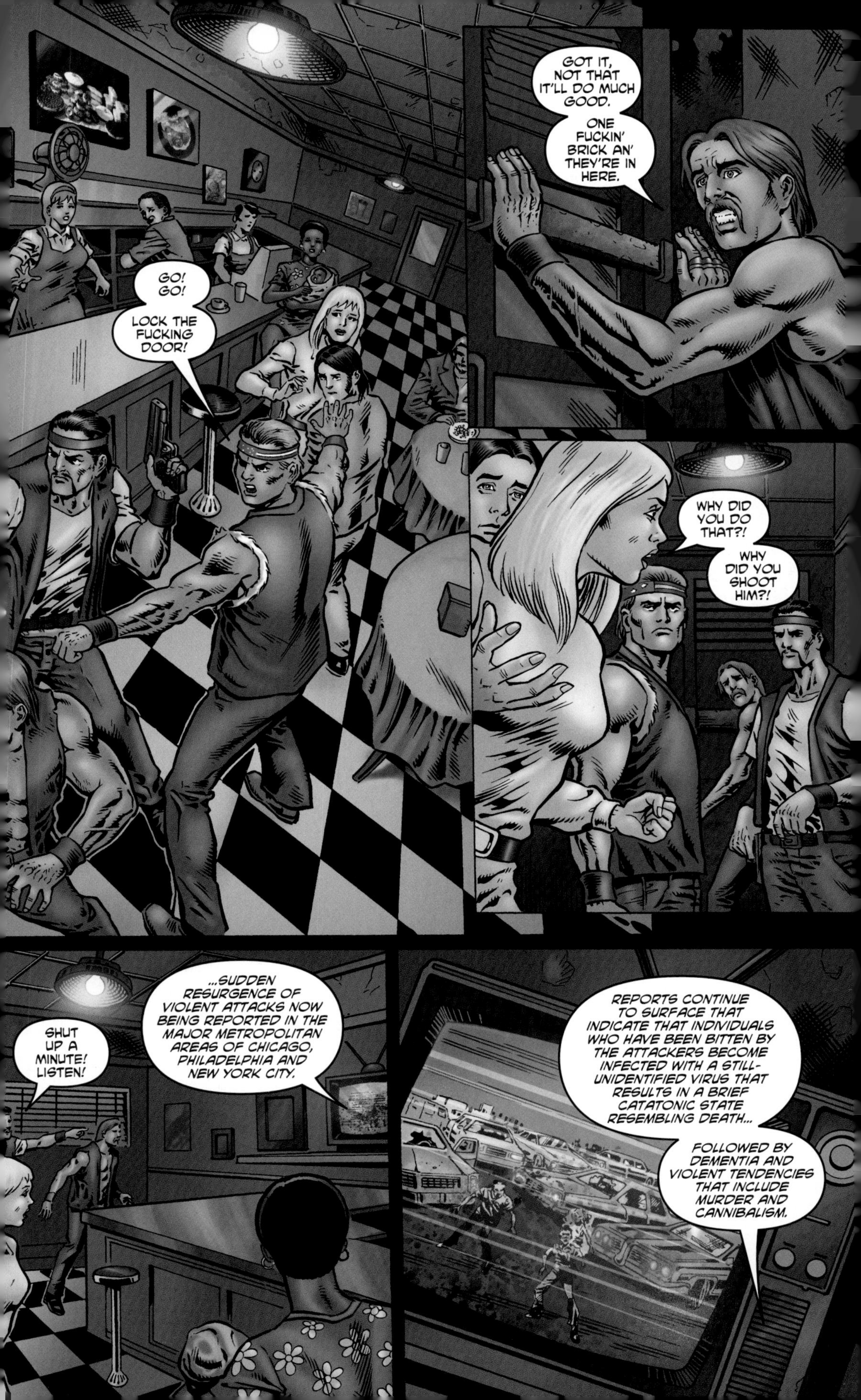
GO! GO!
LOCK THE FUCKING DOOR!
GOT IT, NOT THAT IT'LL DO MUCH GOOD.
ONE FUCKIN' BRICK AN' THEY'RE IN HERE.
WHY DID YOU DO THAT?!
WHY DID YOU SHOOT HIM?!
SHUT UP A MINUTE! LISTEN!
...SUDDEN RESURGENCE OF VIOLENT ATTACKS NOW BEING REPORTED IN THE MAJOR METROPOLITAN AREAS OF CHICAGO, PHILADELPHIA AND NEW YORK CITY.
REPORTS CONTINUE TO SURFACE THAT INDICATE THAT INDIVIDUALS WHO HAVE BEEN BITTEN BY THE ATTACKERS BECOME INFECTED WITH A STILL-UNIDENTIFIED VIRUS THAT RESULTS IN A BRIEF CATATONIC STATE RESEMBLING DEATH...
FOLLOWED BY DEMENTIA AND VIOLENT TENDENCIES THAT INCLUDE MURDER AND CANNIBALISM.

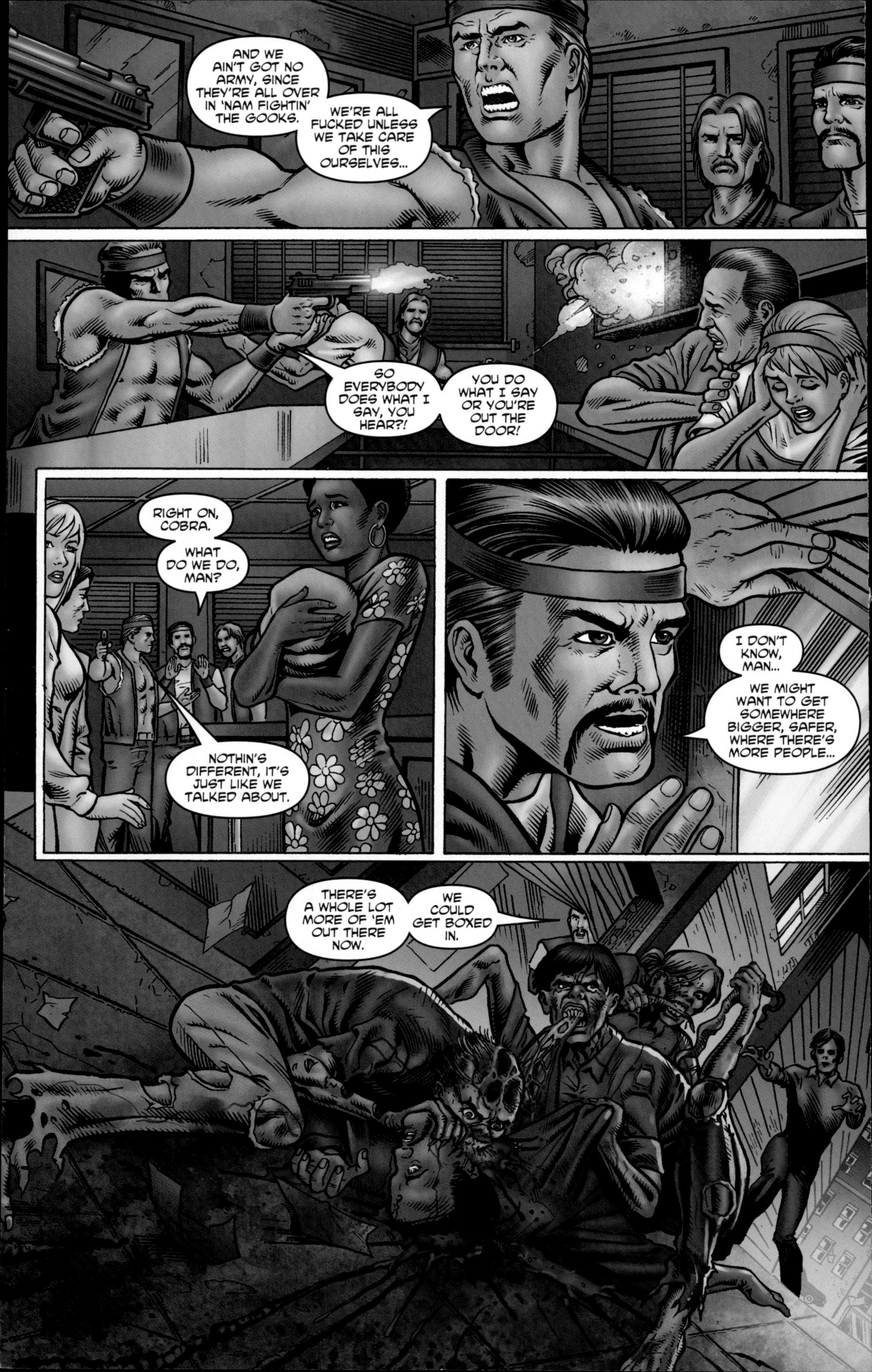
AND WE AIN'T GOT NO ARMY, SINCE THEY'RE ALL OVER IN 'NAM FIGHTIN' THE GOOKS.
WE'RE ALL FUCKED UNLESS WE TAKE CARE OF THIS OURSELVES...
SO EVERYBODY DOES WHAT I SAY, YOU HEAR?!
YOU DO WHAT I SAY OR YOU'RE OUT THE DOOR!
RIGHT ON, COBRA.
WHAT DO WE DO, MAN?
NOTHIN'S DIFFERENT, IT'S JUST LIKE WE TALKED ABOUT.
I DON'T KNOW, MAN...
WE MIGHT WANT TO GET SOMEWHERE BIGGER, SAFER, WHERE THERE'S MORE PEOPLE...
THERE'S A WHOLE LOT MORE OF 'EM OUT THERE NOW.
WE COULD GET BOXED IN.

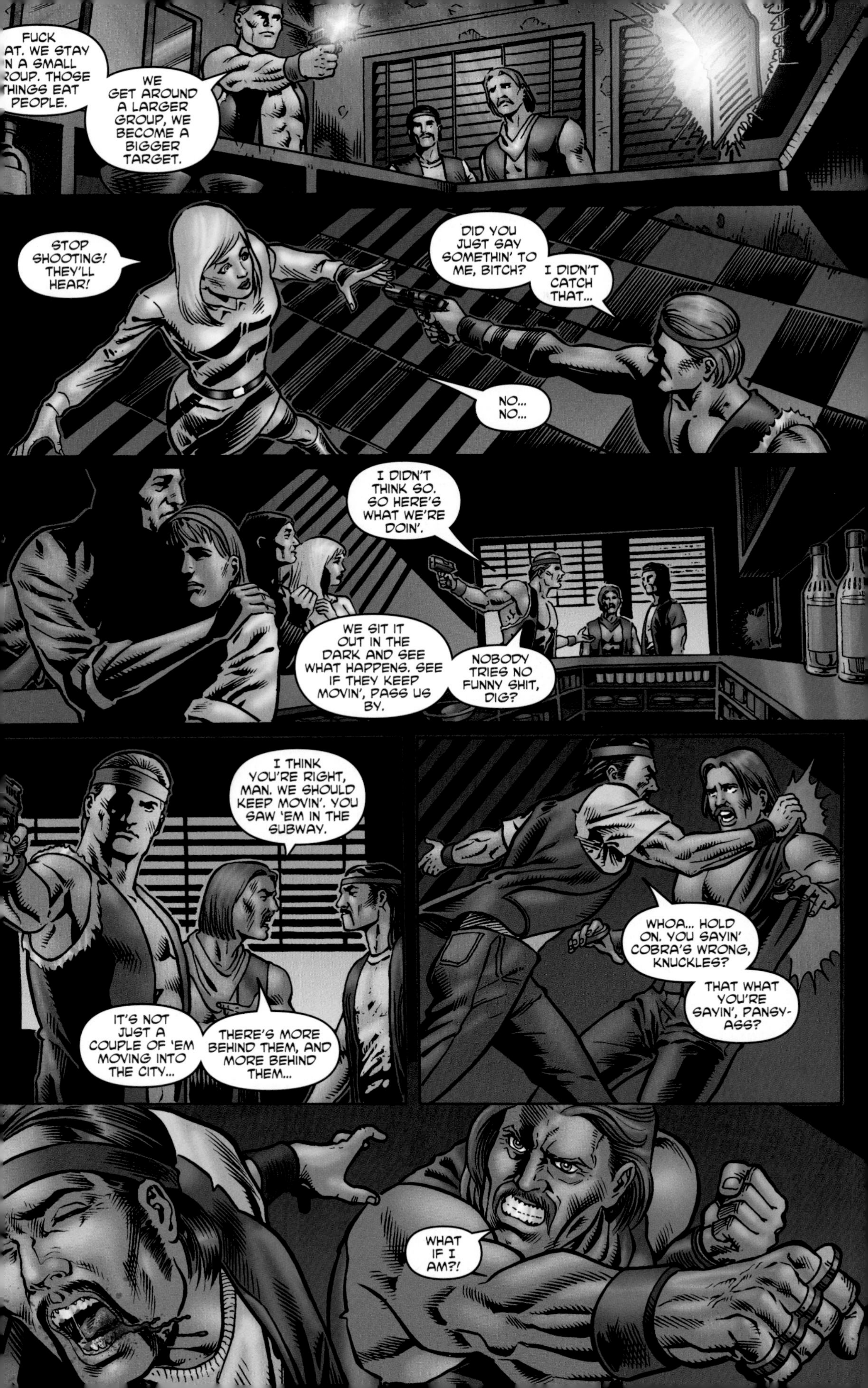
FUCK
AT. WE STAY
N A SMALL
ROUP. THOSE
THINGS EAT
PEOPLE.
WE GET AROUND A LARGER GROUP, WE BECOME A BIGGER TARGET.
STOP SHOOTING! THEY'LL HEAR!
DID YOU JUST SAY SOMETHIN' TO ME, BITCH?
I DIDN'T CATCH THAT...
NO... NO...
I DIDN'T THINK SO. SO HERE'S WHAT WE'RE DOIN'.
WE SIT IT OUT IN THE DARK AND SEE WHAT HAPPENS. SEE IF THEY KEEP MOVIN', PASS US BY.
NOBODY TRIES NO FUNNY SHIT, DIG?
I THINK YOU'RE RIGHT, MAN. WE SHOULD KEEP MOVIN'. YOU SAW 'EM IN THE SUBWAY.
IT'S NOT JUST A COUPLE OF 'EM MOVING INTO THE CITY...
THERE'S MORE BEHIND THEM, AND MORE BEHIND THEM...
WHOA... HOLD ON. YOU SAYIN' COBRA'S WRONG, KNUCKLES?
THAT WHAT YOU'RE SAYIN', PANSY-ASS?
WHAT IF I AM?!

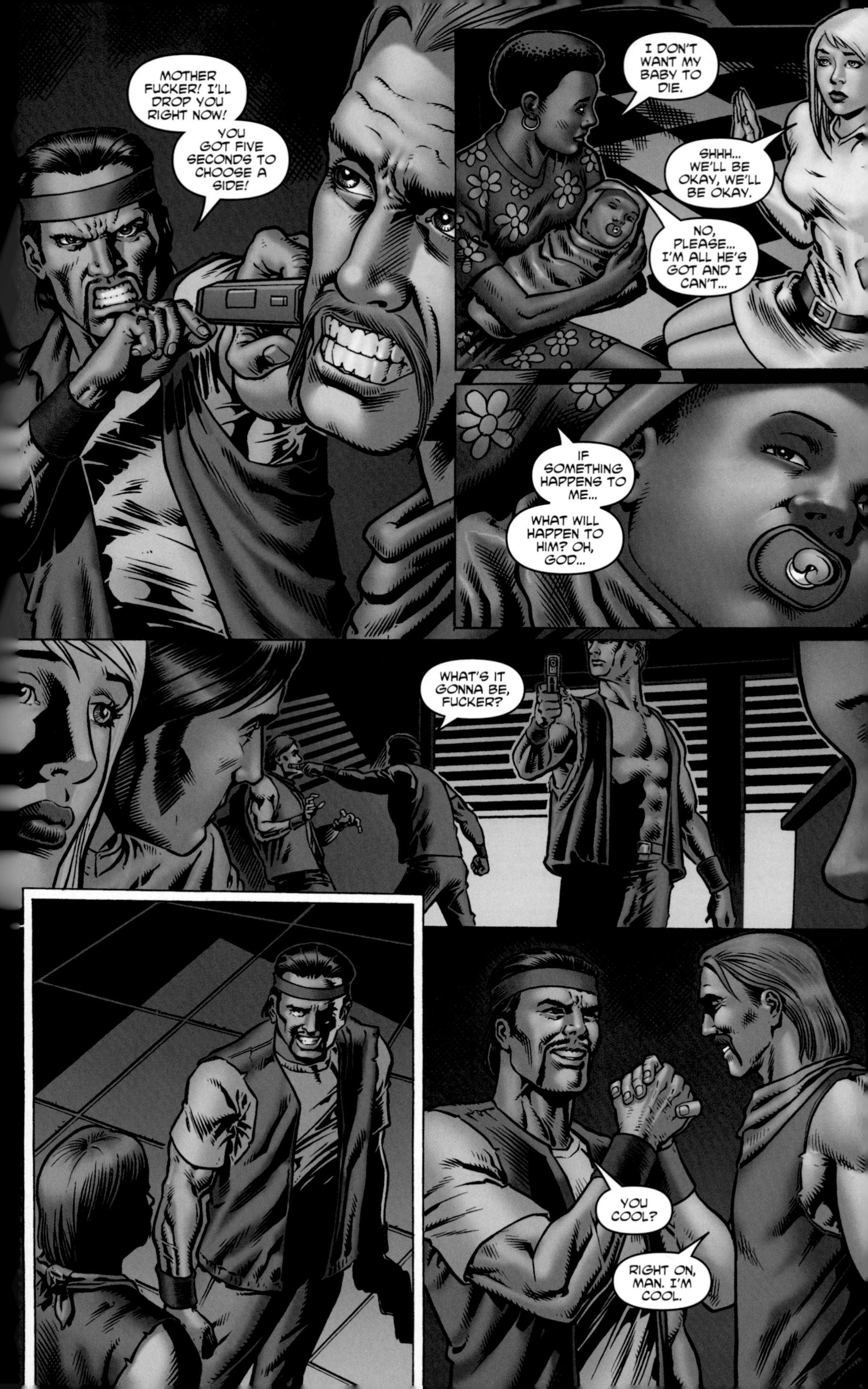
MOTHER FUCKER! I'LL DROP YOU RIGHT NOW!
YOU GOT FIVE SECONDS TO CHOOSE A SIDE!
I DON'T WANT MY BABY TO DIE.
SHHH... WE'LL BE OKAY, WE'LL BE OKAY.
NO, PLEASE... I'M ALL HE'S GOT AND I CAN'T...
IF SOMETHING HAPPENS TO ME...
WHAT WILL HAPPEN TO HIM? OH, GOD...
WHAT'S IT GONNA BE, FUCKER?
YOU COOL?
RIGHT ON, MAN. I'M COOL.

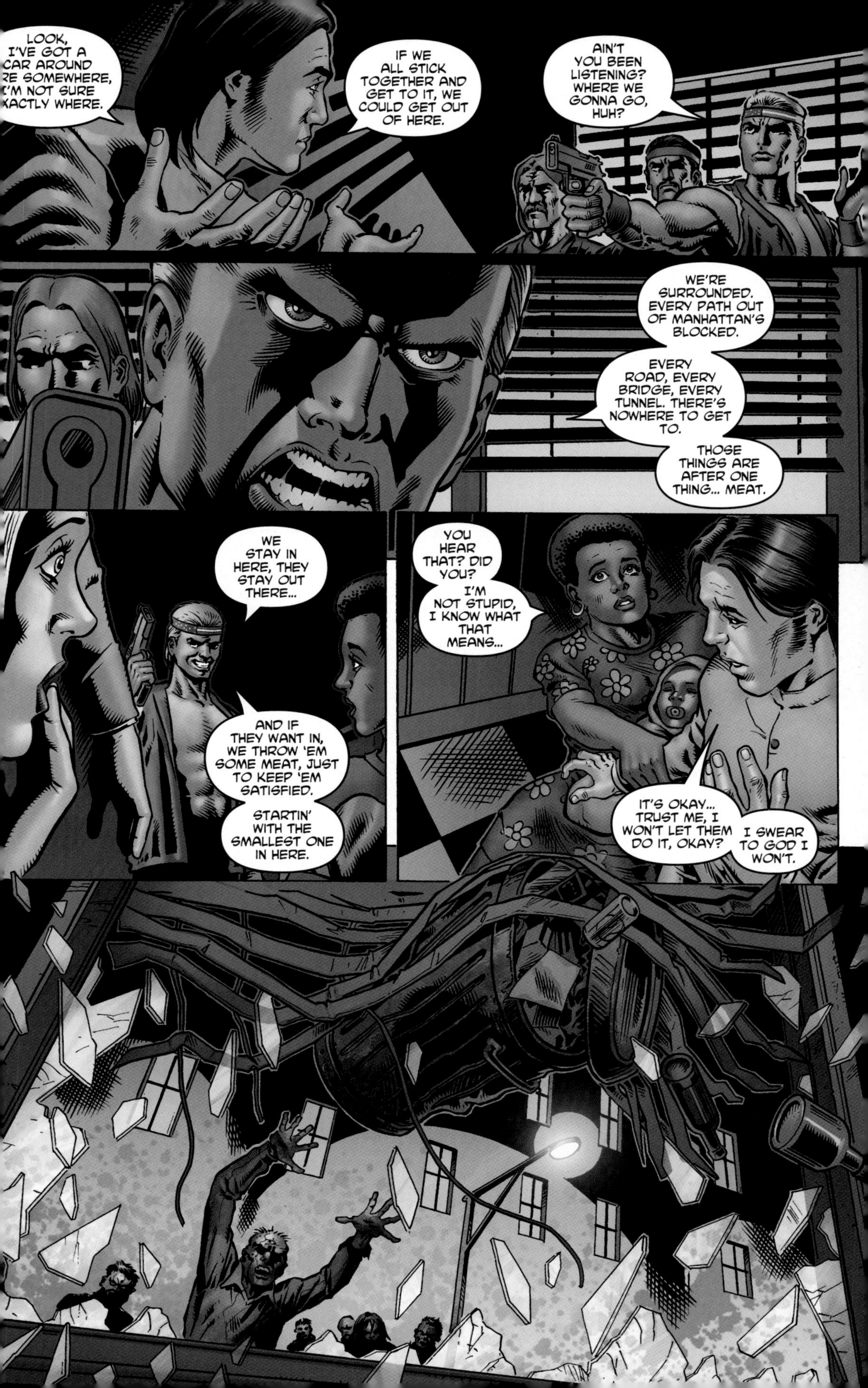
LOOK, I'VE GOT A CAR AROUND RE SOMEWHERE, I'M NOT SURE KACTLY WHERE.
IF WE ALL STICK TOGETHER AND GET TO IT, WE COULD GET OUT OF HERE.
AIN'T YOU BEEN LISTENING? WHERE WE GONNA GO, HUH?
WE'RE SURROUNDED. EVERY PATH OUT OF MANHATTAN'S BLOCKED.
EVERY ROAD, EVERY BRIDGE, EVERY TUNNEL. THERE'S NOWHERE TO GET TO.
THOSE THINGS ARE AFTER ONE THING... MEAT.
WE STAY IN HERE, THEY STAY OUT THERE...
AND IF THEY WANT IN, WE THROW 'EM SOME MEAT, JUST TO KEEP 'EM SATISFIED.
STARTIN' WITH THE SMALLEST ONE IN HERE.
YOU HEAR THAT? DID YOU?
I'M NOT STUPID, I KNOW WHAT THAT MEANS...
IT'S OKAY... TRUST ME, I WON'T LET THEM DO IT, OKAY?
I SWEAR TO GOD I WON'T.

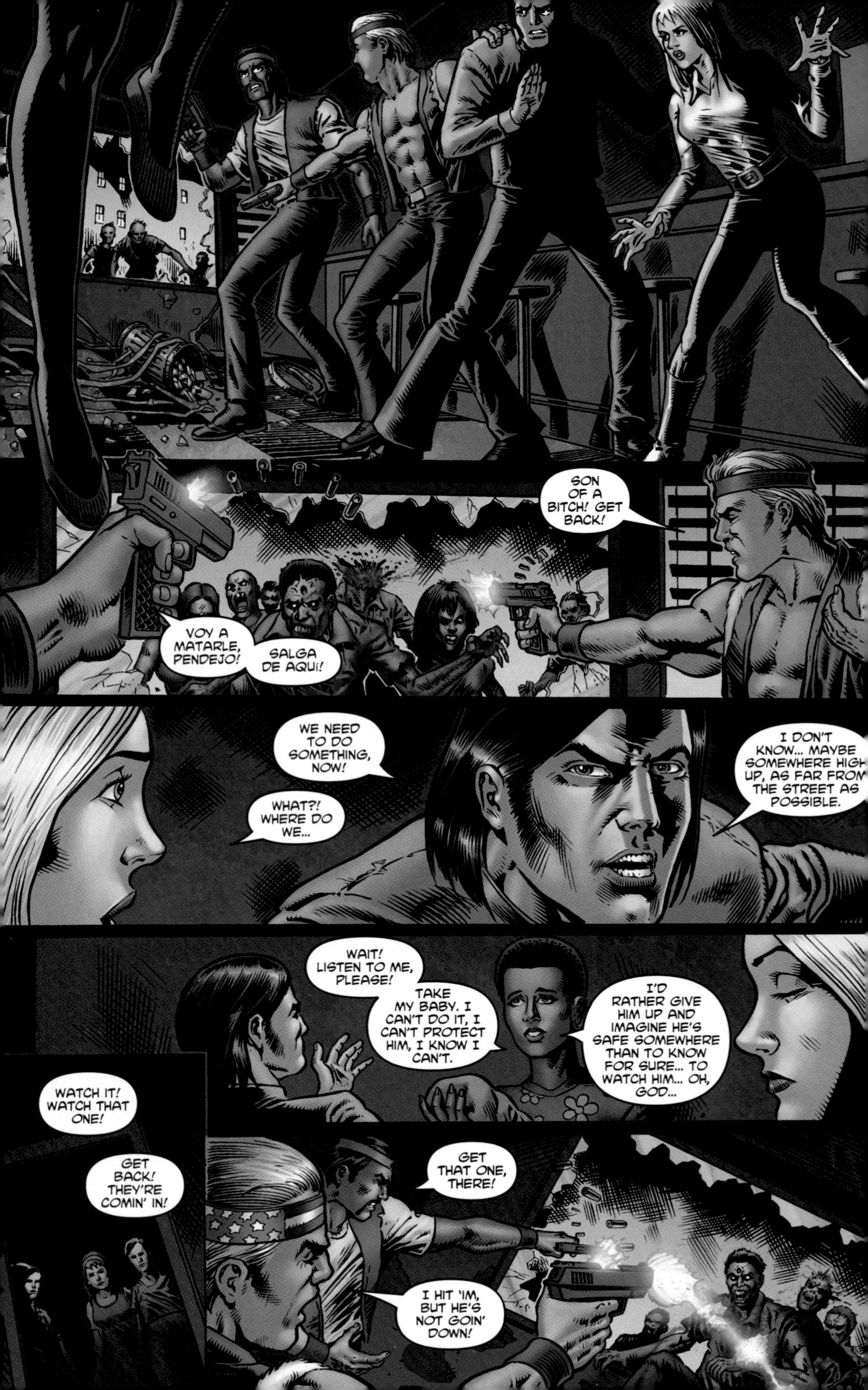
SON OF A BITCH! GET BACK!
VOY A MATARLE, PENDEJO!
SALGA DE AQUÍ!
WE NEED TO DO SOMETHING, NOW!
WHAT?! WHERE DO WE...
I DON'T KNOW... MAYBE SOMEWHERE HIGH UP, AS FAR FROM THE STREET AS POSSIBLE.
WAIT! LISTEN TO ME, PLEASE!
TAKE MY BABY. I CAN'T DO IT, I CAN'T PROTECT HIM, I KNOW I CAN'T.
I'D RATHER GIVE HIM UP AND IMAGINE HE'S SAFE SOMEWHERE THAN TO KNOW FOR SURE... TO WATCH HIM... OH, GOD...
WATCH IT! WATCH THAT ONE!
GET BACK! THEY'RE COMIN' IN!
GET THAT ONE, THERE!
I HIT 'IM, BUT HE'S NOT GOIN' DOWN!

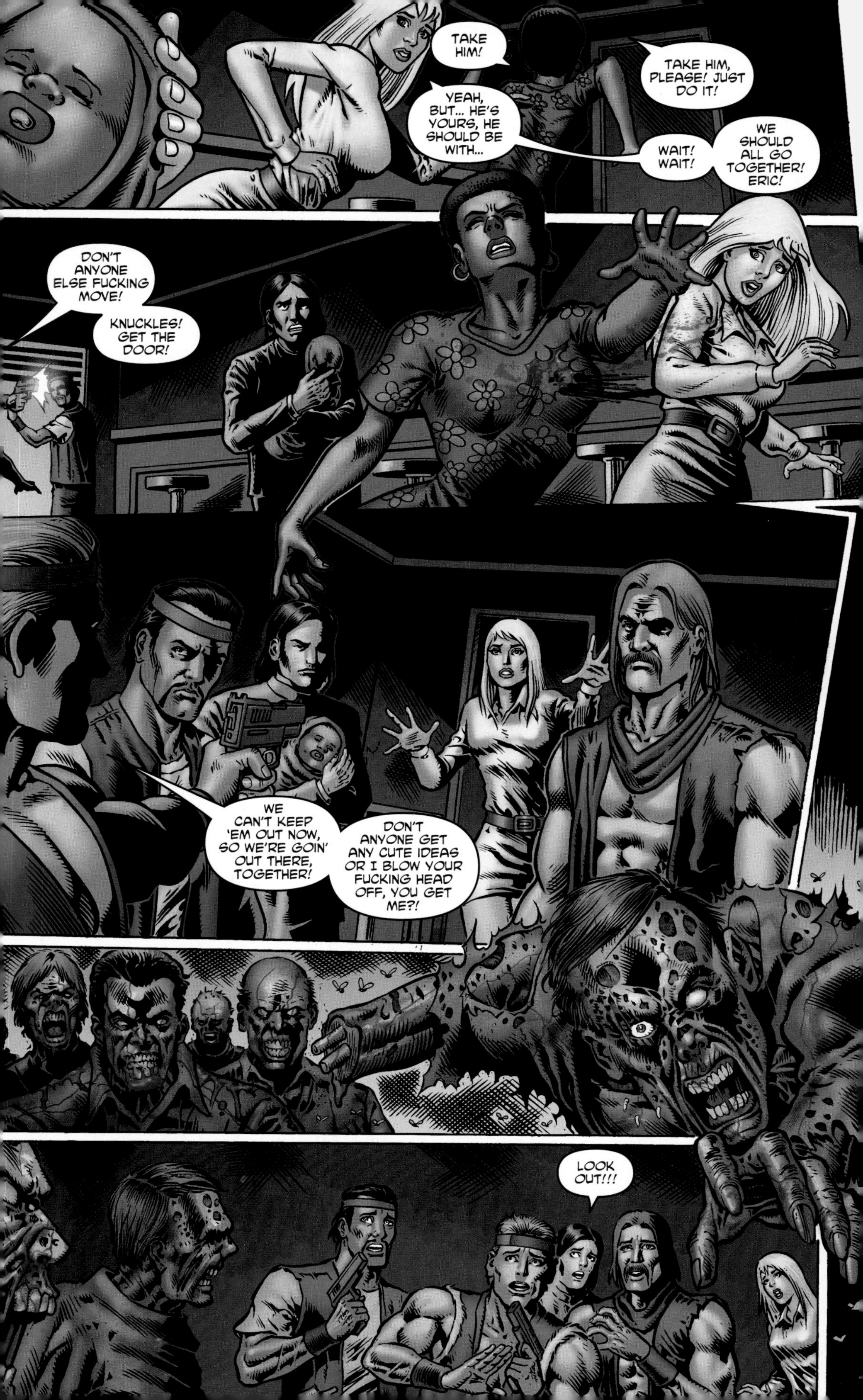
TAKE HIM!
YEAH, BUT... HE'S YOURS, HE SHOULD BE WITH...
TAKE HIM, PLEASE! JUST DO IT!
WAIT! WAIT!
WE SHOULD ALL GO TOGETHER! ERIC!
DON'T ANYONE ELSE FUCKING MOVE!
KNUCKLES! GET THE DOOR!
WE CAN'T KEEP 'EM OUT NOW, SO WE'RE GOIN' OUT THERE, TOGETHER!
DON'T ANYONE GET ANY CUTE IDEAS OR I BLOW YOUR FUCKING HEAD OFF, YOU GET ME?!
LOOK OUT!!!

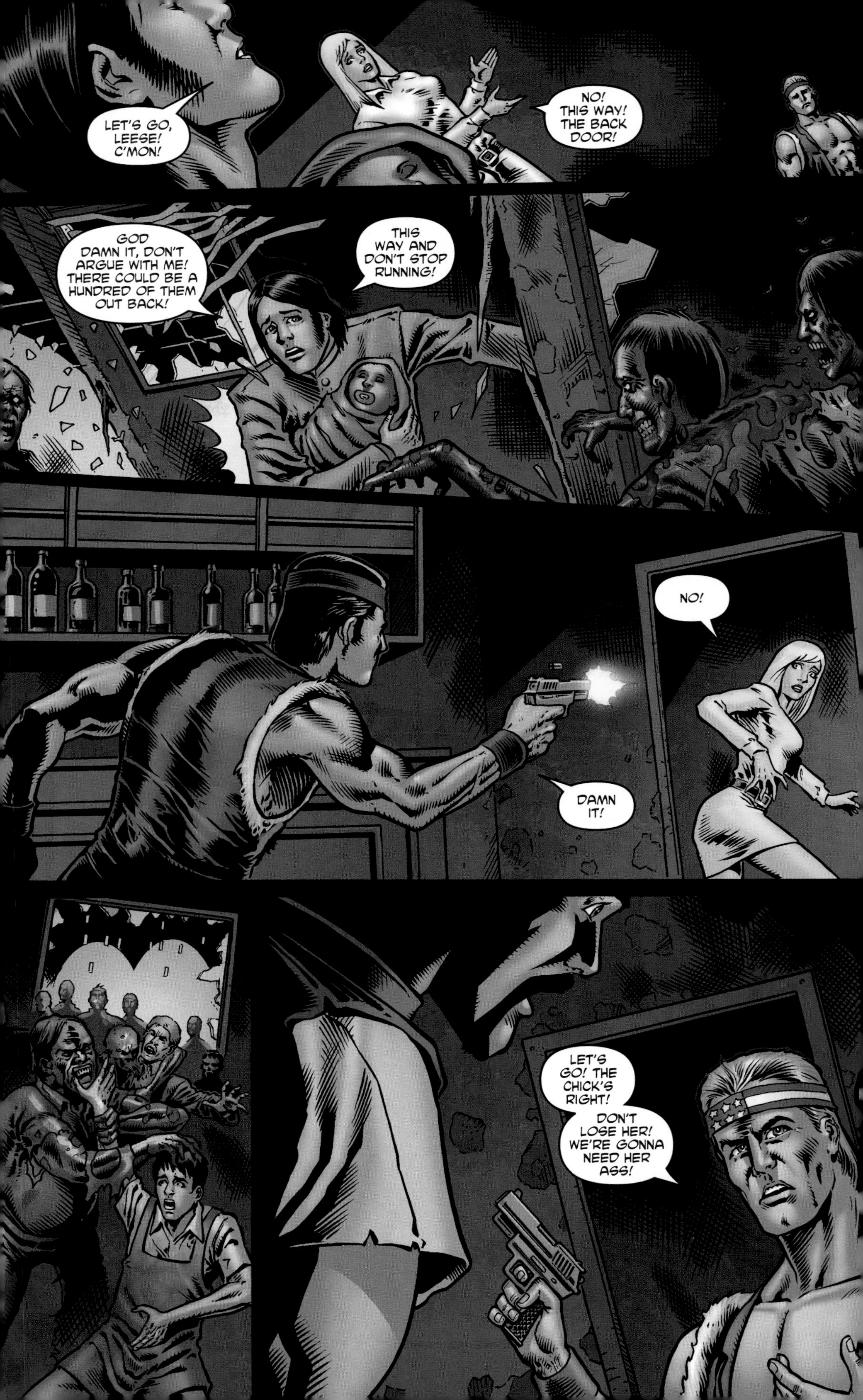
LET'S GO, LEESE! C'MON!
NO! THIS WAY! THE BACK DOOR!
GOD DAMN IT, DON'T ARGUE WITH ME! THERE COULD BE A HUNDRED OF THEM OUT BACK!
THIS WAY AND DON'T STOP RUNNING!
NO!
DAMN IT!
LET'S GO! THE CHICK'S RIGHT!
DON'T LOSE HER! WE'RE GONNA NEED HER ASS!

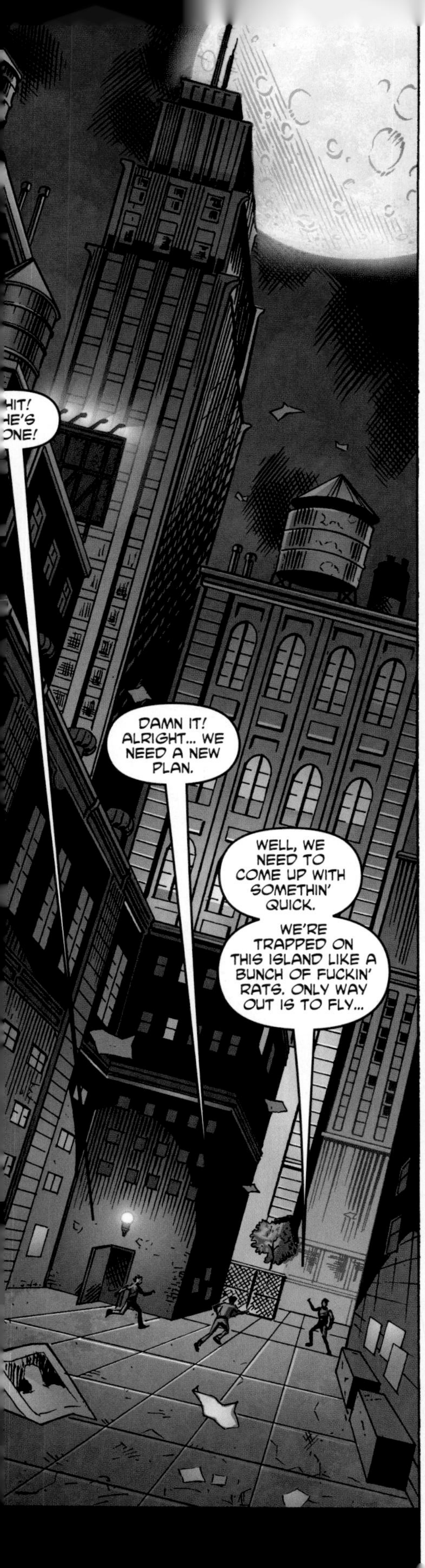
HIT! HE'S ONE!
DAMN IT! ALRIGHT... WE NEED A NEW PLAN.
WELL, WE NEED TO COME UP WITH SOMETHIN' QUICK.
WE'RE TRAPPED ON THIS ISLAND LIKE A BUNCH OF FUCKIN' RATS. ONLY WAY OUT IS TO FLY...

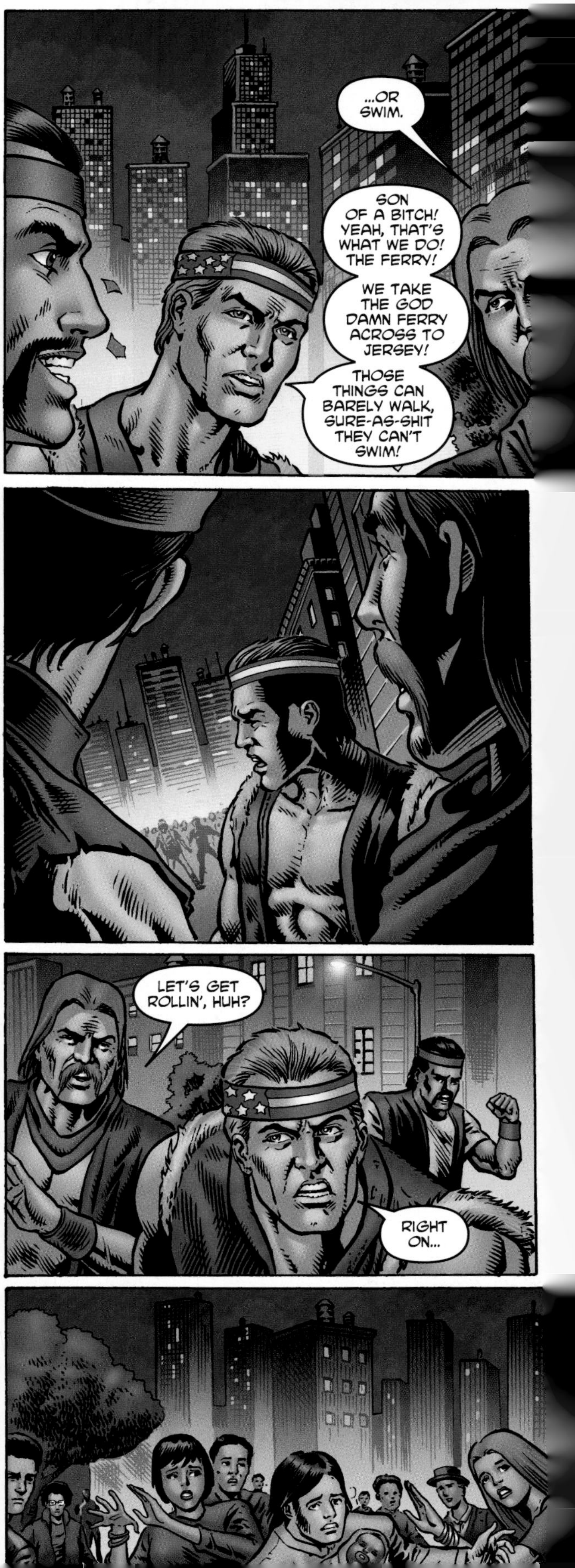
...OR SWIM.
SON OF A BITCH! YEAH, THAT'S WHAT WE DO! THE FERRY!
WE TAKE THE GOD DAMN FERRY ACROSS TO JERSEY!
THOSE THINGS CAN BARELY WALK, SURE-AS-SHIT THEY CAN'T SWIM!
LET'S GET ROLLIN', HUH?
RIGHT ON...

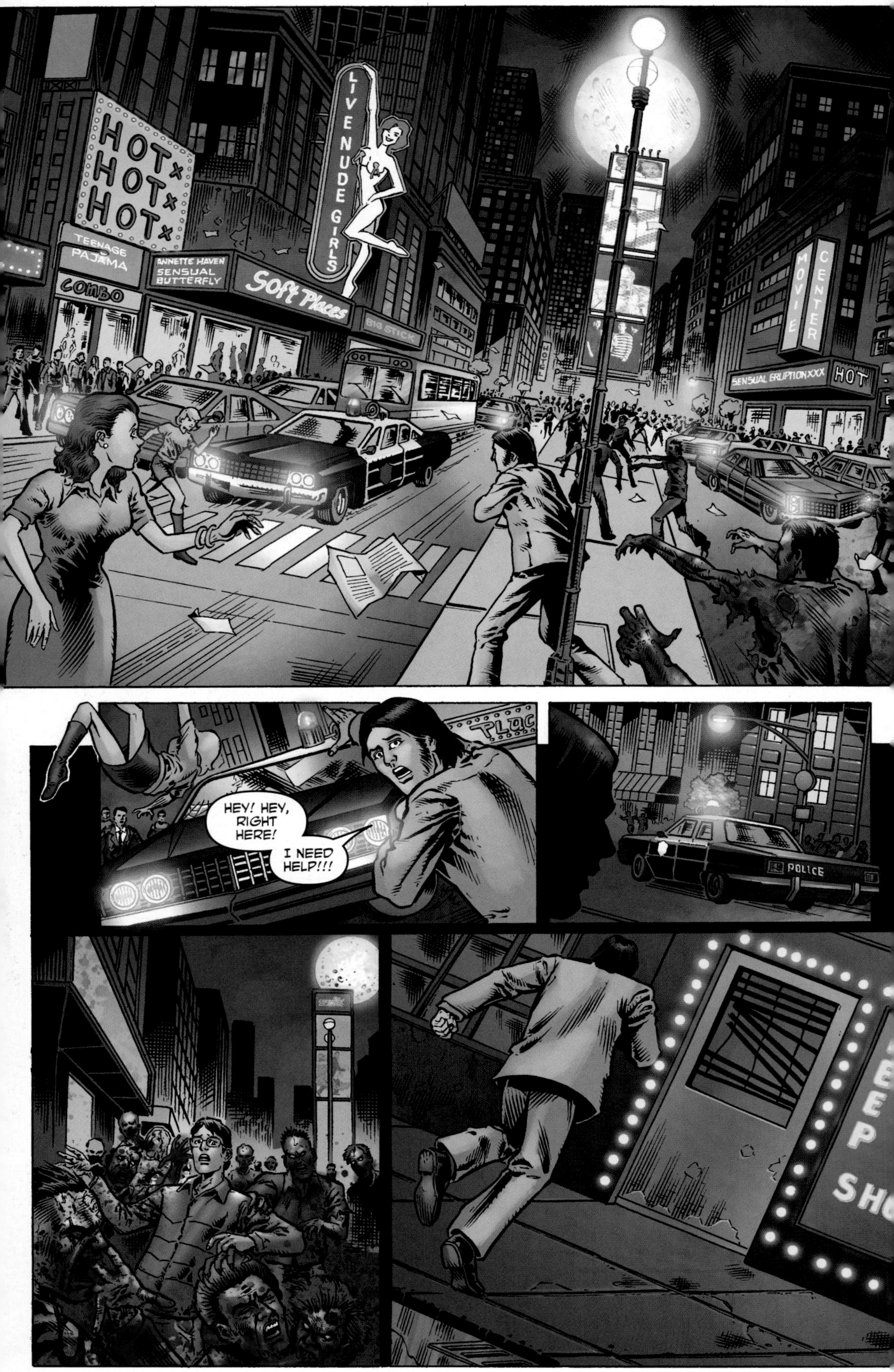
HOT HOT HOT
TEENAGE PAJAMA
COMBO
ANNETTE HAVEN SENSUAL BUTTERFLY
Soft Places
LIVE NUDE GIRLS
BIG STICK
MOVIE CENTER
SENSUAL ERUPTION XXX
HOT
HEY! HEY, RIGHT HERE!
I NEED HELP!!!
POLICE

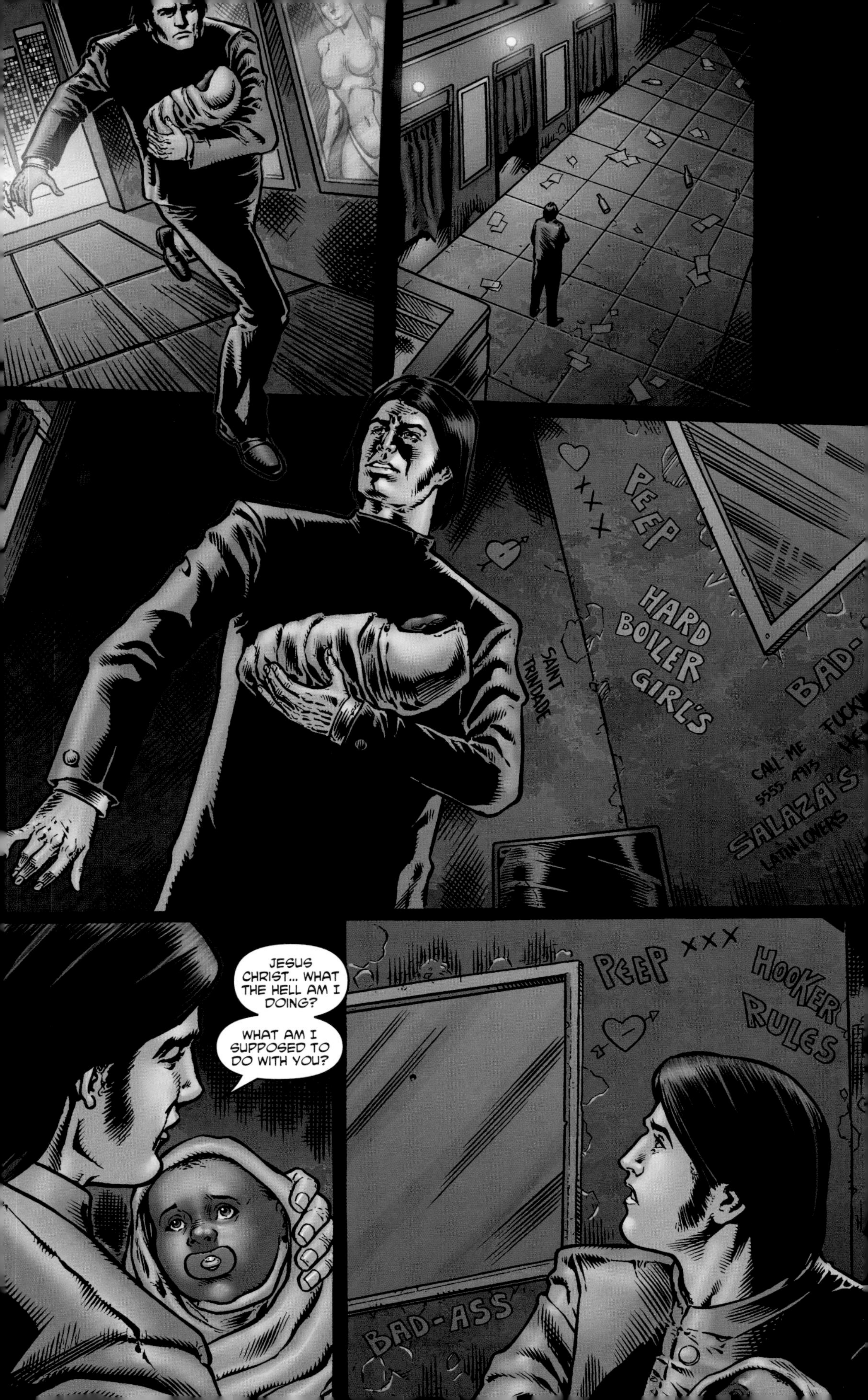
PEEP
HARD BOILER GIRL'S
SAINT TRINDADE
BAD-
CALL-ME 5555-4913
SALAZA'S
LATIN LOVERS
JESUS CHRIST... WHAT THE HELL AM I DOING?
WHAT AM I SUPPOSED TO DO WITH YOU?
PEEP XXX
HOOKER RULES
BAD-ASS

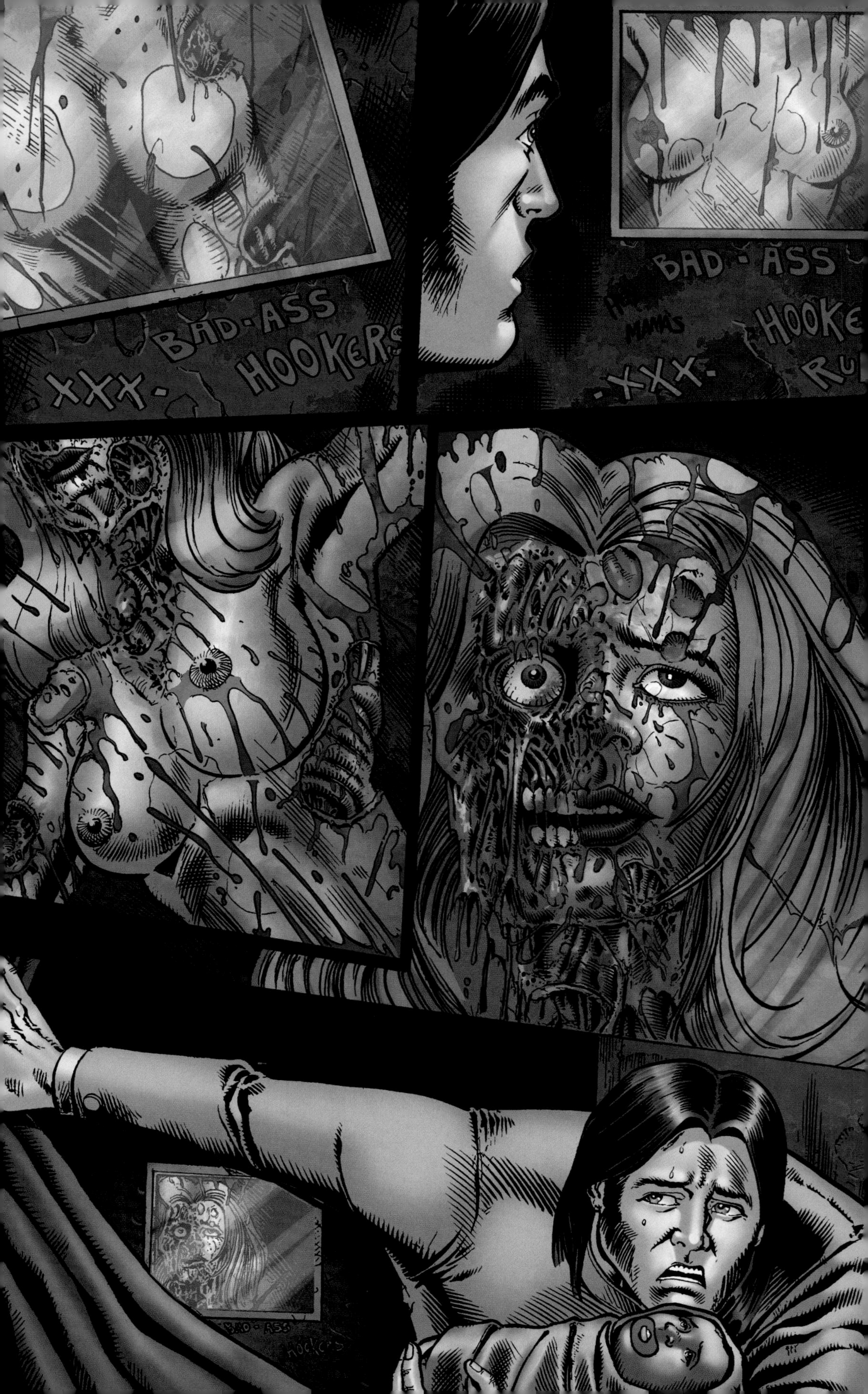
BAD-ASS
HOOKERS
-XXX-
BAD-ASS
MAMA'S
HOOKE
-XXX-
RU
BAD-ASS

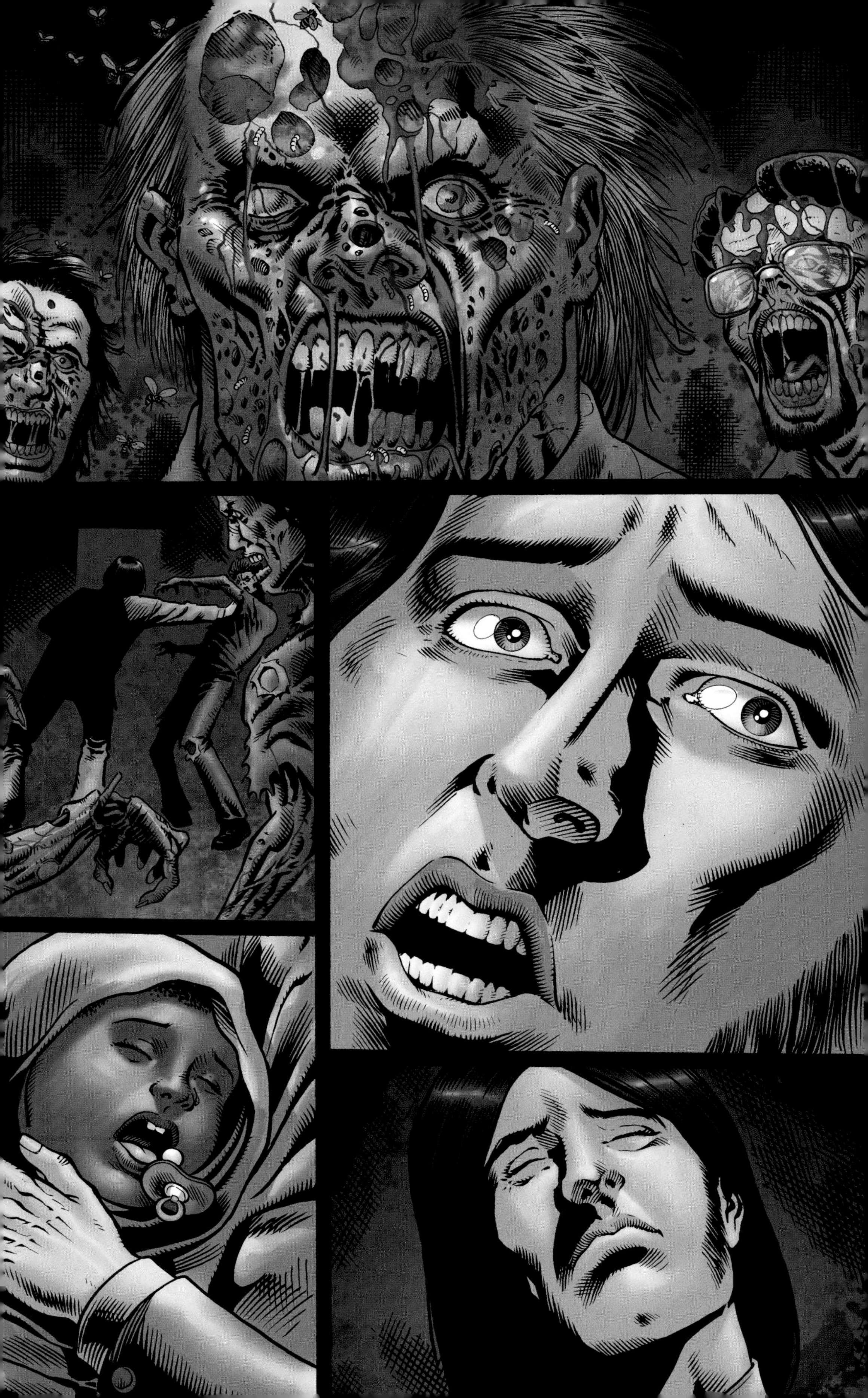

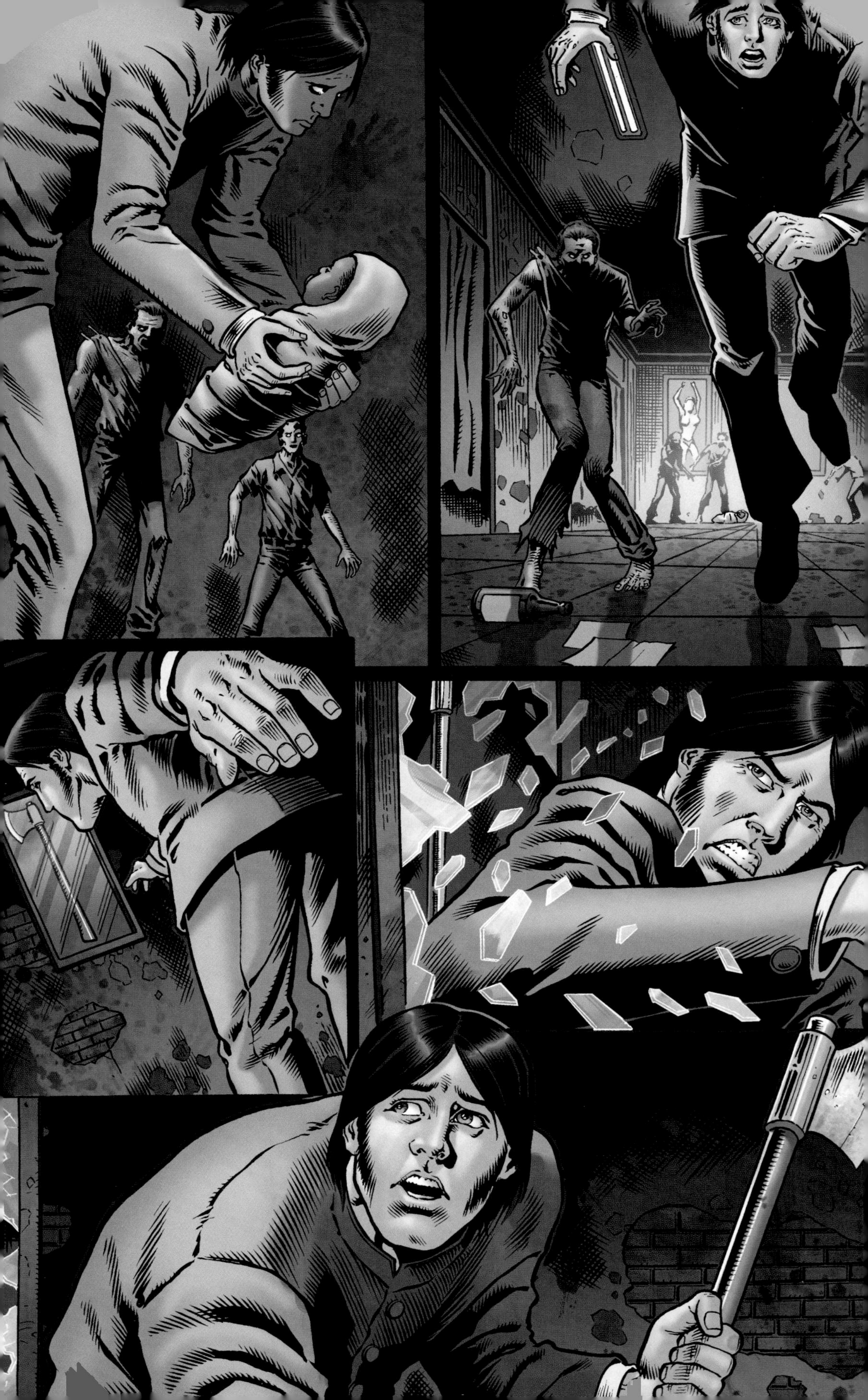

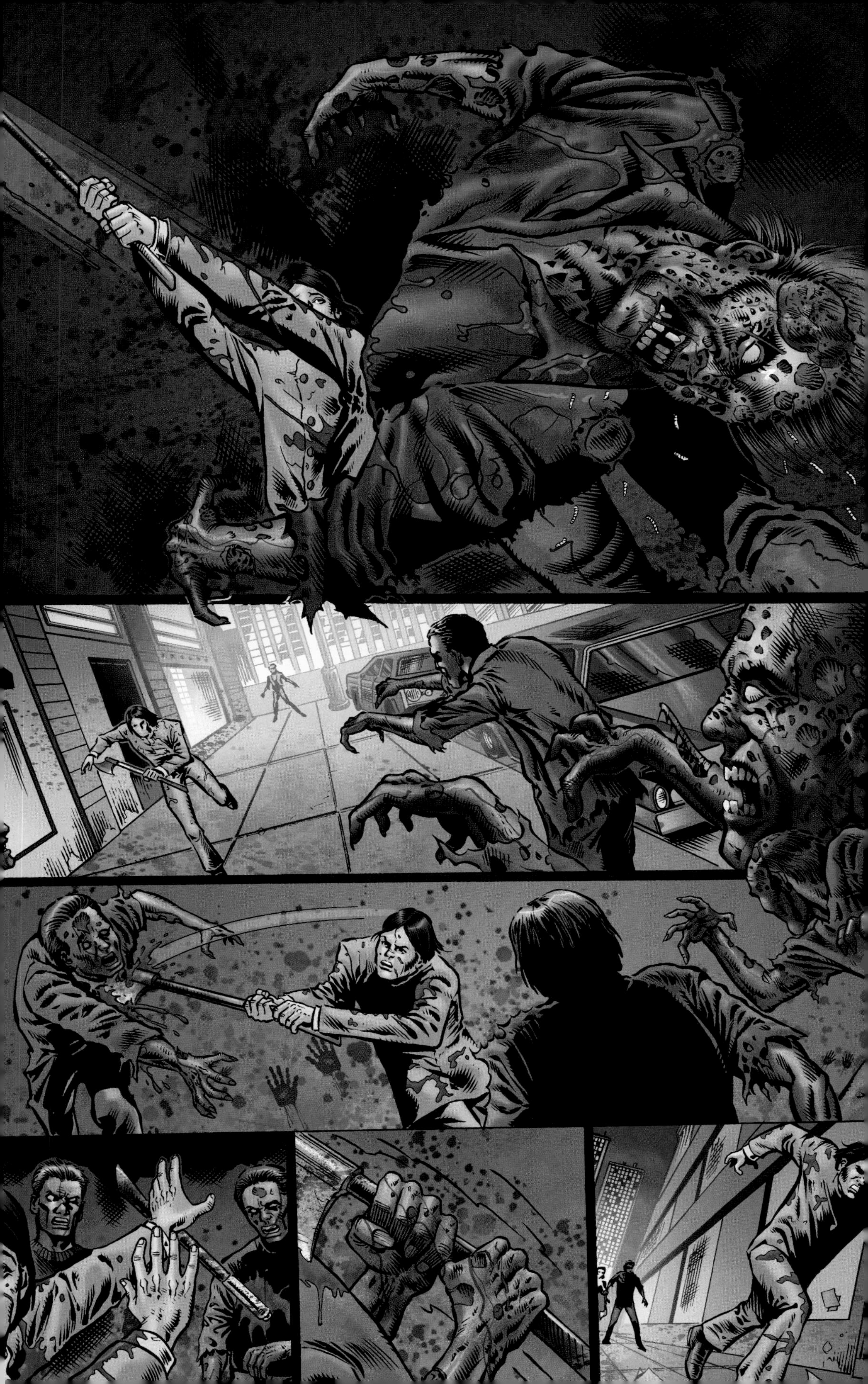

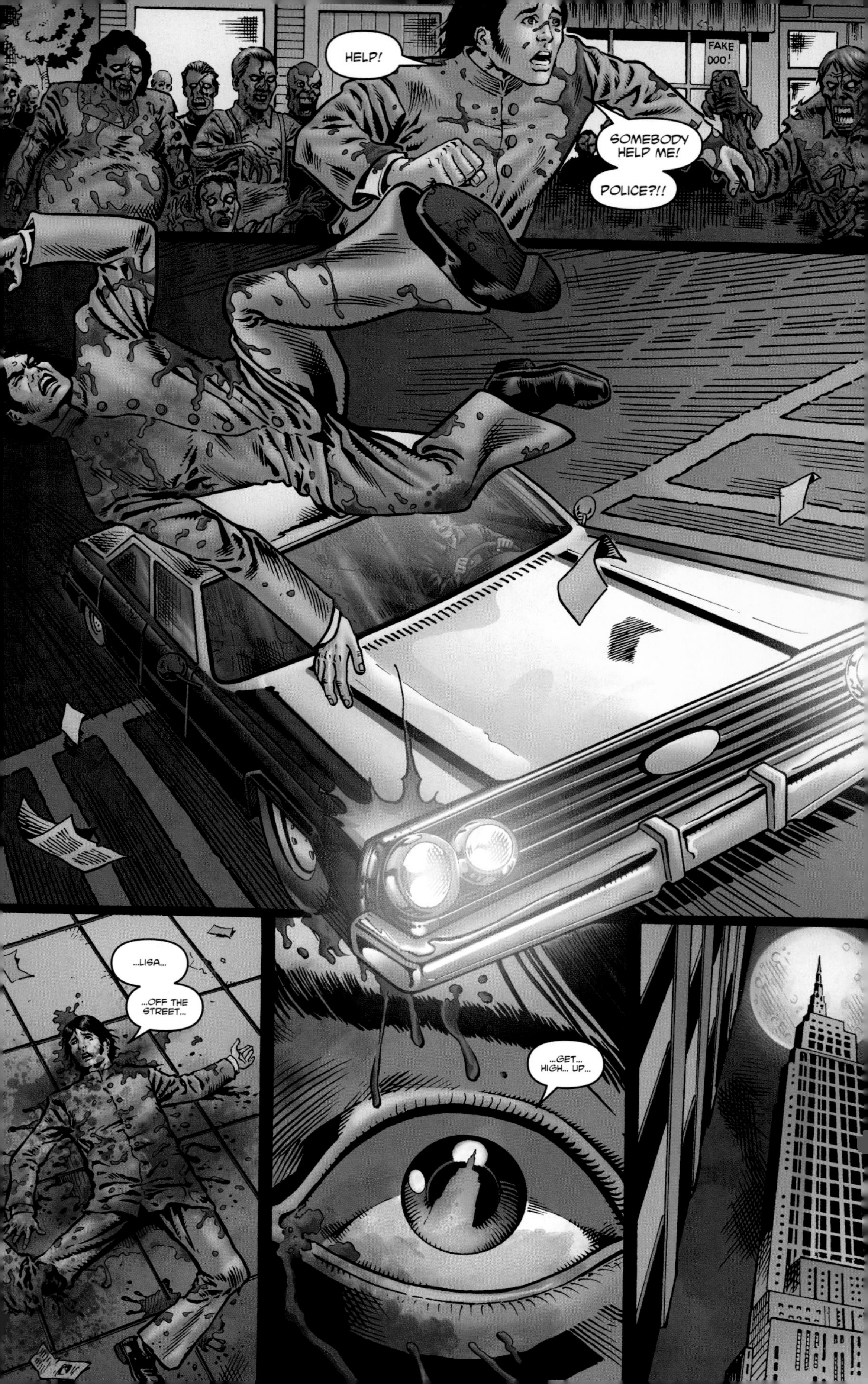
HELP!
SOMEBODY HELP ME!
POLICE?!!
FAKE DOO!
...LISA...
...OFF THE STREET...
...GET... HIGH... UP...

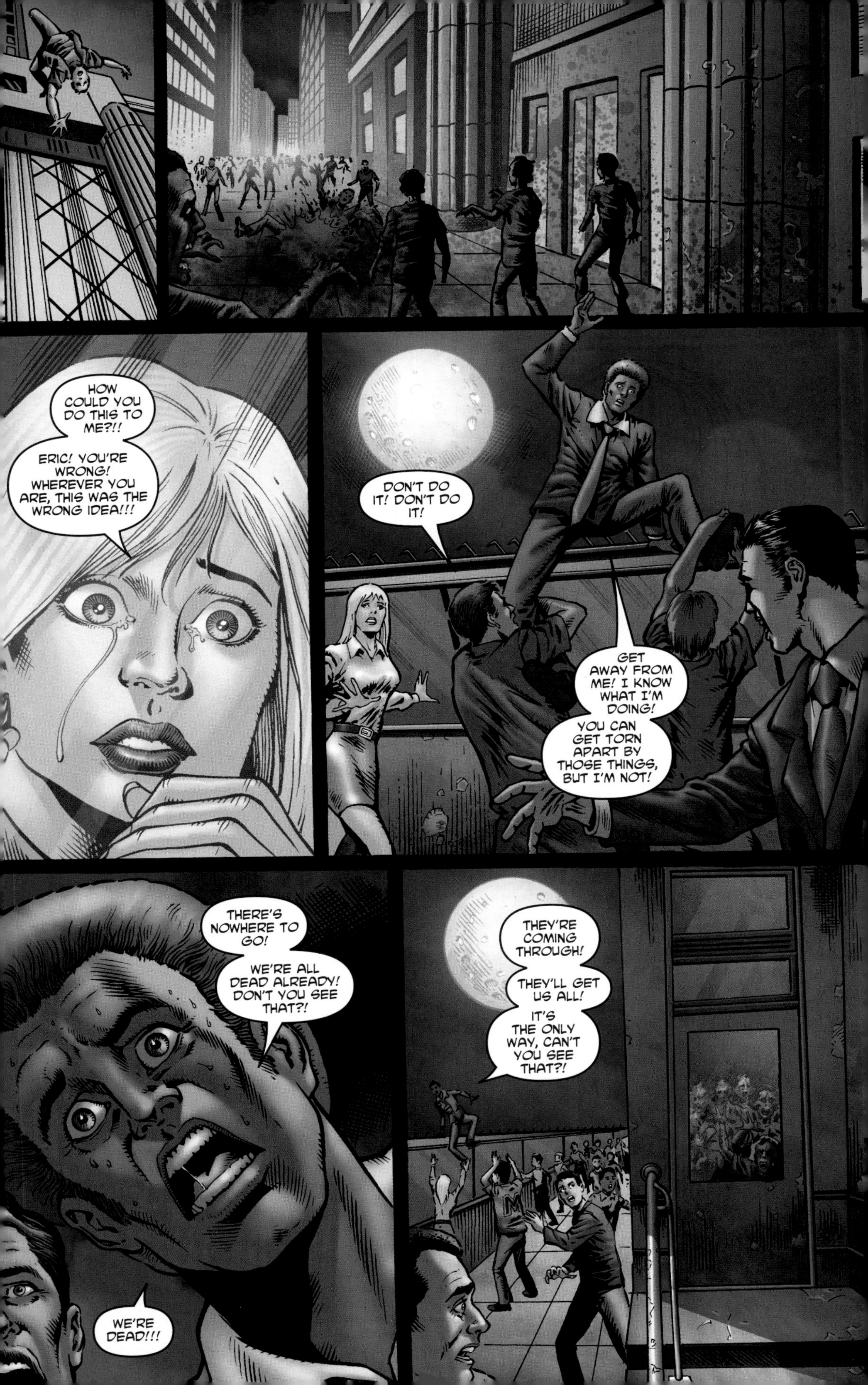
HOW COULD YOU DO THIS TO ME?!!
ERIC! YOU'RE WRONG! WHEREVER YOU ARE, THIS WAS THE WRONG IDEA!!!
DON'T DO IT! DON'T DO IT!
GET AWAY FROM ME! I KNOW WHAT I'M DOING!
YOU CAN GET TORN APART BY THOSE THINGS, BUT I'M NOT!
THERE'S NOWHERE TO GO!
WE'RE ALL DEAD ALREADY! DON'T YOU SEE THAT?!
WE'RE DEAD!!!
THEY'RE COMING THROUGH!
THEY'LL GET US ALL!
IT'S THE ONLY WAY, CAN'T YOU SEE THAT?!

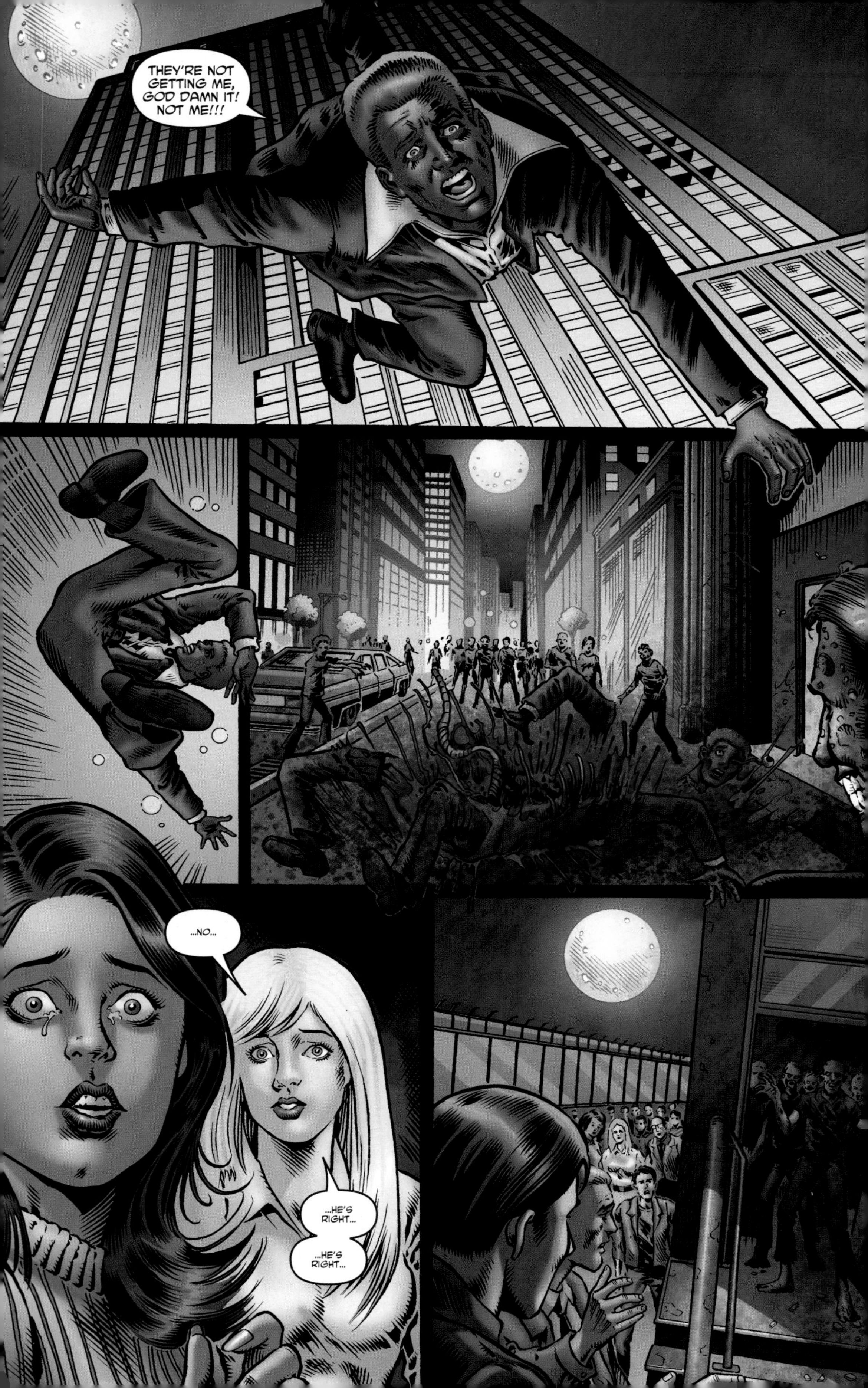
THEY'RE NOT GETTING ME, GOD DAMN IT! NOT ME!!!
...NO...
...HE'S RIGHT...
...HE'S RIGHT...

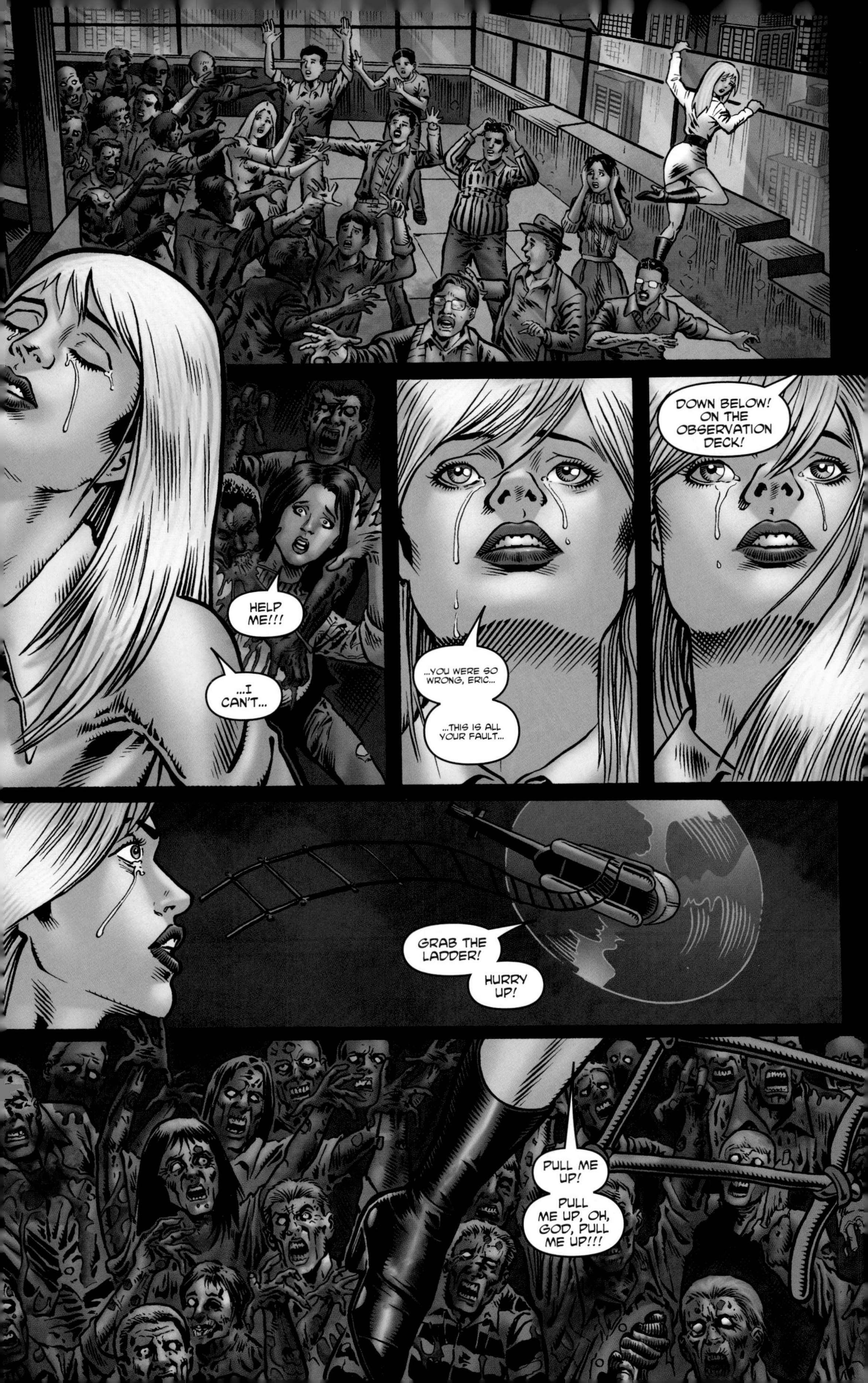
HELP ME!!!
...I CAN'T...
...YOU WERE SO WRONG, ERIC...
...THIS IS ALL YOUR FAULT...
DOWN BELOW! ON THE OBSERVATION DECK!
GRAB THE LADDER!
HURRY UP!
PULL ME UP!
PULL ME UP, OH, GOD, PULL ME UP!!!

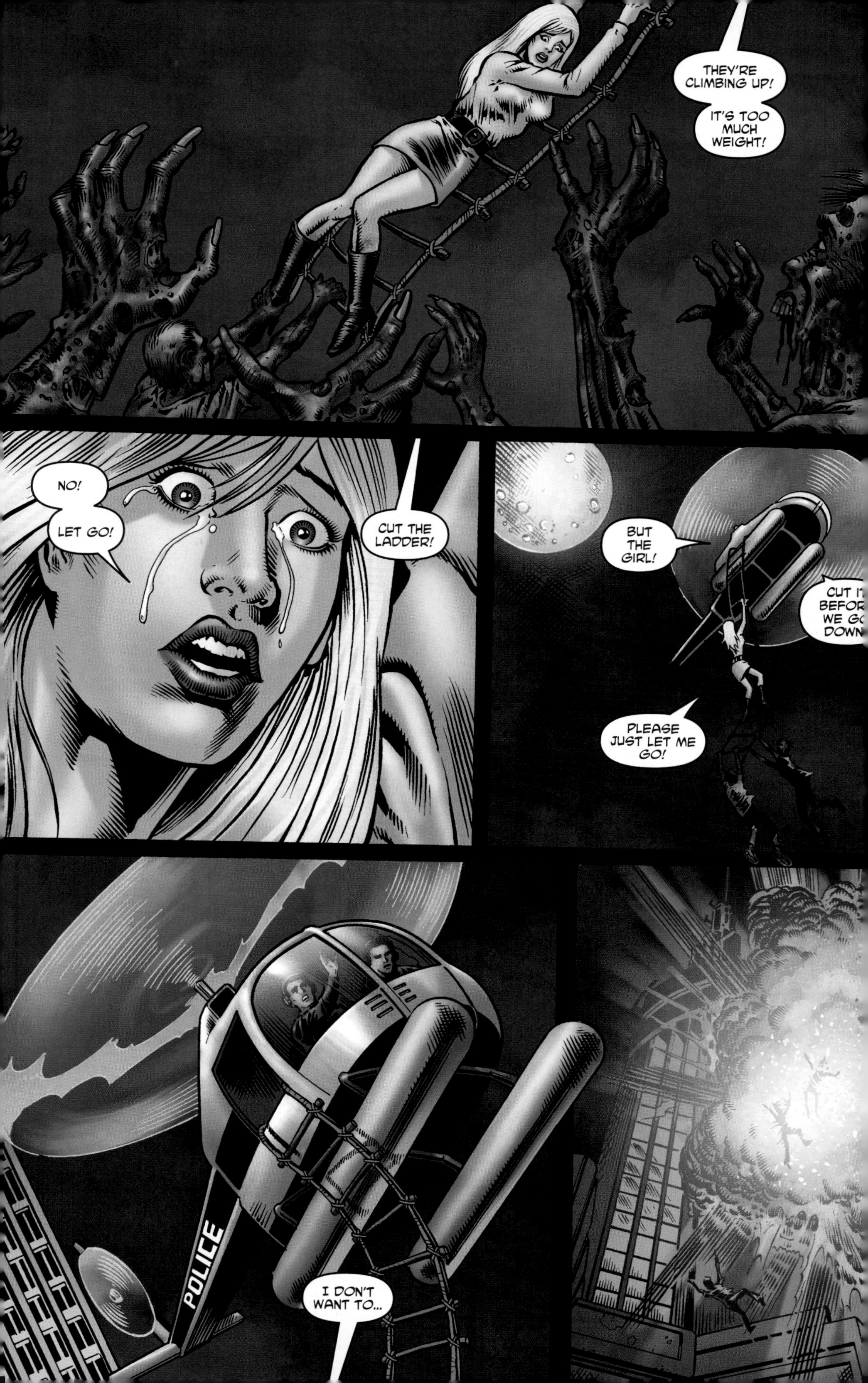
THEY'RE CLIMBING UP!
IT'S TOO MUCH WEIGHT!
NO!
LET GO!
CUT THE LADDER!
BUT THE GIRL!
PLEASE JUST LET ME GO!
POLICE
I DON'T WANT TO...

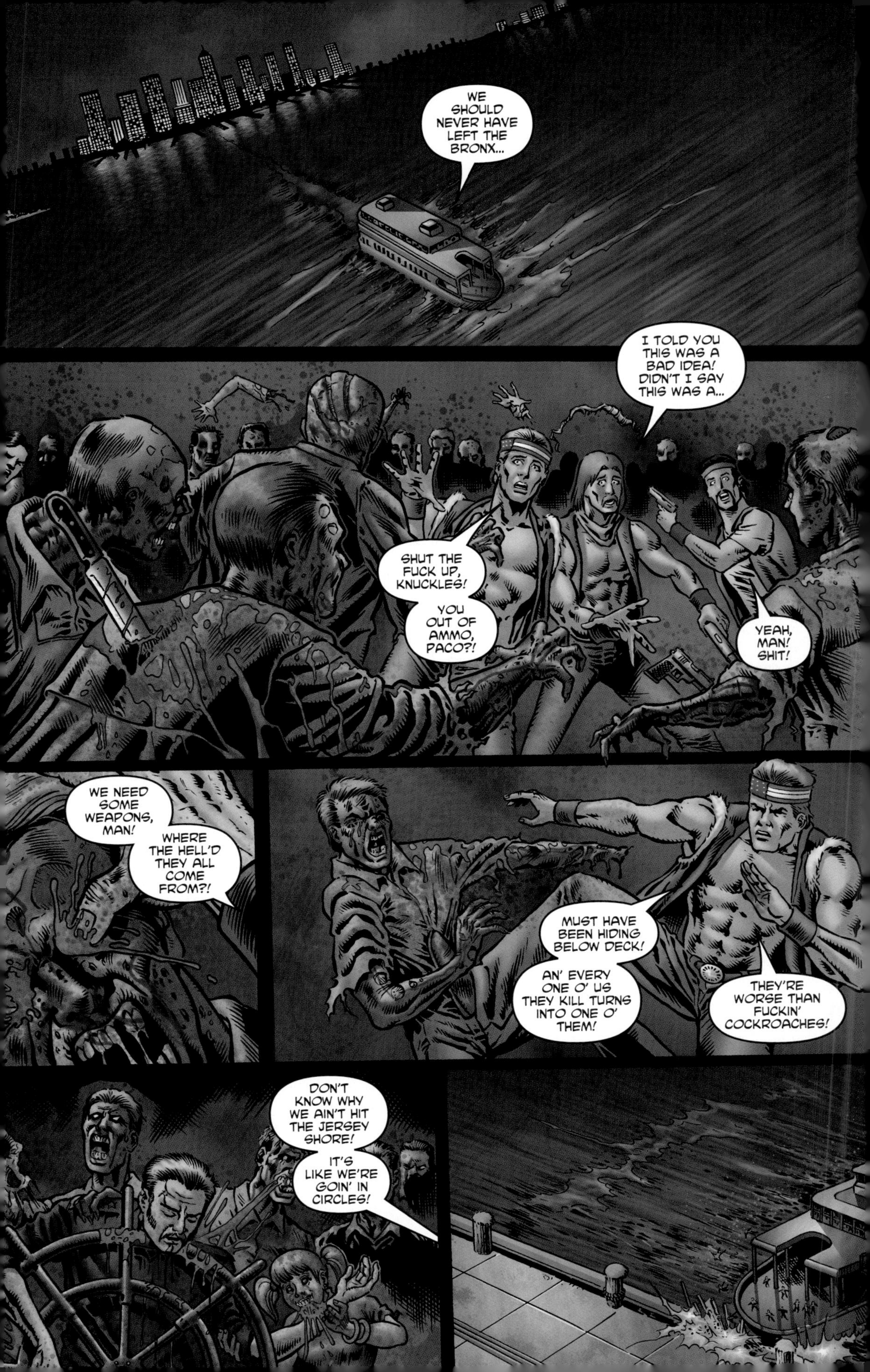

WE SHOULD NEVER HAVE LEFT THE BRONX...
I TOLD YOU THIS WAS A BAD IDEA! DIDN'T I SAY THIS WAS A...
SHUT THE FUCK UP, KNUCKLES!
YOU OUT OF AMMO, PACO?!
YEAH, MAN! SHIT!
WE NEED SOME WEAPONS, MAN!
WHERE THE HELL'D THEY ALL COME FROM?!
MUST HAVE BEEN HIDING BELOW DECK!
AN' EVERY ONE O' US THEY KILL TURNS INTO ONE O' THEM!
THEY'RE WORSE THAN FUCKIN' COCKROACHES!
DON'T KNOW WHY WE AIN'T HIT THE JERSEY SHORE!
IT'S LIKE WE'RE GOIN' IN CIRCLES!

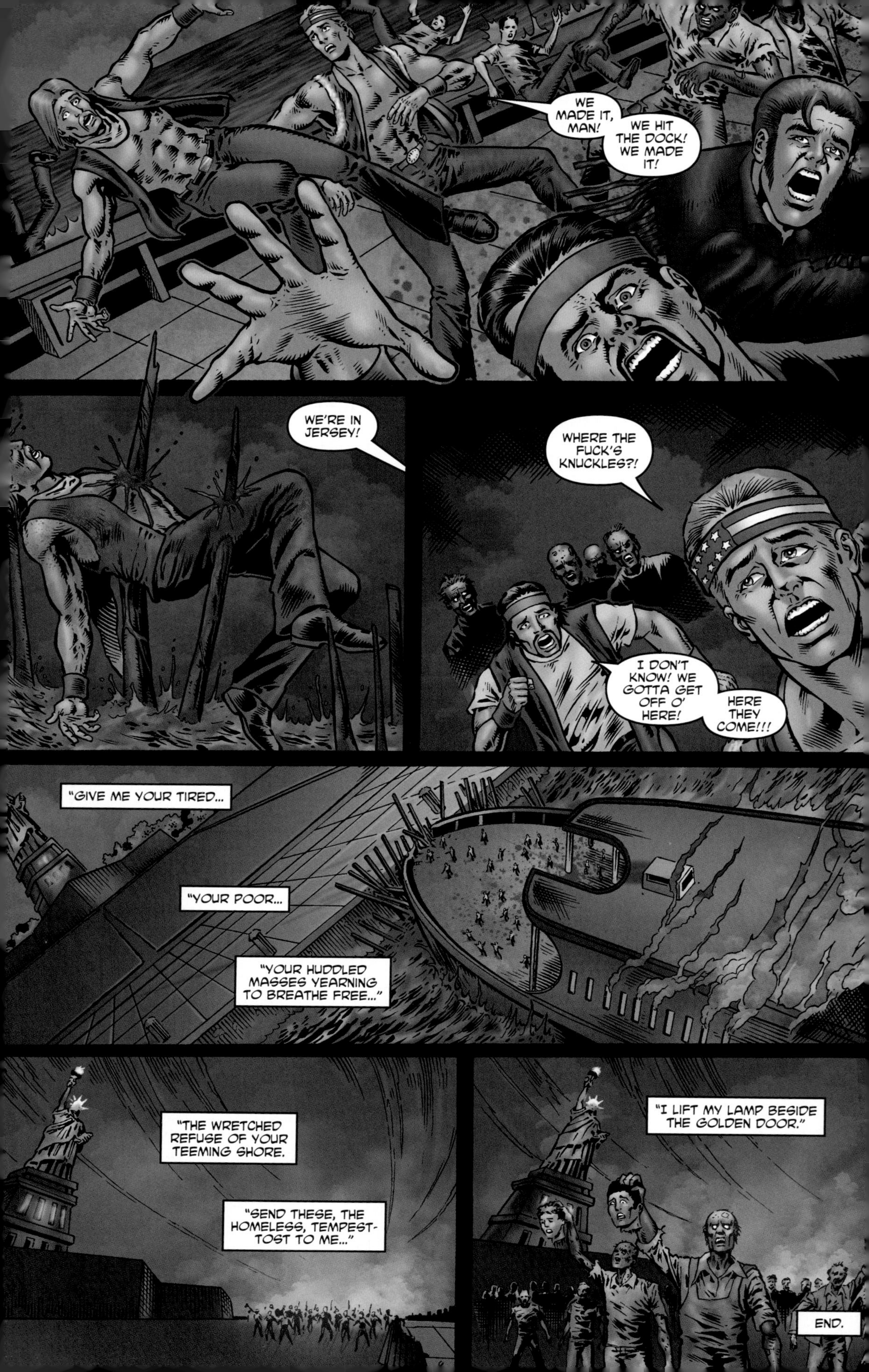
WE MADE IT, MAN!
WE HIT THE DOCK! WE MADE IT!
WE'RE IN JERSEY!
WHERE THE FUCK'S KNUCKLES?!
I DON'T KNOW! WE GOTTA GET OFF O' HERE!
HERE THEY COME!!!
"GIVE ME YOUR TIRED...
"YOUR POOR...
"YOUR HUDDLED MASSES YEARNING TO BREATHE FREE..."
"THE WRETCHED REFUSE OF YOUR TEEMING SHORE.
"SEND THESE, THE HOMELESS, TEMPEST-TOST TO ME..."
"I LIFT MY LAMP BESIDE THE GOLDEN DOOR."
END.

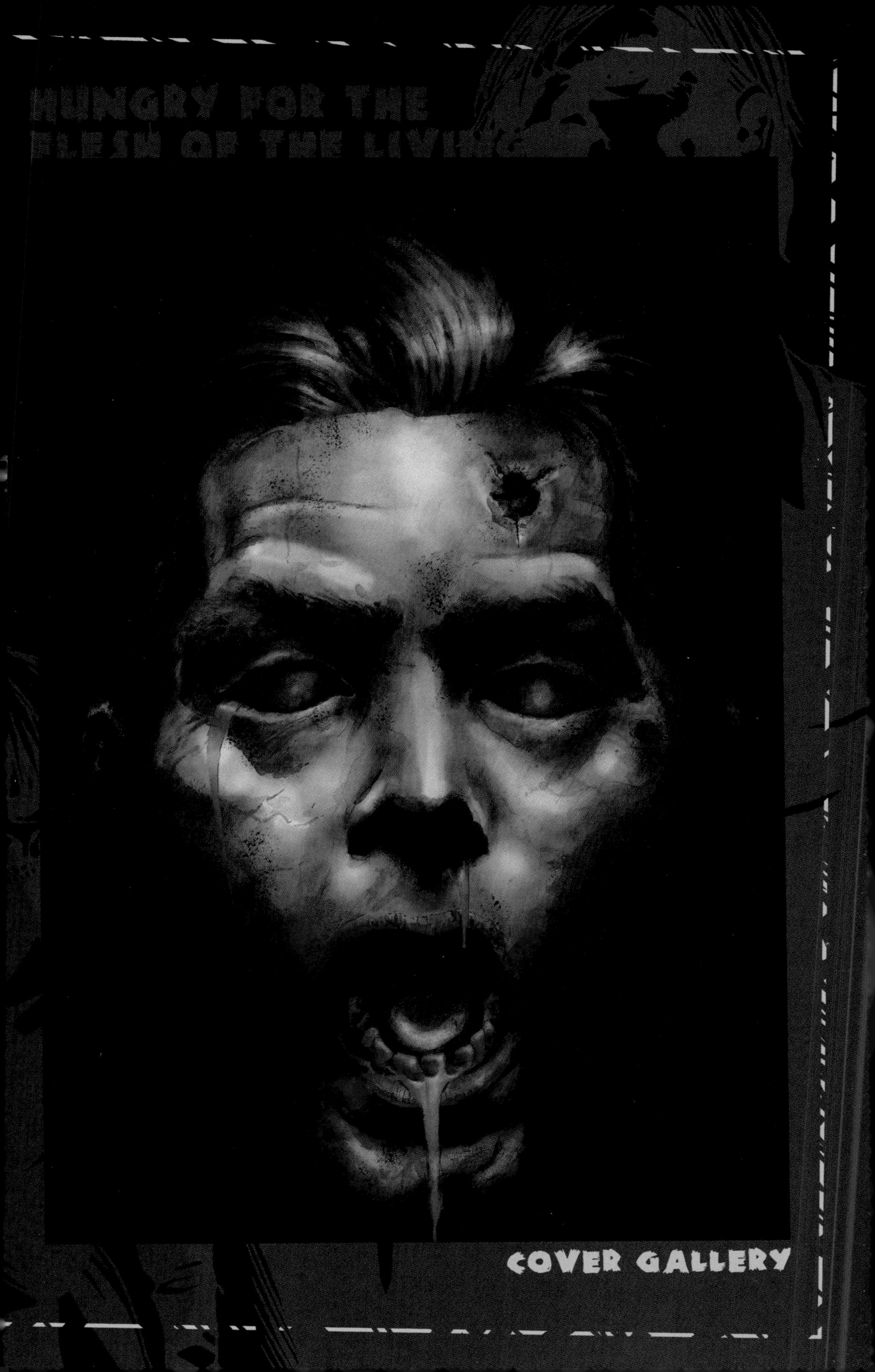
HUNGRY FOR THE
FLESH OF THE LIVIN

COVER GALLERY

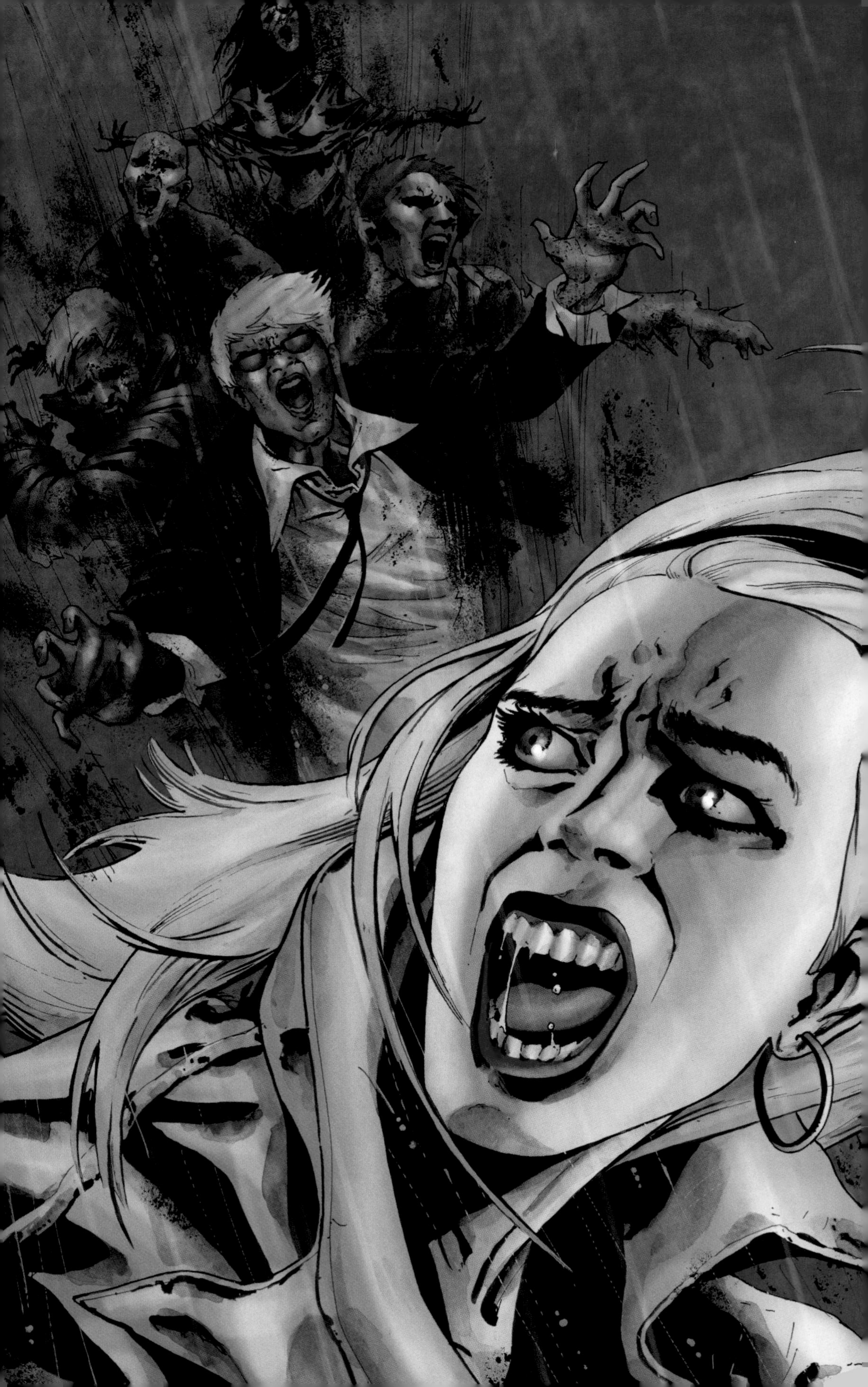

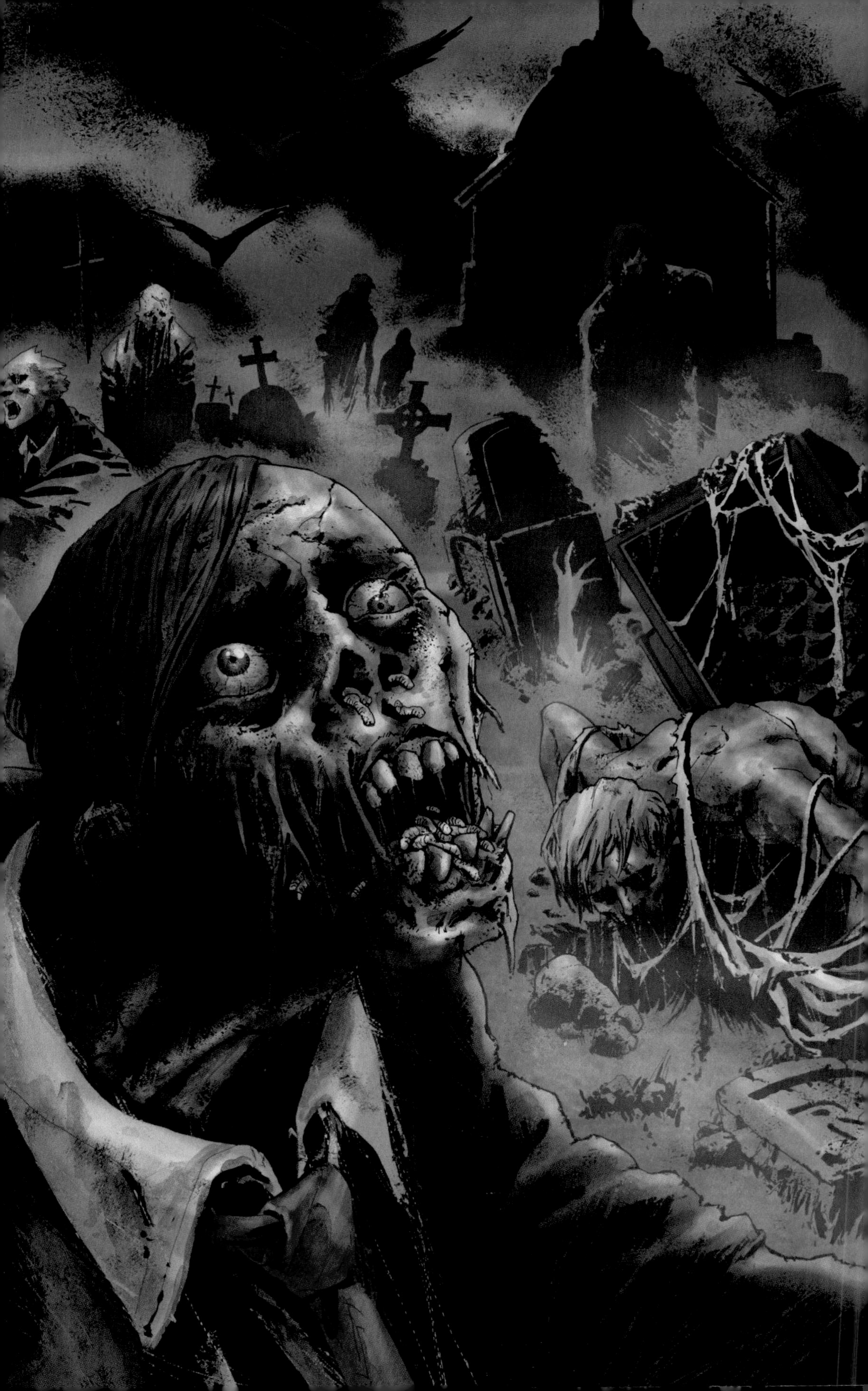

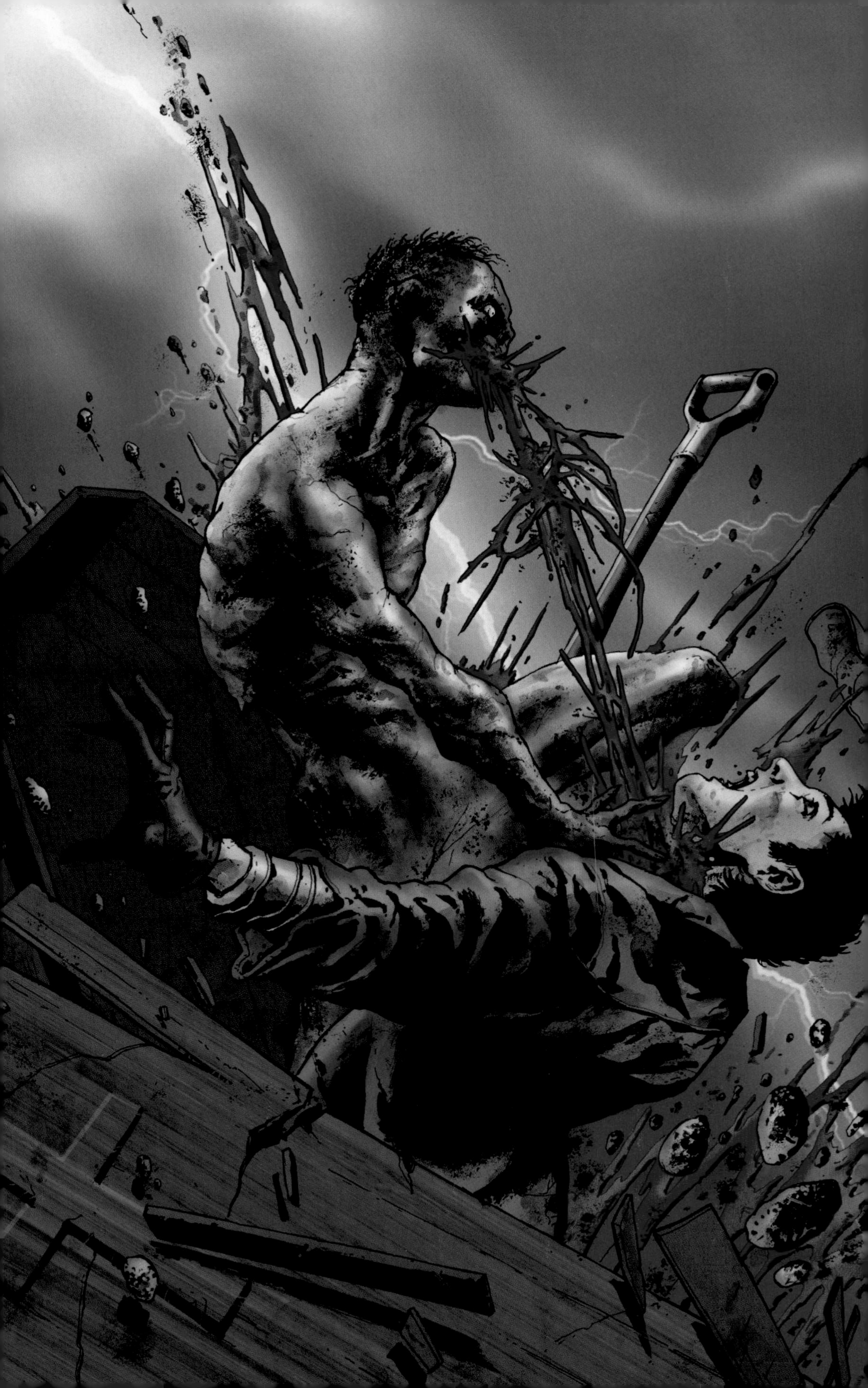

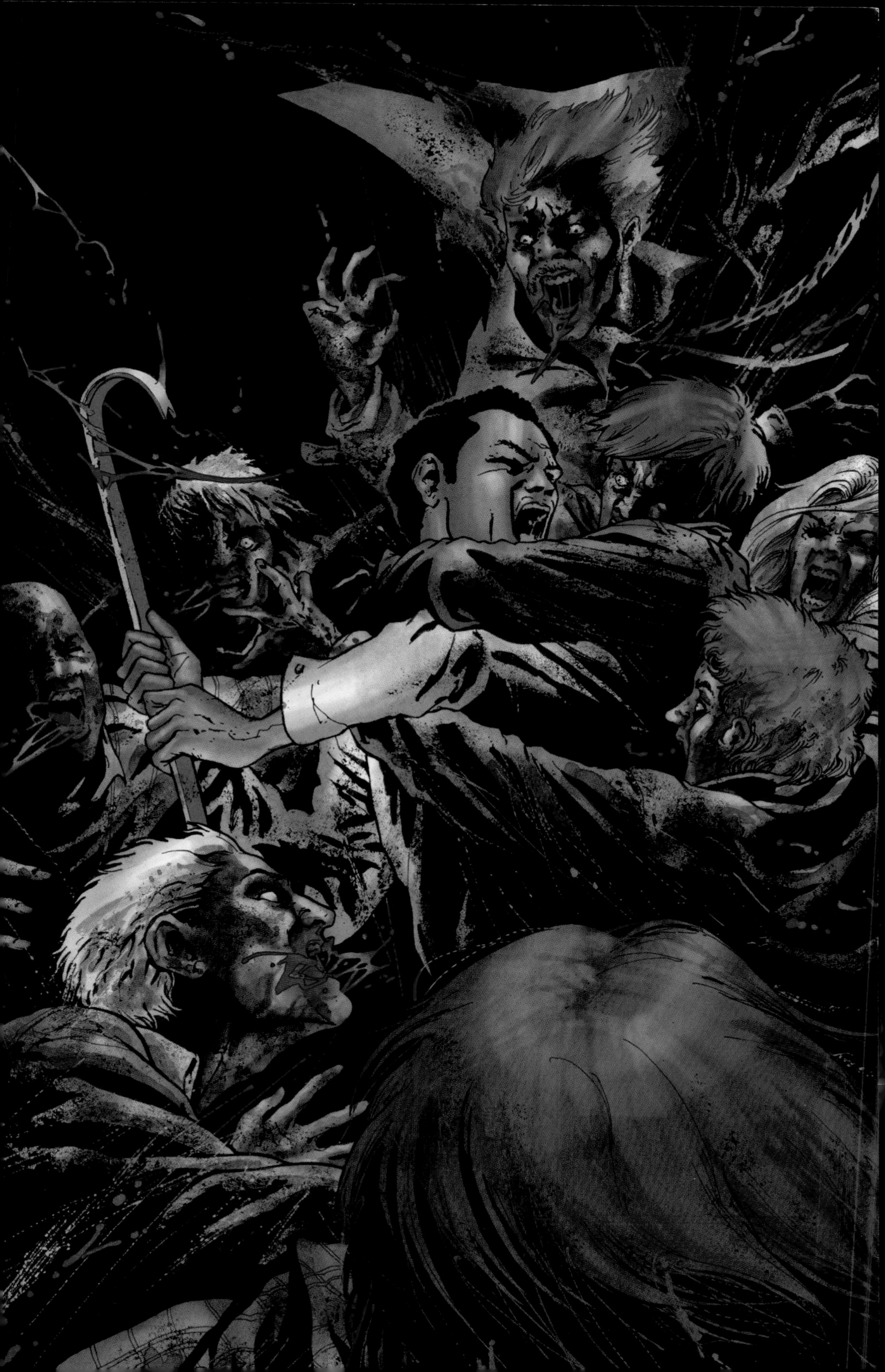

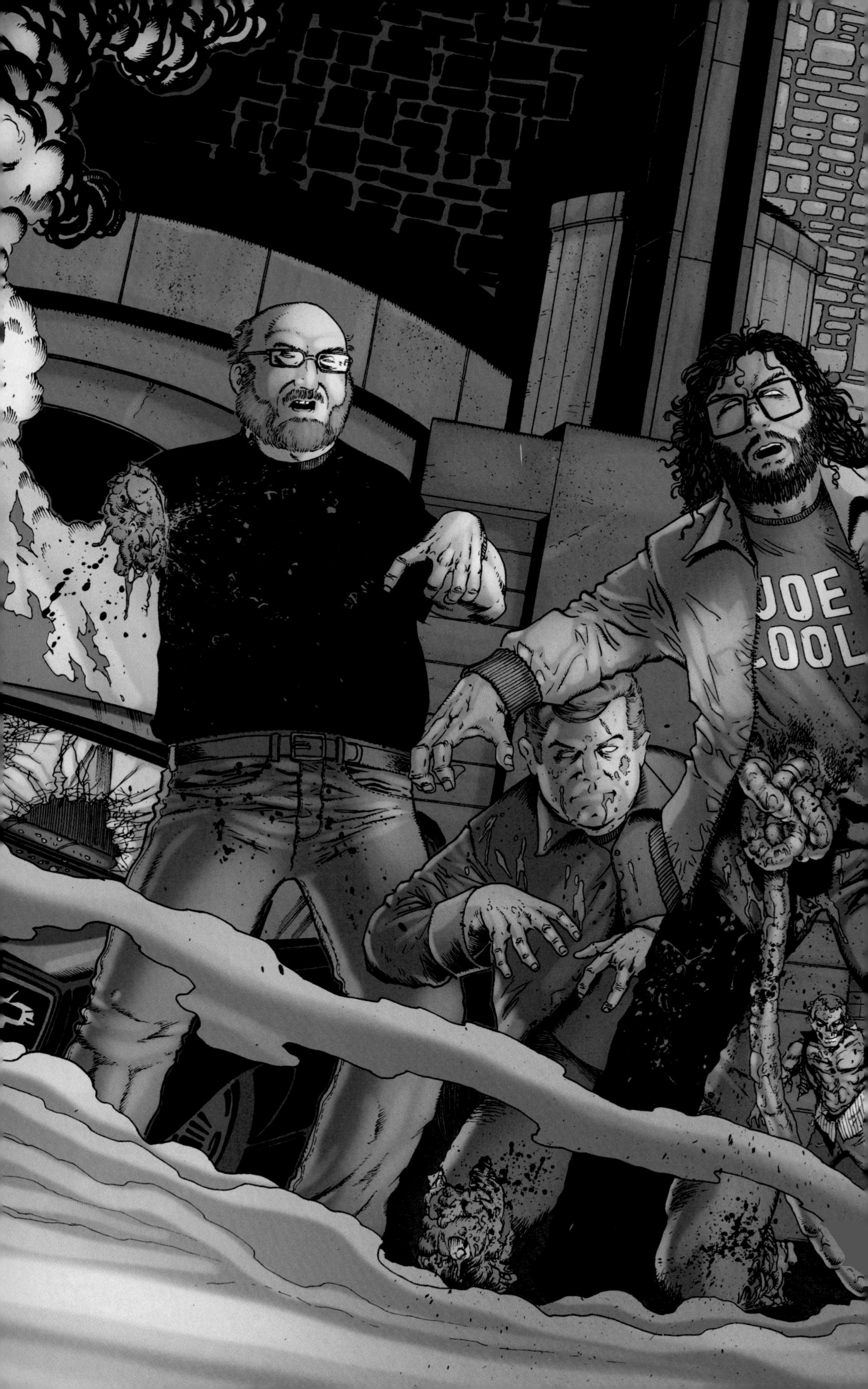
JOE

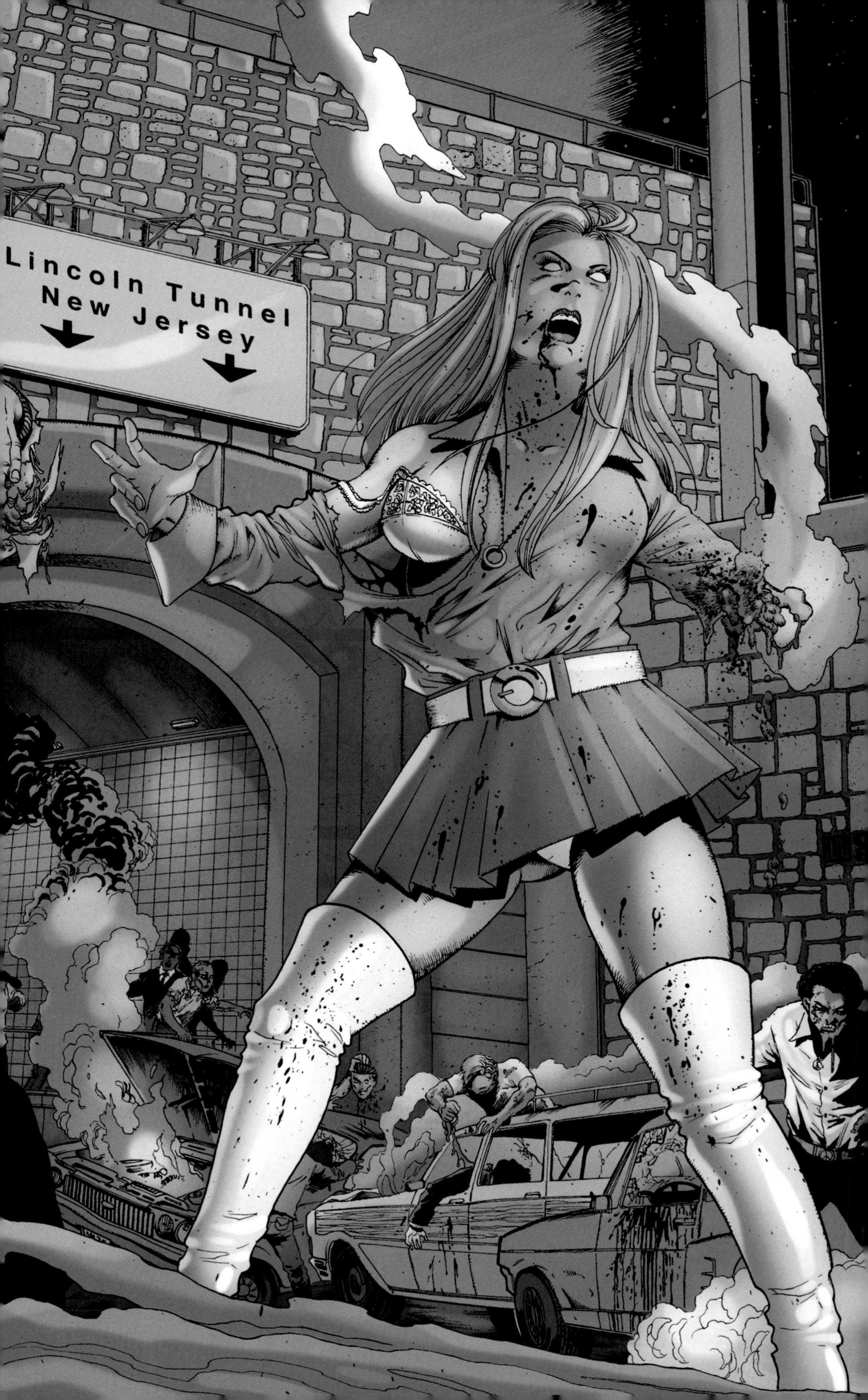

Lincoln Tunnel
New Jersey

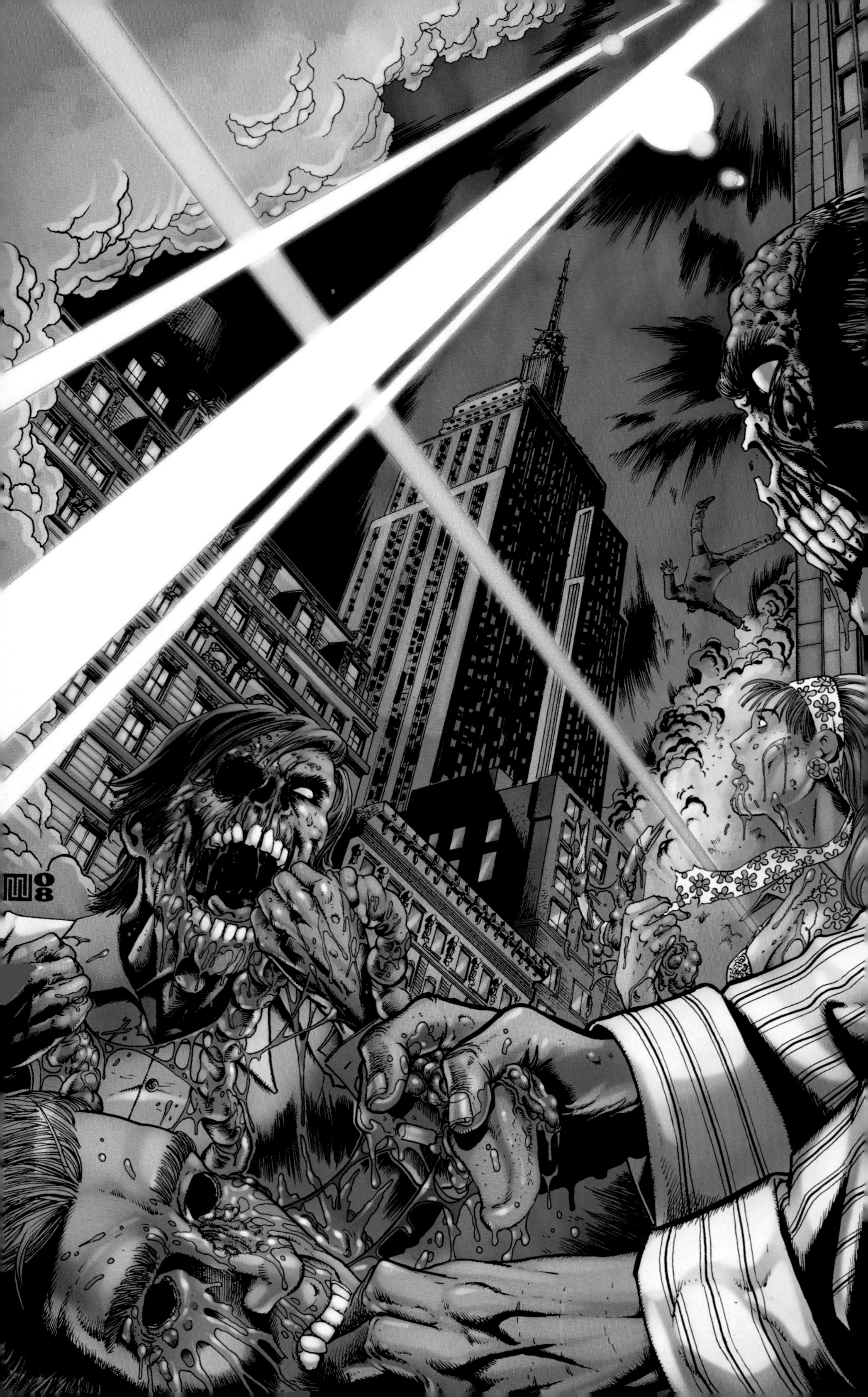

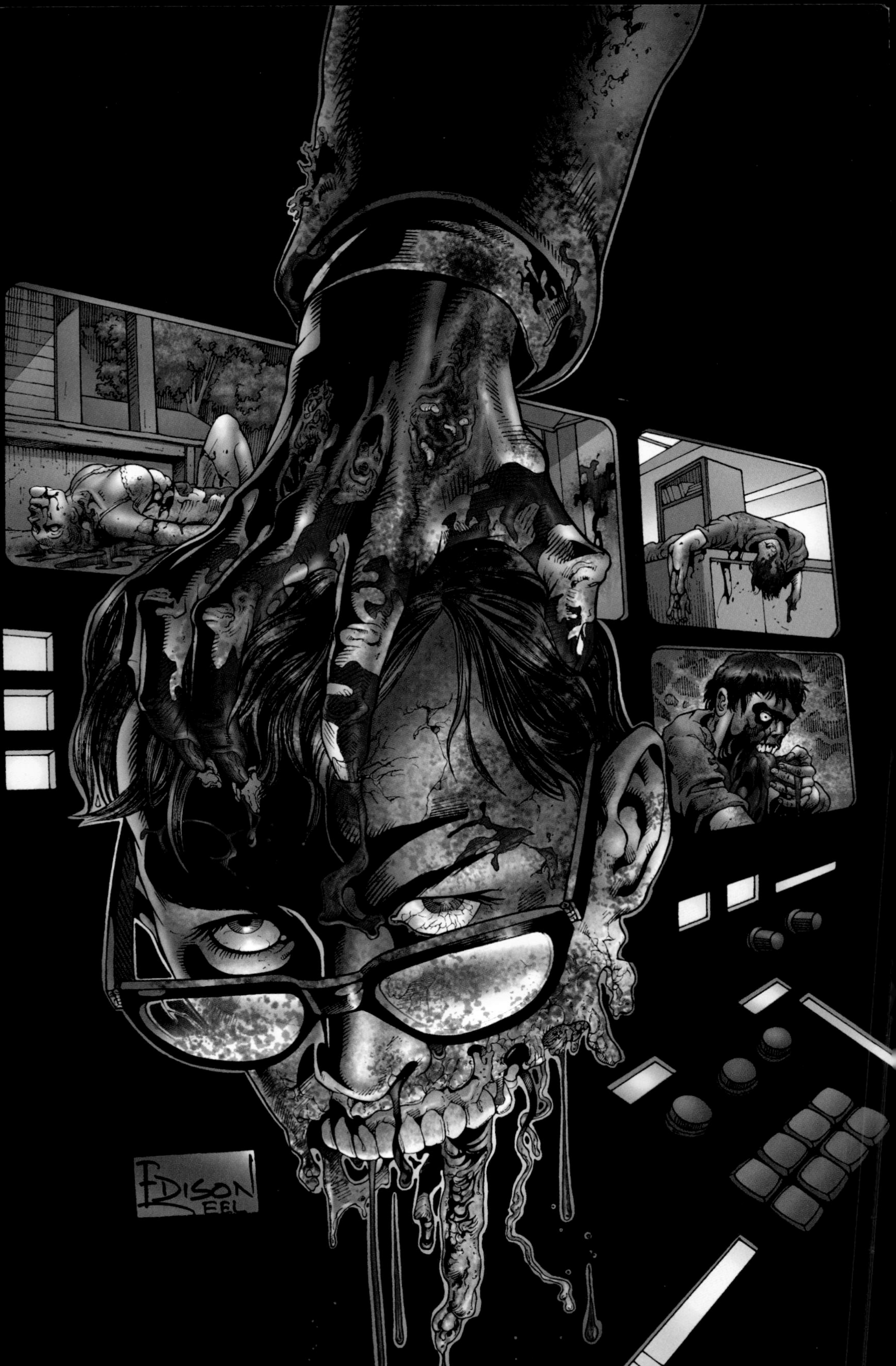
EDISON

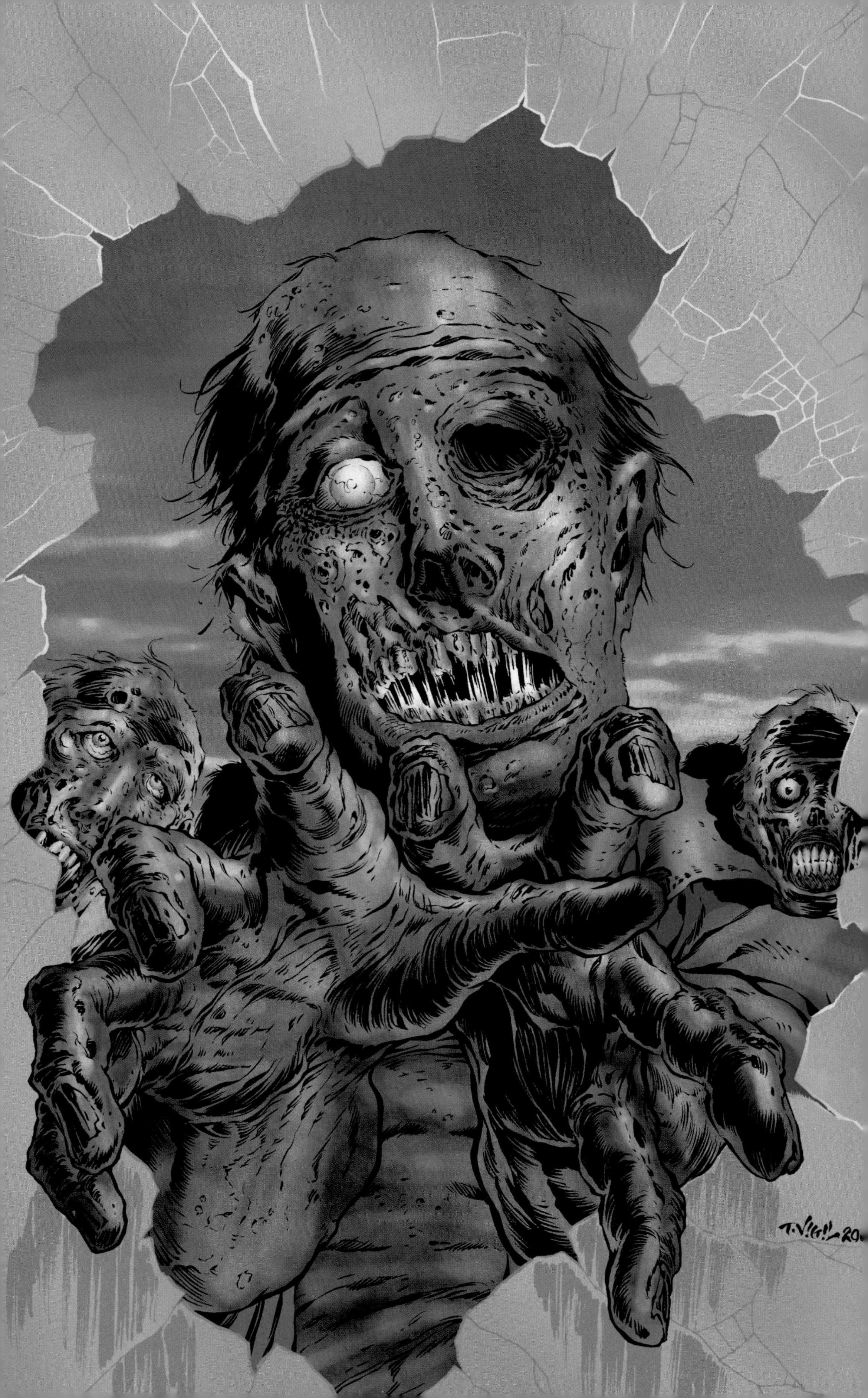

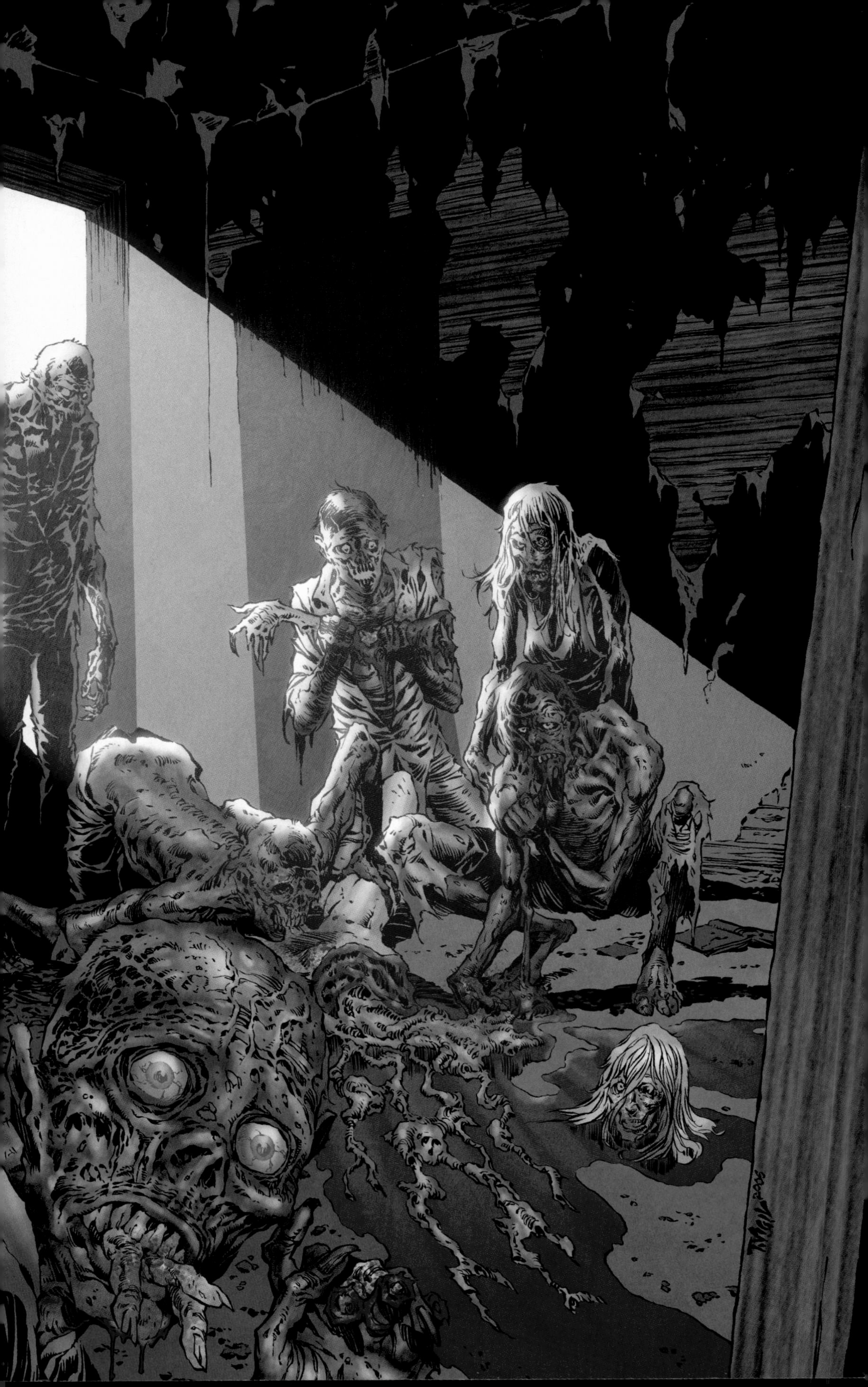

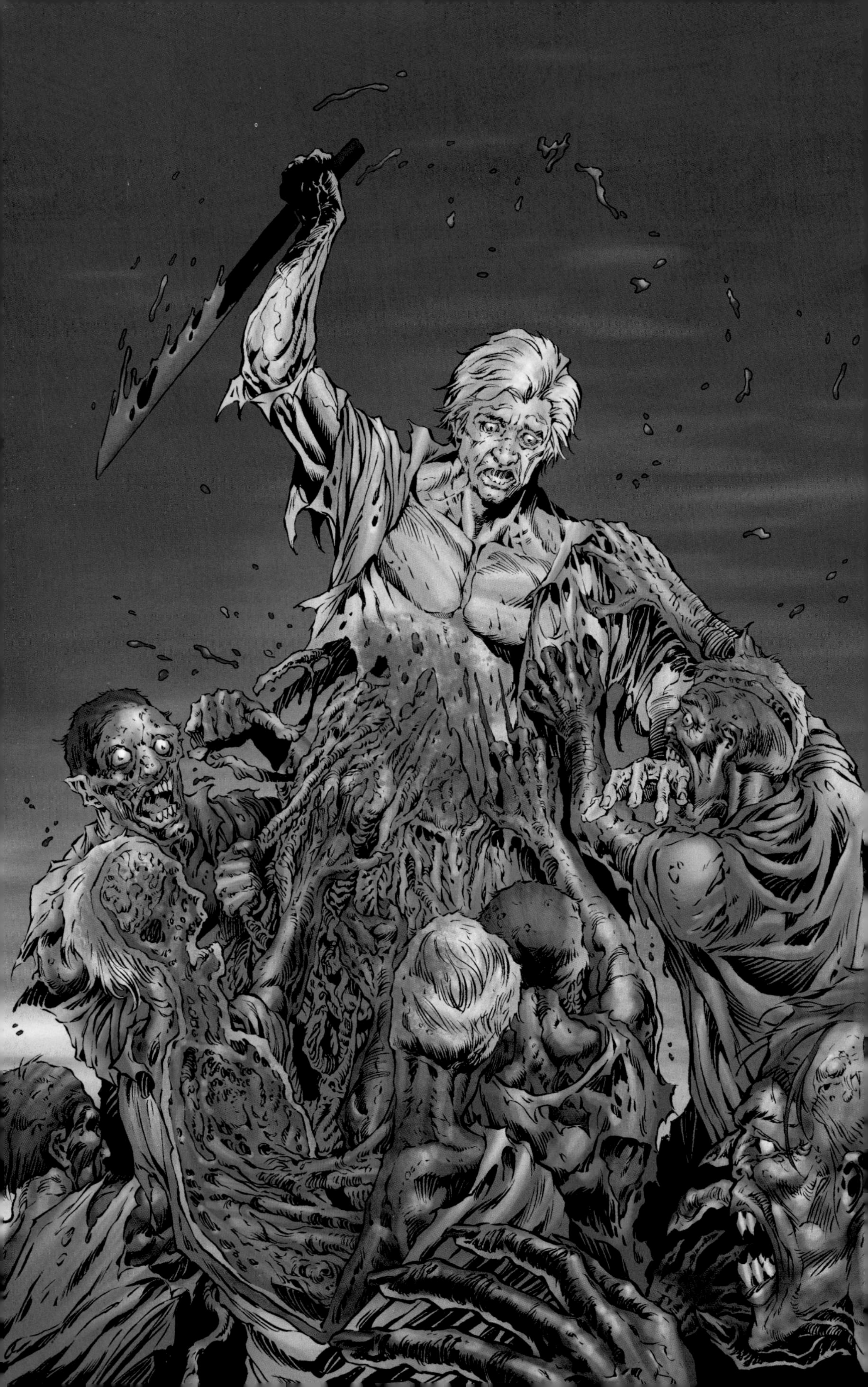

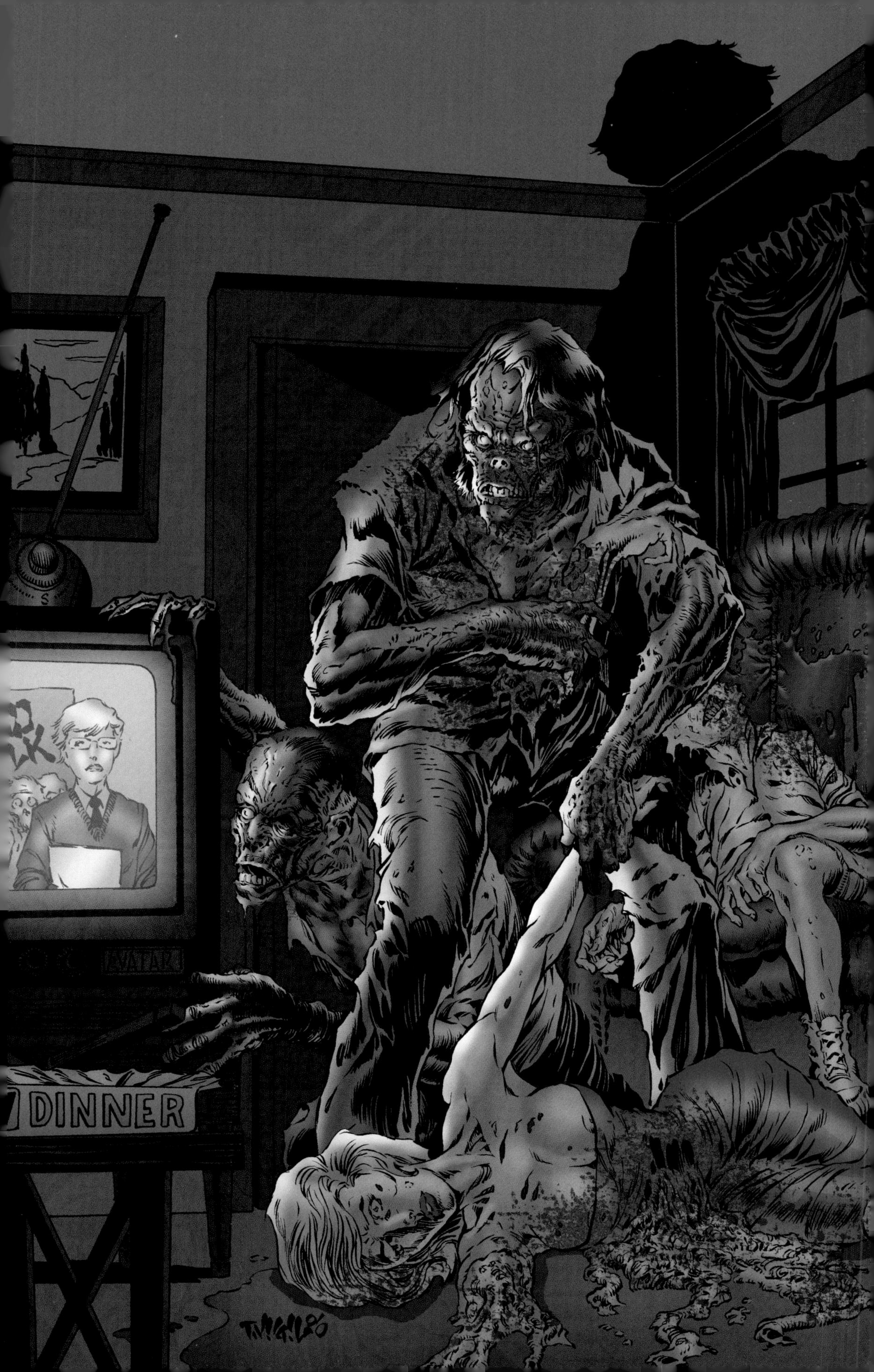
AVATAR
DINNER

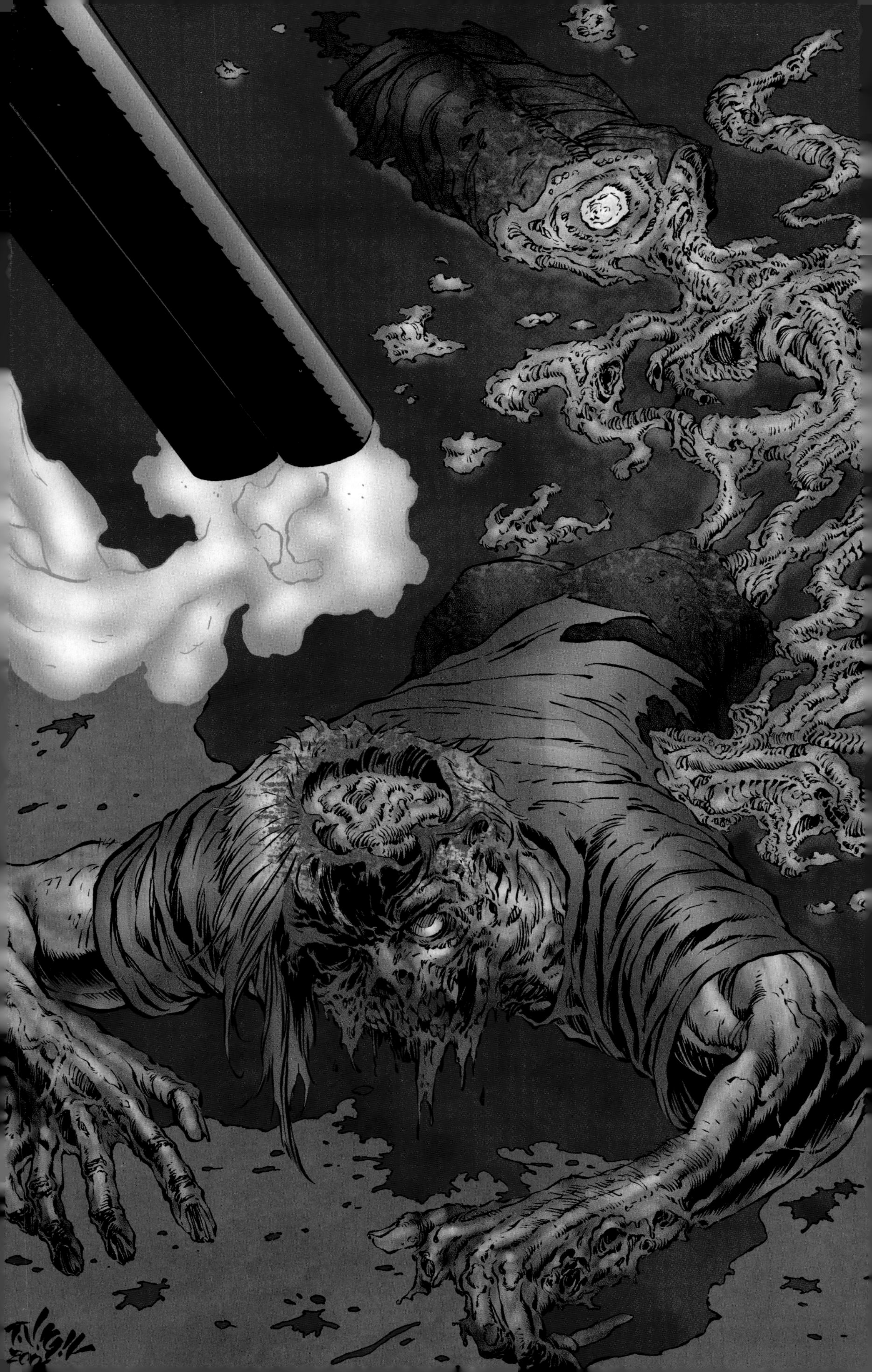

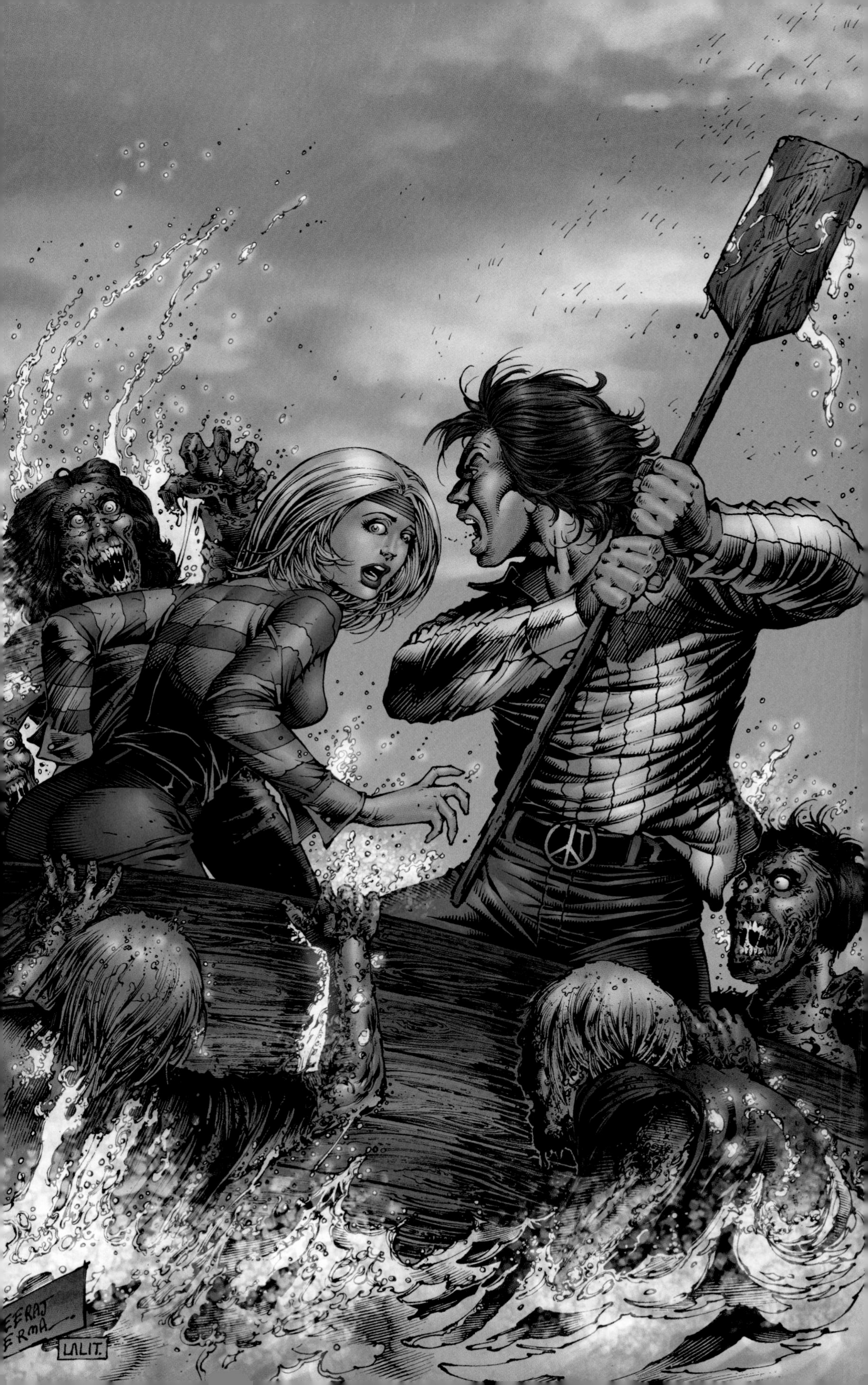
LALIT.

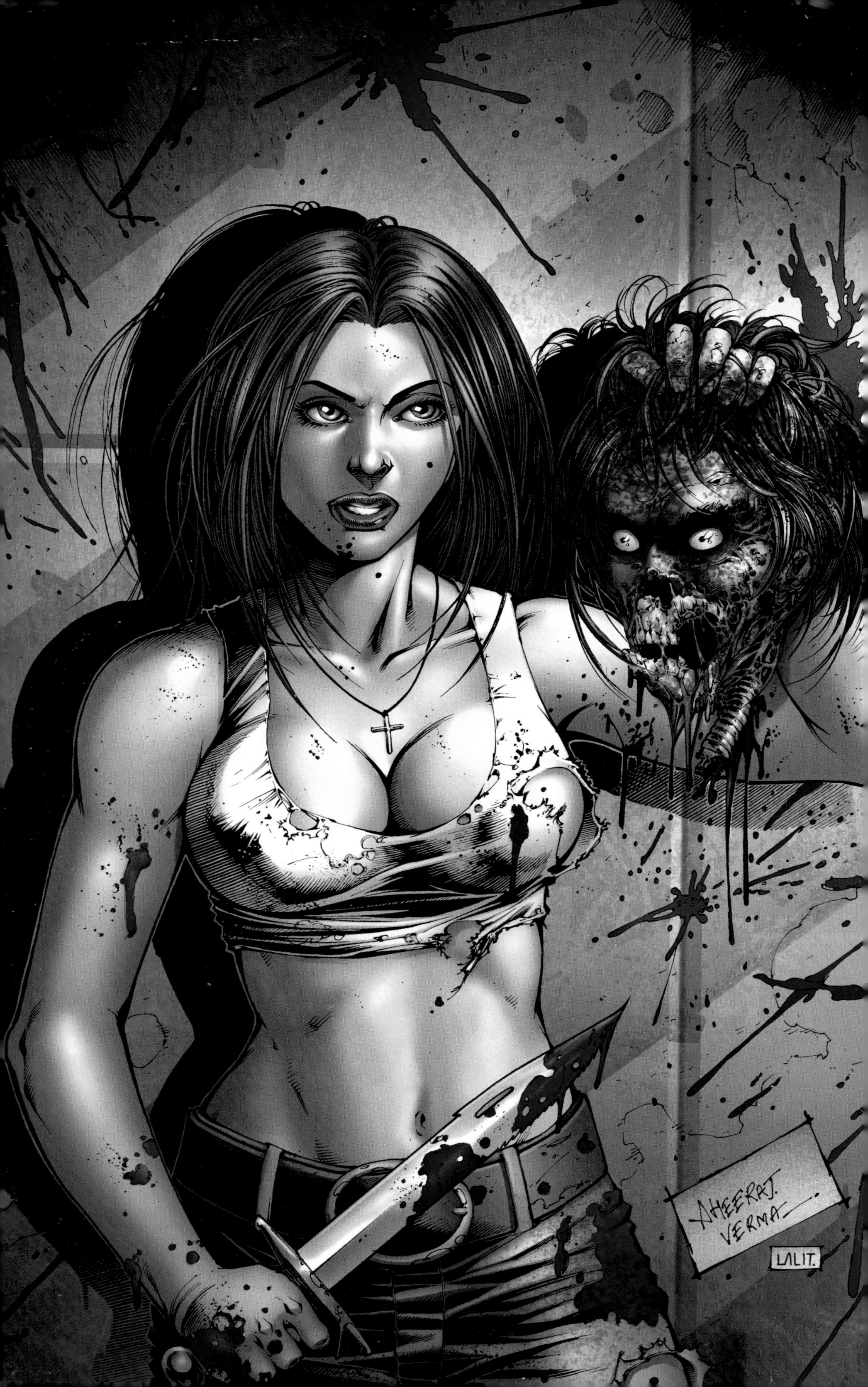
DHEERAJ VERMA
LALIT.